D1557765

Country Risk Assessment

Wiley Finance Series

Country Risk Assessment

A Guide to Global Investment Strategy

Michel Henry Bouchet
Ephraim Clark
and
Bertrand Groslambert

WILEY

Other Wiley Editorial Offices

John Wiley & Sons Inc., 111 River Street, Hoboken, NJ 07030, USA

Jossey-Bass, 989 Market Street, San Francisco, CA 94103-1741, USA

Wiley-VCH Verlag GmbH, Boschstr. 12, D-69469 Weinheim, Germany

John Wiley & Sons Australia Ltd, 33 Park Road, Milton, Queensland 4064, Australia

John Wiley & Sons (Asia) Pte Ltd, 2 Clementi Loop #02-01, Jin Xing Distripark, Singapore 129809

John Wiley & Sons Canada Ltd, 22 Worcester Road, Etobicoke, Ontario, Canada M9W 1L1

Wiley also publishes its books in a variety of electronic formats. Some content that appears
in print may not be available in electronic books.

Library of Congress Cataloging-in-Publication Data

Bouchet, Michel Henry.
   Country risk assessment / Michel Henry Bouchet, Ephraim Clark, and Bertrand Groslambert.
     p.   cm.—(Wiley finance series)
   Includes bibliographical references and index.
   ISBN 0-470-84500-7 (cased : alk. paper)
   1. Investments, Foreign. 2. Country risk. I. Clark, Ephraim. II. Groslambert, Bertrand.
    III. Title. IV. Series.
HG4538.B653   2003
332.67′3—dc21   2003041162

British Library Cataloguing in Publication Data

A catalogue record for this book is available from the British Library

ISBN 0-470-84500-7

Typeset in 10/12pt Times by TechBooks, New Delhi, India
Printed and bound in Great Britain by TJ International Ltd, Padstow, Cornwall, UK
This book is printed on acid-free paper responsibly manufactured from sustainable forestry
in which at least two trees are planted for each one used for paper production.

Contents

Preface

For a long time, country risk belonged to the category of issues that are difficult to understand because information is fragmented or incomplete. Banks knew neither the size of their loan exposure nor to which countries they had lent. Bankers were mesmerized by international eurocredit syndication. Corporations and investors had neither the information nor the means to assess, much less cover, the risks lurking in the shadows of seemingly profitable cross border transactions. Country risk was considered an opaque, unpleasant fact of life better left in the hands of the IMF and the export credit agencies.

In today's global economy wired to the web, however, all this has changed. Information has become abundant, cheap and almost instantaneous as countries compete in transparency to attract foreign direct investment and portfolio capital. The problem is no longer a lack of timely information. It is rather one of deciding which information is important and then knowing how to process it. Country risk involves complex combinations of macroeconomic policy, structural and institutional weakness, bad governance, and regional contagion wrapped in a paradigm of high levels of trade, capital and information flows.

The aim of this book is to provide the framework for understanding the nature of country risk, its sources and its consequences as well as the tools available for judicious country risk assessment in the context of international business and investment. It does so by combining theoretical analyses with a number of practical observations that stem from the authors' market experience with the modest hope of shedding light on a complex but fascinating issue.

Acknowledgments

A number of our colleagues gave us the benefit of their comments and criticism as we were writing this book. We are deeply grateful to them and to our respective institutions, CERAM Sophia Antipolis, ESC Lille and the University of Middlesex. The project of this book received a decisive impetus at the time of the 2001 Finance Symposium jointly organized by IAFE and the CERAM Global Finance Chair that gathered a number of keynote speakers from the international academic community, the rating agencies, the banking industry, and official financial institutions. Lively and fruitful discussions involved a unique combination of scholars including Nobel Laureate Dr. Myron Scholes and Dr. Benoît Mandelbrot, as well as panelists from official institutions such as the ECB, the World Bank, the NY Fed and the BIS. We also wish to thank Michael Payte (Europe Chairman of the International Association of Financial Engineers) and Michael Howell (Crossborder Capital) for useful inputs, as well as Stefano Gori, Georg Merholz, Christoph Moser, and Madjid Touabi for valuable research assistance. We are also indebted to many colleagues in the markets and the scholarly community; too numerous to name individually in this restricted space but nonetheless the target of our everlasting thanks.

Foreword
By Professor Campbell R. Harvey

When I began working in emerging markets more than 10 years ago, the topic was not fashionable and received little attention, mainly because of the cost associated with obtaining comprehensive information, and due to a lack of quality and timely data. On the contrary, at that time, the hot topics were derivatives, M&As, stock market bubbles, LBOs, and the like. When I jumped into this field, emerging markets were regarded as an exotic risk species – good for portfolio diversification and return enhancement strategies but requiring stamina.

Since then, emerging markets have experienced a huge surge of interest generated by their economic dynamism and marked by bouts of volatility and financial crises. By the early 1990s, developing countries were barely recovering from the 1982 global debt crisis only to be rocked by the Mexican peso crisis of 1994, the East-Asian meltdown of 1997, the Russian default of 1998, the Brazilian crisis of 1999 and the ongoing Argentine catastrophe of the new century. Each crisis was a "surprise" to analysts, each was different from the other and they all differed from crises in the more mature capital markets in the OECD countries. All this seems to have awakened investors, traders and businessmen to the importance of country risk assessment and the specific approaches to tackle it.

This book, then, is a welcome initiative. The authors present the content and the tools of modern country risk assessment, both qualitative and quantitative. The book is comprehensive. It includes the traditional techniques of ratings, special reports, Monte Carlo simulations and discriminant, logit and regression analysis, as well as the more modern techniques of value at risk, non-linear and non-parametric estimation, and the sophisticated, cutting edge models developed in the credit risk literature. The authors analyse the advantages and disadvantages of the qualitative and quantitative techniques they describe and show how country risk assessment can be integrated into the overall decision making process. They recognize that country risk assessment must take into account a wide array of parameters including institutions, sociopolitical structures, demographics, culture, religion, economic infrastructure, and legal and regulatory issues. They also recognize that the powerful tools of modern financial theory and practice cannot be neglected either. Their presentation and illustration of risk exposure includes equity and portfolio investment, direct investment, international credit, and trade. They also show that in the last analysis risk assessment is only as good as the quality of the underlying information.

In this uncertain world, I am sure that Michel Bouchet, Ephraim Clark and Bertrand Groslambert have applied their knowledge and wide experience to write a definitive reference book.

Professor Campbell R. Harvey
J. Paul Sticht Professor of International Business
Fuqua School of Business – Duke University
Research Associate – National Bureau of Economic Research

1
Introduction

1.1 AN HISTORICAL PERSPECTIVE

Following the numerous successes it had met with during the flotation of shares and bonds in the capital markets, Baring Brothers was eager to underwrite a loan to be issued by the Buenos Aires Water Supply and Drainage Company. However, the demand was not there and this operation proved to be a failure, leaving the investment bank holding the bulk of the debt. In the meantime, after an extended period of investment boom, the major central banks had decided to substantially increase their discount rates. This tightening of the global liquidity prevented Barings from refinancing at affordable cost and rapidly made its situation untenable. The deterioration of the economic conditions in Argentina hastened an international financial crisis and drove Barings to the verge of bankruptcy. Then, because of contagion effects, Brazil was next on the list. Its currency as well as its stock market collapsed, causing a sharp economic recession.

Does this story sound familiar? Well, any resemblance to an existing situation is probably not coincidental. However, the aforementioned events do not relate one of the recent crises experienced by many emerging markets over the last decade, but actually refer to what is known as the 1890 Baring crisis, more than a century ago. This example illustrates one of the many similarities that can be found when comparing the current period with the prevailing conditions in the nineteenth century.

With the end of Bretton Woods in 1971, and more particularly since the beginning of the 1990s, the world economy has been characterized by its globalization. The fall of communism has permitted the rise of the single American superpower, replacing the *Pax Britannica* of pre-World War I with *Pax Americana*. The economic liberalism that started to be implemented in the industrialized nations by Margaret Thatcher in 1979, and later on was extended to the developing countries by the IMF's adjustment programs, looks like the "laissez faire" policy of the Victorian epoch. Most financial markets are now fully deregulated and capital flows freely circulate all around the world. As a consequence, in the 1990s and for the first time since 1913, the structure of the international capital flows was marked by the return of portfolio investments, especially in the form of bonds and equities. Therefore, exactly like a century ago, "we enjoy at present an undisputed right to place our money where we will, for Government makes no attempt to twist the system into a given channel, and every borrower – native, colonial and foreign – has an equal opportunity for satisfying his needs in London" (*The Economist*, 20 February 1909, in Baring Securities, 1994).

Regrettably and similarly, this also corresponds to a strong increase in the frequency of economic crises. As stated by Krugman (2000) when comparing the current events with the period 1945–1971: "The good old days probably weren't better, but they were certainly calmer." The debt crisis of the 1980s, the Chilean collapse of 1982, the bursting of the European Exchange Rate Mechanism (ERM) in 1992, the debacle of the Mexican peso in 1994, the Asian disaster of 1997, the Russian default and the American bailout of LTCM in 1998, the Argentine chaos in 2001/2002, all demonstrate an accrued volatility of the international economic system. In the same vein, the nineteenth century was regularly shaken by financial crashes. In the years 1836–1839, seven states of the then emerging United States defaulted. A short time later, the railroad boom turned into a speculative bubble and eventually led to the panic of 1857. Turkey, Egypt and Greece defaulted on their debt in 1875–1876. Australia and Canada did the same in 1893, and were followed by Brazil and Mexico in 1914. All through the nineteenth century, speculative mania, financial euphoria, and sharp crises accompanied the economic take-off of the industrial revolution.

Does this mean we are left in exactly the same situation as the one prevalent in the age of the gold standard? Probably not. However, many observers agree on the growing instability of the economic system and believe that "the likelihood of escaping economic and financial crises in the years ahead seems small" (Kindleberger, 2000).

Parallel to this increasing volatility, feeding on and fuelled by globalization, more and more firms invest, trade and compete outside of their home market. Hitherto reserved for the biggest companies, even the smallest firms have started to reason on a global basis. Thus, between 1950 and 2000, the ratio of merchandise exports to world GDP rose from less than 10% to almost 20%. This means that firms are more and more internationally exposed, and national economies are increasingly interlinked. This economic integration translates into a higher sensitivity to foreign events. Consequently, international trade is more and more crucial for companies and countries alike. Furthermore, as the world political leadership is increasingly wielded by the industrialized countries in general and by the United States in particular, there is evidence of a backlash against these countries. In this context, their firms' interests abroad have shown themselves to be especially vulnerable. As the former US Ambassador Paul Bremer outlined: "In the past 30 years, 80% of terrorist attacks against the United States have been aimed at American businesses" (Harvard Business Review, 2002). All this demonstrates the growing importance of a reliable risk management system based on accurate country risk assessment methods.

Forecasting is at the core of all decision-making in the management field. Businessmen must plan and anticipate what the future will bring. They must then make their choices based on their analyses, taking into consideration how today's choices are likely to affect their companies in the future. This implies a certain amount of risk. The ability to look ahead and to take on risk is a major determinant in the frontier between Modern and Ancient times. As Bernstein (1996) put it, "the transformation in attitudes toward risk management has channeled the human passion for games and wagering into economic growth, improved quality of life, and technological progress".

Until the Renaissance, men did not generally try to forecast the future. This was reserved for the Gods. At best, the Gods could possibly deliver their views through an oracle such as the Pythia at Delphi. Starting in the sixteenth century, though, a series of mathematical discoveries enabled mankind to reconsider its position on this issue. Indeed, from this date, Pascal, Fermat, Bernouilli, de Moivre, Laplace and Gauss, to name just a few, progressively built what became the theory of probability. This branch of mathematics created the toolbox to deal with the future in a rational and orderly manner. At the end of the nineteenth century, it led to the conclusion that everything could be measured, either with a deterministic or with a probabilistic approach. Risk was thought to be under control.

However, the twentieth century was to challenge this optimistic vision. Two world wars and the Great Depression showed that even the unthinkable could happen. This altered the perception of risk and caused researchers to redefine it. In the 1920s, Knight introduced the notion of uncertainty as opposed to the notion of risk. Whereas risk can be appraised with probability, uncertainty is not measurable. This distinction was well retranscribed by Keynes (1937) in his famous statement: "By 'uncertain' knowledge . . . I do not merely distinguish what is known for certain from what is only probable. The game of roulette is not subject, in this sense, to uncertainty; nor the prospect of a Victory bond being drawn . . . Even the weather is only moderately uncertain. The sense in which I am using the term is that in which the prospect of a European war is uncertain, or the price of copper and the rate of interest twenty years hence . . . About these matters there is no scientific basis on which to form any calculable probability whatever. We simply do not know."

There may be several reasons why "we simply do not know". First, the system may be too complex to be measured. In this case, the theory of chaos explains the situation by saying that it contains too many degrees of freedom, and is therefore unpredictable in the long run. Alternatively, it may be because we don't have a long enough time series to extrapolate the underlying probability law. For instance, many economic variables follow certain probability laws of "rare events", such as Pareto's law. In order to be accurately estimated, these types of distributions require extremely large empirical databases, which are hardly ever found in real life. Lastly, another argument could lie in the permanently changing and inherently unstable nature of the environment. To draw on the past in order to infer the probability of future occurrences would be completely misleading, if a structural change took place in the meantime.

If the size of the population under scrutiny is sufficiently large (in the billions) to be valid for statistical appraisal and provided it is unaware of the existence of the science of Psychohistory, then Hari Seldom demonstrated that Psychohistory could predict the behavior of human societies over at least 30 000 years. Psychohistory is "a branch of mathematics which deals with the reactions of human conglomerates to fixed social and economic stimuli" (Asimov, 1967). Unfortunately, or rather maybe fortunately, this science has not been invented yet, except in the imagination of the famous science fiction novelist, Isaac Asimov. Today, organization science, political science, economics, or country risk are still light years away from Psychohistory. Nevertheless, we can reasonably expect from them a certain ability to anticipate social changes. The objective of this book is to explore the question for country risk. What is the state of the art in this field? What are the various country risk assessment methods? Do they rely on modern science or are they merely based on intuition and subjective perceptions? Can we reasonably measure country risk with a probabilistic view? Or do we rather face the type of uncertainty as defined by Knight, the one which cannot be addressed with probability laws? In April 1982, *Institutional Investor* ranked South Korea below Mexico. In August of the same year, Mexico defaulted and triggered the international debt crisis of the 1980s. Meanwhile, Korea initiated a period of unparalleled economic growth that would increase its per capita GDP in US dollars fivefold over the next 20 years. In December 1986, *The Economist* tried to detect which countries were at the greatest risk of becoming unstable in the following years. They found that Chile was in the very high-risk category alongside Nigeria and Zaire, while Venezuela and Brazil were in the very low-risk category, like Taiwan and Singapore. As these selected examples clearly illustrate, risk management, and country risk in particular, has proved to be a very difficult task. No one method is able to perfectly assess country risk. However, taken as a whole, the methods of country risk assessment provide a framework for analysis and some necessary guidelines to tackle the issues at hand.

When considering an investment abroad, it is essential that managers do not blindly follow the general consensus. Based on the methods presented in this book, they must take into account their own features, so as to derive their own evaluations. In addition, they should regularly question the validity of their models. They should wonder what could make them defective in the future, whatever their degree of success in the past. As Bernstein (1996) explains: "The science of risk management sometimes creates new risks even as it brings old risks under control. Our faith in risk management encourages us to take risks we would not otherwise take ... Research reveals that seatbelts encourage drivers to drive more aggressively. Consequently, the number of accidents rises even though the seriousness of injury in any one accident declines." Furthermore, the Minsky Paradox of Tranquility is never far away, just waiting to lull investors' awareness. This paradox postulates that after a long enough period of relative tranquility, entrepreneurs and banks tend to become complacent about economic prospects. Little by little, they start to take more risk, going for more debt, and hence making the system more vulnerable. This may be what happened in South East Asia in 1997, when so many investors were trapped, unprepared to bear such a high risk. "Only the pathological weakness of the financial memory, ... or perhaps our indifference to financial history itself, allows us to believe that the modern experience of Third World debt ... is in any way a new phenomenon" (Galbraith, 1994).

Finally, we should keep in mind that it is precisely the difficulty of estimating the risk that can make the investment opportunities attractive. An anecdote by Jean-Louis Terrier, the founder of the French rating firm Nord Sud Export, illustrates this point. A few years ago he had a discussion with one of his clients, a wealthy and quite secretive Belgian entrepreneur, who, every year, was very impatient to read the annual country risk ratings. To Terrier's utmost surprise, the man confessed to him that he wanted to be sure his investments were made effectively in the riskiest countries, those able to generate the highest returns.

1.2   OUTLINE OF THE BOOK

Various definitions and several terminologies exist to deal with the risk related to a foreign investment. In this book, we define country risk as all the additional risks induced by doing business abroad, as opposed to domestic transactions. When a firm starts to expand internationally, it is faced with a new environment, composed of different risks and uncertainties, which it is not used to dealing with. Country risk encompasses all these specific sources of potential difficulties encountered when investing overseas, ranging from political and social risks to macro- and microeconomic risks.

This book should allow the reader to get an insight into the nature of risk when investing in a foreign country. Based on the three authors' experience, it combines a rigorous, theoretical treatment of country risk with some very concrete and practical illustrations. It aims to present and analyze most of the existing country risk assessment methods. It also provides a broad overview of the country risk field with an emphasis on the specific nature of the emerging countries. It should allow professionals to explore the origins of country risk, to understand the assessment process of each method, and to grasp their limits. Each approach has some pros and cons, depending on the nature of the investment and the type of risk under consideration. Practitioners should be able to choose which one is the best suited for their business. They could even decide to develop their own methodology. This text should also prove useful for academics in search of a reference book, and be appropriate for courses in business and economics.

The book is organized in three parts. The first one, comprising Chapters 2 and 3, provides the underlying background for country risk. The second part, from Chapters 4 to 8, investigates the various existing country risk assessment methods. It starts with the most qualitative approaches and ends up with the most quantitative ones. Then, because developing countries exhibit certain specific characteristics that set them apart at a generally higher level of risk, the last part, including Chapters 9 to 11, addresses the major issues specifically related to them. It reviews the economic and financial crises over the last few decades, the possible instruments to mitigate risks, and discusses the available sources of information.

Chapter 2 introduces and defines the concept of country risk. It investigates the numerous streams existing in the literature. Several approaches coexist and can be differentiated depending on their terminology, their definition of risk, the sources of risk they evaluate, or the nature of the investment they consider. Concerning the methodology, a major difference contrasts the quantitative line against the qualitative one. Further distinctions can also be found based on the historical period under examination. Finally, this chapter recapitulates and classifies the various types of country risk. It illustrates each of them with real-world examples.

A major element of country risk revolves around the capacity of the country to generate enough foreign exchange to maintain required levels of imports and service its foreign debt. In Chapter 3, we present the macroeconomic analyses that address this issue. The reader is provided with the theoretical foundations of certain economic and financial notions that are used extensively in the following chapters. We examine the process of internal economic adjustment caused by external disequilibrium. We look at the consequences of a devaluation on relative prices, incomes, and the composition of output and consumption. We then consider the consequences of external disequilibrium when a change in the exchange rate is avoided through offsetting transactions by the monetary authorities. Next, we present the monetary approach to balance of payments analysis and its more sophisticated cousin, the portfolio balance approach. We conclude with a presentation of some of the most commonly used tools for country risk analysis resulting from the foregoing approaches along with some new ratios derived from modern financial theory.

Chapter 4 investigates a range of qualitative assessment approaches to country risk. Qualitative analysis refers to the evaluation of the economic, financial and socio-political fundamentals that can affect investment return prospects in a foreign country. Instead of focusing on a range of ratios, ratings or indices that are supposed to "reduce" a complex situation into one single figure, the qualitative analysis aims at tackling the structures of a country's development process, to shed light on the underlying strengths and weaknesses. Usually, a robust qualitative approach leads to comprehensive country risk reports that deal with the following elements: (i) the social and welfare dimension of the development strategy; (ii) macroeconomic fundamentals; (iii) evolution, structure and burden of external indebtedness; (iv) the situation of the domestic financial system; (v) assessment of the governance and transparency issues; and (vi) evaluation of political stability.

Chapter 5 investigates the rating methods. It differentiates the global country risk approaches from the country credit ratings that are more specifically debt-oriented. The first group encompasses the methodologies developed both by specialized firms such as BERI, PRS, EIU, and by credit export agencies such as Coface. The second cluster gathers the main credit rating agencies, including Fitch, Moody's and Standard & Poor's, as well as country rankings published in *Euromoney* and *Institutional Investor*. They all provide estimations of the relative degree of risk and suggest methods to quantify it. Although some of them claim to be purely quantitatively oriented, they all require a fair amount of human judgment. In general, they correctly describe the present situation and are able to discriminate between very high and very low risk. However, they are sometimes defective, particularly when crises occur.

In Chapter 6, we briefly outline and review a wide range of techniques commonly used in risk assessment. We start with techniques that seek to determine an either/or outcome, such as discriminant analysis and logit and probit models. We then deal with regression analysis and model building and show how Monte Carlo simulations can be combined with model building to produce risk estimates. We also present value at risk and principal components analysis. We conclude the chapter with an overview of non-parametric techniques, artificial neural networks and multicriteria methods.

Chapter 7 focuses on how to quantify country risk and incorporate its effects in the investment decision. First, we look at the credit risk models and see how they can be applied to country risk to estimate default probabilities, maximum debt levels, implied volatility and credit value at risk. We then turn to the problem of country risk in portfolio and foreign direct investment. We show how country risk can be incorporated in the investment decision by adjusting either the cash flows or the required rate of return. We then present several methods for estimating the required rate of return to capture the country risk element. Finally, we show how the cost of country risk can be measured as a hypothetical insurance policy that pays off all losses accruing to political events.

Then, in Chapter 8, we address the issue of country risk from a portfolio investment perspective, and rely on modern portfolio theory to analyze this matter. Even though an *ex ante* optimum portfolio is difficult to build, this chapter recalls the potential benefits to be gained from international portfolio diversification. It explains how the Capital Asset Pricing Model can be extended to an international framework and shows the limits of these theoretical developments. It presents modified versions developed by practitioners such as the Bank of America or Goldman Sachs and shows that, although they do give some very rough estimates of the cost of capital and facilitate comparisons across countries, these practitioners' approaches are basically *ad hoc* and lack theoretical foundation.

With Chapter 9, we start a review of questions mainly concerning the developing countries. This chapter includes a comprehensive review of the debt workout process over the 1982–2002 period. It addresses the combined role of Paris and London Club restructuring negotiations to provide emerging market countries with debt relief and sustainable growth conditions. After two decades of official and private debt reduction, developing countries still remain heavily indebted despite a concerted refinancing strategy and the reduction of financial charges carried out under the aegis of international institutions. The chapter analyzes the evolution of indicators of solvency and liquidity. It concludes that the emerging market countries' debt ratios show little improvement. It observes that protracted signs of slower growth in OECD countries will have a long-term impact on developing countries' trade and capital market access, at a time when commercial banks have to contend with competitive and regulatory pressure to satisfy capital adequacy requirements imposed by supervisory banking authorities.

Chapter 10 addresses the various institutional and financial instruments investors and creditors can rely upon to mitigate country risk. Export cover, investment insurance, and a market-driven menu of financial innovations can enhance liquidity while reducing country risk. As a result of mounting risks in a more complex global market, investors and lenders try to mitigate their vulnerability. This can be done by obtaining "comfort" from official bilateral and multilateral agencies through insurance coverage or co-lender status. It can also be done through market-based instruments that alter an investor's risk exposure, thereby achieving superior risk–return combinations. These financial instruments include asset securitization, asset-backed securities, and debt conversion transactions that provide implicit access to a preferential exchange rate.

Chapter 11 tackles the crucial issue of sources of country risk information. Country risk analysis, indeed, is as good as the quality of the underlying information. The latter is the key behind decision-making, resulting in either good assessment or excess exposure with related losses. To anticipate and assess the riskiness behind macroeconomic discontinuities, investors and creditors need reliable data. As the global economy and the spill-over effects compound the magnitude and abruptness of country risk crises, timely information has never been so crucial in risk assessment and prediction. The chapter presents and assesses the various sources of country risk intelligence from both official and private origins, including international organizations, central banks and private risk agencies, as well as the academic community.

Finally, a comprehensive glossary supplies the reader with a list of risk-related economic and financial concepts with a view to shedding light on current country risk debates in the academic and practitioner communities.

REFERENCES

Asimov I, 1967, *Foundation*. London: Panther Publishing.
Baring Securities, 1994, *Cross Border Equity Flow*. London: Baring Securities, October.
Bernstein PL, 1996, *Against the Gods, The Remarkable Story of Risk*. New York: John Wiley and Sons.
Galbraith JK, 1994, *A Short History of Financial Euphoria*. New York: Penguin Books.
Harvard Business Review, 2002, Doing Business in a Dangerous World. *Harvard Business Review*, Apr, 80 (4), 22–3.
Keynes JM, 1937, The General Theory of Employment. *Quarterly Journal of Economics*, 51, 209–23.
Kindleberger CP, 2000, *Manias, Panics, and Crashes, A History of Financial Crises*. 4th edition. New York: John Wiley and Sons.
Krugman P, 2000, Crises: the Price of Globalization? *Proceedings*, Federal Reserve Bank of Kansas City, August, 75–106.

2

An Overview of Country Risk

2.1 A REVIEW OF THE LITERATURE

The literature on country risk uses several terminologies and has generated various streams depending on the definition that is retained, the sources of risk, the nature of the investment, the historical context, and the chosen methodology. These various approaches will be dealt with in the following paragraphs and are summarized in Table 2.1.

2.1.1 The Terminologies

Just a few years after many American firms were expropriated by the Cuban revolution, the notion of "political risk" began to emerge in the literature of the 1960s, with authors like Usher (1965) or Root (1968). At this time, as Zenoff (1967) wrote: "For many [companies with an overseas subsidiary] this venture is . . . profitable, fast growing, but still the stepchild." Indeed, the international landscape was changing. Decolonization was the order of the day and the newly formed countries were experimenting with their new political autonomy as more and more firms were awakening to the opportunities abroad and gradually increasing their exposure to foreign markets.

At the outset, researchers tried to assess the risk of investing abroad in terms of "investment climate" (Gabriel, 1966 or Stobaugh, 1969a,b). Recognizing that: "[political scientists] still disagree significantly on how to define political stability or instability, on how to measure the phenomenon and on what are the causal forces", Robock (1971) was among the first to advocate the necessity of a definition for this hitherto vague concept. Nevertheless, as the next decades demonstrated, this task proved to be more complex than originally anticipated and is still far from being resolved.

Consider the following quotes:

While there has been increasing academic interest in the intersection of politics and international business, it is still a relatively new and loosely defined field. Kobrin (1979)

Political risk often becomes a catchall term that refers to miscellaneous risks. Brewer (1981)

Despite an increasing familiarity with the term "country risk analysis," there are still many people in banking circles today who argue that such analysis is nothing more than a fancy description of what banks have always done. . . . Merrill (1982)

There is no consensus today as to what constitutes a "political risk," let alone an accepted methodology for anticipating and assessing overseas developments. Simon (1982)

Although political risk is mentioned often in the literature on international business, a consensus on the precise meaning of the term has not yet been achieved. Fitzpatrick (1983)

Researchers and analysts differ widely in the way they define political risk. Desta (1985)

Table 2.1 Various approaches of the literature on country risk

Terminologies	Definition of risk	Sources of risk	Nature of the investment	Historical perspective	Methodology
• Political risk • Country risk • Sovereign risk • Cross-border risk	• Performance variance • Negative outcome	• Sovereign interference • Environmental instability	• Foreign direct investment • Banking commercial loans • Portfolio investment	• 1960s–1970s • 1980s • 1990s–?	• Qualitative • Quantitative

Many in the academic field of political science do not immediately recognize the term "political risk" and do not associate it with their own regular pursuits....   Howell and Chaddick (1994)

The existence of these disparate notions of political instability raises questions about the "construct validity" of any empirical measures used in a study of the effects of political instability.
                Rivoli and Brewer (1997)

As the foregoing quotations show, academics and practitioners are still short of a consensus about the scope of this field of research. The difficulty of reaching a comprehensive definition of "country risk" and agreeing on its meaning is further extended by the various terminologies used to deal with similar and/or overlapping issues. In the literature dealing with the risk of doing business abroad, the two terms most frequently encountered are "country risk" and "political risk". Less frequently, references to "cross-border risk" or "sovereign risk" can be found. "Political risk" is the oldest terminology and appears mostly in academic articles. "Country risk" began to be widely used in the 1970s. It was originally more professionally oriented in the sense that it aimed at addressing the concrete issue of a particular business in a particular country and was generally used by the banking industry. This stream of literature flourished in the aftermath of the international debt crisis of the 1980s. Desta (1985) notes: "Analysts in international lending institutions prefer to use 'country risk' or 'sovereign risk' as opposed to political risk." Reviewing the sovereign rating history and its methodological evolution, Moody's (2002) states: "In 1997, we changed the name 'sovereign ceiling' to 'country ceiling', because the ambiguous term 'sovereign' could be taken to refer sometimes to the country as a whole and sometimes to the government itself as an issuer." Table 2.2 reviews the literature dealing with the definition of country risk and distinguishes between the terms "political risk" and "country risk". The term "country risk" as opposed to "political risk" has been gaining ascendency because it has a broader meaning in that it can include any risk specific to a given country, whereas "political risk" restricts the risks to those that are exclusively political in nature.

2.1.2 Definitions of Country Risk

For some authors, risk is defined as a performance variance, whether it impacts the firm positively or negatively. Robock (1971) explains: "Yet, as in the case of other types of risk, political risk can result in gains as well as losses." For this group of researchers country risk refers to the "probability of occurrence of political events that will change the prospects for profitability of a given investment" (Haendel *et al.*, 1975). As an example, companies involved in the armored car industry in Argentina experienced a dramatic increase of their sales in 2001, because they benefitted from the growing political instability of the country. Kobrin (1979)

Table 2.2 Political risk versus country risk in the literature

Political risk	Country risk
Aliber (1973)	Citron and Nickelsburg (1987)
Aliber (1975)	Cosset *et al.* (1992)*
Alon and Martin (1998)	Davis (1981)
Brewer (1981)	Desta (1985)
Cosset and Suret (1995)	Eaton *et al.* (1986)*
Desta (1985)	Kennedy (1991)
Feils and Sabac (2000)	Marois (1990)
Fitzpatrick (1983)	Meldrum (1999)
Haendel *et al.* (1975)	Meldrum (2000)
Howell and Chaddick (1994)	Merril (1982)*
Kennedy (1991)	Nagy (1978)*
Kobrin (1978)	Rivoli and Brewer (1997)*
Kobrin (1979)	Robinson (1981)*
Marois and Behar (1981)	Roy and Roy (1994)*
Robock (1971)	Wilson (1979)
Root (1968)	
Root (1972)	
Rummel and Heenan (1978)	
Simon (1982)	
Stevens (1997)	
Usher (1965)	

*Articles with a specific focus on the banking industry.

and, more recently, Feils and Sabac (2000) belong to this cluster. Another approach adopts a more practical stance and analyzes risk as a negative outcome. With this meaning, risk will exist if it implies a possible loss or at least, as stated by Meldrum (2000), a potential reduction of the expected return. Root (1972), Simon (1982), Howell and Chaddick (1994) or Roy and Roy (1994) follow this route and consider that, when it occurs, risk negatively impacts the firm's operations and/or investments.

Thus, the notion of risk has different meanings and may be understood either as a performance variance or just as the likelihood of a negative outcome that reduces the initially expected return. However, as evidenced by March and Shapira (1987) or Baird and Thomas (1990), practitioners are more concerned by failing to achieve a given target performance than by the entire set of possible outcomes. Consequently it is more appealing to follow a downside risk approach as opposed to a total risk perspective. Indeed, while investors try to minimize their downside risk exposure, they want to maximize their upside risk sensibility. Some like Miller (1992) retain the concept of risk as performance variance because it "is widely used in finance, economics, and strategic management." Though the concept of downside risk was already mentioned in Markowitz (1959), it is mainly because of computational difficulties in handling this type of model as well as the assumption of normally distributed returns[1] that the variance was favored as a measure of risk. The paper of Nawrocki (1999) reviews the literature and presents the advantages of using a downside risk approach in lieu of a total risk stance. Even though Roy (1952) or Bawa and Lindenberg (1977) had already integrated the notion of downside risk into portfolio theory, it is only more recently that papers like those of Harlow

---

[1] If the returns were normally distributed (and consequently symmetric around the mean) both approaches would yield similar results.

and Rao (1989), Sortino and van der Meer (1991) or Miller and Reuer (1996) explored this route. Estrada (2000) and Reuer and Leiblein (2000) have emphasized the usefulness of the downside risk approach for studying emerging markets and international joint ventures. More-over, many studies such as those of Aggarwal *et al.* (1989), Harvey (1995) or Bekaert *et al.* (1998) have established the skewness of the return distribution at the international level, thus offering a further case for the downside risk line versus the increasingly challenged choice of variance.

A look at the literature over the last 40 years shows that the country risk field, while encompassing a wide range of different situations, always refers to doing business abroad and to the specific risks it engenders, whatever the source of risk and the nature of the industry. Of course, the particular features of each investment or transaction type must obviously be taken into account. Yet, it is also necessary to adopt an overall perspective because the sources of risk all interact with each other and possibly impact several if not all sectors of an economy. For example, the Asian crisis of 1997/1998 that started in Thailand with the devaluation of the Thai baht had some economic causes, notably the misbalance of the current accounts, but also some political roots due to the so-called crony capitalism. Contagion effects then spread the crisis to its neighbors, including Malaysia that reacted on the political front by enforcing foreign exchange controls and restricting transactions in foreign currency. Many Asian economies were badly hit and barely avoided a collapse of most of their industries.

The definition proposed by Meldrum (2000) perfectly reflects these characteristics: "All business transactions involve some degree of risk. When business transactions occur across international borders, they carry additional risks not present in domestic transactions. These additional risks, called country risks, typically include risks arising from a variety of national differences in economic structures, policies, socio-political institutions, geography and curren-cies. Country risk analysis (CRA) attempts to identify the potential for these risks to decrease the expected return of a cross-border investment." This definition rejoins the very early articles of Gabriel (1966) or Stobaugh (1969a,b) that were concerned with how the "investment cli-mate" in a foreign country may differ from the "investment climate" at home. It highlights the specific risks when doing business abroad, outside the national borders of the firm's country of origin. It is worth noting that country risk exists whatever the level of economic development of the country in question. Even the most economically advanced nations may generate a sub-stantial degree of country risk. Finnerty (2001) noted that "many project finance professionals would argue that natural resource projects in the United States are exposed to political risk because of the proclivity within the United States to change the environmental laws and apply the new laws retroactively".

Except for the very tentative work of Meldrum (1999) based on a modified version of a supply-side Solow growth theory model, a comprehensive country risk theory is yet to be formulated. Up to now, the literature is simply building on the implicit assumption that, for a given country, imbalances in the economic, social and political fields are likely to increase the risk of investing there. Because of the multiplicity of the sources of risk, the complexity of their interactions and the variety of social sciences involved, an underlying theory of country risk is still missing. Such a conceptualization would greatly help to identify the variables at stake. It would make it possible to test the respective relevance of the various approaches on offer. So far, most of the research merely consists of a classification and a description of the various potential sources of risk, and the assessment methods turn these elements into numerical variables without any scientific justification. Fitzpatrick (1983) writes on the subject that "the literature is found to define political event risk rather than political risk".

2.1.3 Sources of Risk

A second type of division in the literature is based on the sources of risk. Kobrin (1979) or Desta (1985) identify two main streams. The first one only focuses on the governmental or sovereign interference with business operations. Weston and Sorge (1972) write: "Political risks arise from the actions of national governments which interfere with or prevent business transactions, or change the terms of agreements, or cause the confiscation of wholly or partially foreign owned business property." For this group of authors, such as Zenoff (1967), Aliber (1975), Baglini (1976) or Feils and Sabac (2000), country risk narrowly originates from adverse governmental or sovereign actions. The second stream of literature represented by Robock (1971), Root (1972), Haendel *et al.* (1975) or Rummel and Heenan (1978) refers to the environmental instability and its impact on business conditions. Their line provides a broader perspective and includes not only governmental sources of risk but also any other causes that may impede the efficient functioning of any foreign organization abroad. Fitzpatrick (1983) further refines this second approach and divides it into three categories. He identifies (1) "political risk in terms of occurrences of a political nature", (2) "political risk in terms of an environment rather than in isolation", where any change in the business environment may represent a risk, provided it can impact the firm's operations, and (3) a last category, where authors do not try to conceptualize the notion of "political risk" but rather merely concentrate on the consequences of operating "in countries where the environment is strange and not well understood", as written subsequently by Drake and Prager (1977).

2.1.4 Types of Investment

A third taxonomy can be found in the literature, depending on the nature of the investment undertaken by the foreign firm in the host country. In this manner, Meldrum (2000) analyzes the impact of various sources of risk based on four different investment types: direct investment/ private sector, short term financial/private sector, short term loan to government and long term loan to government. However, most research focuses on a selected category of investment and carries out its analysis in this restricted framework. The three major groupings are (1) foreign direct investment (FDI), (2) commercial bank loans and (3) portfolio investment. Exporters could possibly be considered as a fourth group *per se*. However, they are rarely tackled in this way, probably because, even though their investment abroad stems from a commercial or industrial nature, the sorts of risks they run are more akin to those of the commercial banks or the credit export agencies. As Terrier (2001) puts it: "Obviously an exporter is not subject with an equivalent intensity to the same risks as a foreign direct investor. The former, like his banker for their common debt and his insurance company for possible default, is much less concerned by the political instability of a foreign country than the locally and permanently settled investor."

The first group deals exclusively with foreign direct investment and basically aims at answering the question raised by Stobaugh (1969a): "Where in the world should we put that plant?" Along these lines, Root (1968), Rummel and Heenan (1978), Brewer (1981), Stevens (1997) or Alon and Martin (1998) adopt an overall perspective and discuss country risk for FDI in a general context. Others like Bergara *et al.* (1998) prefer to concentrate specifically on industry-related investments. For example, they investigate the impact of political risk for electric utilities. Their work is often associated with studies of the project finance industry as, for instance, in Schwimmer (1995) or Spillers (1999).

The second group addresses the issue of external debt servicing and tries to assess the likelihood of default or possible debt service difficulties. Among the first articles were those of Frank and Cline (1971), Feder and Just (1977) or Nagy (1978), but as noticed by Morgan (1986): "Following the wave of debt reschedulings by more than thirty countries from 1981 to 1984, there was a pressing need to reassess country risk techniques used by international commercial banks." This explains the burgeoning of the literature on this topic from the 1980s, including Agmon and Dietrich (1983), Abdullah (1985), Feder and Uy (1985), Shapiro (1985), Eaton *et al.* (1986), Citron and Nickelsburg (1987), Cosset *et al.* (1992), Schwartz and Zurita (1992), Rivoli and Brewer (1997).

The last group tackles the influence of country risk on international portfolio investment (i.e. foreign stock markets or international fixed-income investments). Researchers started to extend portfolio theory in an international framework by applying the works of Markowitz (1952) to an international set of investment opportunities. Pioneering studies in this field are by Grubel (1968), Levy and Sarnat (1970), Lessard (1973) or Errunza (1977). In the same spirit, after the seminal paper of Solnik (1974b), many articles such as those of Grauer *et al.* (1976), Sercu (1980) or Stulz (1984) derived the Capital Asset Pricing Model in an international context. For most of these researches "capital markets are supposed to be perfect with free flows of capital between nations" (Solnik, 1974a). However, as noticed later by Solnik (1991): "The political risks of foreign investment might dampen the enthusiasm for international diversification. This political transfer risk might take the form of prohibition on repatriation of profits or capital investment from a foreign country." Jorion and Schwartz (1986) also mention "any other cost of doing investment business abroad" or "any other barrier linked to the country of origin of the security".

Moreover, Adler and Dumas (1983) note that "financial economic theory does not deal easily with such imperfections which tend to segment international capital markets". Consequently, other works attempted to identify the specific features of international portfolio investment and to establish a likely segmentation of these markets. Aliber (1973) explores the possible impact of "political risk" as a source of deviation from the interest-rate parity. Stehle (1977), Errunza and Losq (1985), Bekaert (1995) or Bekaert and Harvey (1995) aim to test the integration of the international capital markets. Groslambert and Kassibrakis (1999) dispute the normal distribution hypothesis of some emerging stock market returns. Finally, some authors concentrate on the practical aspects of international portfolio management. Agmon (1973), Erb *et al.* (1995, 1996a,b), Rajan and Friedman (1997) or Madura *et al.* (1997) try to demonstrate the influence of the country factor when explaining differences in portfolio performance. Although most of these papers do not explicitly refer to the notion of country risk, they address this issue *de facto* either by investigating the return properties and potential diversification benefits from investing abroad, or by studying the barriers to investment and their effect on expected returns. It is worth noticing that the literature on international portfolio investment addresses the issue of country risk in a risk/return framework which is not always the case for other streams, whose results, as Meldrum (1999) has noted, "would benefit greatly from additional research into the theoretical and quantitative relationships between risk and the returns earned in cross-border investments".

2.1.5 The Historical Context

Ultimately, the literature on country risk can be analyzed from an historical perspective. Over the last four decades, research in the field of country risk was mainly driven by a series of crises:

"political crises" in the 1960s and 1970s, "debt crises" in the 1980s and "financial crises" in the 1990s. Each type of crisis induced an explosion of papers that tried to explain *ex post* the causes of the foregoing events. However, very few, if any, adopted a more comprehensive view and tried to extract a general rule from these particular cases.

The period ranging from the 1960s to the end of the 1970s was dominated by studies on multinational corporations (MNCs) and their exposure to political risk. At that time, many countries had just recovered their sovereignty from colonial powers and, little by little, they started to question the benefits of having extremely powerful foreign firms in their backyard. This question reached its climax when it appeared that International Telephone and Telegraph was involved in the coup d'état against Allende's socialist government in Chile in 1973. Over this period, researchers were primarily concerned with the influence of governments on firms doing business abroad. The second stage took place in the 1980s with the advent of the international debt crisis in many developing countries. A large part of the literature was dedicated to creditworthiness assessment. This stream is the same as the one presented above that deals with the matter of external debt servicing. Finally, following the Mexican crisis in 1994 and the Asian meltdown in 1997, a third stage emerged in the 1990s, in order to focus on the financial crises. Currency and banking crises have occurred regularly over the last decades. For instance, Kaminsky and Reinhart (1999) report 102 banking or currency crises from 1970 to 1995, among a sample of 20 industrialized and developing countries. However, as noted by Feldstein (2002) "crises in the emerging market economies since the late 1990s were more global and potentially more damaging to economic and political stability than the crises of the past" and also "the crises that hit Latin America in the 1980s were significantly different from those of the 1990s". In the same vein, Terrier (1999) writes "le risque nouveau est arrivé".

The theoretical underpinnings of the articles about "financial crises" are rooted in the crisis models of Krugman (1979), Flood and Garber (1984), Obstfeld (1994), Calvo and Mendoza (1996) or Krugman (1998). Based on these papers, other authors have attempted to identify early warning indicators of crisis in order to assess the risk of occurrence of this type of event. Frankel and Rose (1996) or Eichengreen *et al.* (1996) concentrate on currency crises, Hardy and Pazarbasioglu (1999) or Demirguc-Kunt and Detragiache (1998) tackle the banking crisis, while Kaminsky (1999) or Goldstein *et al.* (2000) include these two types of crisis in a single approach. Nonetheless, by following an *ad hoc* procedure after each series of economic collapses, these papers run the risk of missing the call in the future. As stressed by Eichengreen and Rose (2000): "The success of future papers in explaining past crises does not mean that they will necessarily succeed in predicting future crises. This creates a real danger that the policy community, if led to think otherwise, will be lulled into a false sense of complacency."

A very illustrative example of the historical evolution of country risk can be found in the various changes in the country risk assessment methods of Coface, the French credit export agency, over the last decades (Clei, 1997, 1998). In the 1980s their analysis was mainly focused on external debt ratios. They then began to include political factors after the Soviet Union's breakup and the Gulf War of 1991. Finally, the Mexican crisis in 1994 led them to consider financial instability as well.

2.1.6 Different Methodologies

Besides the historical classification, a similar one differentiates between the qualitative line versus the quantitative method. While the literature in the 1960s and 1970s was mainly based on qualitative studies aimed at analyzing political risk, it became much more quantitatively oriented in the 1980s and 1990s when trying to predict sovereign default or financial crises. Rummel and Heenan (1978), for example, advocate an integrated methodology combining both quantitative and qualitative tools whereas Ray and Russett (1996) assert that "the scientific or systematic empirical approach to international politics is not dead". Stevens (1997) tests the reliability of the quantitative approach in political risk analysis. The failure to anticipate recent evolutions in international politics or the latest economic debacles has brought some researchers such as Gaddis (1992/93) or Sionneau (2000) to question the "quant perspective". This view is supported by Gori (2002) when he asserts that "social complexity is badly represented by neo-classical economics and rationalistic epistemology".

2.2 CLASSIFICATION AND EXAMPLES OF COUNTRY RISK

Robock (1971), Desta (1985), Miller (1992) or Meldrum (2000) list each type of country risk and describe its characteristics after having classified the main origins. Indeed, in the absence of any comprehensive theory, an accurate and exhaustive classification is necessary in order to make an extensive review of the various specific sources of risk, without missing in the future any possible new factor of instability. This is also necessary to be able to undertake an operational monitoring at the firm's level. Table 2.3 recaps these various groupings.

2.2.1 Natural Disasters

A first but seldom-mentioned line has to be drawn between natural and man-made sources of risk.[2] Natural risks refer to the natural phenomena (seismicity, weather) that may negatively impact the business conditions. As stressed above, in order to belong to the country risk category, the features of the events to be included must be different from those at home. As shown in Box 2.1, these events may impact directly on the firm through the destruction of facilities, for example, but they may also indirectly provoke business interruption because of a shortage of inventories or the impossibility of the workforce attending their plants or offices. This situation can be worsened by weak infrastructure and inefficiencies of the local institutions.

Table 2.3 Sources of risk classification

Socio-political risk			Economic risk		Natural risk
Political	Government policy	Social	Macroeconomic	Microeconomic	
Democratic or non-democratic change in the government	Change in the policy of the local authorities	Social movement intending to influence foreign business or host country policy	Any macroeconomic risk specific to the host country	Any microeconomic risk specific to the host country	Earthquake and other natural disaster

---

[2] Even though it could now be argued that because of global warming, it will be more difficult to discern between natural climate change and human influence. The Intergovernmental Panel on Climate Change (IPCC) at http://www.ipcc.ch/ reviews the scientific, technical and socio-economic information relevant to the understanding of the risk of human-induced climate change.

Box 2.1   Natural disaster risk

Turkish earthquake in 1999 – Anika Therapeutics

Izmit is an important industrial center near Istanbul, Turkey and one of the most exposed regions to the earthquake risk. On 17 August 1999, it was hit by a disastrous quake with a magnitude of 7.6 on the Richter Scale. More than 17 000 inhabitants were killed, 50 000 injured and 600 000 left homeless. About 150 industrial plants, among them 50 multi-national companies with production facilities in this area, were badly affected. Insurance companies estimated the damage at over \$2 billion. But the approximate total economic costs reached \$5 to 10 billion according to Gaci Ercel, head of the Turkish central bank.

Some experts blamed the Turkish government for taking insufficient preventive measures, in spite of knowing for a long time the high exposure of the region to earthquakes, increasing the devastating impact of the quake. Beyond the destruction of property, losses were also caused by disorganization of the workforce since thousands of employees were unable or unwilling to return to work for days. This event illustrated the deficiencies of insurance policies which usually do not cover "human element" losses.

Anika Therapeutics Inc., a biotechnology firm based in Massachusetts, USA, was affected by this catastrophe. The company develops, manufactures and commercializes therapeutic products helping to protect and repair bone and soft tissue. One of its products is Orthovisc®, serving for the treatment of osteoarthritis, and is not approved for use in the United States. Anika Therapeutics derived a substantial share of its revenues from Orthovisc, which was distributed in Israel, Spain and Turkey. As a consequence, the firm was severely hit by the earthquake. Indeed, Biomeks, their Turkish distributor, was obliged to postpone the delivery of the product to local customers, which caused a significant disruption in sales. This obliged J. Melville Engle, chairman, president and chief executive officer of Anika, to announce lower than expected sales for the third quarter 1999 and a net loss of about \$0.02 per share versus a net profit of \$0.07 in the same period of 1998.

2.2.2   Socio-political Risk

Among the man-made sources of risk, two groups can be distinguished: Socio-political risk and economic risk. Socio-political risk includes all possible damaging actions or factors for the business of foreign firms that emanate from any social group, political authority or governmental body in the host country. Following Miller (1992), it can be further split between social risk, government policy risk and political risk.

Social Risk

Social or societal-related risk corresponds to collective actions from organizations such as trade unions, non-governmental organizations (NGOs) or more informal sets of people that, peacefully or not, democratically or not, lobby the local authorities and/or directly the foreign firms, in order to influence their policy and/or their actions. These movements may be from internal origins, as was the case when José Bové the French farm workers' union leader ransacked a McDonald's restaurant in southern France. He and a few other activists caused more than \$100 000 of damage to what he called a "symbol of economic imperialism" (Bové and Dufour, 2001).[3] This type of action may be relatively peaceful. However, in the worst-case scenario, societal-related risk can go all the way to the physical aggression of foreign employees or even kidnapping (see Box 2.2).

Box 2.2   Example of societal-related risk from internal origin

---

Occidental Petroleum Corp. facing terrorism in Colombia

Colombia is in the midst of a 38-year civil war and a "booming kidnapping business" with revenues reaching 4 million euros and a total of 2000 kidnappings in 2001. In such an environment it is difficult both for local and international companies to operate without taking into account potential losses.

When the Cano Limon field was discovered in 1983 with an estimated one billion barrels of reserves, it was seen as a field that would transform the Los Angeles-based Occidental Petroleum Corp. The pipeline is crucial not only to Colombia but also for the US, since last year it provided 2% of US oil consumption.

However, as oil royalties began coming into the region, Occidental began to face a constant threat of terrorism from two guerrilla groups, the National Liberation Army (ELN) and the Armed Forces of Colombia (FARC). They are battling for economic and military control of a northern region and the latter group is trying to put a strangle hold on the former. The attention of the rebel groups is mainly focused on the 750-km pipeline that transports oil from the Cano Limon oil field to a port in the Caribbean and was bombed a record 170 times in 2001. Due to this, it was out of operation for 266 days at a cost of $40 million a month and the production was cut to 19 million barrels, a 58% reduction from the year before. Furthermore, Occidental says that it pays about 50 cents in security costs for each barrel of oil extracted and the costs are climbing as attacks on its pipeline rise. Hence, as part of the 2003 budget proposal, the Bush administration in mid-February proposed spending $98 million (112.5 million euros) to help train local troops in pipeline protection.

These risks may also have external origins, for instance when a firm is obliged to disinvest from certain countries under the pressure of world public opinion (see Box 2.3).

Box 2.3   Example of societal-related risk from external origin

---

Press release from the Free Burma Coalition, 27 January 1997 (extract:)[4]

Purchase, NY – January 27 – PepsiCo, Inc., the $30 billion soft drinks giant, has confirmed its intention to withdraw completely from the Southeast Asian dictatorship of Burma. In a letter released on Friday, Pepsi said "Based on our assessment of the spirit of current US government foreign policy, we are completing our total disengagement from the Burmese market. Accordingly, we have severed all relationships with our former franchise bottler, effective January 15, 1997."

Pepsi had long been a boycott target because of close ties between its Burmese bottler and the ruling Burmese military junta, widely condemned for its human rights violations and suppression of democracy. The bottler, named Thein Tun, had publicly called for the

---

[3] Ironically enough, a little time later, McDonald's decided to use as mascot in France the Gallic nationalist comic-book hero Asterix, which is also José Bové's nickname in reference to his impressive walrus moustache.
[4] Full text available at http://www.freeburmacoalition.org/frames/Press%20Releases/97-1-27.htm

popular democracy movement, headed by Nobel Peace Laureate Aung San Suu Kyi, to be "ostracized and crushed".

Aung San Suu Kyi, in the cover story from the 19 January *Parade Magazine*, appealed to the world community. "Don't support businesses which are supporting injustice in Burma", she said.

Since last July, companies leaving Burma have included Carlsberg, Heineken, London Fog, Motorola, Apple Computer, Hewlett-Packard, Walt Disney, J. Crew and Wente Vine-yards. Eleven US cities, one county, and the State of Massachusetts have passed anti-apartheid-style "selective contracting" laws. More are expected this year, including cities in Canada, the United Kingdom and Australia.

The next focus of the campaign is a small group of oil companies, including Unocal, Total, Arco and Texaco. Unocal and Total are partners with the Burmese junta in a major project to pipe natural gas into Thailand. The United Nations, European Commission, International Labor Organization, and US State Department have all concluded that forced labor is endemic in Burma, and is especially prevalent on infrastructure projects. Numerous groups have reported that forced labor and other human rights violations are directly related to the gas pipeline project.

Government Policy Risk

According to Miller (1992), "social uncertainty can be a precursor to political and policy uncertainty". Indeed, social protests rise from the ground of frustration and aim at altering governmental policy or even more radically the political regime. Government policy risk covers any unanticipated detrimental actions to foreign companies taken by local authorities. This includes expropriation/nationalization, breach of contract including loan repudiation, foreign exchange controls, trade restrictions or trade agreements that could favor some foreign competitors at the expense of others (see Box 2.4).

Box 2.4   Example of governmental policy risk – trade restrictions

Steel trade dispute

In March 2002, serious economic tensions between the European Union and the United States were triggered by a sudden change in attitude from the USA, concerning their trade relationship with the EU. The President of the United States, George W. Bush Jr. announced one of the most comprehensive trade protections for the US steel industry. Tariffs of up to 30% on imported steel are supposed to be imposed. Attempts to protect struggling American steel firms had already been made in the 1980s, when certain import quotas had been negotiated with Europe and Japan. The protectionist action of the American authorities globally raised sharp protests and criticism, especially from European politicians and steel producers.

In 2001 the United States was a net importer of about 23.5 million tons of steel, of which 4.9 million tons were shipped in from the European Union. Experts estimated that about half of these imports could fall away because of those trade restrictions from 2002 on. The immediate consequences of this trade war were found in the stock price of the European steel producers. Thus, on 6 March 2002, the initial drop of one of the largest European steelmakers, Corus Inc., was 5.7%. Corus Inc. is the biggest steelmaker in Great Britain and the fifth biggest in the world. With about 5% of its production delivered to the US market, it is directly exposed to this threat.

The amount of finished steel products sent to the United States could fall by 5 to 16 million tons as a consequence of the restrictions. As an indirect consequence of these trade barriers, it is feared that Brazilian or Korean steel output will be diverted and exported to Europe instead. This could lead to tumbling prices for steel because of the additional supply of 9 million tons and further job losses of up to 18 000 steel workers in Europe.

Loan repudiation or sovereign default concerns a sovereign debtor's unwillingness to service its local or foreign currency obligations. If the sovereign entity's difficulties in servicing its debt are the result of poor economic conditions such as depletion of foreign exchange reserves, this risk would not be treated in the political category but rather in the economic category to be dealt with below. Regarding local currency debt, it is argued that a country cannot be bankrupt since it always has the possibility to print money. Consequently, non-payment on internal debt can be considered as the result of a political choice. For instance, the Russian default on 281 000 million ruble-denominated treasury bills and bonds, representing $43 billion as of August 1998, could have been avoided had the authorities decided to print more money. But of course, on the other hand, this would have generated more inflation and *de facto* have led to an implicit default. Clark and Zenaidi (1999) have developed a model that makes it possible to measure a government's willingness to default.

Foreign exchange controls are usually based on concrete economic difficulties but their timing and implementation remain an economic policy choice. The various answers to the Asian crisis in 1997/1998 illustrate this point. Whereas Indonesia, the Philippines, South Korea and Thailand maintained a policy of free convertibility, Malaysia chose to implement currency controls. The same alternative was offered to the Zedillo administration after the Mexican debacle of 1994. At this time, many international investors feared the risk of foreign currency control and were relieved when the Mexican authorities chose to maintain free convertibility.

Expropriation can take many forms. As explained by Mark Vandewater, a vice-president of international development at the Overseas Private Investment Corporation[5] in Kielmas (1998): "Governments have become extremely sophisticated in how they do this [expropriation]. It's no longer the case of sending tanks to surround the factory and throwing you out." Indeed, government policy risk can include some less dramatic but probably more pervasive events including economic, fiscal and monetary reforms, as well as inadequate provision of public services or inability/unwillingness to enforce regulations in the host country (see Box 2.5).

Box 2.5   Example of governmental policy risk – legal enforcement

Archangel versus Lukoil
At first glance, the area of Verkhotina located near the Arctic Circle region in Russia has nothing to attract multinational corporations, except for the huge potential for diamond mining which dramatically changes the deal. This is also the place of a harsh battle between the Canadian diamond mining company Archangel Diamond Corp., controlled by the

---

[5] Overseas Private Investment Corporation (OPIC) is one of the leading export credit agencies.

Oppenheimer family, and Arkhangelskgeoldobycha, a 74.1% owned subsidiary of Lukoil, the still partly state-owned Russian oil giant.

The story starts in November 1993, when Archangel Diamond Corp., Arkhangelskgeoldobycha and IBME, a third foreign offshore company, founded a joint venture, named Almazny Bereg., with respective stakes of 50%, 40% and 10%. Their common goal was to explore and mine diamonds in the Verkhotina region. At that time, Russian state law did not permit foreign capital companies to hold licenses for diamond fields. Therefore all partners agreed that the native subsidiary of Lukoil should keep the license until the law was changed. In the meantime, Archangel invested over $30 million into the common project for exploration work. In 1996, a very rich diamond field was discovered, the so-called "Grib pipe", with an estimated potential of about $5 billion.

In 1995, the Russian Natural Ministry changed the regulation and authorized foreign companies to hold licenses which should have allowed the transfer of the exploration rights to the joint venture. However, in August 1998, Arkhangelskgeoldobycha had not yet passed the license to Almazny Bereg. In Archangel's opinion, this clearly represented a violation of the agreement that planned the transfer of the rights as soon as legally possible. Consequently, in a first step, the Canadians sought justice at an international arbitration court in Stockholm under UNCITRAL Rules, as an arbitration clause stipulated in one of their agreements. But because of the difficult question of the jurisdiction of such an international court, the matter proved impossible to resolve at this stage. Then, Archangel filed a lawsuit against Arkhangelskgeoldobycha and its mother company Lukoil at a court in Denver, USA. They claimed about $4.8 billion, representing $1.2 billion of lost gains from their share in the diamond fields and $3.6 billion of "punitive damages" for other expenses.

An effective resolution procedure for such disputes between foreign and native investors in developing economies like Russia is a very complicated issue. Archangel's difficulties illustrate the complexity for doing business in a fast-changing legal environment. Although international arbitration according to international rules had been foreseen, the final responsibility of any court was hard to determine. Archangel's president and CEO Timothy J. Haddon declared in *Oil & Gas Today* on 24 August 2001: "...It is a tragedy for all parties, but especially for Russia, where this action clearly demonstrates to the world once again the lack of protection international investors have in regard to corporate governance, rule of law or the simple sense of fairness in doing business...The enforcement of a contract in Russia seems impossible."

Political Risk

Political risk is the last type of socio-political risk. It concerns any potential or actual change in the political system, civil or external war but also includes any democratic evolution that may disrupt the foreign business. For instance, in the past changes in government have resulted in nationalizations/expropriation. Examples of nationalizations of foreign-owned firms occurred in France after the democratic election of Mitterrand as President in 1981, when Roussel-Uclaf, CII-Honeywell and ITT-France, respectively subsidiaries of Hoescht, Honeywell and International Telephone and Telegraph, were acquired by the French government. Expropriation differs from nationalization in the sense that expropriation is a loss of ownership without any compensation. An example of expropriation is found in Cuba in 1960 where, one year after Castro seized power, United Fruit Company, among other American firms, lost the ownership of several hundred thousand acres of property. Even though this type of risk has rarely materialized in the recent past, West (1999) notices: "While no government has engaged in wholesale expropriation for nearly two decades, the possibility of selective expropriations are higher than ever in some countries due to rising nationalism." At the utmost, expropriation can be the consequence of a war between countries as was the case for the German firm Bayer in the USA after the First World War (see Box 2.6).

Box 2.6   Example of political risk – war

Bayer in the USA

Shortly before 1900, one of the most classic painkillers of the twentieth century was born, in the laboratories of the German chemical and pharmaceutical company Bayer AG. After receiving its patents not only for Germany, but also for the United States, Aspirin® very rapidly became one of the most popular and best known drugs worldwide. Franz Kafka is supposed to have said to his fiancée that Aspirin was one of the few substances that brought relief to his tormented psyche. As early as 1908, this drug accounted for more than 30% of Bayer AG's revenues.

Less than a decade later, the United States joined their European allies in the First World War, to fight the German and the Austrian Empire. After the war, to pay for reparations the United States expropriated several German companies, among them Bayer AG. The former properties of Bayer AG were auctioned and Sterling Drug Inc., a US pharmaceutical company, acquired the rights for $5.3 million in 1918. As a consequence, Bayer lost not only its former US subsidiaries, but also the right to use "Bayer-Aspirin" as a trademark.

Until 1986, Bayer AG owned and sold this almost universally recognized brand in more than 70 countries worldwide, except the United States of America, where it could not do any business under its famous brand name because of the expropriation. After more than half a century of struggling for its brand, Bayer made an important step to acquire the full name rights. In 1986, it bought Sterling's over-the-counter line of pharmaceutics for more than $1 billion together with the formal right to again use the name Aspirin in the United States. However, the dispute between Bayer and Sterling about the exact extent of Bayer's rights on the brand was not over. Bayer was obliged to fight several years more, until it was at last granted the full rights in 1994. This now allows the company to offer Aspirin under its proper name and use its famous brand, the "Bayer cross".

2.2.3   Country-Specific Economic Risk

Country-specific economic risk can be broken down into macro risk (directed at all foreign enterprises) and micro risk (directed toward specific sectors of activity or selected firms). Economic risk may result from political mismanagement but, contrary to the socio-political risk discussed above, it should not be the explicit consequence of a political choice.

Macroeconomic risk refers to variability in the economic environment such as output, prices, interest rates, foreign exchange rates, terms of trade, etc. For instance, a period of hyperinflation engulfed many Latin American countries during the 1980s up until the beginning of the 1990s. In the most extreme case, in June 1994 Brazil experienced a monthly inflation rate of 50.75%, equivalent to more than 13 000% on an annual basis. This kind of imbalance badly disrupts day-to-day business and may prove to be very costly as illustrated by the following anecdote. In the mid-1980s, shortly after the implementation of a stabilization plan by the Argentinian government that aimed at curbing the triple-digit inflation rate prevalent at the time, the Argentinian subsidiary of a worldwide leading retailer had decided to promote a credit card policy for its customers. Unfortunately, less than a year after, the failure of the economic plan led to the resurgence of hyperinflation. The retailer started to suffer huge losses because of his credit policy and the program was soon abandoned.

Another crucial source of economic risk lies in the exchange rate. The sudden devaluation of the Mexican peso in 1994/1995 and the Asian currencies in 1997/1998 highlighted this issue. However, it is not confined absolutely to developing countries and can materialize in the most developed countries, such as within the European Community area, as exemplified by the BMW–Rover case in Box 2.7.

Box 2.7   Example of macroeconomic risk – exchange rate

The BMW-Rover case

At the beginning of the 1990s, Bayerische Motoren Werke AG (also known as BMW), a German premium car producer, was in good shape. Sales were steadily increasing. The success of the company was even threatening the leading position of their old rival Mercedes Benz. In 1994, BMW acquired Rover, the last British mass market car maker for £800 million. This happened only two years after a massive devaluation of the British currency, when Great Britain was obliged to exit from the European Monetary System.

At this time, the deal was greeted with euphoria, in particular by the then chairman of BMW, Bernd Pischetsrieder, who was not only known as very anglophile, but also as a relative of Sir Alec Issigonis, the famous designer of the legendary "Mini", one of Rover's strongest brands. This optimism was based on the assumption that it could help BMW challenge new fields. One of the main arguments for the Rover acquisition was to export to foreign, especially emerging, markets.

The very few critical voices, such as BMW board member Wolfgang Reitzle who warned against the bad situation of Rover, were more or less ignored. The objective was to bring Rover back into profits by 2000. Important resources, manpower and about £2 billion of capital were poured into the company. According to Pischetsrieder in *Automotive News* (1998): "I know where Rover has to go, and we're slightly ahead of time. We've got everything under control but the (British) pound."

Unfortunately, BMW did not achieve an improvement in Rover's poor economic position, partly because of the strength of the British pound, which was "hurting Rover's finances" as stated by the chairman in *Automotive News* (1998). Since the devaluation of 1992, the pound had steadily appreciated against most of the European currencies (see Figure 2.1). At the height of its strength, the pound was up to 25% stronger than expected by BMW. On the one hand, Rover found it more and more difficult to export to the continent, while on the other hand, competition from foreign firms intensified.

The market share of Rover at home decreased from over 13% at the time of the merger to only 5% in 1999. After six continuous years in the red, losses reached £750 million. In 2000, shareholders, among them the 50% owning Quandt family, lost patience. Rover was sold to Alchemy Partners, a British consortium, and Pischetsrieder was fired.

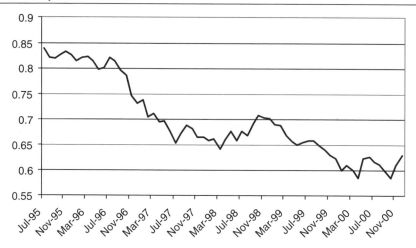

Figure 2.1 Exchange rate: Euro/GBP

Although it involves the economy as a whole, macroeconomic risk does not necessarily negatively impact all foreign businesses. It may only concern certain industries or even merely a few companies. Consequently, assessment of country-specific macroeconomic risk should be firm-specific and done at the individual level. Thus, for instance, even though the Mexican economic crisis of 1994 that followed the devaluation of the peso affected the whole economy, some companies benefitted from this situation to gain some market share abroad. This was the case for Grupo Modelo, producer of Corona beer and partly owned by the American brewer Anheuser-Busch. As stated in its Annual Report 1995: "Grupo Modelo's sales volume decreased less than the overall industry in 1995 to only 0.43% compared to the previous year. Grupo Modelo's domestic and international sales of 25.1 million hectoliters represented 56.4% of the market share of all Mexican Beer sold in 1995. This great accomplishment can be explained by the growing success of products in the International Market, registering an increase of 39.06% in its export volume in 1995 compared to the previous year, which practically compensated the decrease in its domestic market."

Microeconomic risk encompasses all the negative events that may arise at the industry or the firm level. It embraces both risks related to the resources required by the foreign firm to run its business (raw materials, labor, capital) and risks associated with outputs and marketing uncertainties. Quoting Swyngedouw's (1992) neologism, many of these microeconomic uncertainties could be classified as "glocalization" risks, i.e. when a global strategy must cope with local features (see also Robertson, 1995). This category concerns the business environment of the foreign firm in its regular operations. It includes all the risks specific to the host country affecting the business transactions and the management of local operations: production, marketing, finance, supply and logistics, human resources, technology, organizational structure. It also involves the cultural aspects of the risk management and particularly the "safety culture" such as that described by Waring and Glendon (1998). This notion is especially crucial when multinational corporations export "industrial risks" into developing countries, where local infrastructure, regulations, safety procedures or environmental requirements may be less stringent vis-à-vis this kind of risk. A tragic example is Bhopal, India in 1984, when a toxic gas was released into the atmosphere by Union Carbide of India, a subsidiary of the American chemical company Union Carbide Corporation.

Microeconomic risk may also come from specific local customer preference. For instance, trying to increase its market share in Asia, Revlon, the American cosmetic multinational, decided to use Cindy Crawford's image, the famous Western top model, without wondering if it would fit the Asian canon of beauty. In the meantime, L'Oréal, their main competitor, built its advertisement campaign around a Chinese star and struck a blow against Revlon.

Some of the above-mentioned risks can develop at a supranational level. A typical case was provided by the Asian crisis. After the devaluation of the Thai baht in July 1997, it was then the turn of the Philippine peso, the Malaysian ringitt and the Indonesian rupee in August 1997, shortly followed by the Korean won in November 1997, through a kind of domino effect. However, such outcomes do not necessarily call for the definition of a specific "contagion risk". Most of the concerned countries shared the same structural weaknesses that led to the successive meltdowns. Consequently, such risk can be classified as the global materialization of a blend of social and macroeconomic risks. The relatively small impact of the Mexican crisis on Latin American countries in 1995 tends to support this stance.

It should be noted that some of these risks are difficult to identify exclusively within a single category. For instance, when a strike occurs in a foreign company, it may be the result of a particular problem between the firm and its employees in a country where trade unions are possibly more powerful than in the country of origin (microeconomic risk), but it can also be the outcome of a nationwide movement of protest against foreign businesses (social risk). Energy shortages are another example of a difficult-to-classify risk. Indeed, an energy crisis could be due to natural causes when, for instance, it is the result of a severe drought that impedes the operation of hydroelectrical plants. But on the other hand, the government should probably be blamed for public mismanagement, inability to foster the supply of energy and failure to correctly anticipate the demand for electricity. Or, finally, for those countries or states like California, where the electricity sector is only partially deregulated, this could be perceived as a byproduct of a free market and be classified as an economic risk. This kind of situation materialized in Brazil in 2001, when drought caused massive power shortages. This affected many firms, including Flextronics International Ltd of Singapore, an electronics manufacturing services provider. At that time, Flextronics was about to build two more plants near São Paulo. However, the energy problem was so severe that it decided against making this $85 million investment, that would have created 500 new jobs.

REFERENCES

Abdullah FA, 1985, Development of an Advance Warning Indicator of External Debt Servicing Vulner-ability. *Journal of International Business Studies*, Fall, 16 (3), 135–41.

Adler M and Dumas B, 1983, International Portfolio Choice and Corporation Finance: A Synthesis. *Journal of Finance*, Jun, 38 (3), 925–84.

Aggarwal R, Rao RP and Hiraki T, 1989, Skewness and Kurtosis in Japanese Equity Returns: Empirical Evidence. *Journal of Financial Research*, Fall, 12 (3), 253–60.

Agmon T, 1973, Country Risk: The Significance of the Country Factor for Share-Price Movements in the United Kingdom, Germany, and Japan. *Journal of Business*, Jan, 46 (1), 24–32.

Agmon T and Dietrich JK, 1983, International Lending and Income Redistribution: An Alternative View of Country Risk. *Journal of Banking and Finance*, Dec, 7, 483–95.

Aliber RZ, 1973, The Interest Rate Parity Theorem: A Reinterpretation. *Journal of Political Economy*, Nov/Dec, 81 (6), 1451–9.

Aliber RZ, 1975, Exchange Risk, Political Risk, and Investor Demand for External Currency Deposits. *Journal of Money, Credit, and Banking*, May, 7 (2), 161–79.

Alon I and Martin MA, 1998, A Normative Model of Macro Political Risk Assessment. *Multinational Business Review*, Fall, 6 (2), 10–19.

Baglini NA, 1976, *Risk Management in International Corporations*. New York: Risk Studies Foundations Inc.

Baird I and Thomas H, 1990, What Is Risk Anyway? Using and Measuring Risk in Strategic Management. *In:* R Bettis and H Thomas, eds. *Risk Strategy and Management*. Greenwich, CT: JAI Press, 21–52.

Bawa VS and Lindenberg EB, 1977, Capital Market Equilibrium in a Mean-Lower Partial Moment Framework. *Journal of Financial Economics*, Nov, 5 (2), 189–200.

Bekaert G, 1995, Market Integration and Investment Barriers in Emerging Equity Markets. *World Bank Economic Review*, Jan, 9 (1), 75–107.

Bekaert G and Harvey CR, 1995, Time-Varying World Market Integration. *Journal of Finance*, Jun, 50 (2), 403–44.

Bekaert G, Erb CB, Harvey CR and Viskanta TE, 1998, Distributional Characteristics of Emerging Market Returns and Asset Allocation. *Journal of Portfolio Management*, Winter, 24 (2), 102–16.

Bergara ME, Henisz WJ and Spiller PT, 1998, Political Institutions and Electric Utility Investment: A Cross-National Analysis. *California Management Review*, Winter, 40 (2), 18–35.

Bové J and Dufour F, 2001, *The World Is Not for Sale*. London, New York: Verso Books.

Brewer TL, 1981, Political Risk Assessment for Foreign Direct Investment Decisions: Better Methods for Better Results. *Columbia Journal of World Business*, Spring, 16 (1), 5–12.

Calvo GA and Mendoza EG, 1996, Petty Crime and Cruel Punishment: Lessons from the Mexican Debacle. *American Economic Review*, May, 86 (2), 170–5.

Citron JT and Nickelsburg G, 1987, Country Risk and Political Instability. *Journal of Development Economics*, Apr, 25 (2), 385–92.

Clark E and Zenaidi A, 1999, Sovereign Debt Discounts and the Unwillingness to Pay. *Finance*, 20 (2), 185–99.

Clei J, 1997, Les Leçons de la Crise Mexicaine. *Banque Stratégie*, Sep, 141, 21–3.

Clei J, 1998, La Coface Devant le Risque Pays. *Risques*, Déc, 36, 51–4.

Cosset JC and Suret JM, 1995, Political Risk and the Benefits of International Portfolio Diversification. *Journal of International Business Studies*, 26 (2), 301–18.

Cosset JC, Siskos Y and Zopounidis C, 1992, Evaluating Country Risk: A Decision Support Approach. *Global Finance Journal*, 3 (1), 79–95.

Davis RR, 1981, Alternative Techniques for Country Risk Evaluation. *Business Economics*, May, 16 (3), 34–41.

Demirguc-Kunt A and Detragiache E, 1998, The Determinants of Banking Crises in Developing and Developed Countries. *International Monetary Fund Staff Papers*, Mar, 45 (1), 81–109.

Desta A, 1985, Assessing Political Risk in Less Developed Countries. *Journal of Business Strategy*, Spring, 5 (4), 40–53.

Drake RL and Prager AJ, 1977, Floundering with Foreign Investment Planning. *Columbia Journal of World Business*, 12 (2), 66–77.

Eaton J, Gersovitz M and Stiglitz JE, 1986, The Pure Theory of Country Risk. *European Economic Review*, Jun, 30 (3), 481–513.

Eichengreen B and Rose A, 2000, The Empirics of Currency and Banking Crises. *Wirtschaftspolitische Blatter*, 47 (4), 395–402.

Eichengreen B, Rose A and Wyplosz C, 1996, Contagious Currency Crises: First Tests. *Scandinavian Journal of Economics*, Dec, 98 (4), 463–84.

Erb CB, Harvey CR and Viskanta TE, 1995, Country Risk and Global Equity Selection. *Journal of Portfolio Management*, Winter, 21 (2), 74–83.

Erb CB, Harvey CR and Viskanta TE, 1996a, The Influence of Political, Economic and Financial Risk on Expected Fixed Income Returns. *Journal of Fixed Income*, Jun, 6 (1), 7–31.

Erb CB, Harvey CR and Viskanta TE, 1996b, Political Risk, Economic Risk, and Financial Risk. *Financial Analysts Journal*, Nov/Dec, 52 (6), 28–46.

Errunza VR, 1977, Gains from Portfolio Diversification into Less Developed Countries' Securities. *Journal of International Business Studies*, Fall–Winter, 8 (2), 83–99.

Errunza VR and Losq E, 1985, International Asset Pricing under Mild Segmentation: Theory and Test. *Journal of Finance*, Mar, 40 (1), 105–24.

Estrada J, 2000, The Cost of Equity in Emerging Markets: A Downside Risk Approach. *Emerging Markets Quarterly*, Fall, 4 (3), 19–30.

Feder G and Just RE, 1977, A Study of Debt Servicing Capacity Applying Logit Analysis. *Journal of Development Economics*, Mar, 4 (1), 25–38.

Feder G and Uy LV, 1985, The Determinants of International Creditworthiness and Their Policy Implications. *Journal of Policy Modeling*, Spring, 7 (1), 133–56.

Feils DJ and Sabac FM, 2000, The Impact of Political Risk on the Foreign Direct Investment Decision: A Capital Budgeting Analysis. *Engineering Economist*, 45 (2), 129–43.

Feldstein M, 2002, Economic and Financial Crises in Emerging Market Economies: Overview of Prevention and Management. *NBER Working Paper Series*, Working Paper 8837, March, http://www.nber.org/papers/w8837

Finnerty JD, 2001, Securitizing Political Risk Investment Insurance: Lessons from Past Securitizations. *In:* TH Moran, ed. *International Political Risk Management*. Washington: The World Bank, 77–147.

Fitzpatrick M, 1983, The Definition and Assessment of Political Risk in International Business: A Review of the Literature. *Academy of Management Review*, Apr, 8 (2), 249–54.

Flood RP and Garber PM, 1984, Collapsing Exchange Rate Regimes: Some Linear Examples. *Journal of International Economics*, Aug, 17 (1/2), 1–13.

Frank CR and Cline WR, 1971, Measurement of Debt Servicing Capacity: An Application of Discriminant Analysis. *Journal of International Economics*, Aug, 1 (3), 327–44.

Frankel JA and Rose AK, 1996, Currency Crashes in Emerging Markets: An Empirical Treatment. *Journal of International Economics*, Nov, 41 (3/4), 351–66.

Gabriel PP, 1966, The Investment in the LDC: Asset with a Fixed Maturity. *Columbia Journal of World Business*, Summer, 1 (3), 109–19.

Gaddis JL, 1992/93, International Relations Theory and the End of the Cold War. *International Security*, 17, 5–58.

Goldstein M, Kaminsky GL and Reinhart CM, 2000, *Assessing Financial Vulnerability: An Early Warning System for Emerging Markets*. Washington: Institute for International Economics.

Gori S (sgori@mailexcite.com), 2002, A Cognitive Approach to Political Risk Analysis. Working Paper, 26 April 2002. E-mail to B Groslambert (bertrand.groslambert@ceram.fr).

Grauer FL, Litzenberger RH and Stehle RE, 1976, Sharing Rules and Equilibrium in an International Capital Market under Uncertainty. *Journal of Financial Economics*, Jun, 3 (3), 233–56.

Groslambert B and Kassibrakis S, 1999, The Alpha-Stable Hypothesis: An Alternative to the Distribution of Emerging Stock Market Returns. *Emerging Markets Quarterly*, Spring, 3 (1), 22–38.

Grubel HG, 1968, Internationally Diversified Portfolios: Welfare Gains and Capital Flows. *American Economic Review*, Dec, Part 1 of 2, 58 (5), 1299–314.

Haendel D, West GT and Meadow RG, 1975, *Overseas Investment and Political Risk*. Philadelphia: Foreign Policy Research Institute Monograph Series, No. 21.

Hardy DC and Pazarbasioglu C, 1999, Determinants and Leading Indicators of Banking Crises: Further Evidence. *International Monetary Fund Staff Papers*, Sep–Dec, 46 (3), 247–58.

Harlow WV and Rao KS, 1989, Asset Pricing in a Generalized Mean-Lower Partial Moment Framework: Theory and Evidence. *Journal of Financial and Quantitative Analysis*, Sep, 24 (3), 285–311.

Harvey CR, 1995, Predictable Risk and Return in Emerging Markets. *Review of Financial Studies*, Fall, 8 (3), 773–816.

Howell LD and Chaddick B, 1994, Models of Political Risk for Foreign Investment and Trade: An Assessment of Three Approaches. *Columbia Journal of World Business*, Fall, 29 (3), 70–91.

Jorion P and Schwartz E, 1986, Integration vs. Segmentation in the Canadian Stock Market. *Journal of Finance*, Jul, 41 (3), 603–14.

Kaminsky GL, 1999, Currency and Banking Crises: The Early Warnings of Distress. *International Monetary Fund Working Paper*, WP/99/178.

Kaminsky GL and Reinhart CM, 1999, The Twin Crises: The Causes of Banking and Balance-of-Payments Problems. *American Economic Review*, Jun, 89 (3), 473–500.

Kennedy CR, 1991. *Managing the International Business Environment. Cases in Political and Country Risk*. Englewood Cliffs: Prentice Hall.

Kielmas M, 1998, Expropriation by Two Countries Is Alleged. *Business Insurance*, Feb, 32 (44), 3–4.

Kobrin SJ, 1978, When Does Political Instability Result in Increased Investment Risk? *Columbia Journal of World Business*, Fall, 13 (3), 113–22.

Kobrin SJ, 1979, Political Risk: A Review and Reconsideration. *Journal of International Business Studies*, Spring/Summer, 10 (1), 67–80.

Krugman P, 1979, A Model of Balance of Payments Crisis. *Journal of Money Credit and Banking*, Aug, 11 (3), 311–25.

Krugman P, 1998, What Happened to Asia? [online]. Cambridge, MA: Massachusetts Institute of Technology. Available from: http://web.mit.edu/krugman/www/disinter.html [Accessed 1 April 2002].

Lessard DR, 1973, International Portfolio Diversification: A Multivariate Analysis for a Group of Latin American Countries. *Journal of Finance*, Jun, 28 (3), 619–33.

Levy H and Sarnat M, 1970, International Diversification of Investment Portfolios. *American Economic Review*, Sep, 4, 668–75.

Madura J, Tucker AL and Wiley M, 1997, Factors Affecting Returns across Stock Markets. *Global Finance Journal*, Spring–Summer, 8 (1), 1–14.

March JG and Shapira Z, 1987, Managerial perspectives on risk and risk taking. *Management Science*, 33, 1404–18.

Markowitz H, 1952, Portfolio Selection. *The Journal of Finance*, Mar, 7 (1), 77–91.

Markowitz H, 1959, *Portfolio Selection*. New Haven: Yale University Press.

Marois B, 1990, *Le Risque-Pays*. Paris: Presses Universitaires de France.

Marois B and Behar M, 1981, La prévision du risque politique liée aux investissements à l'étranger. *Revue d'Économie Industrielle*, 2ème trimestre, 0 (16), 34–43.

Meldrum DH, 1999, Country Risk and a Quick Look at Latin America. *Business Economics*, Jul, 34 (3), 30–7.

Meldrum DH, 2000, Country Risk and Foreign Direct Investment. *Business Economics*, Jan, 35 (1), 33–40.

Merrill J, 1982, Country Risk Analysis. *Columbia Journal of World Business*, Spring, 17 (1), 88–91.

Miller KD, 1992, A Framework for Integrated Risk Management in International Business. *Journal of International Business Studies*, 23 (2), 311–31.

Miller KD and Reuer JJ, 1996, Measuring Organizational Downside Risk. *Strategic Management Journal*, Nov, 17 (9), 671–91.

Moody's, 2002, *Sovereign Rating History: Special Comment*. New York: Moody's Investors Service, January, 73505.

Morgan JB, 1986, A New Look at Debt Rescheduling Indicators and Models. *Journal of International Business Studies*, Summer, 17 (2), 37–54.

Nagy P, 1978, Quantifying Country Risk: A System Developed By Economists At The Bank of Montreal. *Columbia Journal of World Business*, Fall, 13 (3), 135–47.

Nawrocki DN, 1999, A Brief History of Downside Risk Measures. *Journal of Investing*, Fall, 8 (3), 9–25.

Obstfeld M, 1994, The Logic of Currency Crisis. *Cahiers Economiques et Monétaires*, 43, 189–213.

Rajan M and Friedman J, 1997, An Examination of the Impact of Country Risk on the International Portfolio Selection Decision. *Global Finance Journal*, Spring–Summer, 8 (1), 55–70.

Ray JL and Russett B, 1996, The Future as Arbiter of Theoretical Controversies: Predictions, Explanations and the End of the Cold War. *British Journal of Political Science*, Oct, 26, 441–70.

Reuer JJ and Leiblein MJ, 2000, Downside Risk Implications of Multinationality and International Joint Ventures. *Academy of Management Journal*, Apr, 43 (2), 203–14.

Rivoli P and Brewer T, 1997, Political Instability and Country Risk. *Global Finance Journal*, Fall–Winter, 8 (2), 309–21.

Robertson R, 1995, Glocalization: Time–Space and Homogeneity and Heterogeneity. *In*: M Featherstone *et al.*, eds. *Global Modernities*. London: Sage, 25–44.

Robinson JN, 1981, Is It Possible to Assess Country Risk? *The Banker*, Jan, 71–79.

Robock SH, 1971, Political Risk: Identification and Assessment. *Columbia Journal of World Business*, Jul/Aug, 6 (4), 6–20.

Root FR, 1968, The Expropriation Experience of American Companies. *Business Horizons*, 11 (2), 69–74.

Root FR, 1972, Analyzing Political Risks in International Business. *In:* A Kapoor and PD Grub, eds *The Multinational Enterprise in Transition*. Princeton: Darwin Press, 354–65.

Roy AD, 1952, Safety First and the Holding of Assets. *Econometrica*, 20 (3), 431–49.

Roy A and Roy PG, 1994, Despite Past Debacles, Predicting Sovereign Risk Still Presents Problems. *Commercial Lending Review*, Summer, 9 (3), 92–5.

Rummel RJ and Heenan DA, 1978, How Multinationals Analyze Political Risk. *Harvard Business Review*, Jan/Feb, 56 (1), 67–76.

Schwartz ES and Zurita S, 1992, Sovereign Debt: Optimal Contract, Underinvestment, and Forgiveness. *Journal of Finance*, Jul, 47 (3), 981–1004.

Schwimmer A, 1995, The Battle Intensifies for Project Financings. *The Investment Dealers' Digest*, Feb 13, 61 (7), 12.

Sercu P, 1980, A Generalization of the International Asset Pricing Model. *Revue de l'Association Française de Finance*, Jun, 1, 91–135.

Shapiro AC, 1985, Currency Risk and Country Risk in International Banking. *Journal of Finance*, Jul, 40 (3), 881–91.

Simon JD, 1982, Political Risk Assessment: Past Trends And Future Prospects. *Columbia Journal of World Business*, Fall, 17 (3), 62–70.

Sionneau B, 2000, *Risque-Pays et Prospective Internationale: Théorie et Application*. Thèse de Doctorat, Sciences de Gestion, CNAM.

Solnik BH, 1974a, The International Pricing of Risk: An Empirical Investigation of the World Capital Market Structure. *Journal of Finance*, 29 (2), May, 365–78.

Solnik BH, 1974b, An Equilibrium Model of the International Capital Market. *Journal of Economic Theory*, Aug, 8 (4), 500–24.

Solnik BH, 1991, *International Investments*. 2nd edition. Reading, MA: Addison-Wesley.

Sortino FA and van der Meer R, 1991, Downside Risk. *The Journal of Portfolio Management*, Summer, 17 (4), 27–31.

Spillers CA, 1999, Implications of Economic Turmoil to Emerging Market Project Finance Transactions – A Rating Agency Perspective. *Journal of Project Finance*, Winter, 4 (4), 9–12.

Stehle RE, 1977, An Empirical Test of the Alternative Hypotheses of National and International Pricing of Risky Assets. *Journal of Finance*, May, 32 (2), 493–502.

Stevens FY, 1997, Quantitative Perspective on Political Risk Analysis for Direct Foreign Investment – A Closer Look. *Multinational Business Review*, Spring, 5 (1), 77–84.

Stobaugh RB, 1969a, Where in the World Should We Put that Plant? *Harvard Business Review*, Jan/Feb, 47 (1), 129–36.

Stobaugh RB, 1969b, How to Analyze Foreign Investment Climates. *Harvard Business Review*, Sep/Oct, 47 (5), 100–8.

Stulz RM, 1984, Pricing Capital Assets in an International Setting: An Introduction. *Journal of International Business Studies*, Winter, 15 (3), 55–73.

Swyngedouw E, 1992, The Mammon Quest: "Glocalization", Interspatial Competition and the Monetary Order – The Construction of New Scales. *In:* M Dunford and G Kafkalas, eds. *Cities and Regions in the New Europe: the Global–Local Interplay and Spatial Development Strategies*. London: Belhaven, 39–67.

Terrier JL, 1999, Assurance Crédit Export: Le Risque Nouveau est Arrivé. *Le MOCI*, Sep, 1405, 42.

Terrier JL, 2001, Country Rating 2001–2002. *Mimeo*, Paris: Credit Risk International.

Usher D, 1965, Political Risk. *Economic Development and Cultural Change*, Jul, 453–62.

Waring A and Glendon AI, 1998, *Managing Risk*. London: Thomson Learning.

West GT, 1999, Political Risk Investment Insurance: A Renaissance. *Journal of Project Finance*, Summer, 5 (2), 27–36.

Weston VF and Sorge BW, 1972. *International Managerial Finance*. Homewood, IL: Irwin.

Wilson JO, 1979, Measuring Country Risk in a Global Context. *Business Economics*, Jan, 14 (1), 23–7.

Zenoff D, 1967, Profitable, Fast Growing, But Still the Stepchild. *Columbia Journal of World Business*, Jul/Aug, 2 (4), 51–6.

3
The Economic and Financial Foundations
of Country Risk Assessment

A major element of country risk revolves around the capacity of the country to generate enough foreign exchange to maintain required levels of imports and service its foreign debt. The analysis is often conducted in terms of domestic and external equilibrium. Domestic equilibrium generally refers to full employment and a certain standard of living or growth in the standard of living. External equilibrium refers to the *ex ante* equality between the supply and demand of domestic currency on the foreign exchange markets. Because the balance of payments equation is an accounting identity, the *ex post* supply and demand of domestic currency will always be equal. However, *ex ante* the two can differ and, if they do, the disequilibrium will be reflected in a change in the exchange rate, if the monetary authority does not intervene, or in a change in foreign reserves, if it does intervene. Where country risk is concerned, the problem is a shortage of foreign exchange. Thus, the intervention option is limited by the monetary authority's supply of foreign reserves. Given the relationship between the balance of payments and the country's overall economic performance, both alternatives imply adjustments in the economy's domestic equilibrium. At the time of the gold standard or even fixed exchange rates, this meant a painful deflation where levels of output and consumption were reduced to the point where *ex ante* external equilibrium was restored. This can still be the case. However, in today's world of national currencies and floating exchanges, solutions to major fundamental external disequilibrium usually revolve around a change in the exchange rate.

On the surface, a change in the exchange rate seems to involve nothing more than a change in the price of one currency for another. In fact, the effects, with varying time lags, magnitudes and intensities, penetrate to the core of the economy and ultimately generate a new set of economic conditions with resulting consequences for domestic equilibrium and standards of living, the balance of payments, the supply and demand for foreign currency and the exchange rate. If the adjustments are too painful, governments are often obliged to make matters even worse in the long run by defaulting on their foreign debt. Consequently, balance of payments and exchange rate adjustment are major elements in country risk analysis.

In this chapter we examine the economic adjustment process caused by external disequilibrium. We look at the consequences of a devaluation on relative prices, incomes, and the composition of output and consumption. We then consider the consequences of external disequilibrium when a change in the exchange rate is avoided through offsetting transactions by the monetary authorities. Next, we present the monetary approach to balance of payments analysis and its more sophisticated cousin, the portfolio balance approach. We conclude with a presentation of some of the most commonly used tools for country risk analysis resulting from the foregoing approaches along with some new ratios derived from modern financial theory.

3.1 DEVALUATION

3.1.1 Relative Price Effects: The Elasticities Approach

The elasticities approach to devaluation looks at the relative price effects of a devaluation on the balance of payments, which it analyzes in terms of the supply and demand of exports and imports. Exports are assumed to account for the total supply of foreign exchange and imports for the total demand for foreign exchange. In this framework, there are no capital flows between countries. Foreign exchange can be obtained exclusively by exporting and the only need for foreign exchange is to pay for imports. When disequilibrium occurs, the goal of the devaluation is to bring the supply and demand of foreign exchange into equilibrium. According to the elasticities approach, the key to the success of the devaluation in achieving this depends on the price elasticities of demand for exports and imports as well as on their supply elasticities.

A devaluation implies a fall in the price of exports in foreign currency and a rise in the price of imports in domestic currency. Thus, the higher the demand elasticities, the more exports should rise and the more imports should fall. The role of supply elasticities is to determine the effects of the devaluation on the *terms of trade*, that is, the number of units of imports that one unit of exports will buy (or vice versa). Higher supply elasticities imply a deterioration in the terms of trade. In fact, the deterioration of the terms of trade due to a devaluation is maximum when supply elasticities are infinite, that is, when the exports and imports of the devaluing country are supplied at constant cost. It is minimum when the supply elasticities are zero, that is, when costs rise proportionately in the devaluing country or fall proportionately in the rest of the world.

The outcome of the devaluation depends on the elasticities of the supply and demand for foreign exchange. The elasticity of the supply of foreign exchange depends on two things: the elasticity of foreign demand for domestic exports and the elasticity of the supply of domestic exports. If foreign demand is sensitive to price changes, a decline in export prices resulting from the devaluation will increase the quantities of goods that are exported. The actual decline in export prices depends on the supply elasticity of exports. Thus, the supply of foreign exchange will tend to increase because of the increase in export volume and decrease because of the fall in the foreign exchange price at which this volume can be sold.

Demand is considered elastic when the elasticity is greater than one and inelastic when the elasticity is less than one. In practice, whether or not exports are elastic depends on many things such as the type of product and the market share of the exporter, the affluence of the importer and trade restrictions. Trade restrictions, including tariffs, quotas, oligopolies and cartels, restrict competition and reduce the demand elasticities by reducing the role of prices in buying decisions.

It is also difficult to generalize about export supply elasticities, which, like demand elasticities, depend on many factors such as the type of product, its production function, stocks of intermediate and raw materials, available qualified labor, etc. In the short-run context of a devaluation, we can say, however, that supply elasticities depend to a large extent on the domestic economy's position in the trade cycle. In a downturn, increments in products available for export at little extra cost are more likely to be forthcoming than in the later stages of an expansion when stocks are low and factors of production are being used at close to full capacity.

The elasticity of the demand for foreign exchange depends on two things: the elasticities of the supply and demand for imports. Other things being equal, the effect of a devaluation is to raise the price of imports in domestic currency. If domestic demand is sensitive to price changes, an increase in domestic import prices resulting from the devaluation will decrease the quantities of goods that are imported. The actual rise in domestic import prices depends on the supply elasticity of imports. Thus, the demand for foreign exchange will tend to decrease because of the decrease in import volume. This decrease will be offset to the extent that supply elasticities are not infinite and the price of imports in foreign exchange tends to fall with the fall in demand.

Import demand elasticities are similar to export demand elasticities in that they depend on the type of product, the affluence of the domestic market and trade restrictions. Another important element is the supply of *import substitutes* produced by the domestic economy. When domestic products compete with imports, the higher prices of imported products should cause a switch from imports to domestic substitutes, thereby raising the import demand elasticity.

Where import supply elasticities are concerned, many countries, including most of those that are highly indebted, are in the position of a *price taker*. In other words they are too small to have much effect on world prices. In this case supply elasticities, if not infinite, are likely to be very high. For large, affluent countries like the United States that account for an important share of world trade in many products, the price-taking assumption is less likely to be valid.

In summary, then, the elasticities approach to devaluation analyzes the price effects of exchange rate changes on the balance of payments. A devaluation causes imports to become more expensive in the domestic market and, depending on the demand elasticity, this should provoke a reduction in imports. The devaluation should also cause exports to become cheaper on foreign markets and, again depending on the demand elasticity, this should provoke an increase in exports. The extent to which the domestic price of imports rises and the foreign price of exports falls depends on the supply elasticities of the two types of products. The combined effects of the price elasticities will determine whether the devaluation will be successful in restoring external equilibrium. The *Marshall–Lerner condition* is a more precise statement of the requirements for stable equilibrium in the foreign exchange market. Assuming infinite supply elasticities for imports and exports, it states that devaluation will always improve the trade balance if the *sum* of the demand elasticities for imports and exports is greater than one. The empirical question of actually measuring these elasticities is very difficult because of the variations in the prices, quantities and types of products that are exported and imported. The IMF, however, does estimate demand elasticities for its world trade model (Deppler and Ripley, 1978).

In spite of the empirical difficulties in measuring the relevant elasticities, the elasticities approach is a theoretically sound short-term explanation of the reaction of the balance on current account to exchange rate changes. To the extent that these reactions can be observed and do tend to occur, it has considerable analytical value. However, the approach does suffer from some confusion and inconsistency arising from the use of two units of account, national currency and foreign exchange, in the measurement of the relevant variables. Furthermore, it omits time lags and capital movements but its most important shortcoming is that it neglects devaluation-induced effects on income and expenditure.

3.1.2 Income Effects: The Absorption Approach

The shortcomings of the elasticities approach to devaluation analysis led to the development of what is called the *absorption approach* (Alexander, 1952). The absorption approach builds on the elasticities approach. It points out that the elasticities of the preceeding section are only partial elasticities, that is, the effects of price variations on the quantities supplied and demanded when the other relevant variables remain unchanged. It completes the analysis based on what it calls the total elasticities, that is, the effects of price variations on the quantities supplied and demanded when the other relevant variables have been allowed to change. In other words, the absorption approach takes into consideration the variations in income and consumption caused by the devaluation.

There are three major devaluation-induced effects on income or gross national product (GNP). The first effect has already been considered. It concerns the terms of trade and depends on how much the supply elasticities cause the terms of trade to deteriorate. A deterioration in the terms of trade tends to reduce domestic income. The second effect depends on the demand elasticities and on whether or not the economy is working at full capacity. If the economy is running at less than full capacity, the increased demand for exports and import substitutes should increase output and employment in industries producing these products. If the economy is running at or near full capacity, however, supply elasticities are likely to be low and the increased demand will translate into price increases. The third effect is the most important and concerns resource allocation. Income should increase if the relative price changes induced by the devaluation improve resource allocation by transferring factors of production to sectors where they are more productive. For long-term external equilibrium, this is a key consideration.

Absorption refers to the economy's total consumption of resources. It is equal to private and government consumption plus total gross investment, including variations in stocks. The first and most important effect on absorption results from the relative price changes that cause an *income redistribution* within the domestic economy. Producers of *importables* and *exportables* should experience an increase in income due to the elasticity effects discussed above. Importables and exportables refer to products actually imported and exported as well as their close substitutes produced domestically. Consumers of importables and exportables, however, should experience a reduction in real income due to the higher prices of these products. A second effect on absorption is caused by the desire of investors to maintain their real cash balances. The rise in prices following the devaluation causes a reduction in real cash balances, thereby causing investors to sell stocks and bonds in an effort to maintain them. The resulting fall in bond prices means a rise in the rate of interest. The resulting rise in the interest rate causes a reduction in investment and consumption. Finally, there may be other diverse effects from devaluation such as anticipated price rises inciting immediate consumption or a high import content in investment goods causing a reduction in investment because of the higher cost of imports.

In this context the devaluation will improve the external balance on current account if the increase in income caused by the devaluation is greater than the devaluation-induced increase in absorption. This can be written algebraically in terms of the national accounting equation. Consider the following notation:

S_0 = the spot exchange rate (number of units of domestic currency for one unit of foreign currency)

X = merchandise exports plus exports of all non-financial services plus unrequited transfers (credit)

M = merchandise imports plus imports of all non-financial services plus unrequited transfers (debit)

FS = net investment income [investment income (credit) minus investment income (debit)]

F = net foreign capital not counting the change in reserves (capital account balance minus the change in reserves)

BP = the change in reserves

C = private consumption plus government consumption

I = gross fixed capital formation

Δstk = increase in stocks

The economy's income is equal to its GNP and can be broken down as follows:

$$GNP = X - M + FS + C + \Delta stk + I \tag{3.1}$$

Absorption is equal to $C + \Delta stk + I$ and the balance of payments identity can be written as

$$BP = X - M + FS + F \tag{3.2}$$

The idea is to increase the current account balance $X - M + FS$ by devaluing. This will be the case when the increase in income resulting from the devaluation is greater than the increase in absorption:

$$\frac{dGNP}{dS_0} > \frac{d(C + \Delta stk + I)}{dS_0} \tag{3.3}$$

The new exchange rate is the key to success.

The new exchange rate determines the volume of exports and the division of absorption between imports and domestic importables. In this way the exchange rate fixes the relative price of exports on foreign markets and the relative price of imports on domestic markets. Income and absorption, then, are two distinct functions of the exchange rate, the long-term success of the devaluation depending on the ability of these functions to maintain income greater than, or at least equal to, the level of absorption. In the next sections we examine some of the characteristics of these functions.

Relative Price Effects on Income and Absorption

Besides the relative price changes between exports and imports treated in the elasticities approach, the absorption approach also considers the relative price changes between tradeables (importables and exportables) and *non-tradeables*. Non-tradeables refer to goods and services produced and consumed domestically that are not close substitutes of exportables and importables. The initial effects of a devaluation should increase the domestic price of tradeables relative to non-tradeables. The actual amount of the price increase depends partly on the supply elasticities and partly on the demand elasticities. For exportables, a lower supply elasticity and a higher foreign demand elasticity will cause a larger increase in the domestic price. This is because the lower supply elasticity causes a greater reduction in the supply of exportables to the domestic market as exports increase in response to the increased foreign demand. A lower supply in the face of an unchanged demand will cause prices to rise. For importables the domestic price increase will be greater the higher the supply and the lower the demand elasticities. Higher prices and increased demand for exportables should stimulate output. Higher prices and the substitution of domestic importables for imports should stimulate output in this sector as well. Therefore, there should be a switch in absorption from foreign to domestic importables and the increase in exports should increase domestic income. The ultimate increase will depend on the *foreign trade income multiplier dGNP/dX*. The foreign trade income multiplier is equal to $1/(ds/dGNP + dM/dGNP)$ where $ds/dGNP$ is the marginal propensity to save and $dM/dGNP$ is the marginal propensity to import.[1]

Non-tradeable Goods

The demand for *non-tradeables* is strictly domestic, so its price is not directly affected by a devaluation. However, its cost is directly determined by the international markets, if imported intermediate products, investment goods and raw materials are direct inputs. If importable and exportable goods are consumed by the labor force, its cost is determined indirectly. Higher prices for importables and exportables make direct inputs more expensive. They also reduce labor's real income and lead to demands for higher wages that raise costs.

The income redistribution resulting from the devaluation creates winners and losers, which affects the demand for non-tradeables. The winners in the redistribution are the producers of importables and exportables. If they are consumers of non-tradeables, some of their incremental income will be spent on non-tradeables. This will raise the demand for non-tradeables. The losers in the redistribution are the consumers of importables and exportables. If they are also consumers of non-tradeables, their loss of real income should reduce the demand for non-tradeables. The net effect determines whether overall demand for non-tradeables will increase or decrease. If the winners win more than the losers lose, the effect is positive. If the losers lose more than the winners win, the effect is negative. In fact, an overall decrease is the usual outcome. Thus, it is the reaction of the non-tradeable sector during the period between devaluation and the response of the balance on current account that explains the apparent paradox of the devaluation causing a recession (Pearce, 1961; Gerakis, 1964).

The Wealth Effect

Countries exporting raw materials can see their income negatively influenced by the *wealth effect*. This happens when the supply of exports is inelastic in the long or short term. Commodity exports are often limited in the long term by land, mineral deposits, etc. and in the short term by mines, wells, herds, etc. Since a devaluation increases the wealth of the owners of these resources even if output does not increase, resource allocation can be disturbed if the owners of the inputs count on the effects of relative price movements to increase their wealth rather than increasing it through investments that will increase output. This phenomenon occurred at the international level when oil producing countries limited their output but increased their wealth through higher prices that increased income and the value of their reserves underground.

---

[1] This can be shown as follows. Combine equations (3.1) and (3.2) and subtract C to get saving, denoted as s. Saving is equal to the current account balance plus gross investment:

$$s = B_c + I_g$$

Let investment income be included in exports and imports so that $B_c = X - M$. Then:

$$X + I_g = s + M$$

A change in exports is a change in income equal to dX that will induce a change in savings and imports. Assume that I_g is unaffected. Then:

$$dX = ds + dM$$

and dividing both sides into $dGNP$ gives:

$$dGNP/dX = 1/(ds/dGNP + dM/dGNP)$$

If the exportable products subject to the wealth effect are also wage goods such as in Argentina where beef and wheat, besides being major export products, are also consumed in large quantities by the general population, the consequences can be particularly onerous. The devaluation-induced income redistribution depresses real income and standards of living while the wealth effect tends to perpetuate or prolong the situation.

Strategic Imports

Strategic imports refer to intermediate goods necessary to maintain current levels of output or investment goods necessary to maintain future output. If imports of intermediate goods for current output are reduced, current income will fall by several times the value of the reduction in imports. A reduction in imports of investment goods will reduce the economy's future productive capacity and output.

Time Lags

Time lags are a key element in determining how painful the income redistribution will be. Supply elasticities for individual countries are likely to be very low in the short term, especially for commodities. Most products require a time lag before they can respond to demand signals. A prime example is agricultural products. The season has to be right and the plants take time to grow. Even industrial output requires an interval between the moment that increased demand manifests itself and production can be increased and distributed to meet this demand. Thus, in the short term exports can only increase at the expense of domestic consumption of exportable goods. This will be the case if the domestic prices of exportable goods rise faster than the incomes of those who consume them, thereby exacerbating the income transfer from consumers to producers of exportables.

Structural Change

From the foregoing analysis it is clear that the exchange rate plays an important role in a country's resource allocation. It determines the economy's external terms of trade, that is, the relative prices of exports to imports. It also determines the economy's internal terms of trade, the relative prices of tradeable goods to non-tradeable goods. These relative prices then determine the economy's structure of production and the composition of output and consumption. Thus, if no neutralizing actions are undertaken by the government, a devaluation will initiate a change in the economy's structure of production as the modified relative price structure induces a reallocation of the economy's resources.

There are many forms that a devaluation-induced resource reallocation can take. In the early stages of a devaluation, a temporary, more or less intensive use of labor and capital in the same basic processes such as production cutbacks or overtime are the forms likely to manifest themselves. If the devaluation-induced price signals are not neutralized or reversed by government policy, the later stages are likely to see resource shifts between sectors and the apparition of entirely new processes and technologies as well as the elimination of the production of certain products and the creation of processes for products not formerly produced. The reorganization process will have long and short-term consequences on levels of output and growth. In the case of idle resources and excess capacity, the beneficial effects should be felt relatively quickly. However, as is more likely to be the case, when it is necessary to make investments in order to create the required resources and incremental capacity, the beneficial effects will be longer in coming while the negative effects will be felt immediately. Furthermore, capital losses will appear in industries losing out in the devaluation. Many operations will become unprofitable and have to shut down.

Clearly, there will be powerful forces working against the structural change. These forces often have the upper hand. Losers in the income redistribution will fight to restore their standard of living while industries benefitting from tariffs, subsidies and controls will strive to maintain their privileges. If the income redistribution is allowed to progress and privileges are effectively eliminated, many producers will be forced out of business. The resulting layoffs and reduced output will create political and social pressures that cannot be resisted indefinitely. The time element, then, is crucial to the outcome. How long it takes for the beneficial effects of the resource reallocation to begin to offset the negative effects often determines whether the devaluation will be successful in establishing the conditions for the long-term equilibrium of the external sector.

The J-Curve

How the balance on current account eventually reacts to the elasticities, income and absorption forces of the preceding sections depends on the time it takes for each one to make itself felt. Price elasticities may be smaller in the short run than in the long run. Income and absorption effects may take several years to work themselves through the economy. Structural adjustment may take much longer. Consequently, the time path of the current account balance can take different forms. One of the forms frequently observed is the *J-curve*, an initial worsening of the current account balance followed by a gradual improvement.

The J-curve effect is often explained as the result of flexible prices and sticky quantities due to the fact that the external terms of trade deteriorate faster than quantities of exports and imports can adjust to them (Dornbush and Krugman, 1976; Baldwin and Krugman, 1987). An interesting explanation of why this happens holds that immediately following a devaluation, the anticipation of higher prices for tradeables causes a strong intertemporal substitution effect between tradeables and non-tradeables. Anticipating price rises in tradeables as a result of the devaluation, economic agents rush to make purchases before they occur, thereby causing a temporary reduction in exports and an increase in imports (Gelach, 1989).

There are many combinations of short and long-term supply and demand elasticities that can produce the J-curve effect. The important point to remember is that the J-curve effect depends on different time lags in the adjustment process set off by the devaluation. When it appears, it tends to increase the disequilibrium between the supply and demand for foreign currency.

3.1.3   Stock Adjustments: The Monetary Approach

The monetary approach to the balance of payments is based on the quantity theory of money that links price levels to the money supply. In its most primitive form the quantity theory of money postulates a strict proportional relationship between the price level and the supply of money. For example, suppose we separate nominal GNP into Y, the measure of the flow of real goods and services or real income, and P, the average price level. Let v represent the velocity of money, that is, the rate at which the stock of money circulates through the economy in order to finance transactions, and MO the money supply. Nominal GNP can then be written as:

$$GNP = PY = vMO \qquad (3.4)$$

and

$$P = \frac{v}{Y}MO \qquad (3.5)$$

Equation (3.4) is known as the Fisher equation after the economist Irving Fisher and expresses the identity on which the quantity theory of money is based. Price times quantity equals the money supply times the rate at which it circulates through the economy (for an excellent review of the history of monetary theory, see Marchal and Lecaillon, 1967). It is argued that in the medium term both v and Y are constants. Certain behavioral patterns and institutional features of the economy that only evolve slowly over time make v a constant while Y is a constant because of the hypothesis that the economy is at full employment and will remain there. Thus, from equation (3.5) an increase in the money supply, MO, will increase prices by the proportion v/Y and the rate of increase in prices will be equal to the rate of increase of the money supply.

The money supply is directly related to the external sector through the purchase and sale of foreign exchange. In the absence of neutralizing operations by the central bank, an excess demand for foreign currency decreases the domestic money supply and an excess supply of foreign currency increases it. Changes in the domestic monetary situation induced by disequilibrium in the external sector set in motion a self-correcting process as prices and cash balances adjust to the new situation. The monetary approach concentrates on the relationship between the money supply, prices and real cash balances to explain the balance of payments equilibrium.

Remember that the total supply elasticities of the traditional approach to balance of payments discipline and devaluation theory recognize the importance of price differentials or relative rates of inflation between the devaluing country and the rest of the world. The traditional approach also recognizes the importance of real cash balances in determining the balance of payments equilibrium. In these respects it resembles the monetary approach. It differs from the monetary approach in that it concentrates on flow adjustments such as exports, imports, income and absorption and fails to consider stock adjustments. The monetary approach recognizes money as a stock concept and its importance for the balance of payments equilibrium. Therefore, its analysis is conducted in terms of stock adjustments in the supply and demand for money. A deficit in the balance of trade, for instance, can be considered as a reduction in the level of cash balances in favor of goods and services beyond the domestic economy's productive capacity. A deficit on capital account can be considered as a reduction of cash balances in favor of other types of financial assets or as a level of outstanding credit in excess of the economy's capacity to save.

The monetary approach assumes a stable functional demand for money and considers the world economy as a closed system where optimal prices are those determined in the international marketplace. Relative prices that deviate from those in the international marketplace due to tariffs, subsidies and controls are viewed as sources of sub-optimal resource allocation and impediments to the balance of payments equilibrium. We can outline the monetary approach to the balance in four simple equations (Polak and Argy, 1977).

The first equation in the monetary approach is the balance of payments identity, equation (3.2), reproduced here for convenience, which establishes accounting discipline:

$$BP = X - M + FS + F$$

The second equation is the identity showing that the money supply is partially determined by the external sector:

$$\Delta MO = BP + \Delta D \tag{3.6}$$

where ΔMO represents the change in the money supply and ΔD represents the change in domestic credit.

The first behavioral equation is the Fisher equation (3.4), reproduced here for convenience:

$$GNP = PY = vMO$$

The second behavioral equation explains imports in terms of national income in domestic currency:

$$M = mGNP \tag{3.7}$$

If we combine equations (3.4) and (3.7) we have:

$$MO = \frac{M}{mv} \tag{3.8}$$

Equation (3.8) is the condition for monetary stability. It says that the money supply compatible with external equilibrium depends on the role of imports in the total economy and the economy's velocity of money. Imports are given by the balance of payments identity in equation (3.2). Thus, everything necessary for external equilibrium is known. By rearranging equation (3.6), we can single out the policy variable that the authorities can use to assure external equilibrium:

$$\Delta D = \Delta MO - BP \tag{3.9}$$

The policy variable that the authorities can use to assure external equilibrium is the amount of domestic credit. From equation (3.9) it follows that domestic credit should be regulated with respect to the change in official reserves so that the money supply varies just enough to keep it at the equilibrium level defined in equation (3.8).

If the monetary equilibrium of equation (3.8) is not respected, according to the quantity theory of money on which the monetary approach is based, a nominal money supply that exceeds or falls short of the real cash balances demanded by domestic economic agents will affect the price level. An excess supply of money raises the price level and a shortage lowers it.

It is clear that the monetary approach to the balance of payments is a powerful tool for international financial analysis. Where the traditional approach relies on knowledge of complicated micro- and macroeconomic relationships as well as generally unmeasurable supply and demand elasticities, the monetary approach concentrates on one observable variable, the money supply and the prospective performance of the economy's external sector can be judged by domestic monetary policy represented by domestic credit. This having been said, some caution is in order when applying the theory in the real world. First of all, except in the most unsophisticated financial systems, there is some confusion surrounding the financial aggregates corresponding to the definition of "money" (Barnett, 1983; Belongia and Chalfant, 1989). Secondly, the velocity of money is probably not a constant but rather a stable function of certain variables such as prices, interest rates and wealth (Friedman, 1956).

3.1.4 Stock Adjustments: The Portfolio Balance Approach

The portfolio balance approach to the balance of payments starts from the monetary approach and adds demand functions and equilibrium conditions for bond markets (Kouri and Porter, 1974). The assumption is that investors desire diversified portfolios and, hence, will hold both domestic and foreign assets. Whereas the monetary approach assumes that bond markets always clear, the portfolio balance approach, through supply and demand functions for bonds and equilibrium conditions setting bond supply equal to demand, shows how bond markets clear. With this modification the effects of changing bond supplies and demands can have consequences on interest rates and the exchange rate that differ in the short run from what is forecast in the monetary approach.

Suppose, for example, that the central bank buys domestic bonds on the market. This will increase the money base and, through the reserve ratio multiplier, cause an increase in the domestic money supply. The primitive formulations of the monetary approach predict that, other things being equal, the exchange rate will depreciate by the percentage increase in the money supply. In the portfolio balance approach, the reduction of the supply of bonds in circulation generates an excess demand that will increase bond prices and lower interest rates. Lower interest rates have well-known stimulative effects on investment, output and prices that will affect the exchange rate. This implies that at least in the short run the exchange rate can stray from its long-run PPP equilibrium. We can outline the portfolio balance approach in four simple equations.

Consider the following notation:

$$
\begin{aligned}
W &= \text{country's wealth} \\
B &= \text{demand for domestic bonds} \\
SB^* &= \text{demand for foreign bonds in domestic currency} \\
S &= \text{the exchange rate (number of units of domestic currency for one unit of foreign} \\
&\quad \text{currency)} \\
MO_{1d} &= \text{the demand for money} \\
r &= \text{domestic interest rate} \\
r^* &= \text{foreign interest rate} \\
h, i, j &= \text{the percentage of wealth held in each type of asset with } h + i + j = 1
\end{aligned}
$$

$$MO_{1d} = h(r, r^*)W \tag{3.10}$$

$$B = i(r, r^*)W \tag{3.11}$$

$$SB^* = j(r, r^*)W \tag{3.12}$$

$$W = MO_{1d} + B + SB^* \tag{3.13}$$

The first three equations postulate that the proportions of wealth held as money, domestic bonds, and foreign bonds are functions of the domestic and the foreign interest rates. The demand for money MO_{1d} is inversely related to both the domestic and foreign interest rates. The demand for domestic bonds B is positively related to the domestic interest rate and inversely to the foreign interest rate. The demand for foreign bonds SB^* is positively related to the foreign interest rate and inversely to the domestic interest rate.

According to the portfolio balance approach equilibrium occurs when the quantity demanded of each financial asset equals the quantity supplied. Under the assumption that each financial market is in equilibrium, we can solve for SB^*:

$$SB^* = W - M_{1d} - B = W - i(r, r^*)W - h(r, r^*)W$$
$$= W[1 - i(r, r^*) - h(r, r^*)] \tag{3.14}$$

and

$$S = \frac{W}{B^*}[1 - i(r, r^*) - h(r, r^*)] \tag{3.15}$$

From equation (3.15) we can see that the exchange rate is positively related to W and r^* and inversely related to B^* and r. An increase in wealth resulting from an increase in savings increases the demand for all three financial assets. As the country exchanges domestic currency for foreign currency to purchase the foreign bonds, the domestic currency will depreciate. The same goes for a rise in the foreign interest rate. As the country exchanges domestic currency for foreign currency to purchase the foreign bonds, the domestic currency will depreciate. On the other hand, an increase in the supply of the foreign bond will lower its price and reduce the wealth of domestic residents, which causes them to reduce their holdings of all financial assets. As they sell the foreign bonds and exchange foreign currency for domestic currency, the value of the domestic currency appreciates. The same thing happens if the domestic interest rate rises.

3.1.5 Country Risk: Ratio Analysis

The foregoing approaches to balance of payments analysis identify the variables that form the backbone of the economic and financial aspects of country risk analysis. In fact, most approaches to country risk analysis, including the comparative techniques such as rating systems, the analytical techniques such as special reports, and the econometric techniques such as logit and discriminant analysis and model building, use either the variables specified above or some combination of the variables presented in terms of a ratio.

Variables and Ratios for Economic Risk Assessment

The economic risk of a country refers to developments in the national economy that can affect the outcome of an international economic or financial transaction. For instance, in the case of a portfolio investment, a currency devaluation in a country where an investment is held will reduce the value of the cash flows and returns from the investment in the investor's home currency. In the case of a foreign direct investment (FDI), a recession or economic slowdown will reduce the cash flows and returns to the parent.

Economic risk analysis involves an assessment of the country's ongoing and prospective economic situation. The economic variables currently used in assessing country economic risk figure in the different approaches to devaluation presented above and are the same as those that are commonly used for domestic macroeconomic analysis. They can be separated into variables associated with the domestic economy and variables associated with the balance of payments. The principal domestic economic variables are:

– GNP or GDP (usually measured in USDs or SDRs[2])
– Gross domestic investment (usually measured in USDs or SDRs)

---

[2] SDRs = special drawing rights.

- Gross domestic fixed investment (usually measured in USDs or SDRs)
- Private and public consumption (usually measured in USDs or SDRs)
- Gross domestic savings (usually measured in USDs or SDRs)
- *The resource gap*, defined as the difference between gross domestic savings and gross domestic investment (remember from footnote 1 that this is equal to the current account balance)
- The money supply
- The government budget deficit
- *The GNP deflator* (a Paasche index)[3]
- *The consumer price index* (a Laspeyre index)[4]

The principal variables associated with the balance of payments are:

- Exports of goods and services in USDs or SDRs (X)
- Imports of goods and services in USDs or SDRs (M)
- The trade balance
- The current account balance
- The export price index in USDs or SDRs
- The import price index in USDs or SDRs
- The exchange rate
- Foreign reserves (RES)

Inspired by well-established procedures in corporate financial analysis, the country economic risk analysis is usually carried out by using these two sets of variables to generate a number of ratios designed to serve as indicators of the ongoing and prospective economic situation. One set of ratios aims at assessing the prospects for long-term growth in GDP or GNP. It includes:

- Gross domestic fixed investment/GDP (or GNP)
- Gross domestic savings/GDP (or GNP)
- Marginal capital/output (the number of dollars of increase in investment necessary to increase output by one dollar)
- *Net capital imports/gross domestic fixed investment*
- *Gross domestic savings/gross domestic fixed investment*

The ratio of gross domestic fixed investment/GNP measures the economy's propensity to invest. The assumption here is that a higher rate of investment will lead to increased output and higher rates of growth of GNP. This investment ratio is used along with the marginal

---

[3] A Paasche price index is weighted by current consumption patterns. Thus, if p stands for price per unit and q for the number of units, with superscripts referring to the individual goods and subscripts referring to time, a Paasche price index can be expressed as follows:

$$\frac{\sum_j p_t^j q_t^j}{\sum_j p_0^j q_t^j}$$

Most introductory statistics textbooks deal with the different types of index numbers. See, for example, Grais (1982).

[4] A Laspeyre index is weighted by consumption patterns of the base year. Using the same notation as in the previous footnote, a Laspeyre price index can be expressed as follows:

$$\frac{\sum_j p_t^j q_0^j}{\sum_j p_0^j q_0^j}$$

capital/output ratio to determine growth rates. The marginal capital/output ratio is supposed to measure the marginal productivity of capital and is usually calculated by dividing gross fixed domestic investment in one period by the increase in GNP one or two periods later. A lower ratio signifies a higher productivity of capital and the higher the productivity of capital, the better the outlook for GNP growth.

The net capital imports/gross domestic fixed investment ratio indicates the extent to which GNP growth is dependent on goods produced abroad. A higher ratio indicates that the economy is more dependent. Combined with the gross domestic savings/gross domestic fixed investment ratio, it gives a good idea of how dependent the economy is on foreign resources. A lower domestic savings to domestic investment ratio indicates that the economy is more dependent. Dependence on foreign resources is usually interpreted as a negative insofar as economic risk assessment is concerned. This interpretation is open to question, however. For example, the resource gap can be large due to profitable investment opportunities and the willingness of foreigners to lend. It is hard to see why this should be a negative. On the other hand, in the absence of profitable investment opportunities, the resource gap can also be large due to a high propensity to consume. This, of course, is a negative because it signals that current consumption is being financed with foreign borrowing and that the rate of return on domestic investment is lower than the cost of the foreign resources.

From the monetary approach to the balance of payments, price stability is the key to a stable exchange rate. The set of ratios used as indicators of price stability are:

– Percentage increase in the money supply/percentage increase in GNP (GDP)
– Government budget deficit/GNP (or GDP)

Given the relationship between the money supply, output and prices, the first ratio is a measure of future inflation. The second ratio is used as an indicator of future increases in the money supply under the assumption that a large part of the government deficit will be financed by money creation. Since price instability is considered undesirable, the outlook for price stability should be more favorable when both the government budget deficit and the growth in the money supply are smaller.

The principal ratios for assessing the evolution of the balance of payments are based on the elasticities approach. They include:

– *Percentage change in exports/percentage change in world GNP* (or the GNP of the main customer countries). This represents the income elasticity of the demand for exports
– *Percentage change in imports/percentage change in GDP*. This represents the income elasticity of demand for imports
– *Imports/GDP*
– *Commodity exports/total exports*
– *Official reserves/imports*

A high income elasticity of the demand for exports and a low income elasticity of the demand for imports is usually considered as favorable for the balance of payments. On the other hand, a high ratio of imports to GDP is considered as unfavorable. Because of the well-known volatility of commodity prices, a high ratio of commodity exports to total exports is also considered unfavorable. The ratio of reserves to imports resembles a liquidity ratio in financial analysis. A higher ratio indicates higher liquidity and is favorable.

Variables and Ratios for Financial Risk Assessment

A country's *financial risk* refers to the ability of the national economy to generate enough foreign exchange to meet payments of interest and principal on its foreign debt. Financial risk analysis involves an assessment of the country's foreign financial obligations compared to its ongoing and prospective economic situation. The variables most frequently used in assessing cross-border financial risk include those presented above as well as variables that give information on the country's foreign debt and interest:[5]

– *Total external debt* (EDT) which can be broken down into:
  - *long-term public and publicly guaranteed outstanding and disbursed* (DOD)
  - *long-term private non-guaranteed*
  - *short-term*
  - *use of IMF credit*
– *Total debt service* (TDS) which can be broken down into:
  - interest payments (INT)
  - principal payments

Long-term external debt refers to debt that has an original or extended maturity of more than one year and that is owed to non-residents and repayable in foreign currency, goods, or services.[6] It has three components, public debt, publicly guaranteed debt, and private, non-guaranteed external debt.

Public debt is an external obligation of a public debtor, including the national government, a political subdivision or agency of either, and autonomous public bodies.

Publicly guaranteed debt is an external obligation of a private debtor that is guaranteed for repayment by a public entity.

Private non-guaranteed external debt is an external obligation of a private debtor that is not guaranteed by a public entity.

Short-term external debt refers to debt that has a maturity of one year or less and includes no distinctions between public and private non-guaranteed short-term debt.

Use of IMF credit refers to repurchase obligations to the IMF with respect to all uses of IMF resources, excluding those resulting from drawings in the reserve or first credit tranche.

Total debt service is the sum of (1) principal repayments and interest payments on long-term debt, (2) repurchases and charges on use of IMF resources, (3) principal and interest payments on short-term debt.

The most frequently used tools for assessing a country's ongoing and prospective financial situation are ratios that combine information on a country's external debt with the economic and balance of payments variables presented above. Some of the most common financial ratios are (see, for example, *Global Development Finance*, published by the World Bank):

– *Total external debt/exports* (EDT/X)
– *Total external debt/GNP* (EDT/GNP)
– *Official reserves/total external debt* (RES/EDT)
– *Official reserves/imports* (RES/M)

---

[5] In *Global Development Finance*, formerly the *World Debt Tables*, the World Bank publishes detailed statistics on the foreign debt of over 110 developing countries. The information includes undisbursed debt, commitments, disbursements, principal repayments, net flows, interest payments, net transfers, debt service, average terms of new commitments, debt restructurings, and debt service projections. The information is broken down by type of creditor and type of loan.

[6] These definitions are those given by the World Bank (1989).

- *Long-term public and publicly guaranteed outstanding and disbursed/exports* (DOD/X)
- *Long-term public and publicly guaranteed outstanding and disbursed/GNP* (DOD/GNP)
- *Total debt service/exports* (TDS/X)
- *Total debt service/GNP* (TDS/GNP)
- *Interest payments/exports* (INT/X)
- *Interest payments/GNP* (INT/GNP)
- *Official reserves/long-term public and publicly guaranteed outstanding and disbursed* (RES/ DOD)

In corporate financial theory, financial leverage plays a major role in determining financial risk. Financial leverage is measured by the extent to which the assets of the firm are financed with debt. It shows up as interest expense, causing variability in net income over and above the variability in operating income caused by operating risk. Where macroeconomic financial risk is concerned, the same type of effect is present. Financial leverage shows up as interest expense, causing variability in GDP or GNP over and above the variability caused by economic risk.

The problems with the foregoing ratios as analytical tools for financial risk assessment are grounded in the fact that they have no theoretical underpinning. Rather than the balance sheet (stock) variables used in corporate finance to determine financial leverage, the first set of country financial risk ratios uses the flow variables GNP and exports as proxies. Thus, ratios such as EDT/X, EDT/GNP, DOD/X, and DOD/GNP can be interpreted as a measure of the economy's financial leverage. The lower these ratios, the better the economy's financial position. How reliable these ratios are in signaling an economy's financial position depends on how accurately the variables X and GNP reflect the state of the economy's balance sheet. GNP and the traditional presentation of its component parts can be very misleading regarding the state of an economy's health. Consequently, these ratios should be used with caution.

Other types of leverage ratios used in corporate finance, such as times interest earned and cash flow coverage, seek to determine the extent to which current obligations are covered by current income. The times interest earned ratio relates earnings before interest and taxes to current interest charges while the cash flow coverage ratio relates earnings before interest and taxes to total current financial obligations including payments for interest and principal. Thus, INT/X and INT/GNP resemble a times interest earned ratio and TDS/X and TDS/GNP resemble a cash flow coverage ratio. Lower ratios indicate a better financial position.

Like the former leverage ratios, these latter leverage ratios have no theoretical underpinning. They are conceptually different from the corresponding ratios in corporate finance whose starting point is earnings net of operating costs. The country ratios use exports and GNP which are gross of costs and do not reflect the net flows such as earnings or net exports ($X - M$). Again, their usefulness is suspect and they must be used with caution.

The ratio RES/M complements the leverage ratios and resembles a *liquidity ratio* in corporate finance. Liquidity ratios measure the firm's ability to meet its maturing short-term obligations. The RES/M ratio measures a country's ability to maintain import levels with current cash in hand.

New Accounting Information and Analytical Ratios

As a means of overcoming the shortcomings of the foregoing ratios, Clark (1991, 2002) developed a framework (www.countrymetrics.com) that generates variables and ratios for countries that are compatible with corporate financial theory. The methodology, which we will come back to in Chapter 7, involves estimating an economy's expected cash flows in US dollars at international relative prices and then discounting these cash flows back to the present at the economy's required rate of return. The result is a measure of the economy's international market value, profits and rate of return, analagous to corporate market value, profits and rate of return in financial theory.

These variables – macroeconomic market value, profits and rate of return – can be combined with information on the foreign debt to generate ratios found in standard financial analysis. Some of the most useful include:

$$\text{Debt/Assets} = \text{EDT/Macroeconomic market value}$$

$$\text{Foreign interest coverage ratio (times interest earned)} = \text{Macroeconomic profits/INT}$$

$$\text{Cash flow coverage ratio} = (\text{Macroeconomic profits} + \text{depreciation})/$$
$$(\text{INT} + \text{principal repayment})$$

$$\text{Degree of financial leverage} = \text{Macroeconomic profits/(Macroeconomic profits} - \text{INT})$$

The debt/assets ratio is the standard leverage ratio in financial analysis that indicates the country's capital structure. The coverage ratios show the extent to which current financial obligations are covered by current income. Contrary to the ratios in the preceding section such as INT/X or TDS/X, they are based on net exports $(X - M)$. This is important because the ability to meet foreign debt obligations depends on net exports.

The degree of financial leverage ratio, defined as the percentage change in macroeconomic profits accruing to domestic residents for each percentage change in total macroeconomic profits, complements the three preceding ratios. Whereas the interest and cash flow coverage ratios indicate the economy's ability to meet external obligations in the absence of supplementary foreign resources, the degree of financial leverage indicates the vulnerability of this ability due to fluctuations in expected profits.

Ratios can be extremely useful but they must be used with caution and good judgment. Ratio interpretation can be aided by trend analysis and comparison with ratios of other countries. Trend analysis is useful because ratios only capture one period. By examining several periods, it is often possible to determine a tendency toward a stronger or weaker position. Comparing ratios across countries in similar economic conditions makes it possible to develop a basis against which ratios can be judged. Even when ratios diverge from those of the other countries, however, it does not necessarily mean that something is wrong. It could actually mean that the country is doing something better than the others. The analyst must develop in-depth knowledge of the country, its customs, and its government in order to interpret what the ratios really mean. Be that as it may, ratios are useful and popular and play a major role in contemporary country risk analysis.

REFERENCES

Alexander SS, 1952, Effects of a Devaluation on a Trade Balance. *Staff Papers*, Apr, II (2), 263–78.
Baldwin R and Krugman P, 1987, The Persistence of the U.S. Trade Deficit. *Brookings Papers on Economic Activity*, 1, 1–43.
Barnett WA, 1983, New Indices of Money Supply and the Flexible Laurent Demand System. *Journal of Business and Economic Statistics*, Jan, 1, 7–23.
Belongia MT and Chalfant JA, 1989, The Changing Empirical Definition of Money: Some Estimates from a Model for Money Substitutes. *Journal of Political Economy*, 97 (2), 387–97.

Clark E, 1991, *Cross Border Investment Risk: Applications of Modern Portfolio Theory*. London: Euromoney Publications.

Clark E, 2002, *International Finance*. London: Thomson.

Deppler MC and Ripley D, 1978, The World Trade Model: Merchandise Trade Flows. *Staff Papers*, Mar, XXVIII (1), 147–206.

Dornbush R and Krugman P, 1976, Flexible Exchange Rates in the Short Term. *Brookings Papers on Economic Activity*, 3, 537–75.

Friedman M, 1956, The Quantity Theory of Money, A Restatement. *In:* M Friedman, ed. *Studies in the Quantity Theory of Money*. Chicago: University of Chicago Press.

Gelach S, 1989, Intertemporal Speculation, Devaluation and the J-Curve. *Journal of International Economics*, 27, 335–45.

Gerakis AS, 1964, Recession in the Initial Phase of a Stabilisation Program: The Experience of Finland. *Staff Papers*, Nov, XI (1), 434–45.

Grais B, 1982, *Statistique Descriptive*. Paris: Dunod.

Kouri PJK and Porter MG, 1974, International Capital Flows and Portfolio Equilibrium. *Journal of Political Economy*, May/Jun, 443–67.

Marchal J and Lecaillon J, 1967, *Les Flux Monétaires*. Paris: Editions Cujas.

Pearce IF, 1961, The Problem of the Balance of Payments. *International Economic Review*, Jan, II (1), 1–28.

Polak JJ and Argy V, 1977, Credit Policy and the Balance of Payments. *In:* International Monetary Fund, *The Monetary Approach to the Balance of Payments*. Washington: IMF, 205–225.

World Bank, 1989, *World Debt Tables 1989–1990*, vol. 2. Washington: World Bank, xii–xvi.

4

Country Risk Assessment
Methodologies: The Qualitative,
Structural Approach to Country Risk

ARGENTINA is bust. It's bankrupt. Business is halted, the chain of payments is broken, there is no currency to get the economy moving and we don't have a peso to pay Christmas bonuses, wages or pensions.

Eduardo Duhalde, Argentina's President (1 January 2002)

4.1 INTRODUCTION

The globalization of the world's trade, financial and technology markets has created a new world environment, full of opportunities, but fraught with uncertainty and spill-over risks. The last two decades have been disrupted by a number of financial crises in emerging market countries. These crises have taken a variety of upheaval forms, ranging from external debt crises (most developing countries in 1982–1985), exchange rate crises (Mexico and CFAF zone[1] countries in 1994; Brazil and Russia in 1998; Argentina and Turkey in 2001–2002), and banking system crises (Asian countries in 1997–1998). Whatever the root causes of the economic and financial crises, most of them boiled down to balance of payments disequilibria with resulting debt servicing difficulties. The latter materialize in protracted arrears, moratoria, rescheduling and restructuring negotiations.

These crises have been very costly for both the countries and their creditors. Losses have been heavy and long-lasting for the local populations as well as for bondholders, international banks and foreign investors. In addition, ramification and contagion effects have increased the financial vulnerability of other countries through a variety of market channels, illustrating that emerging markets are often considered as one single asset class in investors' portfolios.[2] The IMF's 1998 WEO indicates that the impact of the Asian crisis was the main factor contributing to a full 1% slowing of growth in the world economy in 1998. The global slowdown, which began in the middle of 2000, has been accentuated by the events of September 11, and by the protracted stock exchange and emerging markets crises in 2001–2002. All in all, it takes between two and three years in currency crisis episodes for economic growth to return to the pre-crisis average trends.

Despite the conventional view that emerging markets constitute highly volatile, fiscally unsound, politically fragile economies, the fact is that emerging market debt often outperformed other investments in developed markets. These countries are analogous to "start-up" companies. Given modest scope for growth in OECD countries, emerging markets provide investors with

---

[1] 14 countries in West and East Africa constitute a monetary zone linked to the French franc since 1948, and to the euro since 2002: the "Communauté Française d'Afrique".

[2] Since the beginning of 1998, the year that Russia defaulted, emerging market bonds have provided investors with total returns of about 22%, according to JP Morgan's Emerging Markets Bond Index Plus. This is a sizeable premium over returns of about 18% on the benchmark S&P500 US stock index during the same period. (Bronstein, 2001).

portfolio diversification opportunities, and exporters with market rebalancing options. Solid country risk assessment is, therefore, a prerequisite for balanced risk management in both advanced and developing economies.

Country risk stems from the possibility that a foreign country's borrower, importer or corporate partner may be *unable or unwilling* to fulfill its contractual obligations toward a foreign lender, exporter and/or investor. Contractual obligations can be related to loans, bonds, equity investment, exports and imports, and procurement of services. Country risk is not limited to developing economies and it exists whatever the level of economic development. Even OECD countries may generate a substantial degree of country risk related to investment projects and trade flows. Trade barriers, environmental laws, unfair competition, and exchange rate volatility challenge investors in the most advanced nations as well as in emerging countries. Given the wide range of risks that can make a foreign investment more volatile, one approach alone will give only a partial picture of the risk. Risk appraisal thus requires a combination of converging approaches. In this chapter, we present a range of qualitative assessment approaches to country risk.

Qualitative analysis refers to the assessment of the economic, financial and socio-political fundamentals that can affect the investment return prospects in a foreign country. Instead of focusing on a range of ratios, ratings or indices that are supposed to "reduce" a complex situation into one single figure, the qualitative analysis aims at tackling the structures of a country's development process to shed light on the underlying strengths and weaknesses. How to explain Thailand, the Philippines and Korea's sudden currency collapses in mid-1997 while the three countries still had robust growth in the absence of major fiscal imbalances and inflation, and enjoyed stable credit ratings? How to account for substantial profit opportunities in Cuba (tourism, mining, trade lines, collateralized credits) while the country faces substantial structural weaknesses and a huge debt burden? How to justify European banks' appetite in mid-2002 for snapping up a big chunk of Iran's first international bond issue since the 1979 Islamic Revolution?

The answer lies in four shortcomings of the quantitative approach to country risk:

1. Two countries facing similar ratios and financial indicators may face considerably different socio-economic structures.
2. Quantitative data are either not available on time, or data are incomplete, wrong or distorted.
3. Interpretation is made exceedingly difficult given mixed and often contradictory signals.
4. Figures seem sound but are subject to considerable volatility due to regional contagion, herd instinct, and external shocks including downgrading by rating agencies. As Coface's Deputy-Director Clei (1998) points out regarding the inherent biases of the rating approach: "Risk specificities of ranked countries cannot be accounted for by such a uniform approach. It is thus important to consider ratings as helpful decision-making tools that must be supported by a more qualitative analysis integrating all these specificities."

This is why a comprehensive assessment of country risk requires careful consideration of the overall macroeconomic and social situation. Clearly, the approach cannot ignore numerical data but the latter are merely inputs that feed an analysis aimed at highlighting the economic, socio-political, financial and institutional structures of the country's development process.

Usually, a robust qualitative approach leads to comprehensive country risk reports that tackle the following six elements: (i) the *social and welfare* dimension of the development strategy;

(ii) *macroeconomic* fundamentals; (iii) *external indebtedness* evolution, structure and burden; (iv) domestic *financial system* situation; (v) assessment of the governance and transparency issues; and (vi) evaluation of *political stability*.

4.2   ANALYSIS OF WELFARE AND SOCIAL INDICATORS OF THE DEVELOPMENT PROCESS

The objective of cross-border investment is to reach profit rates higher than in more mature markets. The reverse side of the coin, clearly, is country risk. Unless investment, trade or lending is short-term oriented, foreign firms keep their fingers on the pulse of long-term trends in emerging countries, including development prospects and market scope. There is no market scope without growth and there is no development without economic growth. Development, however, is about much more than the rise or fall of national economies. Growth is a precondition for self-sustaining development as well as for enlarging people's choices. Annual GDP evolution, however, captures only a portion of a country's long-term development prospects. Accordingly, development means economic growth coupled with those conditions that make it self-sustaining. These conditions include democratic legitimacy, robust and stable institutions, and efficient public affairs management. Politics and policies thus matter for social and economic development.

Fundamental for building up a firm development base is an enabling environment including access to education, nutrition and health services, political and cultural freedom, and a sense of participation in decision-making, that all combine to produce decent standards of living. These criteria, although apparently remote from investment yields and debt servicing, constitute key, basic components of country risk. There is, indeed, a close correlation between human development indicators, as measured by the UNDP, and country risk. If one observes those countries that suffer strong setbacks in the UNDP's (2002) development index, namely Zambia, Romania, Zimbabwe, Bulgaria, Congo-Brazzaville, Cameroon, Ukraine, Kenya, Malawi, Lithuania and Moldavia, there is little doubt they do not constitute attractive investment markets, with the exception of specific niches. The reverse, however, is not necessarily true and a country such as Cuba, despite robust development features (life expectancy, literacy, commitment to health and education), is widely considered as a high-risk country.

The World Bank attempts to encapsulate development prospects into a so-called "development diamond" that portrays four socio-economic indicators for a given country and compares them with the average of a regional group of countries. These indicators comprise life expectancy, access to safe water, per capita GNP, and primary school enrollment. Population growth and life expectancy are crucial data for assessing country risk. Stable or declining population does not improve long-term market prospects. Rapidly rising population, however, will exert pressure on the government's budget and on the country's infrastructure. It will also generate demands for social services. Demography has a lasting impact on economics and geopolitics. Higher fertility rates and immigration in America than in Europe, for instance, produce not only a larger population but also a society that is younger, more ethnically mixed and, on balance, more dynamic.

Life expectancy is a good illustration of the overall quality of a country's enabling environment for sustainable development. It also illustrates the government's commitment to the adoption of a basic human needs strategy. In Africa, 19 countries out of 45 experience

Table 4.1   Basic and social indicators

Basic environmental indicators:
• Geographic situation, land area
• Natural resource endowment and self-sufficiency in raw material
• Physical infrastructure (ports, telecommunications, roads, power, transportation)

Social indicators:
• Population growth, human capital, life expectancy
• Labor force and unemployment, urbanization
• Age and gender structure of the population, family planning
• Health care
• Illiteracy and public expenditure on education
• Poverty and income distribution
• GDP per capita based on PPP[a]
• Development diamond (life expectancy, primary school enrolment, GNP per
  capita, primary school enrollment)

[a]Usually, the World Bank Atlas uses a three-year average of conversion factors to convert GNP data in national currencies to US dollars. The conversion factor is the average of the official exchange rate after adjustment for differences in relative inflation. The three-year average smoothes fluctuations in prices and exchange rates for each country. The resulting GNP in US dollars is divided by the mid-year population for the latest of the three years to derive GNP per capita.

life expectancy below 50 years (World Bank, 1997). As Hansen (1978) points out: "In most LDCs, the general development strategies of the 1950s and 1960s emphasized limiting consumption, raising savings and investment rates as rapidly as possible, investing heavily in the protected modern industrial sector of the economy, and concentrating government expenditures on 'economic' rather than 'social' overhead projects." Policymakers did so with the support of IFIs on the assumption that this market-driven approach would ensure rapid economic take-off, the benefit of which would in turn "trickle down" to the entire population in the form of growing per capita income. This standard development strategy has led to unemployment, foreign aid dependency and overindebtedness, as well as social upheaval. It showed also that the rationale of the free market as an organizing device may not be appropriate in structurally poor societies. The role of the state as providing a conducive institutional framework to development is essential and must be properly assessed by the risk analyst. Part of the job of the forecaster and the firm's strategy adviser is to spot longer-term trends that are rooted in basic social and development indicators.

Table 4.1 illustrates a number of basic indicators. They are prerequisite for an in-depth analysis of the structures of a country's development process.

4.3   ANALYSIS OF THE MACROECONOMIC STRUCTURES OF GROWTH

The second element in the qualitative analysis deals with macroeconomic fundamentals as key explanatory variables behind growth success versus financial crises.[3] This approach aims at taking into account most, if not all, the variables that feed or hinder the economic development

---

[3] Barry Eichengreen and Ashoka Mody, however, noticed that the analysis of market access shows the observed changes in economic fundamentals explain only a fraction of market conditions in the period leading up to the recent crisis in emerging markets (Eichengreen and Mody, 1998).

process, including the following: institutional reforms, budget and monetary policy, capital accumulation, resource gap financing, trade openness, financial intermediation, balance of payments sustainability, etc. The most important challenge is the county's capacity to pre-serve sustainable growth. Excessive growth, be it of spending, debt, money supply, GDP, investment, or domestic credit, will create bubbles and costly imbalances that will require adjustment.

Growth crisis can stem from endogenous or exogenous influences that will affect each of these variables. The qualitative or "structural" approach deals with the relationships between the domestic economy and the international environment as a source of strength and/or weakness for the country's growth. As Krugman (1998, p. 54) noted: "The benefits of outward-looking policies that take advantage of the possibilities for international trade and capital flows are well understood in economic theory and are also demonstrated by development experience. By linking itself to the world economy, however, a country also exposes itself to external shocks. Coping with such shocks is often the most crucial test facing policymakers in developing countries."

The economic literature regarding the root causes of economic growth traces back to a large number of thinkers. Quesnay, the Physiocrats and Adam Smith in the eighteenth century consider that population and agricultural production are two key ingredients of long-term growth. The limited availability of land was the centerpiece of classic economics as developed by David Ricardo and, from a different standpoint, by Thomas Malthus in the late eighteenth century. Marx in the nineteenth century emphasized the inherently contradictory process of capital accumulation in market capitalism while Keynes shed light on the need to guide Smith's invisible hand in a managed capitalist system. He focused on the role of the state in promoting domestic stabilization policy to minimize the ups and downs of economic activity, particularly to avoid mass unemployment and runaway inflation.

With various relative emphasis, growth has long been considered as a byproduct of cap-ital accumulation and factor productivity. Faced with a number of protracted economic and financial crises in the twentieth century, however, economic theory had to adjust its analytical framework to cope with a stubborn reality: growth cycles are interrupted by abrupt swings in output, employment, liquidity and overall welfare. After World War II, conventional wis-dom considered that growth is the byproduct of a combination of factors including domestic and external resources, solid infrastructure, adaptive and efficient institutions, and the central guidance role of the state in an otherwise decentralized market economy. Whatever the focus on specific factors, growth is seen as a byproduct of capital accumulation, whether it regards capital as physical (land, infrastructure), human (education, incentives), or institutional. Once a critical mass of capital is reached, development should prevail.

Regarding the pace of economic development, a consensus emerged in the international community that capital inflows should rise to make medium-term programs of adjustment with growth feasible in emerging countries (World Bank, 1986). Foreign capital, both public and private, can speed up the transition from developing to advanced economies. However, in a challenging article in the aftermath of the first oil shock, Peter Drucker (1974) attacked the belief that capital resources from abroad can "develop" a country. He points out that productivity is the key and that "underdevelopment" is the inability to obtain full performance from domestic resources. Developing countries have, almost by definition, more capital than they productively employ. What these countries lack is the full ability to mobilize their resources – whether human resources, capital or physical resources – and to embark on institutional capacity-building. Although Drucker is right to point out that productivity and competitiveness are low in many, if not most, emerging market countries, the fact is that the 1990s have added another exogenous growth crisis trigger. The globalization in financial and trade relations brings new risks of destabilizing speculation and capital flow volatility that stem from the spill-over and regional contamination threats.

Given the challenge to sum up the key ingredients of self-sustaining growth, the risk analyst is better off concentrating on the root causes of growth and financial crises in emerging and developed countries. Crisis analysis will cast light, in turn, on growth conditions. Although crises have occurred for as long as there have been financial markets, the crises in the emerging market economies since the late 1990s were more global and potentially more damaging to economic, trade and political stability than the crises of the past. Given the variety of internal and external shocks, one can identify a typology of "crisis models".

The "first-generation" crisis is that analyzed by the Bretton Woods institutions, focusing on fiscal imbalances in the form of government budget deficits, which cause the loss of international reserves until governments are unable or unwilling to defend fixed exchange rates. Financial crises are rooted in macroeconomic disequilibria that show up in a protracted balance of payments deficit. This deficit is itself the byproduct of an expansionary monetary policy that generates domestic inflation in a context of overvalued exchange rate policy. The monetary approach to the balance of payments, developed by Harry Johnson and the IMF Research Department in the 1960s and 1970s, provides the conceptual framework for both the imbalance diagnosis and the adjustment therapy through contractionary domestic demand policy (see Chapter 3). As Feldstein (2002) notices: The "devalue-and-deflate" became a standard part of the IMF prescription for dealing with currency crises even when such explicit deflation strategy was not necessary.

The "fundamentalist" approach to financial crises, centered upon unsustainable expansionary domestic policy and economic overheating, has been refined by Krugman (1979). He adds the role of monetary financing of budget deficits that leads to the eventual collapse of a fixed exchange rate regime. This approach is consistent with the debt crisis of the 1980s[4] and the European Monetary System crises in the early 1990s.

Second-generation models, introduced by Obstfeld (1985), focus on the domestic impact of high real interest rates as a policy tool to defend the exchange rate parity in a context of speculative attack and falling reserves. Market perception and portfolio shifts are key variables behind reserve levels and exchange rate depreciation. This model is relevant to analyzing the 1995 Mexican crisis[5] as well as the 1998 Russian crisis. Although this model incorporates the destabilizing role of international speculation and capital flight, it does not give much importance to that of bad governance, business climate, regulatory framework and institutional deficiencies.

The abruptness of the 1997–1998 Asian crisis, the regional contamination that engulfed most emerging countries in the aftermath of the Thai baht devaluation, as well as the protracted crisis in Argentina in 2001–2002, exemplify that current knowledge about growth and crisis in developing countries has proven inadequate for analyzing recent events. In the mid-1990s, Krugman popularized the controversial view (originally presented by Young, 1995) that the economic miracle of the "Asian tigers" was due to an unsustainable rate of capital and labor inputs. An attempt to formalize a third-generation model has been developed by

---

[4] For an observation of the root causes of the debt crisis in Latin America, see Dornbush (1985).
[5] Following the nearly 50% nominal depreciation of the peso between December 1994 and the year to end-1995, consumer prices soared 50% over the course of that year, real GDP fell by more than 6%, and open unemployment doubled to 7.4%.

Krugman (1999), by Roubini (1998), and by Radelet and Sachs (1998). In various ways, they focus on the role of financial intermediation and speculative short-term capital flows as crisis triggers. Radelet and Sachs emphasize the role of financial panic that stems from large-scale foreign capital flows into underdeveloped financial systems. A financial panic is an adverse equilibrium outcome in which short-term private creditors suddenly withdraw their loans from a solvent borrower, while there is no lender of last resort. Krugman (1998a) emphasizes moral hazard problems related to implicit government guarantees on unregulated domestic banks, with resulting inflated asset prices. Moral-hazard-driven lending provides a sort of subsidy to investment, with self-fulfilling loss of confidence. This approach to financial crisis indirectly touches on governance, as it devotes attention to reckless government spending, nepotism, crony capitalism and hidden subsidies (Krugman, 1998b), as well as to creditor panic and ruthless speculation, as worsening conditions precipitate crises.

These new approaches to the underlying roots of growth and crisis are thus more subtle and comprehensive than the early "policy slippage" approach of the Bretton Woods institutions. Growth is considered as a multifaceted process that is based on robust infrastructure, sound institutions, good governance, conducive regulatory framework, coupled with a supportive international environment. Nevertheless, the "refined" analysis of economic growth in developing countries still puts modest emphasis on the countries' structural dependency on capital markets, including the crucial dimension of market psychology.

In the late 1980s, Krugman (1988, pp. 54–79) already called attention to the sharp swings in virtually every aspect of the international economy and to the specific channels through which an unstable world economy affects emerging countries. External shocks comprise reduced foreign exchange earnings, rising payments to the rest of the world, abrupt reduction in market access and destabilizing speculative attacks. In sum, price, quantity and perception can move adversely. The latter is emphasized by Williamson (2002) to shed light on "multiple equilibria", in which macroeconomic fundamentals end up affected by market expectations that become the deciding factor. The 2002 protracted Argentine financial crisis and its spill-over risk to the entire Western Hemisphere gave analysts an opportunity to revisit the linkages between the development process and the global markets. Williamson argues that the possibility of multiple equilibria arises with the fundamentals in "intermediate" range, thereby leading to speculative attacks that will make the macroeconomic situation "tilted" toward a crisis outcome. This shift depends on the market's willingness to roll over debt payments and to provide financial conditions for the supply of capital that do not increase the debt burden excessively. See Table 4.2.

All in all, the nature of economic and financial crises has evolved substantially since World War II. This is not so because country governments make different policy mistakes. Crises are always rooted in a combination of overspending, monetary expansion and unsustainable exchange rates. What is new, however, is the nature of the multiple linkages between the global economy and developing countries. The magnitude and transmission speed of external economic and financial disturbances are such that, often, the market perception becomes crucial regarding macroeconomic policy sustainability. Market expectations, in turn, tend to shape policy options available to countries that attempt to cope with adverse shifts in the economic environment. In the global economy, like in beauty contests, perception does matter.

To perform the qualitative approach to economic growth, the analyst requires a range of inputs. National accounting data provide the broadest picture of a nation's economic performance. They also provide a basis for forecasting and policymaking. However, because statistical methods, coverage, practices and definitions differ widely among national sources, full comparability cannot be assured, and the indicators must be interpreted with care. In

Table 4.2   Modelling financial crisis: the generations approach

---

First-generation model (Krugman, 1979)

Fixed exchange rate + budget deficit + monetary expansion = drop in FX reserves ⇨ financial crisis + devaluation

Second-generation crisis model (Obstfeld, 1985)

Unsustainable fixed parity + current account deficit ⇨ portfolio shift = capital outflows = reserves exhaustion ⇨ exchange rate depreciation

Third-generation crisis model (Krugman, 1997; Radelet and Sachs, 1998)

Weak financial intermediation institutions + bad governance + moral hazard ⇨ speculative short-term capital flows = debt overhang and official reserve drop ⇨ financial panic and bank liquidations

Second-generation adjusted model of self-fulfilling crisis (Williamson, 2002)

Macroeconomic fundamentals in intermediate situation (growth, inflation, current account, budget, debt) ⇨ "multiple equilibria" depending on market psychology:

1. regional contamination + speculative attacks = "bad equilibrium" = *default*
2. IMF + G7 bail-out + robust adjustment credibility = "good" equilibrium = sustainable debt servicing = *capital market access*

---

addition, the statistical systems in many developing countries are still weak, particularly in Africa, and this affects the availability and reliability of the data they report. Intercountry and intertemporal comparisons thus require analytical backup before interpreting the data. To facilitate cross-country comparisons, values of many national series are converted from the national currencies to US dollars, by using the appropriate conversion factor, official exchange rate or the prevailing market rate. Income data are often expressed in constant prices for monitoring real changes and on a PPP basis to eliminate price and exchange rate distortions.

Table 4.3 depicts the main macroeconomic aggregates that will support the risk and opportunity analysis of any given country.

Table 4.3   Macroeconomic and policy data for country risk analysis

---

1. *Domestic economy assessment*
- National accounts, GDP evolution and composition, sector analysis
- Informal economy, savings and investment ratios
- Trade structure and terms of trade, trade openness ratio, commodity prices and markets

2. *Macroeconomic policy evaluation*
- Prices and exchange rate: domestic inflation (CPI and GNP deflator), real effective exchange rate, parallel market rate
- Government finance: budget policy, privatization, public sector borrowing requirements
- Monetary and credit policy: money supply growth, reserve money, claims on government and on private sector, real interest rates
- Legal and regulatory environment (customs, taxation, company law, flexibility of labor markets)

3. *Balance of payments analysis*
- Trade balance, resource gap and current account balance
- Capital accounts, international reserve assets, errors and omissions
- Non-debt-creating flows: FDI, foreign transfers, grants and ODA
- Liquidity ratios: import coverage ratio, current account/GDP
- Structure and composition of external capital sources
- Exceptional financing and use of IMF credit compared with country's quota

---

Box 4.1   Krugman's modeling of the Asian crisis with special regard for asymmetric information and crony capitalism (Moser, 2002)

Paul Krugman was one of the most prominent critics* of the IMF measures taken during and after the Asian crisis. He questioned the sustainability of the praised "Asian Miracle", but also argued that Asia was bound to run into diminishing returns eventually. Generally speaking, Krugman blames bad governance and lack of transparency in most Asian countries, resulting in the poor state of banking regulation and weak financial institutions.

Crony capitalism and moral-hazard-driven overinvestment
In most South-East Asia countries, unregulated *financial intermediaries* have held large portfolios of liabilities with an implicit government guarantee. Overinvestment and the resulting "inflation" of asset prices, in turn, made the financial institutions seem sounder than they were. Then the implosion of the unsound financial system revealed more sober prospects, driven by the losses of the existing institutions, reducing asset prices and producing a self-reinforcing collapse of asset values.

Crony capitalism – sometimes also referred to as nepotism or more bluntly corruption – summarizes the excessively cozy relationship between government and business. In South Korea the government took an active role in the allocation of capital between industries as an integral part of long-term development strategies. Domestic banks built up considerable credit exposure to highly-leveraged and diversified multinational companies – the *chaebols* – under pervasive government pressure. The implicit backup of the government provided the banks with a kind of hidden subsidy to investment, which in turn induced moral-hazard-driven lending.

According to Krugman, crony capitalism has led asset prices to get driven to their "*Pangloss value*": They rose much higher than they would do in an efficient market without asymmetric information and implicit guarantees. The same mechanism that props up the prices in the boom period, reinforces the deflationary effects in the downturn (boom–bust cycle). This can be induced by the election of a reformist government (no implicit guarantees any longer), by the IMF (fight against "crony capitalism"), or simply by an exogenous shock that forces the first intermediaries to shut down. Their bankruptcies can not only show the vulnerability of the system and therefore decrease confidence, but also simply lower the prices for assets as competition between potential investors loosens. In this context, *self-fulfilling financial crisis* can occur, in which plunging asset prices undermine banks, and the collapse of the banks in turn ratifies the drop in asset prices.

*Other renowned critics include Jeffrey Sachs and Joseph Stiglitz.

4.4   EXTERNAL INDEBTEDNESS, LIQUIDITY AND SOLVENCY ANALYSIS

Although the most visible element of emerging market crises is debt servicing suspension or, at worst, sheer defaulting, the root causes of the debt crises are still complex and the subject of endless academic debates. In particular, policymakers and economists around the world focus on such fundamental questions as:

(A) What are the relationships between external debt and domestic growth?
(B) Is external indebtedness a transitory but necessary ingredient behind long-term sustainable growth? And what is the quantitative effect of debt on growth?
(C) Beyond what threshold level does debt impair economic growth and generate liquidity and solvency imbalances? And, conversely, are official debt reduction workouts key elements for restoring growth and market access?

Economic theory suggests that external debt is a temporary phenomenon that supplements domestic savings, bridges the resource–investment gap and speeds up the growth process toward the "take-off" stage of sustaining development (Bouchet, 1987). The conventional approach stipulates that as long as borrowing countries invest capital inflows in productive investments with high return rates, and without sizable adverse shocks, growth should increase and generate the proceeds for timely debt repayments. The key condition is that the investment project yields a return that is above the international cost of capital, when the project's costs and returns are measured at appropriate shadow prices (i.e., taking into account the distortions in incentives in the borrowing country's economy).

Reality, however, shows that countries do not grow smoothly out of external indebtedness. Two different theoretical approaches underlie attempts to predict the risk of default. One approach regards default as arising out of an unintended deterioration in the borrowing country's capacity to service its debt. The other, in contrast, views the rescheduling of (or default on) a country's external debt as a rational choice made by the borrower based on an assessment of the costs and benefits of rescheduling or defaulting.

In the debt-service-capacity approach, the probability of default is seen as a function of the unsustainability of a given level of external debt, either as a result of short-term illiquidity or of long-term insolvency reflected in liquidity problems. It is assumed that the debtor's budget constraint is breached, either because of short-term economic mismanagement, long-term structural problems, domestic policy, or domestic shocks such as harvest failures, or because of external shocks such as an increase in international interest rates, deterioration in a country's terms of trade, and slowing growth in industrial countries. With this approach, a number of key economic variables could serve as indicators of future liquidity and solvency problems, including export growth rates, current account balance, real exchange rate, as well as various liquidity and solvency indicators.

The probability of default will increase for at least three reasons. One, the debt is not invested as it should be but instead is used to finance current consumption spending and/or the black hole of the government budget deficit, or the debt is recycled in international bank accounts via capital flight. Two, the debt composition, in terms of maturity, currency or interest rates, is such that the borrowing country becomes highly vulnerable to external shocks and to imported crises via a contraction of capital availability for refinancing or via more severe financial conditions linked to floating interest rates or higher spreads. Sachs highlights the importance of the role of "global shocks" for both the eruption of the 1982 debt crisis and the 1997 Asian financial crisis. Three, the country is subject to "debt overhang" in that the accumulated debt is larger than the country's repayment capacity and expected debt servicing obligations will discourage domestic investors and exporters, as well as foreign creditors. If the discounted sum of current and future trade balances is less than the current debt, the country can never service the debt out of its own resources, and it will have to borrow forever, in an amount growing at the real interest rate.

Capital flight and low domestic investment will then result from the implicit "tax" creditors exert on the country's resources to service the external debt. Krugman and Sachs have shown that a heavy debt burden also acts like a high marginal tax rate on economic adjustment in that, if the economy successfully embarks on tight austerity, much of the benefit accrues to the foreign creditors. This situation supports the efficiency case for debt relief (Sachs, 1989, p. 28). The debt overhang is illustrated by a debt "Laffer curve" which posits that larger debt stocks tend to lead to lower probabilities of debt repayment and shrinking market value of bank claims, hence a hindrance to growth.

All in all, these three arguments considering the non-linear effects of debt on economic growth have been examined in an IMF study looking at nearly 100 developing countries over a 30-year period (Pattilli, 2002). The study concludes that the overall contribution of debt to growth turns negative beyond a critical point. Likewise, in an effort to promote US aid flows with strong conditionality attached, a Heritage Foundation study shows that compound annual GDP per capita growth of those countries having received substantial US official development aid between 1980 and 2000 is close to zero (Brett, 2002). For instance, the Philippines received more than US$4 billion during the period, in constant 1999 dollars, while the per capita GDP level remained stubbornly flat at US$ 1170.

The "classic" analysis focuses on the following relation: *Weak fundamentals + large relative debt = debt overhang + deteriorating creditworthiness*. As we have seen earlier in Section 4.3, this view has been challenged by Williamson during the 2002 Argentine and Brazilian crises. Williamson argues that a heavy debt burden is not a sufficient trigger to a debt crisis when a country's fundamentals are strong enough to service the debt depending on the market's psychology. Otherwise, the negative market's perception will generate a self-fulfilling crisis. The markets' choice between focusing on the good versus the bad debt equilibrium is influenced by a range of variables including the political situation, the policymakers' credibility, the independent status of the central bank, the support of IFIs, etc.

For the risk analyst, assessing the growth-maximizing level of debt, beyond which a crisis becomes more likely, requires first "measuring" external indebtedness and the extent of debt overhang. This is more difficult than just looking at the nominal amount of accumulated debt. As shown in Chapter 11, the sheer amount of debt is not so easy to grasp either, given the diversity of sources and the unequal quality of debtor and creditor reporting systems. The first priority is to measure the external debt relative to macroeconomic indicators such as GDP and official reserve assets, etc. to obtain solvency indicators. Solvency indicators should illustrate stock/stock relationships, linking the country's debt obligations with its overall assets and its hard currency liquid reserves. Solvency indicators, however, are not sufficient *per se* to assess a country's financial weaknesses. The main reason is not related to Citibank Chairman Walter Wriston's shortsighted claim that "contrary to banks, countries don't go bankrupt", but rather to the need to relate stock indicators with flow relationships as well as tackling the debt composition. In the aftermath of the Second World War, both Britain and the USA had a debt to GDP ratio larger than 200%. In 2002, Japan, faced with the threat of protracted deflation, had a solvency ratio close to 140%. However, Japan has strong domestic savings, its debt is denominated in local currency and held mostly by domestic investors.

The second avenue is to measure the "real" weight of the debt through its net present value – a measure that takes into account the fact that a significant part of the external debt is contracted at a below-market interest rate. This is being done by the World Bank to calculate eligibility criteria to the HIPC's Debt Reduction Initiative. The real debt burden should comprise forward foreign exchange transactions as well as key contingent liabilities.

The third avenue is to focus on debt flows versus debt stocks, i.e., on debt servicing payments relative to export receipts as scaling factors to obtain a range of liquidity indicators. The latter combine financial relationships between flows of obligations and earnings. For the borrower, as Sachs pointed out, the happy state of affairs depends on nominal interest rates remaining below the growth rate of dollar exports of the debtor countries, or real interest rates remaining below the growth rate of real exports, in order to stabilize the debt-to-export ratio (Sachs, 1989, p. 7). Several rules of thumb have been suggested for managing the level of external liabilities, such as limiting the total debt service ratio to a specific number, around 20%. Greenspan and Guidotti suggest the adoption of a "liquidity-at-risk" standard whereby countries should be expected to hold sufficient liquid reserves to ensure that they could avoid new borrowing for one year with a certain *ex ante* probability, such as 95% of the time. That is, usable foreign exchange reserves should exceed scheduled amortizations of foreign currency debts (assuming no rollovers) during the following year (Greenspan, 1999). Greenspan calls for strengthening this rule to meet the additional test that the average maturity of a country's external liabilities should exceed a certain threshold, such as three years. The constraint on the average maturity ensures a degree of private sector "burden sharing" in times of crisis, since the market value of longer maturities would doubtless fall sharply. Short-term foreign creditors, on the other hand, are able to exit without loss when their instruments mature. If the preponderance of a country's liabilities are short term, the entire burden of a crisis would fall on the emerging market economy in the form of a run on reserves.

However, the country's ability to sustain any particular debt ratio depends on a wide number of internal and external factors including the outlook for exports (markets, demand/supply conditions and prices), import requirements, exchange rate competitiveness, terms of trade, interest rate developments, and the flexibility to adjust policies and economic structures (Table 4.4).

The fourth priority is analyzing the volume and stability of net flows and net transfers, i.e., the amount of financing that is actually available in the country's economy to finance key imports, infrastructure investment and debt repayments. Net flows, indeed, are equal to gross capital inflows from all creditors minus debt repayments, while net transfers are equal to net flows minus interest payments. For many emerging market countries, depending on current interest rates and the size and conditions of the "inherited" debt, net transfers turn negative. This situation both precipitates and accentuates the financial crisis. As the debt crisis emerges, then the net outflow is exacerbated as either short-term debts are not rolled over or as maturing-term debts cannot be replaced with new credits. Countries suddenly confront a liquidity "swing" from financial surplus to a payments gap.

Finally, the risk analyst should tackle the debt's structure in order to assess the impact of the financial conditions of capital flows upon the debt servicing capacity. The analysis of the debt

Table 4.4   Solvency (stock) and liquidity (flow) indicators of external debt burden

Solvency indicators	Liquidity indicators
• Debt/GDP	• Debt servicing ratio (debt payments/ export earnings of GSI)
• Net external debt/Exports of GSI	• Interest payments/Exports of GSI
• Debt/Exports of GSI	• Current account/GDP
• Debt/Official reserve assets	• Reserves/Imports of GSI
• Short-term debt/Liquid reserves + contingent credit lines	• Growth rate of exports of GSI/Average interest rate
• Short-term debt/Outstanding debt	• Average maturity of external liabilities

Table 4.5   The Institute of International Finance: Thailands external indebtedness assessment

External debt ($ million)	1995	1996	1997	1998	1999	2000e	2001f	2002f	2003f
Total external debt	100473	112826	109399	105000	95252	79790	71662	64122	61165
% GDP	59.7	61.9	72.4	93.8	78.1	65.3	63.0	55.6	51.7
% Exports of GSI	135.6	149.7	143.6	151.7	127.8	93.6	91.2	80.1	72.5
Medium/long-term	48331	65111	70945	75594	74261	65227	58868	52053	49676
Short-term	52142	47715	38275	28671	19653	13212	11564	10689	9959
Interest arrears	0	0	180	735	1337	1350	1230	1380	1530
% Total external debt ($)	70.8	71.7	68.2	65.3	61.5	59.6	60.4	61.7	61.9
Debt service payments	1995	1996	1997	1998	1999	2000e	2001f	2002f	2003f
Total debt service	9290	10409	18067	16830	14749	11166	12871	13359	10000
% Exports of GSI	12.5	13.8	23.7	24.3	19.8	13.1	16.4	16.7	11.8
Interest payments due	4888	6054	6707	6546	5884	5440	4050	2950	2900
% Exports of GSI	6.6	8.0	8.8	9.5	7.9	6.4	5.2	3.7	3.4
Amortization paid	4402	4355	11360	10284	8866	5727	8821	10408	7100
% Exports of GSI	5.9	5.8	14.9	14.9	11.9	6.7	11.2	13.0	8.4

(*Source*: Institute of International Finance, reproduced with permission)

composition (regarding creditors, debtors, floating/fixed rate, currency, maturity) will illustrate the "quality" and sustainability of the country's market access.

Two main institutions, one public and one private, provide not merely debt-related information as described in Chapter 11, but comprehensive analysis on the "quality" of the growth-cum-debt process, namely, the International Monetary Fund and the Institute of International Finance. The two organizations tackle the relationships between the volume and root causes of the country's borrowing requirements, as well as the country's market access and the immediate and lasting impact on the debt outstanding.

Table 4.5 illustrates the information provided by the IIF to its member banks regarding Thailand's liquidity and solvency situation, as of mid-2002.

The IMF is also a robust source of quality information on emerging market countries' debt situation. Country government Letters of Intent to the IMF's managing director include useful information on the annual external debt ceilings as well as on the maturity composition of new money flows. In addition, the annual Art. IV consultation reports provide information and analysis on the country's overall external debt strategy.

4.5   THE SAVINGS–INVESTMENT GAP AND DOMESTIC FINANCIAL INTERMEDIATION

As Stanley Fischer (1988) noted so succinctly: "The 1982 debt crisis had three causes: imprudent macroeconomic management, capital flight and over borrowing by the debtor countries; imprudent lending by the international banks; and the increase in real interest rates, decline in commodity prices, and recession associated with counter-inflationary policies in the OECD." All in all, Fischer distributes the blame equally to each actor involved in the first global debt crisis, with the notable exception of the IFIs where he came to work as World Bank Chief Economist. This view of the origins of the debt problem, not surprisingly, is shared by the IMF Institute (1992).

The 1997–1998 financial crisis that emerged in Asia and contaminated later on nearly all LDCs had little to do with the previous crisis scenario. Many of the East Asian economies had robust savings mobilization and high living standards, large foreign investment flows, and buoyant economic growth without inflation or fiscal imbalances. The crisis stemmed from a combination of overvalued exchange rates and the accumulation of short-term debt by the private sector. But the root causes of these two "crisis triggers" is to be found in basic flaws in the region's domestic financial sectors, including the following: directed credit and "administered" interest rates; the lack of international standards in regulation, accounting, and operating policies; poor and non-transparent supervision; the lack of medium or long-term local currency debt markets; and the scarcity of adequate equity in both the financial and corporate sectors. This financial debacle led to a new round of protracted crises and painful macroeconomic adjustment coupled with strict financial and corporate sector reforms. As Camdessus (1999) says, sharing the blame equally on both sides of the borrowing/lending equation: "The 1997–98 emerging markets crisis revealed deficiencies in the international financial system both on the debtor side – in the national policies and institutions – and on the creditor side – notably in the capacity of investors to undertake adequate risk assessment and of supervisory authorities to monitor properly their activities."

The emergence of new financial instruments along with innovative institutional developments have been striking in the banking system of most emerging market countries in the past 15 years, particularly in Asia. As the World Bank (1998) summarizes: "To facilitate the development of financial institutions, restrictions on lenders were eliminated, and innovative ways of doing business were adopted. Financial deregulation and liberalization were attempted in parallel. Technological change helped the volume of private international capital flows to grow at unprecedented rates."

The Asian crisis confirmed that Ragnar Nurkse's point was well taken when he said: "Capital is made at home." He referred to the need for vibrant domestic financial intermediation to finance sound local currency-generating investments. Domestic capital formation is the driving force behind any country's development, and effective domestic financial institutions are one of its most important facilitators. They are the key channel between savings from a broad variety of sources and productive investment, and their institutional efficiency is a key factor of a country's sustainable economic growth. World Bank research shows that a 10% increase in financial depth (liquid liabilities) is associated with an increase in per capita GDP growth of 2.8%, a remarkable rise (IFC, 1998). See Table 4.6.

Table 4.6   Financial systems' institutional efficiency factors

- Banking system development and efficiency
- Level and structure of interest rates; real interest rates evolution
- Financial liberalization (broad money/national income)
- Stock market development and efficiency (capitalization, value traded, listed companies, transparency)
- Non-bank credit and the role of securities markets in providing corporate funding
- Interbank market and secondary market in government securities
- Development of financial instruments and financial innovation
- Institutional development and structural reforms
- Legal restrictions on capital movements
- Role of national authorities for effective prudential supervision and deposit insurance schemes
- Legal, accounting, management and supervisory infrastructures

Box 4.2   Financial system crisis and moral hazard

According to Frederic Mishkin (1996, 2001), a financial system performs the essential function of channeling funds to those individuals or firms that have productive investment opportunities. Thereby, the system is challenged by asymmetric information, which can occur in two different forms.

Ex ante: Adverse selection takes place before the transaction occurs when potential bad credit risks are the ones who most actively seek out a loan as they are willing to pay a higher price, i.e. to accept a higher risk premium represented by higher interest rates. This phenomenon was first described by George Akerlof* who pioneered "asymmetric information" analysis (Akerlof, 1970).

Ex post: Moral hazard problems occur when participants have the same information when the relationship is established, while informational asymmetry arises from the fact that, once the contract has been signed, the principal cannot (adequately) observe the action of the agent. So, the principal faces the asymmetric information *ex post*. Traditional examples of moral hazard come from the insurance sector. Insurance companies want the policyholder to try to avoid accidents. However, once the insurance contract is signed, the agent tendentiously takes more risk than he would have previously taken, as he doesn't have to bear all the costs on his own. This issue was raised with an increasing frequency after several large-scale bail-out packages were delivered by the IMF as the "lender of last resort" in the 1990s and early 2000s. Regarding financial intermediation, one can assume that the credit taker will take more risk than expected after having received the loan. In order to minimize the moral hazard problem, lenders have to impose restrictions on borrowers and to monitor the borrower's actions. This is at the root of the IFIs' financial conditionality attaching macroeconomic adjustment "strings" to emergency loans. To avoid a financial crisis, lending institutions must fulfill their "natural" duty of scrutinizing their clients. This process of collecting information is even more necessary in emerging markets, as the empirical evidence confirms (see, for instance, Dell' Arriccia *et al.*, 2000).

*George Akerlof was one of three economists – along with Joseph Stiglitz – to be awarded the Nobel Prize in 2001 for his contribution to asymmetric information research.

4.6   GROWTH, CRISIS AND GOVERNANCE

Whereas country risk analysts focused on debt ratios and growth rate indicators in the 1980s, a consensus is emerging to place governance at the heart of the development process. Corporate and sovereign governance get the headlines of academic articles and magazines. The US Justice Department's investigation against Enron, which collapsed into bankruptcy court proceedings in late 2001, shed light on corrupt practices linking Enron and developing country governments. Claims of corruption in Enron water projects have arisen in many countries, including Ghana, Colombia, Bolivia, Panama, Nigeria, India, Mozambique and the Dominican Republic. The Enron and Worldcom debacles also shed light on deeply-rooted corrupt corporate practices in the most advanced economic country in the world!

Increasingly, World Bank and IMF macroeconomic conditionality incorporates "governance" criteria to determine eligibility access to official financing flows. Public sector institutional reform is at the heart of good governance. The latter comprises the IFIs' "second-generation reforms" that affect the relationship between the state, the market, and civil society. These reforms aim at strengthening the so-called "social capital", a concept that Fukuyama (1992) defines as "group solidarity and trust in human communities". Today, to get market access and show robust creditworthiness to rating agencies, emerging market countries must demonstrate that they adhere to high transparency and governance standards. As Michalet (1999) puts it: "One key aspect of the investment climate is the assessment of political stability as well as transparency and efficiency of the legal and judiciary system." In country risk analysis, governance has become the name of the game.

What is the importance of governance in economic growth and, vice versa, to what extent does weak governance precipitate financial crises and deteriorating creditworthiness?

1. *What is governance?* The issue of governance is relatively new in public administration. It emerged only in the early 1990s when the role of international financial institutions was put under the scrutiny of OECD countries' parliaments and NGOs. The latter challenged the IFIs as throwing taxpayer money at corrupt regimes and as bailing out incompetent governments in developing countries.

Governance, however, has been a topic of interest in the academic literature since the mid-1960s. It is a concept that traces back to the Greek philosophers, Montesquieu and Tocqueville. It can be defined as all the values that drive the regulation and ultimate finality of the exercise of power in private and public institutions. It includes issues such as transparency, sound and efficient administration, government accountability for the use of public funds, the rule of law, and social inclusion.

Whereas governance might seem a catch-all concept, corruption can be used as a useful proxy to observe, measure and compare the perception of governance across time and across countries. The World Bank and the IMF have a short and straightforward definition of corruption: *it is the abuse of public power for private benefit* (Tanzi, 1998). It refers to the exchange and delivery of services for payments, privileges and undue compensations. According to the Asian Development Bank,[6] corruption involves "behavior on the part of officials in the public and private sectors, in which they improperly and unlawfully enrich themselves and/or those close to them, or induce others to do so, by misusing the position in which they are placed". For country risk analysis purposes, we define corruption as *rent-exacting power by public agency officials with a view to exchanging discretionary public preferences* (bribe-taking by officials in public procurement, license, contract, tax breaks and subsidies, market share . . .) *for private gains* (speculation, insider information, cash payment . . .). It involves a patron–client relationship.

2. *Where does corruption come from?* Corruption is the symptom of deeply-rooted institutional problems in a country's public sector. Corruption is a phenomenon linked to a high pace of social change combined with weak institutional development. Social change, indeed, brings challenges to rent seeking, and when not accompanied by commensurate institutional capacity building, change goes with regulation vacuum and corruption. The latter, indeed, is observed in countries that face systemic transition challenges, i.e., those countries that had centrally planned economies which move toward market-driven economic policies, albeit with loose institutions: Vietnam, Laos, Cambodia, Albania, Ukraine, Algeria, Russia and, indeed, most former CIS nations. The lack of transparency in legal, regulatory and accounting frameworks, as well as in processes, creates loopholes in fast-changing societies. In that sense, economic liberalization and public sector reform reduce opportunities for corruption, given that the latter

---

[6] See "What is Corruption", World Bank seminar. www1.worldbank.org/wbiep/decentralization/courses/turkey

places a premium on the ability to bypass local bureaucracies and obtain privileges from all-powerful government officials.[7]

Samuel Huntington (1968) has observed distorted social behavior in fast-changing societies. The political scientist considers that in rapidly changing nations, from modernization to modernity, new exogenous demands on government cannot be adequately channeled through efficient economic and political institutions, hence mounting corruption. Corruption, thus, is one measure of the absence of effective political institutionalization. Corruption, like violence, results when the absence of mobility opportunities outside politics, combined with weak and inflexible political institutions, channels ambitions into politically deviant behavior. All in all, Huntington holds that modernization breeds corruption. The latter may be functional to the maintenance of a stable political system in the same way that reform is. Examples of countries where corruption itself may be a substitute for reform include Cameroon, Ivory Coast, Democratic Republic of Congo, Burma, Turkmenistan and Ukraine, *inter alia* (Bouchet and Groslambert, 2000). It serves to reduce social demands and group pressures for policy changes. It helps to foster loyalty through patronage and it reduces the probability of political upheaval. It helps, at least in the short term, to preserve legitimacy and loyalty in the face of social and economic change. Corruption buys time and creates adhesion.

If one follows Huntington, one can graphically illustrate the rise in corruption with a tension between rapid social change that is at the heart of the modernization process, and a lag in the process of institutional change (see Figure 4.1). Corruption, then, boils down to a weakness in the process of social mobilization in emerging countries. Institution building is a prerequisite to channel social mobilization with a view to prevent political upheaval and corruption. In different words, Nye (1967) refers to the same balancing challenge when he writes: "Political development refers to the recurring problem of relating governmental structures and processes to social change."

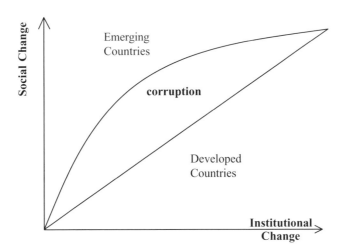

Figure 4.1   Governance: a by-product of balanced structural change

---

[7] Poland is an interesting case where the former Finance Minister and Central Bank Governor, Leszel Balcerowicz, has set up a special committee to shrink the number of unnecessary public regulations that hinder private sector business development.

This political science approach to stability and social change can be observed "at work" in Lehman Brothers–Eurasia Group's stability index (http://www.legsi.com) designed specifically to measure economic and political stability in emerging markets. The underlying analytical framework focuses on institutional efficiency, government effectiveness and political institutionalization in developing countries. Likewise, the Global Competitiveness Report (World Economic Forum, 2002) focuses on the set of institutions, market structures and economic policies supportive of high rates of economic growth in the medium term. Growth is considered as a byproduct of global competitiveness and the latter is perceived as stemming from efficient government institutions, market transparency and good governance.

3. *How does corruption relate to social and economic development?* There is an extensive economic literature on the subject of corruption and development, which is another way to say that there is little consensus on precisely how to define, measure and assess corruption and its related impact on social and economic change. One can identify three main theoretical approaches.

The first approach considers corruption as a "normal" ingredient of fast change in backward societies. Weak governance and rampant corruption are to be expected "naturally" in developing country economies. Both Huntington (1968, p. 386) and Harberger (1988) illustrate deeply-rooted feelings among Western-educated economists that corruption is a *fatum* in developing countries. Huntington concludes bluntly: "In terms of economic growth, the only thing worse than a society with a rigid, over-centralized, dishonest bureaucracy is one with a rigid, over-centralized, honest bureaucracy." Huntington and Haberger's fatalistic stance stems from a linear analysis of history where countries are not so much "underdeveloped" or "emerging" but rather backward with regard to Western democracies.

The second approach considers that governance is a policy choice. Consciousness of, and respect for, public welfare, whatever the degree of modernization, influences the process of social change. It regards the code of socio-cultural values as stronger in those societies that praise and reward social cooperation, converging goals and altruistic behavior. Sen (1973), for instance, notices that individuals can attain their self-interested objectives only if they behave as if they were altruistic. Auguste Comte (1830), Emile Durkheim (1893), Karl Marx (1865) and Max Weber (1904) have all noticed the role of moral values and have stressed the contribution of belief and ritual in social life, thereby integrating moral–religious norms into the economic framework. These norms induce participation in social life with resulting collective action and cooperative relationships. Weber (1904), in particular, concluded that moral virtues play a central role in capital accumulation and economic development. This approach considers that it is the intersection of moral values and socio-economic behavior that matters. In practical terms, it follows that corruption can be encouraged or discouraged by donors, capital markets, and international institutions.

The third approach boils down to observing the role, either positive or negative, of corruption in economic development, from a practical point of view. Is corruption useful in the process of development, at least in the short term? Does corruption bring with it misallocation of resources or does it provide private incentives for entrepreneurship and stimulus for elite integration and social mobilization?

A first group of economists holds that corruption may be positive as a way to "grease the wheels" of rigid social and institutional structures. This position is held among Western academic circles, *inter alia*, by Leff (1964), Lui (1985), Beck and Maher (1986) or Lien (1986). They regard corruption as providing useful flexibility in fast-changing social and economic structures. In the economic field, they mirror the *fatum* approach of the political scientists in the political economy field. Corruption provides a role of income redistribution in poor countries with rigid institutional fabrics. In the context of pervasive and cumbersome regulations in developing countries, corruption may actually improve efficiency and help growth. As Bardhan (1997) summarizes it: "Economists have shown that, in the second best-world when there are pre-existing policy induced distortions, additional distortions in the form of black-market, smuggling . . . may actually improve welfare even when some resources have to be spent in such activities."

A second group of economists looks at corruption as a sub-optimal allocation of resources. According to Rose-Ackerman (1975, 1978), Shleifer and Vishny (1993) or Mauro (1995), corruption has a negative impact on economic potential in a country, leading to distortions in resource distribution and income inequalities. It discourages savings and investment. It contributes to rent seeking, it stimulates capital flight and brain drain, and it creates "externalities". Corruption, thus, is a specific and important component of governance, with large impact on growth, stability and business prospects.

The focus upon the negative impact of corruption on growth is accentuated by the globalization of capital markets and the instantaneous transmission of information. Increasingly, countries strive to convince private investors, both domestic and foreign, that higher standards of governance will make the business environment more conducive to investment, savings and growth dynamism. They try to make the bureaucracy more efficient and the legal framework more transparent. Conversely, corruption lowers country risk ratings, while discouraging foreign direct investment, triggering capital flight and precipitating financial crisis. This view is widely shared to analyze Argentina's protracted difficulties in early 2002 that reflect the lack of independent judiciaries and widespread corruption. As Miguel Kiguel puts it: "Argentina's biggest problem is institutional and political – not economic. Hence the priority should be restoring stability with public-sector and institutional reform to deal with a complete vacuum of law."[8]

4. *Corruption as a determinant of financial and economic crises.* Governance, corruption and accountability in government policy are a relatively new and loosely-defined field in country risk analysis. Until recently, there was no hint of incorporating the role of bad governance in the business climate, savings mobilization, and capital flow situation in the classic macroeconomic framework. Even in analyzing the impact of political risk upon the firm, most analysts reduce political risk to abrupt upheavals under the form of brutal events such as nationalization, regime change and expropriation (Kobrin, 2001). Though rampant or institutionalized corruption clearly increases uncertainty, hence country risk and opportunity costs, traditional political and economic risk analysis fails to tackle it as a major risk input.

Krugman's (1998a, 1999) approach to financial crisis indirectly touches on governance, as it devotes attention to reckless government spending, nepotism, crony capitalism and hidden subsidies, as worsening conditions that precipitate crises. The issue of governance also touches on the IFIs' conditional lending. Since the IMF and the World Bank have become major and vocal proponents of enhanced governance in developing countries, there is growing attention devoted to their own consideration of transparency in the lending decision-making process. Bouchet and Groslambert (2002) have examined the extent to which official multilateral institutions incorporate governance in comparison with private capital markets and investors. They found a stronger correlation between high corruption and low lending with private capital flows than with official credits.

---

[8] Peru's leader calls on world to provide aid for Argentina, *Financial Times*, 5 February 2002, p. 8.

The new world economic environment has changed the structural relations between countries and the global economy as well as the relations between countries and, within countries, between the state, the private sector and private citizens. Despite more attention devoted to governance in multilateral arenas, country risk analysts still focus on the state as a homogeneous actor in the allocation of goods and services. Country risk still looks at the probability that the state will nationalize, repudiate, devalue and suspend debt servicing. There is little attention devoted to internal power competition within the state as well as to those cross-border actors who challenge the supremacy of the state, namely, global companies, mafias, multinational criminal organizations, NGOs, supranational institutions, and the like. Today, global market forces increasingly bypass the state. Corruption is the byproduct of a state that resists losing its traditional legitimacy, centered on territorial integrity and money supply control. Corruption, then, is the symptom of a rigid institutional system that is unable to move toward a new role of conductor and regulator of market forces. As such, corruption and bad governance are central to country risk assessment.

5. *How to measure corruption in country risk analysis.* Corruption's raw material is made of bribery, abuse of public power, illicit taxes. Regular surveys of international investors' perception of corruption can shed light on the intensity of corruption while providing a comparative picture across time and across countries of rent-exacting power by public agency officials. Country risk analysts can use at least nine main sources of data on governance, including the following:

- Transparency International's annual surveys of corruption practices in nearly 90 countries since 1995.
- The World Bank's database of corruption in developing countries. The World Bank's Board approved a new anticorruption strategy in 1998 as part of a broad and integrated program for improving public sector performance and economic policies (World Bank, 1998).
- PricewaterhouseCoopers' Opacity Index aimed at measuring the lack of clear, accurate, formal and widely accepted practices in a country's business environment. It focuses on the relative state of corrupt business practices, the transparency of the legal system and the

Box 4.3   Transparency International's analysis and measure of corruption

TI is a non-governmental organization devoted to combating corruption, with a network of more than 80 national chapters around the world. In the international arena, TI raises awareness about the damaging effects of corruption, advocates policy reforms, works toward the implementation of multilateral conventions, and subsequently monitors compliance by governments, corporations and banks.

A major tool to curb both the supply and demand of corruption is access to information. The Global Corruption Report is an annual evaluation of the state of corruption around the world. The first report was published in late 2001. The TI Corruption Perception Index attempts to measure perception of corruption. It ranks 91 countries in terms of a "corruption score" since 1995. It is a composite index, drawing on a number of different polls and surveys carried out among business people, academia, and risk analysts, including surveys of residents, both local and expatriate. Since 1999, TI has published an additional index that ranks exporting countries according to their propensity to give bribes. The Bribe Payers Index underlines the fact that corruption in international business is a two-way street.

www.transparency.org/

regulatory framework. It represents a quantitative approach to measuring opacity and its resulting extra risk premium that stems from the additional business and economic costs.

- The Institute for Management Development's World Competitiveness Report which analyzes 49 industrialized and emerging economies around the world based on an Executive Opinion Survey of more than 3500 respondents since 1989. Its analysis of the institutional framework addresses issues such as state efficiency, transparency of government policy, public service's independence from political interference, bureaucracy as well as bribery and corruption.

- Freedom House, founded nearly 60 years ago, and devoted to promoting human rights, free market economics and the rule of law. As such, its staff, helped by a number of US academic experts, focuses on corruption levels in a number of developing and transition economies around the world. Since 1972, FH has published an annual assessment of the state of freedom in various countries and territories on the basis of political rights and civil liberties. In many cross-country researches on growth performance, the political freedom and civil liberties index has been used as a proxy for the political infrastructure of nations and a measure of democracy. Several studies concluded that the positive relation between income levels and democracy is mostly attributable to the former's impact on the latter rather than the other way around.[9]

- The World Economic Forum's Global Competitiveness Report which covers 75 major economies of the world since 1979 (www.weforum.org). Global competitiveness is defined as the set of institutions and economic policies supportive of high rates of economic growth in the medium term.

- The Political and Economic Stability Index of Lehman Brothers and Eurasia aimed at measuring the relative stability in around 20 emerging markets by integrating political science theories with financial market developments. The evaluation of key components of political and economic stability uses a combination of quantitative and qualitative data to produce monthly scoring. Stability components include institutional efficiency, political legitimacy, political violence, economic performance, and government effectiveness.

- The Political and Economic Risk Consultancy (PERC) which provides risk intelligence focused on Asian countries, with emphasis on corruption and business costs. Annual business environment reports compare various socio-political variables in 14 individual Asian countries, based on surveys of a large number of senior expatriates (see Chapter 5 for more details about ICRG).

- The International Country Risk Guide (ICRG) which measures and tracks corruption perception in government, law and order, expropriation risk, as well as the quality of bureaucracy both across 130 countries and across time, since 1982. These measures stem from the subjective assessment of experts around the world.

4.7 THE "QUALITATIVE" AGGREGATE APPROACH TO POLITICAL RISK

The preceding section has already dealt with the issue of political risk in fast-changing societies. Political risk is also discussed regarding the rating approach in Chapter 5, and political risk insurance is discussed in Chapter 9.

---

[9] World Bank, Indicators of Governance and Institutional Quality. www1.worldbank.org/publicsector/indicators.htp

Political risk has never been so much on the front burner as since the 11 September 2001 terrorist attack on the United States. The attack illustrated that there is no sanctuary, since the most advanced nation in the world was the target of brutal and unprecedented large-scale damage. The attack also confirmed, if need be, that developing countries have no monopoly on political risk. Investors are confronted with many political risks in OECD countries, including the hazards of regulatory change, contract frustration, strikes, social unrest and NGO action. To avoid costly surprises, multinationals reassess their political risk models and test ranges of new safeguards, combining intelligence, analysis and insurance. The troubled world of global business has made risk analysis a growth industry.

The qualitative approach to risk considers political risk as a byproduct of an "imbalanced" development process. Economic change produces tensions and centrifugal forces unless a process of institutionalization and social mobilization absorbs and integrates those forces into the development process. However, contrary to the analysis of the components of economic growth or the stability of the domestic financial system, "hard data" are not available in political risk analysis. Number-crunching is of no use. And political risk indexes, with their impressive mathematical precision, can be substitutes for thought.

Information is often scattered and difficult to combine. It includes ethnic tensions, social upheaval, riots, strikes, civil strife damages, and coups d'état. It requires, thus, a substantial amount of expert insight, judgmental inputs and subjective analysis. The various components of political power and influence must be fully identified and understood as well as the credibility of the state's decision-makers. Power might thus be located where it is not expected initially, i.e., in informal pressure groups, in non-governmental organizations, private associations, and the like. A region-wide survey of Latin American politics in mid-2002 showed that the population was losing faith in politicians and institutions of government. The survey also found that support for democracy was eroding and that more than half of the population was calling for an authoritarian regime in order to reverse the protracted economic and social crises in the continent.[10]

Contrary to the balance of payments analysis, political risk monitoring incorporates, implicitly or not, underlying assumptions regarding how politics is structured and how politics relates to economic and social change. The definition of such concepts as stability, order, upheaval or democracy is rarely specified. Ideology and value judgments are often rooted somewhere in political risk analysis. An underlying theory of social change must be clearly defined and stated before embarking on political risk assessment. In particular, a solid theory will help develop a systematic view of factors driving political risk and link them to the risk management strategy.

Six non-rating-based approaches to political risk can be described briefly.

(i) The first approach is the so-called "grand tour" approach that relies on the field company intelligence. Practically, the firm will dispatch a team of specialists to "recognize" the socio-political situation and to test the market risks and opportunities. A bureau will be opened before a branch gets established. Local consultants will get hired. The technique is highly subjective as the country's original flavor can be misleading, incorporating too much emphasis on first-hand impressions.

(ii) The second approach intends to lessen the degree of amateurism of the previous technique, by relying on "old hands", i.e., seasoned experts coming from the academic, intelligence

---

[10] Latins lose faith in politicians, *Financial Times*, 27 August 2002, p. 4.

and diplomacy networks. Former foreign-service officers as well as other analysts from governments and universities are recycled by banks and multinational corporations and sent into countries to assess the current and upcoming political situation. Political scientists will get hired to provide a "rigorous" analysis of the structure of local politics. Given the principle that more information is better than less, expert evaluations of political risk are likely to be more reliable when based on a larger number of specialists. Most international banks and multinational companies retain such experts on a consulting basis, either *ad hoc* or in "in-house" advisory groups. These professional outsiders bring their intimate knowledge of the countries' political complexity as value-added in the decision-making process. Their task is to analyze political uncertainty and to translate it into political risk assessment. Anticipating political changes will lead to plotting how to cope with them. This method is also known as the "expert system".

(iii) The third approach is the well-known checklist technique. This technique boils down to asking the right questions and making sure one tackles them, one by one, and in the right order. Stone (2001) suggests an application of the checklist to managing kidnap risk. The sequence of priorities goes as follows:

- Conduct a thorough assessment of the risk of being kidnapped;
- Implement any necessary security measures;
- Ensure that protection extends to family members;
- Consider undergoing a kidnap survival course;
- Consider kidnap insurance.

(iv) The fourth approach is the Delphi technique based on expert surveys. The key to the effective use of a panel of country specialists is a properly designed questionnaire. The responses are compared and synthesized to produce high-risk/low-risk assessments. However, the method is based on averaging responses so as to produce consensus, thereby eliminating the extremes that carry, usually, the most interesting information.

(v) The fifth approach consists in political risk modeling. This technique assumes a series of linkages between social and political changes that lead to upheaval. As Llewellyn (2001) notices: "In designing a model, the relationships between abstract concepts, such as authoritarianism, and acts of damage to the investor need to be grounded in social science knowledge and research." Modeling requires, first, a careful identification of those main factors driving political risk. Zonis (2001) has developed a political risk framework to focus on the key sources of risk. Risk can be broken into three basic areas, according to Zonis:

- External drivers on which the investor has little influence (riots, coups, weak institutional framework, corruption, pressure groups, etc.).
- Interaction drivers (local communities, labor force, NGOs, shareholders, etc.).
- Internal drivers (information-related problems, company management, human capital).

Modeling then requires a detailed analysis of the structures of political power in the country so as to identify influence circles. Those power circles, in turn, will be examined regarding their relative strength, their evolution and trajectory regarding possible alliances, and their impact on business prospects. Forecasting is then based on correlation and probability calculations. Extrapolation and analogy will be used to analyze additional countries with similar structural attributes.

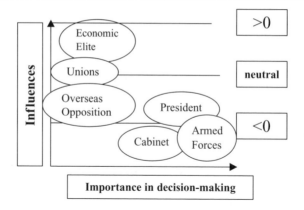

Figure 4.2 The Prince model's power structure (simplified presentation)

(v) Finally, the power base or *Prince model*[11] involves identifying key sources of power and centers of influence, both informal and official. This power structure analysis is based on a general political forecasting framework that relies on questionnaires. The answer to the question "where does power stem from in country *x*" leads to a systematic breakdown of the political power structure. PRS Group's political risk appraisal services produce forecasting reports based on the identification of key actors. Each of the actors is assigned a number to measure its positive or negative impact on a company's strategy. The experts forecast the three most likely regimes to be in power five years from the present, and then predict how they will behave toward businesses and investment strategies. In late 1981, PRS (formerly Frost & Sullivan) characterized as follows "Saddam Hussein's moderately pro-international business policies": "The current regime is increasingly favorable to foreign, or at least Western, business" (Frost & Sullivan, *World Political Risk Forecasts*, Iraq, 10/81).

A Prince chart records the position of major individuals, groups and institutions in a political system toward the vents and actions that could affect international business in the country. A probability score is attached to each and every actor, according to its influence and pertinence. The probabilities calculated in the Prince model represent the likelihood of an event, but not its effect on international business. A second step is to adjust the probability estimates to determine the likelihood of loss to international business from political instability and government restrictions. The most outstanding feature of the calculation process is that it is eclectic and relies heavily upon the judgment of a panel of experts for each country. The decision structure in Figure 4.2 illustrates the probability of a government change, in country *x*, based on the relative influence of major political actors, within and outside the given country.

4.8   CONCLUSION

In conclusion, risk is a multifaceted challenge. Reducing risk to a single, abrupt shock such as default, coup d'état or contract repudiation, misses the subtle and gradual forms of risk

---

[11] The Prince Model is described in layman's terms in Coplin and O'Leary (1976). Prince is an acronym for the four steps in the process, namely: probe, interact, calculate, execute

emergence in cross-border investment. In addition, risk is not to be reduced to developing countries. The September 11 terrorist attack on the United States, the protracted ETA guerilla action in Spain, as well as recent examples of rampant nationalization in France, show that there is no sanctuary and thus LDCs have no monopoly on country risk.

Assessing risk, be it economic or political, requires a thorough understanding of the development process. The latter is much more than GDP growth or even GDP per capita growth. It is a sequential process of building, not just macroeconomic stability, but also interdependent factors such as quality of governance, flexible institutions, societal capacity to advance technological capability, and evolving government and corporate organizational structures. This complexity has a twofold implication. (i) Country risk is not to be reduced to straight national government interference. Instead, it must take into account the full range of discontinuity sources that stem from the political power structure as well as the institutional organization that enhances or hinders the development process. (ii) The more open a country, the more diversified and market-driven its economic system, but also the more prone it is to importing external shocks that result from the global environment's spill-over effects.

Even though country ratings provide the analyst with a quick comparative tool for assessing country risk, the pitfalls are too large to ignore the merits of the qualitative, structural, approach to development. Country rating might boil down to ignorance ranking. A global, integrated, approach has the merit of gathering a broad range of expertise including economists, political scientists, diplomats, statisticians, and development experts. This unique combination of expertise enforces the consideration of development as a multifaceted process of social and economic change.

The World Economic Forum attempts to synthesize the sequence of development stages, describing the various steps a country is to experiment with before graduating from developing to more advanced stages. Resource-based and factor-driven economies depend greatly on mobilizing primary factors of production. They gradually become technology-importing economies before becoming knowledge-based economies where investment-driven growth harnesses global technologies to local production. At a later point of innovation-driven economic development, the country reaches high rates of social learning and ability to shift to new technologies. This process is full of risks and opportunities for local and global investors.

Although describing the rising complexity that is built into the development process, this sequential model has a similar flavor as the old, mechanical, rigid and ideology-biased "take-off approach" of Walter Rostow in the 1960s. Efficiency is assumed to be rooted in free markets. It gives a policy priority to reaching global competitiveness while reducing the state's functional role to support indigenous firms and to attract FDI. In addition, development is seen as an accumulation toward a critical mass of capital, be it physical, human or institutional.

To be sustainable, the development process needs adaptive structures and institutions. What the risk analyst should look at are the institutional and structural rigidities that raise the country's vulnerability to internal and external upheavals. Clearly, the quantitative and qualitative approaches to country risk are not exclusive from each other. Common sense suggests relying on an integrated analysis that combines ratings and scoring, econometric correlations, and an analysis of the underlying multiple components of a country's development. As Rummel and Heenan (1978) conclude: "The most effective analysis combines insight and wisdom with management science."

Table 4.7 Standard country risk assessment report

---

1. Introduction: Map and graphs
(History, political system, ethnical features, culture and religion)

2. Survey of geographical features, human and natural resources. Analysis of sustainable growth strategy based on major social and development indicators
Sources: www.UNCTAD.org; www.undp.org; www.worldbank.org

3. Macroeconomic analysis
Sector analysis, strengths and weaknesses, trade openness, structure of
export/import flows (partner/product composition)
Inflation, budget, public sector borrowing requirements
Savings/investment ratios, financial intermediation credit and monetary policy
GDP growth evolution and prospects, income distribution, underground economy, etc.
Sources: IMF/WB/regional development banks: IADB/AfDB:AsDB/EBRD, EIU, Coface, CIA
http://www.ntu.edu.sg/library/statdata.htm

4. Balance of payments analysis
Trade balance, current and capital accounts, reserves, errors and omissions
Sources: IMF (IFS), IIF, central banks

5. Debt flows and stock analysis
Liquidity and solvency indicators
Debt sustainability analysis (debt structure: creditors, debtors, maturity, currency, interest rates)
Sources: World Bank/OECD/BIS/IMF
www.bis.org
Secondary market discounts: Bradynet, EMTA/IFR
Bond spread evolution: JP Morgan

6. Legal and regulatory framework conducive to private investment
Sources: IFC

7. Governance and transparency assessment
Sources: Transparency International
CONCLUSION: risk and opportunity assessment

Table 4.8 Main sources of country risk intelligence

---

www.imf.org
www.worldbank.org
IFC Emerging Stock Market Factbook (www.ifc.org)
Inter-American Development Bank (www.iadb.org/)
Web sites of central banks (www.zagury.com/cbanks.htm)
International banking and financial market developments (www.bis.org)
Handbook of Economic Statistics, Central Intelligence Agency (www.cia.us)
Countrymetrics (www.countrymetrics.com)
Political and Economic Risk Consultancy, Ltd. – PERC Gateway to news and country data
BERI (Business Environment Risk Index)
Credit Risk International
Frost & Sullivan
Institute for International Economics (Washington, DC)
Institute of International Finance, Inc. (Washington, DC)
The Economist Intelligence Unit (London) (www.eiu.com)
The Davos World Economic Forum (www.weforum.org)
The Harvard Institute for International Development (Boston)
New York University (www.ntu.edu.sg/library/statdata.htm)
Morgan Stanley Capital International Data
Coface (www.coface.org)

Table 4.8   (*continued*)

Bradynet Info (www.bradynet.com)
International Finance Review (London): Secondary market prices and bond issues
Political Risk Services (country risk indices)
Global Risk Assessment, Inc. – Country Risk Services (www.grai.com)
Euromoney Magazine (country risk indices)
Institutional Investor Magazine
Global Finance Magazine
Oxford Analytica, Inc. – On-line daily analysis and custom country risk services
                                        ****
Transparency International (corruption and governance) (www.transparency.org/cpi)
Freedom House (www.freedomhouse.org)
PricewaterhouseCoopers (www.opacityindex.com/)
Lehman Brothers Eurasia Group's Stability Index (www.legsi.com)
World Competitiveness Yearbook – IMD (http://www02.imd.ch/wcy)
Rabid Tiger Project Jeff Deutsch's Political Risk Consulting and Related Research
Dr. Nouriel Roubini (NYU)
Professor Campbell Harvey (Duke University)

REFERENCES

Akerlof G, 1970, The Market of Lemons: Quality Uncertainty and the Market Mechanism. *Quarterly Journal of Economics*, 84, 488–500.

Bardhan P, 1997, Corruption and Development: A Review of Issues. *Journal of Economic Literature*, Sep, 1322.

Beck PJ and Maher MW, 1986, A Comparison of Bribery and Bidding in Thin Markets. *Economic Letters*, 20, 1–5.

Bouchet MH, 1987, *The Political Economy of International Debt*. Greenwood, IL: Quorum Books.

Bouchet M and Groslambert B, 2000, Côte d'Ivoire: Trois Défis Majeurs. *Jeune Afrique-L'Intelligent*, 5 Déc, 2082.

Bouchet M and Groslambert B, 2002, *Governance and Market Access*. Working Paper, CERAM-Sophia Antipolis, March.

Bronstein H, 2001, YearAhead: Despite Argentina, Big Returns Seen for Latin American Debt. *Yahoo Finance*, 27 December.

Camdessus M, 1999, Address to the IOSCO on Transparency and Improved Standards. *IMF Survey*, Jun, 28 (11).

Clei J, 1998, La Coface devant le Risque-Pays. *Risques*, Déc, 36, 52.

Comte A, 1830, *Cours de philosophie positive*, I, Paris.

Coplin WD and O'Leary M, 1976, *Everyman's Prince: A Guide to Understanding your Political Problems*. North Scitate, MA: Duxbury.

Dell'Arriccia G, Gödde I and Zettelmeyer J, 2000, *Moral Hazard and International Crisis Lending: A Test*. IMF Working Papers, preliminary draft, 7 November.

Dornbush R, 1985, External Debt, Budget Deficits and Disequilibrium Exchange Rates. *In: International Debt and the Developing Countries*. World Bank Symposium, 213–35.

Drucker PF, 1974, Multinationals and Developing Countries: Myths and Realities. *Foreign Affairs*, Oct, 53, 121–34.

Durkheim E, 1893, *De la division du travail social*, Paris.

Eichengreen B and Mody A, 1998, *What Explains Changing Spreads on Emerging Market Debt: Fundamentals or Market Sentiment?* NBER Working Paper no. w6408, February.

Feldstein M, 2002, *Economic and Financial Crises in Emerging Market Economies: Overview of Prevention and Management*. NBER Working Paper no. 8837, March, 18.

Fischer S, 1988, Economic Development and the Debt Crisis. *World Bank PPR Working Papers*, Jun, 8.

Fukuyama F, 1992, *The End of History and the Last Man*. New York: The Free Press/MacMillan.

Greenspan A, 1999, Remarks Before the World Bank Conference on Recent Trends in Reserve Management. Federal Reserve Board, 29 April.

Hansen RD, 1978, The Political Economy of North–South Relations: An Overview and An Alternative Approach. *In:* A Fishlow, A Diaz-Alejandro, R Fagen and R Hansen, eds. *Rich and Poor Nations in the World Economy*. New York: McGraw-Hill, 231.

Harberger AC, 1988, Policymaking and Economic Policy in Small Developing Countries. In: R Dornbush and L Helmers, eds. *The Open Economy*. EDI Series in Economic Development. Oxford: Oxford University Press, 243–63.

Huntington SP, 1968, *Political Order in Changing Societies*. New Haven, CT and London: Yale University Press.

IFC, 1998, *Financial Institutions, Lessons of Experience*, 6, 11.

IMF, 1992, *Macroeconomic Adjustment: Policy Instruments and Issues*. IMF Institute, Aug, 67.

Kobrin SJ, 2001, *Political Risk: A Review and Reconsideration*. Massachusetts: MIT.

Krugman P, 1979, A Model of Balance of Payments Crises. *Journal of Money, Credit and Banking*, 11 (3), 311–25.

Krugman P, 1988, External Shocks and Domestic Policy Responses. *In:* R Dornbusch and FL Helmers, eds. *The Open Economy*. EDI Series in Economic Development. Oxford: Oxford University Press.

Krugman P, 1998a, *What Happened to Asia*. Mimeo, January.

Krugman P, 1998b, *Will Asia Bounce Back?* Speech for CSFB, Hong Kong, March, 1–7.

Krugman P, 1999, Balance Sheets, Transfer Problem, and Financial Crises. Mimeo prepared for the festschrift volume in honor of Robert Flood, January.

Leff NH, 1964, Economic Development Through Bureaucratic Corruption. *The American Behavioral Scientist*, 8 (2), 8–14.

Lien DH, 1986, Notes on Competitive Bribery Games. *Economic Letters*, 22, 337–41.

Llewellyn DH, 2001, Introduction: Applications for Management. In: *The Handbook of Country and Political Risk Analysis*. PRS Group, 7.

Lui FT, 1985, Equilibrium Queuing Model of Bribery. *Journal of Political Economy*, 93 (4), 760–81.

Marx K, 1865, *Le Capital, IV, Economie II: Matériaux pour l'Economie*, Chap. IV, Les Crises – Critique de la Théorie Ricardienne. Paris: La Pléiade, 1968.

Mathieu N, 1998, The Evaluation Framework. *In:* World Bank Evaluations Department, *Financial Sector Reform*. Washington, DC: World Bank, 1.

Mauro P, 1995, Corruption and Growth. *Quarterly Journal of Economics*, Aug, 681–711.

Michalet C-A, 1999, *La Séduction des Nations*. Paris: Economica, 41.

Mishkin FS, 1996, *Understanding Financial Crises: A Developing Country Perspective*. NBER Working Paper no. 5600.

Mishkin FS, 2001, *Financial Policies and the Prevention of Financial Crises in Emerging Markets Countries*. NBER Working Paper no. 8087.

Moser C, 2002, *Financial Crisis Models with a Special Regard to Self-Fulfilling Prophecy and Asymmetric Information*. University of Innsbruck, unpublished, February.

Nye J, 1967, Corruption and Political Development: A Cost–Benefit Analysis. *American Political Science Review*, Jun, 61, 417–27.

Obstfeld M, 1985, Floating Exchange Rates: Experience and Prospects. *Brookings Papers on Economic Activity*, 2, 369–450.

Pattilli C, Pourson H and Ricci L, 2002, External Debt and Growth. *Finance & Development*, Jun, 39 (2), 32–5.

Radelet S and Sachs JD, 1998, The East Asian Financial Crisis: Diagnosis, Remedies, Prospects. *Brookings Papers on Economic Activity*, 1, 1.

Rose-Ackerman S, 1975, The Economics of Corruption. *Journal of Public Economics*, 4, 187–203.

Rose-Ackerman S, 1978, *Corruption: A Study in Political Economy*. New York: Academic Press.

Roubini N, 1998, An Introduction to Open Economy Macroeconomics, Currency Crises and the Asian Crisis 3. What Causes Long Run Growth? The Debate on the Asian Miracle. http://www.stern.nyu.edu/globalmacro/Part

Rummel RJ and Heenan DA, 1978, How Multinationals Analyze Political Risk. *Harvard Business Review*, Jan/Feb, 71.

Sachs JD, 1989, *Introduction: Developing Country Debt and The World Economy*. Chicago: University of Chicago Press.

Schaefer BD, 2002, *The Millennium Challenge Account: An Opportunity to Advance Development in Poor Nations*. The Heritage Foundation Lectures no. 753, June.

Sen A, 1973, Behavior and the Concept of Preference. *Economica*, August.

Shleifer A and Vishny RW, 1993, Corruption. *Quarterly Journal of Economics*, 108, 599–617.

Stone M, 2001, Scourges that strike at the heart of global business. Mastering Risk, *Financial Times*, 12–13. www.ftmastering.com/risk

Tanzi V, 1998, *Corruption Around the World*. IMF Working Papers 45, no. 4, December.

UNDP, 2002, *Human Development Index 2002 Presentation*, Table 1.2, http://hdr.undp.org

Weber M, 1904, *The Protestant Ethic and the Spirit of Capitalism*. New York: Scribner, 1958.

Williamson J, 2002, *Is Brazil Next?* International Economics Policy Briefs no. PB-02-7. Institute of International Economics, August.

World Bank, 1986, *Financing Adjustment with Growth in Sub-Saharan Africa*. Washington, DC: World Bank, 12.

World Bank, 1997, *African Development Indicators*. Washington, DC: World Bank.

World Bank, 1998, *Helping Countries Combat Corruption: The Role of the World Bank*. Washington, DC: World Bank.

World Economic Forum, 2002, *Global Competitiveness Report 2002*. Executive Summary. www.weforum.org

Young A, 1995, The Tyranny of Numbers: Confronting the Statistical Realities of the East Asian Growth Experience. *The Quarterly Journal of Economics*, August.

Zonis M, 2001, Driving defensively through a minefield of political risk. Mastering Risk, *Financial Times*, 10–11. www.ftmastering.com/risk

5

Assessment Methodologies: Ratings

The rating or rank ordering comparative approach aims at providing an overall view of relative risk when facing foreign investment decisions. Brealey and Myers (2000) have noted that "businesspeople have good intuition about *relative* risks, at least in industries they are used to, but not about absolute risk or required rates of return". Thus, the objective of these rating methodologies is to rank countries as a function of their degree of risk. Since it is much easier to estimate a relative level of risk than an absolute level of risk, once a rating has been established, it is then more straightforward for the international manager to determine an appropriate required rate of return by comparing with similar existing investments in other countries. Clei (1994), for example, a country risk executive at Coface, the French credit export agency, writes: "The country risk ranking is necessary both to check the overall consistency of the assessments and to price the guarantees, since the premium rate charged by Coface is a function of several parameters of which the most important is the risk category of the host country." Thus, the rating approach is widely used by professionals, inasmuch as it allows them to quantify, to price, or to set some limits depending on the level of the country risk.

There are as many rating methodologies as there are rating entities, depending on different types of investment and the various sources of risk. As mentioned previously, since there exists no comprehensive theory of country risk, all these methods are purely empirical. Most of them are derived from a predetermined checklist. They rely on quantitative evaluations and/or qualitative indicators that provide a more or less explicit score. These scores are then translated into a rating. These methods can be divided into two groups. A first cluster tackles the whole spectrum of foreign investments and consequently is concerned with all the possible kinds of risk as identified in Chapter 2. The objective of the institutions belonging to this group is to provide *global country risk rankings*. A second group focuses exclusively on debt and only considers *country credit ratings*. International bond investors and commercial banks as well as potential borrowers in the international capital markets are their main target.

5.1 GLOBAL COUNTRY RISK RATINGS

This first section refers to the global ranking methods that aim at developing a holistic approach to country risk. These systems assess the general investment climate for any kind of foreign investor and rank various countries based on their respective degree of risk. This approach is developed by firms specialized in country risk ranking, and by credit export agencies.

5.1.1 Specialized Ranking Firms

Specialized ranking firms include many countries in their analysis. They evaluate the degree of risk for each country, establish a rank and then sell their research to third parties. Clients are

We wish to thank Jenny Clei (Coface), Ted Haner (BERI), Jean-Louis Terrier (Credit Risk International) and Mary Lou Walsh (PRS Group) for answering various questions related to rating methodologies.

mainly firms with overseas operations or investments that wish to gauge the risk of their business. The following paragraphs present a selection of the most widely used ranking techniques that have been developed by these organizations. The list is far from exhaustive and similar products are offered by firms such as Rundt's, DRI·WEFA, or Control Risks Group.

Business Environment Risk Intelligence (BERI)[1]

The Geneva-based firm, Business Environment Risk Intelligence SA, was founded in 1966 by Haner, one of the pioneers in political and country risk assessment (Haner, 1965, 1966) when he was director of international activities of the American Cement Corporation. Three times a year, BERI produces its Business Risk Service (BRS). The BERI index covers about 50 countries and has been available since the mid-1970s. As such, it constitutes one of the oldest consistent time series in the field. Four types of ratings are provided by BERI. They are the *Political Risk Index (PRI)*, the *Operations Risk Index (ORI)*, the *Remittance and Repatriation Factor (R Factor)*, and the *Composite Score*, which represents a combination of the other three. For each of them, an assessment of the present situation as well as a one-year and a five-year forecast are published. The PRI and ORI originate from a Delphi method[2] process undertaken and monitored by the BERI team of analysts.

The *Political Risk Index* aims at assessing the social and political environment of a country. It is built on the opinion and scores provided by 100 experts with a diplomatic or political science background. These specialists are asked to grade 10 socio-political variables divided among three categories: internal causes, external causes and symptoms.[3]

Internal causes of political risk:

- Fractionalization of the political spectrum and the power of these factions.
- Mentality, including xenophobia, nationalism, corruption, nepotism, willingness to compromise.
- Fractionalization by language, ethnic and/or religious groups and the power of these factions.
- Social conditions, including population density and wealth distribution.
- Restrictive (coercive) measures required to retain power.
- Organization and strength of forces for a radical government.

External causes of political risk:

- Dependence on and/or importance to a major hostile power.
- Negative influences of regional political forces.

Symptoms of political risk:

- Societal conflict involving demonstrations, strikes and street violence.
- Instability as perceived by non-constitutional changes, assassinations and guerilla wars.

The experts rate each variable from zero (highest risk) to seven points (lowest risk), summing up to a total score between zero and 70. Moreover, up to 30 bonus points can be added up for the eight internal and external causes criteria, resulting in an overall possible score between zero and 100. Then, BERI splits the PRI's country results into four categories from prohibitive risk

---

[1] See http://www.beri.com and BERI (2001a) for a more detailed description. Information reprinted with permission of Beri S.A.
[2] The Delphi method aims at facilitating the formation of a group judgment through a well-structured and controlled process. It aims at bypassing the shortcomings of traditional group discussion such as "follow the leader tendency" and other social biases.
[3] See Howell and Chaddick (1994) for an in-depth discussion of these variables.

(0–39 points), high risk (40–54 points), moderate risk (55–69 points), up to low risk (70–100 points). PRI's one-year and five-year forecasts are obtained by asking the experts to give their overall feeling on the business operations climate, and not by detailing each variable's prevision. The experts' opinions are then averaged after discarding the extremes.

The goal of the *Operations Risk Index* is to assess the general business climate. Like the PRI, it is derived from another panel of 100 experts with international experience, and whose opinion is processed through a Delphi method. It grades the degree of hospitality of a country and how welcoming it is vis-à-vis foreign investment. It deals with both economic and regulatory environments, and also tries to gauge any possible discrimination against foreign business. Fifteen criteria are taken into account and given between zero (unacceptable conditions) and four points (superior conditions). They are assigned various weightings so that the total ORI score scales from zero to 100, with the same type of grouping as for the PRI:

- Policy continuity
- Economic growth
- Currency convertibility
- Labor costs/productivity
- Short-term credit
- Long-term loans and venture capital
- Enforceability of contracts
- Attitude toward foreign investors and profits
- Degree of privatization
- Monetary inflation
- Balance of payments
- Communications and transportation
- Local management and partners
- Bureaucratic delays
- Professional services and contractors

ORI's one-year and five-year forecasts are obtained in the same way as for the PRI.

The *Remittance and Repatriation Factor* addresses the issue of repatriation and convertibility in a foreign currency. Contrary to the two previous indices, the R factor does not rely solely on expert judgments. It is essentially "produced by a large computer program that manipulates over 14 000 cells of data and makes hundreds of calculations", as stipulated mysteriously on BERI's information web page (BERI, 2001b). It estimates a country's ability and willingness to implement and maintain a fully convertible system so that foreign firms may freely repatriate profit and capital in any currency and also import any goods paid in a foreign currency. The R factor is computed from four sub-indices: legal framework (20% of the R factor), foreign exchange generation (30%), accumulated international reserves (30%), and foreign debt assessment (20%). The resulting scores are grouped with the same risk categories as for PRI and ORI. BERI (2001a) states that "forecasts are the result of regression analyses, trends in the ratings, and senior staff judgment". Moreover, they specify that "wholly quantitative forecasts proved unreliable".

The *Combined Score* is a simple average of the PRI, ORI and R factor. It aims at providing an overall assessment of the country's riskiness through a Profit Opportunity Recommendation (POR) that differentiates countries between "No Business Transactions", "Trade Only", "Non-dividend Cash Flow", and "Investment Quality".

Nord Sud Export (NSE)

Founded in 1981 by Jean-Louis Terrier,[4] Nord Sud Export is now part of the French media group Le Monde. It publishes a bimonthly information letter covering about 100 developing countries. The country ratings list is calculated once a year, starting in 1982. NSE provides two types of complementary rankings. The first one is the opportunity rating, and assesses the market potential for a foreign investor. The second is the traditional country risk rating. This latter is computed from four categories of risk parameters: *sovereign financial risk, financial market risk, political risk*, and *business environment risk*. Each parameter is the product of the weighted average of very narrowly defined individual criteria, taken from a series of 60 variables. Each of them is graded on an eight-unit scale, from zero (worst) to seven (best). NSE emphasizes its willingness to follow as objective an assessment process as far as possible. In order to do so, they refuse to use expert panels, and rely mainly on quantitative criteria (43 out of 60). As for the remaining 17 qualitative items, Terrier (2001) states that they "are rated according to rigorous 'rating grids' which reduce the level of subjectivity".

Parameter 1: sovereign financial risk.

- Factor 1 (weight 4/10): importance of the public debt in the economy. Computed from six quantitative variables.
- Factor 2 (weight 4/10): sovereign default risk. Computed from four quantitative variables and two qualitative criteria.
- Factor 3 (weight 2/10): non-convertibility risk. Computed from two quantitative and one qualitative variables.

Parameter 2: financial market risk. This risk category was previously aggregated with the sovereign risk set in a more general financial risk grouping. They were split after the Mexican and Asian crises when the specific influence of financial markets was evidenced.

- Factor 4 (weight 4/10): fundamental macroeconomic equilibrium. Computed from four quantitative items.
- Factor 5 (weight 3/10): risk of unexpected and sharp devaluation. Computed from four quantitative variables.
- Factor 6 (weight 3/10): systemic risk and economic volatility. Computed from five quantitative variables and one qualitative criterion.

Parameter 3: political risk. This parameter addresses the social and political features of a country, and that may generate a specific risk.

- Factor 7 (weight 3/10): homogeneity of the society. Computed from three quantitative and one qualitative variables.
- Factor 8 (weight 5/10): regime and government stability. Computed from three quantitative and four qualitative criteria.
- Factor 9 (weight 2/10): external conflicts. Computed from two quantitative and two qualitative items.

Parameter 4: business environment risk. This risk category gauges the quality of the business conditions and the "hospitality" of a country.

---

[4] Jean-Louis Terrier is now president of Credit Risk International and advisor to Nord Sud Export.

- Factor 10 (weight 4/10): attitude toward foreign investments. Computed from four quantitative and one qualitative variables.
- Factor 11 (weight 3/10): labor conditions. Computed from two quantitative and two qualitative variables.
- Factor 12 (weight 3/10): quality of the governance. Computed from two quantitative and three qualitative variables.

NSE also differentiates between two broad types of investors: *exporters* and *direct investors*. Exporters are seen as more short-term oriented and more concerned by sovereign credit risk and payment delays. On the other hand, direct investors are perceived as more long-term oriented and more sensitive to political instability. Two different ratings are established, depending on the nature of the investment. Ranking for *exporters* is based on 30% of parameter 1 sovereign financial risk, 40% of parameter 2 financial market risk, 10% of parameter 3 political risk, and 20% of parameter 4 business environment risk. Ranking for *direct investors* is computed from respectively 10%, 30%, 30%, and 30% of the aforementioned risk parameters.

Once rated, the country is allocated to one of the seven following classes of risk: 1, dangerous (0–159 points); 2, very high (160–269); 3, high (270–319); 4, quite high (320–379); 5, moderate (380–429); 6, low (430–539); 7, very low (540–700). Then, NSE translates these classifications into recommendations in terms of margin rate premium for exporters, and risk premium above the home country internal rate of return for direct investors.

The NSE method does not aim at extrapolating to obtain future scenarios but focuses only on present conditions, in order to estimate the level of risk. Finally, NSE stresses that this country risk rating must not be taken as a tool *per se*, but must be jointly analyzed with the country opportunity rating, which is developed in parallel by the firm.

Political Risk Services (PRS)[5]

After having been part of the IBC Group,[6] the USA-based Political Risk Services Group was purchased in 1999 by Mary Lou Walsh, its then managing director. The PRS Group publishes Political Risk Services (PRS) as well as the International Country Risk Guide (ICRG). The PRS Group was founded by William Coplin and Michael O'Leary at the end of the 1970s. The PRS analyses were initially published in the World Political Forecasts of Frost & Sullivan under the name World Political Risk Forecasts (WPRF), and are now disseminated via the PRS Group's Country Reports. They cover 100 countries and are updated on a quarterly basis. They provide 18-month and five-year forecasts of risk to international business. The PRS originality lies in its rating system process.

The PRS method is built from the Coplin–O'Leary Rating System whose underlying architecture is based on the Prince model[7] (Coplin and O'Leary, 1972). It can be seen as a kind of "modified Delphi technique" (Howell and Chaddick, 1994) that treats and systematically processes several experts' opinions for each country under review. PRS usually relies on three experts per country and tries to select teams with diversified backgrounds. It separately considers three types of risk, depending on the nature of the investment: financial transfers (convertibility from local to foreign currency and repatriation), foreign direct

---

[5] See http://www.prsgroup.com and PRS (2001b) for a more detailed description. "Political Risk Services" forecasting methodology, reprinted with permission of the publisher and copyright owner, The PRS Group, Inc, East Syracuse, NY, USA.

[6] IBC's name was changed to Informa Group following its merger with LLP Group in 1998.

[7] The Prince model is a rather simple, straightforward, and systematic method that deals with power analysis. It was developed by Coplin and O'Leary at the end of the 1960s and aims at predicting the outcome of any collective action. It is mainly used in political science analysis.

investment (any direct control of overseas assets), and exports (any risk and difficulties faced by exporters).

Firstly, experts look at a series of 17 variables, and evaluate the current degree of risk or restriction (current base level) on a four-unit scale: 0 (low risk), 1 (moderate risk), 2 (high risk), and 3 (very high risk). These risk factors are split between 18-month and five-year forecasts, and are described below.

18-month forecasts:

1. Turmoil: actions that can result in threats or harm to people or property by political groups or foreign governments.
2. Equity restrictions: limitations on the foreign ownership of businesses.
3. Operations restrictions: general quality of the operational business environment, including regulations, efficiency of the officials, and degree of corruption.
4. Taxation discrimination: possible discrimination vis-à-vis foreign businesses, due to formal and informal tax policies.
5. Repatriation restrictions: formal and informal rules regarding the repatriation of profits, dividends and investment capital.
6. Exchange controls: degree of freedom and easiness to convert local currency to foreign currency.
7. Tariff barriers: the average and range of financial costs imposed on imports.
8. Other import barriers: formal and informal quotas, licensing provisions, or other restrictions on imports.
9. Payment delays: degree of punctuality with which government and private importers pay their foreign creditors.
10. Fiscal and monetary expansion: assessment of a country's fiscal and monetary policy as to whether it can generate a healthy business climate or create economic disorders.
11. Labor policies: government policy, trade union activity, and productivity of labor forces.
12. Foreign debt: relative size of the foreign debt and the ability of the country's public and private institutions to service it in due time.

For the five-year forecasts, in addition to the 12 previous criteria, five other elements are taken into consideration.

Five-year forecasts:

13. Turmoil: same item as in the 18-month list but on a five-year horizon.
14. Investment restrictions: the current base and likely changes in the general climate for restricting foreign investments.
15. Trade restrictions: the current base and likely changes in the general climate for restricting the entry of foreign trade.
16. Domestic economic problems: the ranking of the country according to its most recent five-year performance record in per capita GDP, GDP growth, inflation, unemployment, capital investment and budget balance.
17. International economic problems: the ranking of the country according to its most recent five-year performance record in current account (as a percentage of GDP), the ratio of debt service to exports, and the annual percentage change in the value of the currency.

Secondly, experts try to identify the three most likely political regimes that will be in power, in 18 months and five years respectively. Each political scenario is assigned a probability of occurrence. Then, they assess the potential impact of each of the three possible political regimes on the 17 previously described criteria. For each variable, experts must forecast how its degree of risk will be modified by the regime under consideration. They quantify this change according to the following rule: -1.0 (less risk), -0.5 (slightly less risk), 0 (same risk), $+0.5$ (slightly more risk), $+1.0$ (more risk). These numbers are weighted by the probability of occurrence of the regime in question and then added to the current base level of risk.

For example, suppose the experts estimate that the regime XYZ has a 40% probability of seizing power in 18 months and that this will worsen the repatriation conditions (variable #5) so that it will generate more risk for this item ($+1.0$). If the current prevalent environment on this specific issue is seen by the experts as high risk (2), the 18-month impact of this anticipated regime on this criterion would be $40\% \times 1.0 = 0.4$, to be added to the current level (2), resulting in an 18-month forecast of 2.4 for item #5.

Finally, for each of the three types of investment previously identified (financial transfer risk, direct investment risk, export market risk), PRS focuses on a preselected number of relevant criteria.

The 18-month rating for *financial transfer risk* is calculated as the average of four items: repatriation restrictions (#5), payment delays (#9), fiscal and monetary expansion (#10), foreign debt (#12). The five-year grade is obtained from the average of the 18-month rating, the five-year level of turmoil forecast (#13), and the international economic problem score (#17).

The 18-month rating for *direct investment risk* is based on the average grade of seven factors: turmoil (#1), equity restrictions (#2), operations restrictions (#3), taxation discrimination (#4), repatriation restrictions (#5), exchange controls (#6), labor policies (#11). The five-year grade is the average of the 18-month rating, the five-year level of turmoil forecast (#13), the investment restrictions (#14), and the domestic economic problems (#16).

The 18-month rating for *export market risk* is built from the average of six variables: turmoil (#1), exchange controls (#6), tariffs (#7), other import barriers (#8), payment delays (#9), foreign debt (#12). The five-year score is given by the average of the 18-month result, the five-year level of turmoil forecast (#13), trade restrictions (#15), and the domestic economic problems (#16).

Under each of these three approaches, countries are classified in one of the following 12 categories: D− (most risky), D, D+, C, ..., B+, A−, A, A+ (least risky).

One of the main distinctive features of the PRS method is that it first anticipates the possible future political regimes, and only after that estimates the potential impact of each regime on the predetermined variables.

International Country Risk Guide (ICRG)[8]

Founded in 1980, the International Country Risk Guide was initially published in the newsletter International Reports. Like PRS, it has been, since 1992, a product of the PRS Group. ICRG covers about 140 countries. It produces three distinct risk categories on a monthly basis: *political*, *economic* and *financial*, as well as a *composite risk* rating derived from the previous three indices. ICRG assesses the current situation and makes forecasts over one-year and five-year time horizons.

The *political risk* rating aims at gauging the country's degree of stability. It is obtained from the subjective assessment of ICRG editors that transform qualitative information into numerical scores through a series of preset questions. This index is calculated as the sum of

---

[8] See http://www.icrgonline.com and PRS (2001a) for a more detailed description.

12 social and political qualitative components. The score may vary between zero and 100 points. Below 50 is considered as very high risk; 50–59.9 is high risk; 60–69.9 is seen as moderate risk; 70–79.9 is low risk; and 80–100 is perceived as very low risk.

Political risk components:

- Government stability (max. 12 points) is determined by government unity, legislative strength and popular support.
- Socio-economic conditions (max. 12 points) derives from unemployment, consumer confidence and poverty.
- Investment profile (max. 12 points) results from contract viability/expropriation, profits repatriation and payment delays.
- Internal conflicts (max. 12 points) is based on civil war, terrorism/political violence and civil disorder.
- External conflicts (max. 12 points) is a function of war, cross-border conflict and foreign pressures.
- Corruption (max. 6 points) is estimated from the length of time a government has been in power continuously.
- Military in politics (max. 6 points).
- Religious tensions (max. 6 points) is determined by the degree of religious freedom, and the capacity of several religious groups to live in harmony.
- Law and order (max. 6 points) depends on the strength and impartiality of the legal system, as well as on an assessment of popular observance of the law.
- Ethnic tensions (max. 6 points) is evaluated as a function of the degree of tolerance and compromise between various ethnics.
- Democratic accountability (max. 6 points) gauges the degree of responsiveness of a government to its people. ICRG differentiates between five types of governance: alternating democracy, dominated democracy, *de facto* one-party state, *de jure* one-party state, and autarchy.
- Bureaucracy quality (max. 4 points). ICRG tries to assess the ability of the local bureaucracy to administrate the country without drastic changes in policy or interruption in government services.

The *economic risk* rating evaluates the economic strengths and weaknesses of a country. It is built on a set of five purely quantitative components (ratios). It goes from zero to a maximum of 50 points. The 0%–24.9% range is considered as very high risk; 25%–29.9% is high risk; 30%–34.9% is seen as moderate risk; 35%–39.9% is low risk; and 40%–100% is considered as very low risk.

Economic risk components:

- GDP per head (max. 5 points), compared to the average of the total GDP of all the countries covered by ICRG: the lower in the GDP per head ranking, the riskier the country is supposed to be.
- Real GDP growth (max. 10 points): the more growth, the lower risk is assigned by ICRG.
- Annual inflation rate (max. 10 points): the more inflation, the riskier the country is.
- Budget balance as a percentage of GDP (max. 10 points): the more deficit, the riskier the country is.
- Current account as a percentage of GDP (max. 15 points): the more deficit, the riskier the country is.

The *financial risk* rating is concerned with the country's ability to pay its way. It assesses the country's capacity to generate enough hard currency so that it can assume its foreign financial obligations. It is based on five criteria that can add up to 50 points. It has the same risk category ranges as the economic risk rating.

Financial risk components:

- Foreign debt as a percentage of GDP (max. 10 points): the higher the ratio, the riskier the country.
- Foreign debt service as a percentage of exports of goods and services (max. 10 points): the higher the ratio, the riskier the country.
- Current account as a percentage of exports of goods and services (max. 15 points): the lower the ratio, the riskier the country.
- Net international liquidity as months of import cover (max. 5 points): the shorter the coverage period, the riskier the country.
- Exchange rate stability (max. 10 points) is gauged on the appreciation/depreciation rate of the local currency versus the US dollar: the more volatile (whether it is appreciation or depreciation), the riskier the country.

The one-year and five-year forecasts are derived from the ICRG staff's forecasts for each of these components. For the financial and economic components, experts try to use the forecasts produced by the relevant government or official institution as much as possible. However they are often obliged to make subjective extrapolations, especially for the five-year time horizon. The political, economic and financial risk categories are eventually combined into a *composite risk* rating with respectively 50%, 25% and 25% weights. Furthermore, each criterion is available to clients so that they can build their own personal rating system.

The Economist Intelligence Unit (EIU)[9]

Part of the London-based The Economist Group,[10] The Economist Intelligence Unit was founded in 1949. It presents itself as the "world's leading provider of country intelligence" (EIU, 2002). Since 1997, its Country Risk Service product has delivered country risk ratings for 100 developing countries on a quarterly basis. The EIU method flows from experts' answers to a series of 77 predetermined qualitative and quantitative questions. It results in a 100-point index (the higher the score, the riskier the country), which is divided into five bands from A (lowest risk) to E (highest risk). Four general risk categories are analyzed (political risk, economic policy risk, economic structure risk, liquidity risk), and are combined into an overall risk index. In addition to this broad macro measure of risk, EIU produces other more investment-specific micro risk ratings (currency risk, sovereign debt risk, banking sector risk) that address the particular needs and concerns of certain groups of investors.

The *political risk* assessment is based on a set of 11 subjective points split between issues of political stability and political effectiveness.

The *economic policy risk* addresses the quality of the economic policy management as well as the level of the economic performance. This index is computed from 27 criteria, among which 15 are subjectively estimated. They are shared across five groups: monetary policy, exchange rate policy, fiscal policy, trade policy, regulatory environment.

---

[9] See http://store.eiu.com and EIU (2001) for a more detailed description.
[10] It also separately owns *The Economist* news magazine.

The *economic structure risk* is concerned with the growth potential, but also with the degree of dependence of the country vis-à-vis foreign capital. It also estimates the fragility of the economy in case of an external shock. It is a kind of solvency indicator. This rating is based on 29 questions among which 11 are subjective, relative to five subcategories: global environment, growth, current account, debt, financial structure.

The *liquidity risk* focuses more specifically on the country's short-term financial strengths and weaknesses. It gauges any potential imbalance between resources and obligations. It is based on 10 questions of which two are subjective.

These four risk indices are aggregated into an overall rating with a 22%, 28%, 27%, and 23% weighting respectively. Contrary to the BERI, PRS or ICRG approaches, but more like the NSE method, EIU uses only historical data and current expert estimation. It bases its assessment on the existing situation, without trying to predict the evolution of the relevant parameters.

5.1.2   Export Credit Agencies

In order to facilitate international trade and to promote their exports, many countries have fostered the creation of public or state-backed specialized institutions, usually named credit export agencies. Their mission is twofold: they provide country risk insurance and they assist exporters through financial support and funding. Among the most famous are EDC (Canada), Coface (France), Hermes (Germany), Sace (Italy), ECGD (UK), or Exim Bank (USA).[11] In some cases, official multilateral agencies provide investors with insurance for non-commercial risk. This is the case of the Multilateral Investment Guarantee Authority, a Washington-based specialized subsidiary of the World Bank Group. Most of these agencies collaborate and exchange information within the International Union of Credit and Investment Insurers (better known as the Berne Union).

The credit export agencies may cover a large class of risks that starts with the standard default payment of a foreign client, including sovereign entities, and goes on to hedging against economic slowdown in a foreign country. These risks are usually categorized between country risk at the macro level, and commercial risk at the micro level. As Coface (2002a) put it: "The country rating measures the average corporate payment default risk in a given country and indicates to what extent a company's financial commitments are affected by the local business, financial and political outlook." Thus, credit export agencies are concerned not only with credit rating and sovereign default like a bank, but they also deal with several other types of risk arising from the local business environment and possibly affecting the foreign firm's financial commitments, including equity investments.

As explained above, the rating serves as a basis for setting premium rates, and is widely used by most credit export agencies. However, a few avoid using this system, among them MIGA: "unlike many insurers – private and public – MIGA does not utilize a country rating system to calculate premium rates" (Bellinger, 2001).

In order to regulate the industry and to avoid subsidies and trade distortions, the OECD credit export agencies agreed, in 1999, on a common risk classification scheme. This agreement led to the implementation of seven categories of country and sovereign risk, for each of which a minimum premium rate was accepted. This classification is obtained from an econometric model based on three sorts of quantitative criteria: the default history of the country, its financial situation, and its economic situation. In addition, some qualitative political considerations may

---

[11] A list of credit export agencies from the OECD countries is available at http://www1.oecd.org/ech/act/xcred/ecas.htm

be taken into account to determine the final risk category of the country. According to Estrella (2000), and based on seven export credit agencies, there is a very high consistency across their respective classifications: the rank correlation coefficients of export credit agency ratings vary between 0.951 and 0.995.

Cosset and Roy (1994) studied EDC, the Canadian export credit agency. They tried to replicate its ratings, based on certain publicly available economic variables. Using the EDC 1990 country risk classifications and economic data as of 1989, they found that with only few explanatory variables, it was possible to correctly reproduce the agency's rankings. The main determinants were related to certain external debt indicators, which does not constitute a surprise because of the period under consideration. The short-term ratings were also dependent on the GDP per capita and the GDP growth rate, whereas the current account to GDP ratio had an influence on the long-term notes.

Focusing on the methodology of Coface, which is the self-proclaimed worldwide leader of the industry,[12] the following paragraphs will illustrate the export credit agency rating approach. Incorporated in 1946 by the French government as a public sector institution, Coface was privatized in 1994 and floated on the Paris Bourse in 2000. However, it "still covers the political risk on behalf of the French State with its guarantee and with the goal of promoting French exports" (Gherardi, 1998).

At least every three months, their team of seven analysts produces country risk ratings called @rating for about 140 countries. These ratings try to assess the likelihood of default for short-term commercial transactions (up to six months). Their methodology has evolved over the last decades, so that it takes into account the new sorts of risk that appeared during this period. The assessment process is based on quantitative criteria shared across seven groups: political factors, risk of currency shortage, sovereign risk, risk of a sudden devaluation, risk of a systematic crisis in the banking sector, cyclical risk, payment behavior.

The *political factors* subset deals with the political risk in its strict meaning. It measures the likelihood of external and internal conflicts, the degree of religious or ethnic tensions, as well as any potential social disturbances. It also evaluates how these factors could undermine the execution of contracts in progress.

The *risk of currency shortage* assesses the country's economic and financial situation. The financial factor analyzes the balance of payments position and the external financing requirement. It also monitors the short-term debt level. The economic situation deals with the economic performance, the level of development, and includes the country's vulnerability in case of external shocks.

The *sovereign risk* is concerned with the state's capacity to fulfill its obligations. It monitors the public finance sector as well as some of the more qualitative aspects such as the fight against corruption or the degree of the administration's independence vis-à-vis business and political groups.

The *risk of a sudden devaluation* estimates the likelihood of a financial crisis resulting from massive capital flight. It is obtained from three sub-indices: the vulnerability index, the degree of exposure to a confidence drop, and the level of market confidence. The vulnerability index is a function of the level of dependence vis-à-vis foreign short-term investments and the economy's ability to resist speculative attacks. The degree of exposure to a drop in confidence depends on the possible exchange rate overvaluation, the situation of the trade balance, and the existence of financial bubbles. The level of market confidence is computed from financial

---

[12] Their motto is "the first worldwide company rating system" (Coface, 2002b).

Information reprinted with permission of Coface.

market data such as the evolution of interest rates, stock market prices, and the discount on the secondary debt market.

The *risk of a systemic crisis in the banking sector* focuses on the soundness of the banking system. It evaluates both the financial health of the local banks, and the regulatory framework in which they evolve.

The *cyclical risk* estimates the risk of a strong economic slowdown that could occur independently of the five above-mentioned cases. It is based on short-term growth forecasts.

The final criterion examines the *payment behavior* for short-term transactions in a given country. Thanks to Coface's extensive worldwide network of clients and partners, it can be updated very regularly and followed almost without any time delay. The inclusion of this parameter in their rating process distinguishes the export credit agencies' methodology from other methods.

Coface defines several types of country each of which is assigned a specific weighting grid. This rating process results in seven cohorts of risk, ranging from A1 to A4 for the investment grade categories, and from B to D for the speculative grade categories. Finally, it is worth noting that, even though this model is purely quantitative, *in fine*, the grade is given by a rating committee that may decide not to follow the model's result, thus leaving the final decision to the analysts' judgment.

5.1.3 Summary of Global Country Risk Ranking Methods

Built on the underlying assumption that "careful data collection and analysis can generate rules for anticipating politico-economic events in a robust way that does not depend on problematic theory" (Ascher, 1989), and because no comprehensive theory of country risk has yet been developed, all these country risk ranking techniques rely simply on checklists of predetermined indicators. These criteria are carefully selected and weighted by the model's designer, from his own experience or from an historical data analysis.

Howell (2001) identifies various types of country risk ranking methods. Type I is only concerned by the present situation of a country and assumes a correlation between its current features and possible future problems. This is the way followed by NSE, EIU or Coface. Type II also deals with a series of factors that are supposed to characterize a country's environment. However, unlike Type I, experts are asked to forecast the future level of these criteria over various time horizons. Illustrations of Type II are BERI's one and five-year forecasts, or ICRG's 18-month and five-year ratings. Howell (2001) presents a Type III, which only differs from Type II in the sense that variables in the Type III models are not general attributes of the country in question, but are directly linked to potential losses for foreign businesses, such as the "nationalization" parameter. Most of the Type II approaches also contain some Type III variables and it is quite difficult to draw a strict distinction between these two methods. The last model is the Type IV. Instead of directly forecasting the future outcomes of specific criteria, it starts by anticipating the possible governments in power in the future. Only then, does it try to assess the impact of each alternative on a set of predetermined factors.

All these methodologies, whatever their type, are based on expert judgment. Even the most quantitative criteria are evaluated subjectively in order to determine their relevance, or in order to allocate appropriate thresholds. Is the GDP per head a relevant parameter for assessing country risk? Does a 2% current account deficit make a big deal? Does it represent a low, a moderate, or a high risk? Why should the composite score be made of 35% of that, plus 40% of this, and 25% of that? Everything depends on the expert's choice. Even though some approaches try to mitigate the criticism of subjectivity by relying on expert panels, such as those using a Delphi process, the problem remains. As the vice-president of coordinating and planning at Conoco said: "If you pretend to quantify things by your subjective judgment, it is not very helpful. You can't boil things down to numerical indices" (Business Week, 1980). Rummel and Heenan (1978) also note that: "The strength of the Delphi technique rests on the posing of relevant questions. When they are defective, the entire structure crumbles."

West (2001), senior advisor with MIGA, goes further. Referring to the PRS model, he states that:

> ... while one may have a lot of respect for the extensive academic work of William Coplin and Michael O'Leary, the preparation of these indices and the measures that compose them are open to serious questions. Moreover, there has always been a serious problem with the assignment of weights. The fact that the political risk component is exactly twice the weight of financial and economic components, and that this two-to-one ratio is true across all countries and many decades is very convenient. Aside from its convenience, though, there is not a shred of theoretical justification underpinning that weighting. Similarly, there has been no attempt to provide ex post facto evidence that this two-to-one weighting ratio is accurate. Other systems like PRS could be subjected to similar critiques.

It is true that, one year before the Mexican financial crisis of 1994/1995, Coplin and O'Leary (1993) wrongly predicted that: "The most promising aspect of Mexico's long term business outlook is for a stable, improving relationship with international investors." Another example of the difficulty of correctly anticipating such crises is given by the October 2001 NSE rating of Argentina that, just a few months before its economic collapse, graded this country as moderate risk for exporters and low risk for direct investment. Coface also acknowledges its system's failure to anticipate the Mexican crisis or to predict the domino effect of the Thailand meltdown on Asian countries (Gherardi, 1998). Over the last decades, no rating system has been able to consistently anticipate the main manifestations of country risk, and this is true for most events among all global country risk rating publishers.

In order to test the reliability of these models, Howell and Chaddick (1994) are among the very few who studied their predictive power and their ability to anticipate losses. They only focus on the political component of country risk, and investigate the degree of correlation between the 1986 projections of The Economist[13] socio-political factors, the BERI Political Risk Indices (PRI), and the Political Risk Services (PRS) ratings, on the one hand, and on the other hand, a loss indicator for the period 1987–1992. This loss indicator was mainly built from the OPIC[14] documentation of losses due to political risk. They find very low correlation coefficients of 0.33, 0.51 and 0.57, for The Economist, BERI and PRS respectively. The coefficients of determination[15] (R^2) are also quite weak at 11% for The Economist and 26% for BERI (the coefficient for PRS is not provided). Howell and Chaddick (1994) analyzed the various criteria making up each index and, based on historical data, rebuilt a posteriori a new rating system. Thus, they were able to create other, more statistically efficient models. However, no out of sample testing was done.

Howell (1992), concentrating on The Economist rating and analyzing the period 1987–1991, extends this approach to the economic factors and to the overall score. In this case, he finds a lower correlation coefficient for the socio-political variables (0.10), but notices that the result

---

[13] The Economist model is distinct from the EIU approach.

[14] OPIC is an American credit export agency.

[15] R^2 measures the ability of the risk rating to explain the losses. It represents the percentage of the variations in the losses that are explained by the variation in the indices.

is improved when taking the overall score into consideration (0.17) and significantly better when considering the economic indices alone (0.25). However, results are still weak.

Meldrum (2000) also measures the predictive power of four risk services, the Standard & Poor's ratings, and the author's own company-specific manufacturing risk measure. He explores the relationship between these ratings and the returns earned by US manufacturing firms on their direct investment abroad (data taken from the Bureau of Economic Analysis), between 1994 and 1997. He observes that:

Risk measures from external services [...] performed poorly as predictors of one- to two-year-ahead manufacturing foreign investment returns. Some of that inability may be caused by differences in the specific investment for which the risk measures were created, some may be caused by weaknesses in the risk measurement system.

Indeed, the advantage of being synthetic and offering at a glance an overall assessment of country risk can also turn into one of the main weaknesses of these global country risk ranking methods. As far back as 1980, Gordon Rayfield, a political analyst with General Motors stated that: "I don't think there is a lot of meaning in a BI or BERI kind of study. An analysis done for a group of clients with different needs has to confine itself to such a high level of superficiality that its value is limited" (Business Week, 1980). In order to counter this drawback, more and more country risk agencies offer and emphasize the possibility for their clients to make up their own specific index, so that it can be better adjusted to their own needs and their particular situation. This, for instance, is the case of ICRG or PRS, that provide their customers with the detailed political information as well as financial and economic data from which their ratings are built. Following this line, Meldrum (2000) gives a concrete illustration of how a firm can create its own *ad hoc* risk measure.

Another type of critique raised by West (2001) concerns the static feature of ratings. *A priori*, there is no reason for a criterion to keep the same weight forever. This explains why most of these rating methods are regularly updated, usually after the event. There is also no justification for a factor to be as crucial or to have the same graduations in countries as different as Nigeria or Brazil, for example. Goldstein *et al.* (2000) illustrate this point by writing that "a 25 percent decline in stock prices would be considered a signal of future currency crisis in Malaysia and Sweden but not in Mexico, where volatility is historically much higher". To circumvent this issue, some models, such as NSE, avoid analyzing developed economies and only tackle the developing countries, assuming that they share more or less the same common characteristics. Others, like Coface, devise several weighting schemes for various types of countries.

A further flaw of these methods arises from their linear aggregation process. Indeed, once a variable is assigned a weight, it can only impact the final outcome between zero and 100% of its original weight. However, under certain circumstances, it seems reasonable to think that, when a situation reaches a certain threshold, feedback effects could be generated. A sort of chain reaction may start that could make the factor in question much more decisive in the overall assessment of the country risk than originally accounted for in the model. In addition, other criteria could be impacted and see their relative importance revised as well. This is why approaches such as that of Goldstein *et al.* (2000) refuse to rely on the linear regression techniques, and prefer to use non-parametric methods.[16] The Asian crisis exemplified this problem, where cumulative and contagion effects coupled with herd behavior turned an *a priori* seemingly manageable situation into a very chaotic process.

---

[16] Non-parametric methods are presented in Chapter 6.

However, even though these approaches do not forecast country risk events as well as could be expected, they do incorporate a non-negligible amount of information about the level of risk. Looking at between 28 (in 1984) and 48 (in 1995) national stock market indices, Erb *et al.* (1996) found that the ICRG ratings were able to predict the cross-section of expected returns. Based on this fact, they implemented a successful portfolio strategy that, *a posteriori*, was able to deliver some substantial abnormal returns. Consequently, this shows the ratings' ability to contain relevant information for international investors.

Finally, these global country risk methods may prove useful, provided they are only taken for what they are: a first rough grid of analysis that aims at providing as exhaustive a weighted checklist as possible or a means of limiting the analysts' subjectivity, or providing a single axis of analysis for comparing countries. From an operational point of view, the rating process offers managers, CEOs and investors the possibility of comparing and quantifying risks. As Terrier (2001) put it: "From a methodological point of view, to quantify in order to compare is disputable, but to decide without quantifying is still more questionable."

5.2   COUNTRY CREDIT RATINGS

This section investigates the country credit rating methods, which aim at assessing the ability and willingness of a given country's issuer to honor its financial obligations. Country credit risk can be defined as the specific risk generated because the debt issuer is from a different country than the lender. Accordingly, although we may find some divergence between firms about what exactly they are rating, all these methods deal with debt from a global perspective and, therefore, they all have to include the notion of country risk in their analytical process. These ratings tackle bank loans, bonds and short-term credits. They may consider debt denominated in foreign as well as local currency. They can also address the overall impact of country risk on the so-called country or sovereign ceiling.

Country credit risk comes in addition to the pure microeconomic credit risk that is specific to the individual debt issuer. It can be divided between macroeconomic and political risk due to the local characteristics of the country where the debt is issued and transfer risk, in case the debt is issued in a currency different from that of the borrower. Transfer risk arises because the debt issuer may not be able to secure access to foreign exchange in case of a balance of payments crisis and/or because of foreign exchange controls. When the borrower is a sovereign entity, country risk is assimilated into sovereign risk.

The international banks of the main European financial centers were at the origin of the sovereign credit rating industry in the nineteenth century. Crédit Lyonnais was a pioneer in this field, when, in 1871, it set up a research department called Service d'Etudes Financières. One of the goals of this department was to study borrowing countries (Flandreau, 1998). In the aftermath of the Great Depression, most of these international activities were downsized, and did not regain importance until the 1970s when Citibank implemented a formal approach to country risk assessment (Kennedy, 1991). A survey carried out in 2000, in the banking industry, found that nowadays "robust methods exist for generating country risk ratings and incorporating those ratings into the economic capital allocation process. Some banks have developed models to generate specific capital cushions for country risk using processes analogous to existing obligor credit risk models" (Institute of International Finance, 2000).

The situation is similar for the credit rating agencies. Although Moody's issued its first sovereign credit ratings in 1919, and recorded up to 50 government issued debt ratings in 1929, this sector, as evidenced in Figure 5.1, only started to redevelop from the end of the 1980s

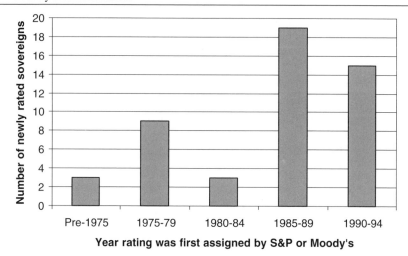

Sources: Standard & Poor's; Moody's Investors Service (in Cantor and Packer, 1995), Reproduced with permission.

Figure 5.1   Growth of the sovereign ratings business

(Cantor and Packer, 1995). Nowadays, the sovereign credit rating industry includes various types of institutions, among which we find banks, magazines and credit rating agencies.[17]

5.2.1   Credit Rating Agencies

The role of credit rating agencies is to collect information about borrowers' creditworthiness and issue ratings on their probability of default. Most agencies, including Fitch, Moody's and Standard & Poor's, aim at establishing a relative likelihood of default in comparison to other issuers, and not an absolute probability of financial distress (Estrella, 2000). Their main economic role and raison d'être is to share information between a large number of potential investors at affordable cost. Generally, ratings are initiated at the request of the issuer, either as a compliance to local regulations, or because it may help to tap the market by providing more transparent information from an independent source. In this case, costs are supported by the borrower, and usually represent about three basis points of the issued amount (Smith and Walter, 2001). However, in some cases, some of these institutions are compensated with subscription fees paid by investors. Occasionally, agencies do provide unsolicited ratings on their own.[18] The next paragraphs present the sovereign credit rating methods of the top three global agencies, Fitch, Moody's and Standard & Poor's. These firms have the largest worldwide exposure, rate firms from every type of industry, and according to Reisen and von Maltzan (1999), cover about 80% of sovereign credit ratings.

5.2.2   Fitch[19]

Headquartered in London and New York, Fitch is part of the French conglomerate Fimalac. It is the result of consecutive mergers of Fitch with IBCA in 1997, and then, with Duff & Phelps and Thomson Financial BankWatch in 2000.

---

[17] A comprehensive list of these institutions was established by Estrella (2000).

[18] Smith and Walter (2001, pp. 36–39) discuss this issue and the possible underlying motivations for doing so.

[19] See http://www.fitchratings.com for more details about Fitch rating methodology.

Fitch covers about 80 sovereign and country ratings. The bulk of the rating activity revenues come from the rated body's fees, even though it also generates some sources of proceeds from its research department.

According to Fitch (2002), if the sovereign borrowers:

... retain the right to print their own money,[20] the question of default is largely an academic one.[21] The risk instead is that a country may service its debt through excessive money creation, effectively eroding the value of its obligations through inflation. When a sovereign nation borrows in a foreign currency, however, there is a more serious risk of outright default since the sovereign borrower cannot print the means of servicing the debt.

Therefore, the objective of Fitch sovereign ratings is "to assess the sovereign's ability and willingness to generate the foreign exchange necessary to meet its obligations" (Fitch, 2002). Because a government may have the legal authority to impose foreign exchange controls, creditors of borrowers in the country are faced with transfer risk. Borrowers may not be provided with foreign currency by the local central bank, and consequently face the impossibility of honoring their obligations. In addition, because sovereign default has such a negative consequence on the national economy, Fitch usually considers the sovereign rating as a benchmark and a ceiling for other issuers domiciled in the same country. Nonetheless, under certain circumstances, some companies deserve above-ceiling grades, when they have demonstrated their ability to maintain some latitude with respect to their foreign exchange position, irrespective of what the country's situation is.

However, in another document, Fitch (2001) distinguishes between sovereign local versus foreign currency ratings, and notes that, at least for the lower-rated countries, it is worthwhile making a distinction. Indeed, since "the threat of a government imposing foreign exchange controls is irrelevant" for local currency debt, it may be useful to raise the sovereign foreign currency ceiling by introducing a sovereign local currency grade. The local currency grade is usually higher than the foreign currency ceiling and consequently, provides a broader range of ratings.

Based on the modern history of default or near-default, the agency has developed some models and established a list of criteria likely to predict potential problems. They result in a percentage score for each sovereign issuer. In order to feed their reflection, analysts use publicly available data as well as specific information drawn from questionnaires sent to the authorities of the country under consideration. Later, the country is visited by teams of at least two persons, and locals from the political, business and administration world are interviewed (see Box 5.1 for an example).

Box 5.1   Country visit by credit rating agencies.

World's top three credit rating firms to visit Korea beginning next week

The world's top three credit rating agencies – Fitch IBCA, Moody's Investor Service and Standard & Poor's – will make official visits to Korea beginning next week.

The three firms said that they will dispatch taskforces which will meet with government authorities and heads of local commercial banks.

Fitch IBCA will dispatch a sovereign credit rating taskforce, while the taskforce of Moody's and S&P will likely focus on credit evaluation of local banks, the Ministry of Finance and Economy announced on Thursday.

---

[20] However, it is worth noting that as central banks become fully independent, governments' room for maneuvering is more and more limited.

[21] This is not always correct as exemplified by the Russian government default on its domestic debt in August 1998.

Fitch IBCA said that it will during February 19–21 visit the MOFE, Financial Supervisory Commission, the Bank of Korea and the Korea Development Institute to examine the restructuring progress and macro-economic status of Korea. The results of the inspections will be released at end-April. Fitch IBCA has currently set Korea's sovereign credit rating at BBB+.

Meanwhile, Moody's Investor Service will send its taskforce next week, beginning with inspections on Hanvit and Kookmin banks on the 21st, Housing & Commercial Bank on the 22nd and Koram and Hana banks on the 23rd. The credit rating agency is also expected to make an official announcement regarding its stance on the Kookmin–Housing & Commercial Bank merger.

S&P is also expected to dispatch an inspection team during mid-March, and will visit Kookmin Bank on March 13th and Shinhan Bank on March 15th.

(Cho Hyun-jung, HYPERLINK "mailto:hokie@mk.co.kr"; hokie@mk.co.kr)

Source: BUSINESS KOREA, Feb 16, 2001.
Item: 2W82001200102168723.

During the rating process, Fitch is primarily concerned with the *country's external debt position*: its exact amount, its nature, and how it can be serviced. The firm also pays attention to other types of external liabilities, such as foreign holdings of direct and portfolio investment, that could threaten the overall situation of the economy and cause rapid and massive outflows. However, many other variables are also scrutinized. *Government policy* is assessed as well as the structural features of the country that determine its long-run, potential growth rate. Fitch emphasizes its willingness to evaluate the *standard financial and macroeconomic indicators*, like the fiscal and monetary policies and their impact on the current account balance as well as the more *long-term factors*, such as the level of unemployment, thereby assessing the country's ability to develop consistently and harmoniously. Furthermore, they make it clear that they give a lot of importance to the *policy coherence* as presented by their counterparts.

Their analysis is then directed toward the *tradeable sector*. By carefully studying the degree of diversification and competitiveness, they try to anticipate prospects for the current account. As for the policy review, it also seeks to determine the underlying structural capacity of the country's tradeable sectors. They investigate the economy's aptitude to be more competitive by looking at the level of openness, and the investment share in GDP.

Although they play down its importance because of the end of the cold war and the advent of the "new world of global finance" (Fitch, 2002), Fitch still acknowledges the weight of *political risk* in the sovereign credit risk rating. They split this issue between internal and external political risks. The former estimates the degree of political and social tensions, as well as the authorities' ability to gain support from the population. The latter focuses on the likelihood of conflicts with foreign countries, and studies the country's level of involvement on the international stage, its relationships with other nations and multilateral institutions.

Finally, Fitch's teams of analysts run stress tests and try to assess the economy's *ability to overcome international exogenous shocks*, particularly in regard to its external debt level.

Fitch has established a checklist of criteria to be reviewed, so as to support the methodology presented above. They are grouped among the 14 following subsets:[22]

- Demographic, educational and structural factors
- Labor market analysis
- Structure of output and trade
- Dynamism of the private sector
- Balance of supply and demand
- Balance of payments
- Analysis of medium-term growth constraints
- Macroeconomic policy
- Trade and foreign investment policy
- Banking and finance
- External assets
- External liabilities
- Politics and the state
- International position

With respect to corporate foreign currency ratings, Fitch follows a three-step process. It starts by assessing the company's debt as if it were located in the highest (AAA) possible rated country. Then, it evaluates the country's features and its specific impact on the firm and its operating environment. Finally, it focuses on the specific foreign exchange issue (transfer risk).

Fitch provides both short and long-term ratings, for which two different models were developed. The short-term notes refer to less than 12-month forecasts and are much more focused on the issue of liquidity. They may stand above their corresponding long-term grade, provided the country is capable of managing its short-term obligations. More attention is placed on the level of foreign exchange reserves compared to imports, as well as on the prospect of sudden and rapid capital outflows. The short-term notes are F1 (highest credit quality), F2 (good credit quality), F3 (fair credit quality), B (speculative), C (high default risk), D (default).

The long-term ratings refer to time horizons of one year and above. They are split between investment grade for which the chance of default is very low, and speculative grade which indicates a much more substantial probability of distress. Investment grade is AAA (highest credit quality), AA (very high credit quality), A (high credit quality), BBB (good credit quality). Speculative grade starts from BB (speculative), followed by B (highly speculative), CCC, CC, C (high default risk), and lastly DDD, DD, D (default). The three default grades differentiate the expected degree of financial recovery for the unfortunate investor.

Finally it is worth noting that Fitch (2002) stresses how sovereign credit rating is a difficult task when compared to standard corporate rating: "It is important, though, that investors realize the limitations of this exercise, which is necessarily far less certain than our ability to analyze either bank or corporate risks of default." They argue that due to the lack of historical data

---

[22] Their components are detailed at http://www.fitchratings.com/corporate/reports/report.cfm?rpt_id=116361

and because of the small size of the statistical samples, they cannot assess the credit risk as precisely as for companies. Fitch (2002) concludes by stating that:

The rating of sovereigns depends more on the art of political economy than on the science of econometrics. It depends on the careful judgment of experienced analysts about the durability of policy and the values of policy-makers as much as on a hard-nosed assessment of the prospects for a nation's export potential.

5.2.3 Moody's

After having been part of Dun & Bradstreet for almost 40 years, Moody's was spun off in September 2000, and is now a freestanding firm, listed on the New York Stock Exchange. With a team of about 25 sovereign analysts and around 100 countries covered, this company, that issued its first rating in 1909, is a leader in this sector. As with Fitch and Standard & Poor's, its credit rating business is supported by the issuers' fees.

Moody's global credit rating methodology has evolved noticeably over the last few years, and is now well structured and defined.[23] Moody's explicitly differentiates between local and foreign currency ratings.

The local currency rating assesses an issuer's ability to repay its local currency obligations, and consequently is not concerned with foreign exchange restrictions. For each country, a local currency guideline is published that provides the local currency ceiling. This gives the highest grade possibly attributed to any locally-domiciled debt issuer. This also reflects the country-specific operating environment, and because grades are globally comparable, it represents a measure of country risk (excluding foreign currency problems). A default on its local currency debt by a government would certainly imply significant negative consequences for the rest of the country's local debt issuers. However, these latter may be rated above the government's local currency debt, provided they demonstrate a very strong cash-flow-generating capacity. Thus, by lifting the sovereign ceiling constraint, the introduction of local currency ratings proved particularly useful for the best issuers domiciled in countries with low foreign currency country ceilings (Moody's, 1999b).

The foreign currency rating deals with the likelihood of default on foreign currency denominated debt. In addition to the aforementioned local specific country risk, the foreign currency grade also takes into consideration the question of foreign exchange availability.[24] Like for the local currency, Moody's publishes a country ceiling[25] for the foreign currency instruments. Even though a debtor's local currency financial situation is sound, in case of an external payments crisis, its ability to get access to foreign currency is fairly limited. Moreover, this limitation is often compounded by the local government's willingness to keep hard currency for its own uses. For that reason, and contrary to the local currency ratings, the foreign currency government debt rating is usually the highest and serves in most instances as the foreign currency country ceiling. However, when it is estimated that a government would probably choose not to impose a blanket moratorium, as some recent examples, such as Ecuador, have shown, Moody's is likely to make some exceptions to this rule. Moody's approach is summarized in Table 5.1.

Moody's ratings for the foreign currency debt of any issuer follow a two-step process (Moody's, 2001b). They first assess the intrinsic credit quality of the institution under

---

[23] See Moody's (1999a,b, 2001a, 2002).

[24] However, in some very exceptional situations, it does not prevent Moody's from assigning a higher foreign currency than local currency grade.

[25] Moody's (2002): "In 1997, we changed the name 'sovereign ceiling' to 'country ceiling', because the ambiguous term 'sovereign' could be taken to refer sometimes to the country as a whole and sometimes to the government itself as an issuer."

Table 5.1   Moody's global credit rating approach

	Local currency	Foreign currency
Ceiling	The *local currency guideline* rating gives the highest grade possibly attributed to any locally-domiciled debt issuer, in a given country. This also reflects the country-specific operating environment, and because grades are globally comparable, it represents a measure of the country risk (excluding foreign currency problems).	The *foreign currency country ceiling* provides the highest foreign currency rating that can be attributed in a given country. It represents country risk, including possible external payments problems.
Government issuer	The local currency government rating is not necessarily a ceiling for other local currency debt issuers.	Moody's rating of the foreign currency debt issued by the local government generally represents a ceiling for other foreign currency debts.
Non-government issuer	Non-government debt rating is not necessarily capped by government debt.	Foreign currency rating is generally constrained by the country ceiling which is usually the same as the government rating.

consideration, as if it were a local currency debt issuer, and then they consider the foreign currency ceiling of the country where the issuer is domiciled. If it is lower than the local currency rating of the firm under review, this is the one that is retained. Otherwise the issuer's domestic currency rating is also applied to the foreign currency denominated debt.

According to Moody's (2001b): "In light of this diversity of theories, the country risk analyst is best advised to take an eclectic approach, borrowing from a variety of traditions of thought and avoiding dogmatic limitation to a single one." Following this line, a rating analysis[26] takes into consideration the structures of social interaction, social and political dynamics, as well as the economic fundamentals. It also defines external debt, computes the net debt, compares the debt burden across countries, and investigates the short-term debt.

Structures of Social Interaction

This refers to the various social components of a country, the way they organize each other, the way they manage conflicts of interest, and their possible degree of dissatisfaction. It deals with the political structure and the underlying social contract. This also includes an examination of the economic structures and the economic policy. It ends with a social behaviorial study, that tries, in particular, to anticipate the possible social reactions to any potential austerity program.

Social Action

This analysis intends to bring tangible dynamics to the previous subset. It aims at estimating what kind of policy could concretely be implemented in the socio-political fields, and what kind of responses it would induce.

---

[26] See Moody's (2001b) for more details.

Political Dynamics

This category looks at the ability of a political structure to promote economic growth. It evaluates the efficiency and the degree of corruption of the administration. It also considers the nature of its relationships with its neighbors, as well as its membership in international organizations. It ponders the likely reactions in case of a political change, and the country's ability to overcome any adverse shock.

Economic Fundamentals

The analysis here focuses on the way the country manages and develops its national wealth and the consequences it has on its ability to service its financial obligations. The nation's resources and their exploitation are studied. The characteristics of the import/export sectors are investigated, in order to identify any possible structural problems. Likewise, international capital flows are examined, so as to assess the country's external financial position. Finally, Moody's explores the country's ability to implement an austerity program, in case it might need one to resolve a deteriorating external current account.

Analyzing Debt

Moody's defines external debt as all foreign currency denominated debts, issued both by public and private institutions. Among various practices for calculating the net debt, Moody's chooses to focus on the gross debt number less the short-term liquid interbank claims of the banking system only. Then, for comparison purposes, the debt numbers are normalized with the introduction of external debt to GDP and external debt to exports ratios. However, Moody's stresses the difficulty of relying on quantitative ratios and emphasizes the need to carefully interpret their relative meaning. Finally, because short-term debt may have an impact on a country's ability to service its long-term obligations, its structure and its evolution are regularly monitored. The possibility of receiving short-term financial assistance from foreign countries or international organizations is also taken into account.

In conclusion, this process of analysis generates a set of possible scenarios, which are assigned a subjective probability weight. Moody's determines the country rating by retaining the probability of the worst-case option.

For evaluating the risk of default, Moody's (2001b) underlines the importance of qualitative judgment as opposed to quantitative analysis: "The debt-rating process cannot be ratio-driven because the ratios are based on past experience, and they provide only a glimmering of guidance in forecasting the future." In another document, Moody's (1999c) explains its general methodology and specifies:

Because it involves a look at the future, credit rating is by nature subjective. The role of the rating committee is to introduce as much objectivity to the process as possible by bringing an understanding of the relevant risk factors and viewpoints to each and every analysis. For each rating, Moody's relies on the judgment of a diverse group of credit risk professionals to weigh those factors in light of a variety of business scenarios for the issuer and then come to a conclusion on what the rating should be. [...] the rating process is guided by a common set of basic analytical principles such as global consistency, an emphasis on qualitative factors, and a focus on the long term.

Moody's long-term ratings are shared between the investment grade ratings: Aaa (best quality), Aa (high quality), A (strong payment capacity), Baa (adequate payment capacity), and the speculative grade ratings: Ba (moderate protection of interest and principal payments), B (small assurance of interest and principal payments), Caa (likely to be or already in default), Ca and C (in default or other market shortcoming). Short-term ratings (less than a year) are named Prime-1, Prime-2 and Prime-3 for the investment grade category and Non-Prime for the speculative grades.

5.2.4   Standard & Poor's [27]

Along with Fitch and Moody's, Standard & Poor's (S&P) is one of the three giants of the credit risk rating industry. It is a division of the publishing company McGraw-Hill and generates income from the fees it charges on rated debt issuers. It covers about 90 sovereigns.

S&P's definition of sovereign credit ratings is different from those of Fitch in the sense that it does not mention the issue of foreign exchange or foreign currency availability. It is merely ascertained as "an assessment of each government's ability and willingness to service its debt in full and on time" (Standard & Poor's, 2002). Consequently, S&P sovereign credit ratings explicitly encompass both local and foreign currency debt. Contrary to Moody's, S&P takes the view that "sovereign ratings are not 'country ratings' ". However, considering the economic impact of governmental policy as well as the political influence of the government on any organization within its borders, S&P's sovereign ratings serve as a benchmark for other issuers of the same country: "The credit rating of an international borrower most often is at, or below, the rating of the sovereign in the country of domicile" (Standard & Poor's, 2002).

The S&P rating approach is both quantitative and qualitative. It is based on a checklist of 10 categories: political risk, income and economic structure, economic growth prospects, fiscal flexibility, general government debt burden, off-budget and contingent liabilities, monetary stability, external liquidity, public and private sector external debt burdens. Each group is graded from one to six. Nevertheless, S&P underlines the absence of any system of predetermined weightings.

The *political risk* factors gauge the impact of politics on economic conditions, as well as the degree of government support in the population. It also tries to forecast any public security issue, including international affairs.

Income and economic structure deals with the structural features of the country. It assesses its degree of economic development and the maturity of its economic system. It evaluates any potential weakness such as over-leveraging of the private sector, and tries to identify any obstacle to the country's economic growth.

Economic growth prospects estimates the potential economic growth rate. It is based, among others, on savings and investment rates.

The *fiscal flexibility* group of indicators reflects S&P's view on the country's past and expected fiscal policy performance. It monitors the fiscal balance and how efficiently the budget is managed.

On average, the lower the *general government debt burden*, the higher the S&P sovereign ratings are. However, this trend is invalidated for a few, exceptionally indebted countries, like Japan, Belgium or Italy, whose level of national wealth alleviates the weight of servicing this debt.

The *off-budget and contingent liabilities* criteria focus on non-financial public sector enterprises as well as the health of the financial sector. From time to time, for example, when

---

[27] See Standard & Poor's (2002) for more details.

economic conditions deteriorate, both of these sectors may transform themselves into huge contingent liabilities for the government that require a bail-out with taxpayer money. Consequently, S&P monitors them carefully.

According to S&P price inflation can prove to be very damaging for a country's economy and its political stability. Since *monetary stability* is essential in controlling inflation, S&P tries to anticipate its evolution.

Within the *external liquidity* risk category, S&P conducts an analysis of the current account balance. It looks at the gross external financing gap in relation to the amount of foreign exchange reserves, and investigates the country's degree of dependence vis-à-vis external capital flows as well as its ability to overcome any unexpected shock. S&P discriminates between the highest investment grade sovereigns and the rest of the cohort whose reliance on foreign investment is much more acute.

The net *public sector external debt burden* is given by the difference between total debt and the financial assets of all governmental and public institutions. The *private sector external debt* position is given by borrowings from non-residents minus deposits with and lending to non-residents. As stipulated by Standard & Poor's (2002), private sector indebtness deserves to be scrutinized, since it can fall under the state's responsibility in case of economic crisis. Public and private sector external debt positions are estimated with regard to the current account receipts. However, their characteristics (type of lender, maturity, currency, fixed or floating rates) are also taken into account, so as to discriminate between their concrete impact in terms of debt servicing.

Usually, S&P assigns higher ratings to local currency debt than it does to foreign currency debt. This discrepancy mainly results from the scarcity of foreign currency reserves in comparison to foreign liabilities, and the difficulty in securing foreign currency financing.

S&P assigns short-term and long-term ratings. The short-term time horizon is usually below one year, while the long-term rating is based on what "rating committees consider reasonable 'worst-case' scenarios over a five-year time horizon" (Standard & Poor's, 2002). These ratings aim at describing the capacity of the issuer to meet its financial commitments. The long-term notes are AAA (extremely strong capacity), AA (very strong), A (strong), BBB (adequate). They constitute the investment grade group in opposition to the speculative cohort made of BB (could be faced with inadequate capacity), B (same as BB but still more vulnerable), CCC (currently vulnerable), CC (highly vulnerable). SD (selective default) and D (default) concern those issuers who failed, either partly or in full, to honor their financial obligations. The short-term notes are A1 (strong capacity), A2 (satisfactory), A3 (adequate), B (vulnerable), C (currently vulnerable), SD (selective default) and D (default).

5.2.5 Country Rankings Published in Magazines

A few international financial magazines publish regular country rankings based on various criteria. Among them, *Euromoney* and *Institutional Investor* focus on a country's ability and willingness to assume its obligations.

Euromoney

Euromoney, which claims to be "the world's most authoritative source of information on trends in international banking and capital markets" (Euromoney, 2002), is a UK-based monthly magazine. Its country risk ranking was first issued in 1982, and is published on a semi-annual basis, in March and September, coinciding with the spring and fall meetings of the IMF.

Since its inception, the *Euromoney* methodology has changed several times (Euromoney, 1987). There is not much information available about it, and it is presented in a very lapidary style in Euromoney (1998, 2001). Although Euromoney (1998, 2001) does not specify which kinds of investment it addresses, when looking at the retained criteria and due to their specific type of readers,[28] we can reasonably infer, following Cosset and Roy (1991), Haque *et al.* (1998) or Estrella (2000), that the *Euromoney* ranking deals with debt. Haque *et al.* (1997) stipulate: "The ratings [. . .] measures a country's ability and willingness to service its financial obligations."

The *Euromoney* methodology is built from a blend of quantitative criteria and qualitative factors coming from surveys with about 40 political analysts and economists. They are grouped between political risk (25% weighting), economic performance (25% weighting), debt indicators (10% weighting), debt in default or rescheduled (10% weighting), credit ratings (10% weighting), access to bank finance (5% weighting), access to short-term finance (5% weighting), access to capital market (5% weighting), and discount on forfeiting (5% weighting). Once all countries are assessed for each criteria, the best scorer is given the full weighting of the considered category (25%, 10%, or 5%), while the lowest performance scores zero. The other in-between countries are attributed a fraction of the weighting, based on a linear interpolation of the two extremes.

The *political risk* indicator is "specifically derived as risk of non-payment or non-serving of payment for goods or services, loans, trade-related finance and dividends, and the non-repatriation of capital" (Euromoney, 2001). It results from a poll of country experts, brokers and banking representatives.

The *economic performance* is the average of the GNP per capita score, and the *Euromoney* poll of economic projection results. This latter statistic is obtained from a questionnaire sent to 30 economists,[29] who are asked to forecast the countries' economic performance for the forthcoming two years.

The *debt indicators* are derived from a formula using the following ratios: total debt stocks to GNP, debt service to exports, and current account balance to GNP.

The *debt in default or rescheduled* is calculated from the ratio of rescheduled debt to debt stocks.

Surprisingly, *Euromoney* ratings are partly built on other publishers' ratings. The *credit ratings* are the average of the Fitch, Moody's and S&P sovereign ratings, once they are converted into numerical values.

Access to bank finance is given by the ratio of disbursements of private, long-term unguaranteed loans to GNP, with a better score for the higher ratios.

Access to short-term finance is provided by the OECD consensus group and by the US Exim Bank and NCM UK coverage.

A survey of the heads of debt and loan syndications gives the score for *access to capital markets*.

Discount on forfeiting is obtained from data supplied by certain international investment banks.

---

[28] *Euromoney* readers are mainly professionals in the financial sectors, such as bankers, risk analysts or corporate treasurers.
[29] See Euromoney (2001) for the list of the economists with their respective institution.

In this way, about 180 countries are graded on a scale from zero to 100, from the worst to the best. *Euromoney* does not mention any specific time horizon. However, since experts are asked to make some two-year predictions of the economic performance, we can speculate that this implicitly represents their time span.

Institutional Investor

Initiated in 1979, Institutional Investor (II)'s Credit Ratings are published twice a year by the US *Institutional Investor* magazine and cover about 150 countries. Shapiro (2001) explains that II specifically concentrates on the issue of the countries' creditworthiness. However, he does not indicate if it refers to government debt or if it includes private debt as well, nor does he mention if it concerns local or foreign currency instruments.

Every six months, *Institutional Investor* reviews between 75 and 100 bankers[30] from all over the world and asks them to rate countries based on their perception of creditworthiness. Cruces (2001) indicates that: "Bankers are surveyed during a two month window that ends about 45 days before the actual publication of the ratings." They are not allowed to grade their institution's home country. The banks' answers are then averaged, with a higher weight for the most international institutions, and for those having a more sophisticated country risk assessment model. The II ratings are based on advanced quantitative models and other, more subjective appraisals and reflect the international banking sector view of country credit risk. The resulting score scales from zero (very high chance of default) to 100 (least chance of default) (Shapiro, 2001). Like *Euromoney*, II does not talk about the time horizon of its assessment.

In a study made in 1994, Shapiro (2001) analyzed the bankers' criteria when answering the II survey. Results are ordered by degree of importance and presented in Table 5.2.

For emerging countries, the debt service factor comes first, but surprisingly enough, political outlook comes second, well before financial reserves and current account, trade balance, foreign direct investment, or access to capital markets. If this analysis were redone today, after the Mexican and Asian crises, its outcomes would probably be significantly different. This view is

Table 5.2 Bankers' criteria for the Institutional Investor's Credit Rating

Factors	Order of importance		
	OECD countries	Emerging countries	Rest of world
Economic outlook	1	3	4
Debt service	2	1	1
Financial reserves and current account	3	4	3
Fiscal policy	4	7	6
Political outlook	5	2	2
Access to capital markets	6	9	9
Trade balance	7	5	5
Inflow of portfolio investments	8	8	8
Foreign direct investment	9	6	7

Source: Shapiro (2001).

---

[30] Cruces (2001) specifies that, from 1999, some mutual fund managers and economists were added to the panel of bankers.

supported by a survey of 36 international banks undertaken in 2000 (Institute of International Finance, 2000). In the banks' quantitative analysis, the issue of debt service remains in first position, but the political factors are closely followed by balance of payments problems and the fiscal balance. As the Institute of International Finance (2000) explains:

Several banks felt that during turning points, as illustrated especially by the periods immediately before the Asian and Russian crises, models based on historical relationships can be inadequate and that assessments based on intimate knowledge of the country can add vitally to assessing country risk.

5.2.6 Summary of Country Credit Rating Methods

Determinants of Country Credit Ratings

Excluding the *Euromoney* methodology, the other country credit risk approaches prove difficult to detail precisely, either for strategic reasons, which make the raters reluctant to give precise information on their system, or because they involve a substantial amount of subjective judgment which is hard to translate into an explicit analytical process.

In the face of this challenge, several researchers tried to replicate these ratings, using readily available public information, in order to incorporate them into an analytical model. While Feder and Uy (1985), Oral *et al.* (1992), Cosset *et al.* (1993), or Lee (1993) only focus on *Institutional Investor*, Cosset and Roy (1991), Haque *et al.* (1996, 1997, 1998) investigate *Euromoney* as well.[31] Others such as Cantor and Packer (1996b), Ferri *et al.* (1999), or Mulder and Perelli (2001) look at the credit rating agencies. Finally Cruces (2001) or Monfort and Mulder (2000) tackle both the magazine and agency ratings.

Using a panel of Moody's and Standard & Poor's ratings for 49 developed and emerging countries, as of September 1995, Cantor and Packer (1996b) try to identify their determinants. Among eight factors under review, they find that income per capita, GDP growth, inflation, external debt, level of economic development, and history of default do have significant explanatory power. To their surprise, fiscal balance as well as external balance coefficients are not significant. Contrary to the seemingly complex methodology used by the rating agencies, Cantor and Packer (1996b) claim that, with only few variables, "the model's ability to predict large differences in ratings is impressive". Indeed, their regression is able to explain more than 90% of the sample variation.

Monfort and Mulder (2000), in a very comprehensive investigation, review four previous studies[32] and run their own regressions. They only focus on emerging countries as "rating behavior for industrialized countries may be quite well different". They cover II, S&P, and Moody's from the first semester 1995 to the first semester 1999. Their results are consistent with Cantor and Packer (1996b) except for the income per capita variable. Other factors are taken into consideration and prove to be statistically significant: current account over GDP, terms of trade, export growth rate, and investment over GDP. The explanatory power of these models remains at a very high 80%.

However, Monfort and Mulder (2000) challenge the validity of these regressions, including the Cantor and Packer (1996b) results, for not taking into account the serial correlation of the statistical series, shown clearly in Cruces (2001). Dividing their time span between three

---

[31] Haque *et al.* (1996, 1997, 1998) also include The Economist Intelligence Unit.
[32] Cantor and Packer (1996b), Jüttner and McCarthy (1998), Haque *et al.* (1996), Eichengreen and Mody (1998).

subperiods, they show that the relationship is not stable, a result already found with Lee (1993) when comparing the periods 1979–1982 and 1983–1987. Implementing a more robust dynamic specification, in order to cope with this issue, Monfort and Mulder (2000) demonstrate that ratings do exhibit a strong inertia. Except for the terms of trade and history of default criteria, all the factors mentioned above and retained in the static model are significant. Moreover, introducing an external crisis indicator, they establish that ratings are strongly influenced by crisis occurrences: "Countries are downgraded following a major crisis, possibly because they do not perform as expected." Rating agencies justify this point by explaining that, during a crisis, new information about the way countries are able to manage their problems is revealed and taken into account. For instance, Fitch realized that "it over-estimated the sophistication of Asian policymakers, who have proved good fairweather navigators but very poor sailors in a storm" (Fitch, 1998).

Using a slightly different panel, Mulder and Perelli (2001) confirm most of these outcomes. They emphasize the importance of the investment to GDP ratio, and note that debt to exports, as well as the rescheduling history (contrary to Monfort and Mulder, 2000) are the main sources of change in the level of the ratings. In addition, in the aftermath of the Asian crisis, they discover a structural break in the determinants of ratings. From 1997, the short-term debt over reserves ratio becomes significant, highlighting the growing attention paid by the rating agencies to this criterion. Fitch confirmed that: "Both the agencies and the IMF had understated the impact that high levels of short-term debt could have on the official reserves of South Korea and other Asian economies" (Luce, 1998).

An earlier paper of Cosset and Roy (1991), looking at *Euromoney* and *Institutional Investor*, had already stressed the weights of the propensity to invest and the debt to export ratios as the main determinants of country ratings. In their study, the GNP per capita was also very significant, probably because they did not separate industrialized and emerging countries.

We can observe that, contrary to the rating agencies' explanations, political factors are not included as significant criteria in the papers mentioned above. Accordingly, Haque *et al.* (1998) "examines the relative importance of political and economic variables in the determination of a country's standing". They find that "political events and variables do not add any additional information once economic factors have been accounted for".

Another interesting feature of the country credit ratings was established by Cruces (2001). Investigating the statistical properties of S&P, Moody's and II series, he evidenced a high level of predictability in the credit rating revisions: "A positive revision has a probability of two-thirds of being followed by another positive revision six months later." This fact was also established by Erb *et al.* (1996) for the changes in the II grades.

It is also worth noting the strong degree of consistency between the credit rating agencies and the export credit agencies, as shown in Table 5.3 (Estrella, 2000).

Finally, although the regressions presented above show a high explanatory power with a very low number of explanatory variables, it is important to remember that all these methods rely in large part on human evaluation. As noted by Haque *et al.* (1997):

While the criteria for assessing credit risk summarized in the table suggest a precise relationship between a country's credit rating and the political, economic, and financial variables specific to that country, the judgment of the rating analysts plays an important role, both in evaluating economic and political variables (e.g., drawing conclusions about the degree of political stability) and in determining how much weight should be attached to different variables within each group of factors. Thus, a fair amount of subjective judgment goes into the final evaluation.

Table 5.3   Spearman correlation coefficients

	Moody's	S&P	Thomson[a]	Average export credit agencies
Moody's	1 (100)[b]			
S&P	0.94558 (80)	1 (86)		
Thomson	0.95030 (82)	0.95842 (72)	1 (87)	
Average export credit agencies	0.91227 (100)	0.85957 (86)	0.93016 (87)	1 (201)

[a] Part of Fitch since 2000.
[b] Number of countries in parentheses.
Source: Estrella (2000). *Credit ratings and complementary sources of credit quality information*, Bank for International Settlements.

Forecasting Capacity

Because they are only focused on one type of investment, the country credit rating methods could be expected to deliver a better performance than the global country risk methods previously studied. However, the Mexican crisis of 1994 and the Asian crisis of 1997 raised a host of concerns regarding their ability to correctly estimate the risk level.

Although credit rating agencies claim that they focus on the likelihood of default and do not aim at predicting crises, Goldstein *et al.* (2000) notice that, at least in emerging countries, "many default episodes have been preceded by banking and/or currency crises". Consequently, Reinhart (2001) asserts that "there is a strong link between currency crises, banking crises and default". She concludes: "Hence, if the credit ratings are forward-looking, financial crises in EMs [emerging markets] should be systematically preceded by downgrades." If we buy this line, credit rating agencies visibly failed to anticipate these dramatic events, which, between July 1997 and November 1998, led to "the largest and most abrupt downgrades in the modern history of sovereign credit ratings" (Mathieson and Schinasi, 1999).

A semi-annual *Institutional Investor* survey, based on bankers' opinion delivered a few months before the Thai baht collapse, was released in September 1997. *Institutional Investor* (1997) titled its article: "It's like growth stocks: led by Eastern Europe and Latin America, sovereign risk has never looked better." Analyzing the Asian situation, it noticed that "the Asia-Pacific region showed no-change in its regional rating". This partly explains why Reinhart (2001), while studying the rating agencies' ability to predict banking and currency crises, found that signals provided by II were very poor.

Similarly, Luce (1998) reports that Fitch "admitted that it and its larger rivals Standard & Poor's and Moody's Investors Service of the US had largely failed to predict the recent turmoil in Asia". As revealed by Cantor and Packer (1996a), this failure was not unprecedented. Looking back at the era of the Great Depression, they recall that about "70% of all sovereign debt (excluding Canadian debt) issued in the United States between 1926 and 1929 defaulted before the end of 1937", among which "a majority of the defaulting countries had investment grade ratings from this agency [Moody's] in 1929". Cantor and Packer (1996a) add: "Moody's was one of many parties taken by surprise by the extent of the sovereign default wave." Likewise, Standard & Poor's decision to grade Mexico BB+ with a positive outlook for upgrade just before the country's collapse, in 1994, prompted *a posteriori* some fierce criticisms. This brings Goldstein *et al.* (2000) to conclude that sovereign ratings are not good indicators of crises.

"It's about time that rating agencies are regulated . . . the damage they cause is horrendous . . . whenever they downgrade a country, it becomes poor" (Banoo, 1998). This remark made by Dr. Mahathir, the Prime Minister of Malaysia, clearly illustrates how powerful and influential the credit rating agencies are perceived to be. However, Reisen and von Maltzan (1999) show that they have not used this capacity to curb excessive capital inflows and outflows. On the contrary, Reisen (1998) estimates that: "Sovereign credit ratings are reactive rather than preventive. As a result, they tend to amplify boom–bust cycles in emerging-market lending." Investigating the Mexico 1994/1995 and the Korea 1997/1998 cases, Kräussl (2000) finds mixed results. He confirms Reisen's (1998) conclusion for Mexico, but thinks that rating agencies had no impact on the Korean situation.

Focusing on periods of financial turbulence, Kuhner (2001) confirms this flaw. He finds "that in an environment of enhanced systemic risk, informational intermediaries such as rating agencies cannot be expected to act as stabilizing institutions, providing reliable early warning signals or all-clear information". And later he concludes: "[these] findings raise considerable skepticism about the role of rating agencies when there is enhanced systemic risk." Monfort and Mulder (2000) investigate the Basel proposal for a new capital adequacy framework[33] that suggests using country credit ratings as a reference for emerging countries. They too question the pro-cyclical characteristic of the rating agencies. Most rating agencies, however, claim they rate through the cycles, meaning they intend to assess a borrower's creditworthiness independently of the business cycle, whatever the economic conditions. Contrary to this assertion, Monfort and Mulder (2000) observe that ratings were influenced by the Asian crisis. In addition, they note that, because of the shortness of the sovereign rating history and due to the small size of the statistical sample, "the relation between sovereign ratings and repayment risks is not well tested".

As noted by Mathieson and Schinasi (1999), rating agencies were not the only ones to miss the point: "It appears that spreads as well as market analysts (as represented by Institutional Investor and Euromoney ratings) provided signals similar to those of the credit rating agencies." This view is shared by Kräussl (2000) when he writes: "This suggests that in Asia, the markets as well as analysts and rating agencies failed to foresee the financial crisis and the corresponding rise in default risk." According to Reinhart (2001), this mistake is explained by a selection of the wrong crisis indicators, such as the debt to exports ratios, and the lack of care for more sensitive variables such as "liquidity, currency misalignments, and asset price behavior". In addition, Cantor and Packer (1996a) argue that because "agencies must consider factors that not only affect solvency but also those that may independently affect the willingness to pay", measuring sovereign credit risk is much more difficult than assessing US corporations' creditworthiness.

These problems are summarized by Monfort and Mulder (2000):

These estimation results for rating agencies cast doubt on the usefulness of ratings during crisis periods. The empirical evidence suggests that the ratings do not quite see through crisis (they react with a lag to crises), and respond negatively to what usually are equilibrating trends in the real effective exchange rate, and thus could be destabilizing.

---

[33] See, for instance, Estrella (2000).

And in the same vein, Reinhart (2001) concludes that:

As to the ability of rating changes to anticipate financial crises, the empirical tests presented here on sovereign credit ratings and financial crises suggest that sovereign credit ratings systematically fail to anticipate banking and currency crises.

These analyses are very pessimistic regarding the country credit ratings' ability to predict crises. Sovereign ratings seem to be much more uncertain than corporate ratings, at least for developing countries and in times of systemic risk. However, rating agencies answer these critics by claiming that this is not their objective, which only consists of estimating the risk of default. Even though many countries were on the verge of bankruptcy and would have probably defaulted if not rescued by international financial aid, "under the definitions of default employed by the agencies, there were no sovereign defaults on any rated foreign-currency-denominated security in the period 1975–98" (Mathieson and Schinasi, 1999). Moreover, they argue the rating agencies were not taken by surprise and had correctly anticipated the subsequent episodes of default by Ecuador in 1998, Russia in 1999 and Argentina in 2001.

5.3   CONCLUSION

The comparative rating approaches provide a method to estimate the relative degree of risk, and try to quantify it. They turn some ratios and expert opinions into a note or a letter, along with a grading scale. They are more or less quantitative oriented, but they all require a good amount of human judgment. They are based on pre-established lists of relevant factors which, sometimes, are given an *a priori* fixed weighting. The determinants of these ratings have largely evolved over the last decades, following the fundamental changes on the international political and economic scene.

The main criteria for country risk classification retained by the majority of these institutions are:

- *Political and social risk*
  - Internal
    - Political effectiveness
    - Corruption
    - Political instability
    - Internal tension or conflict
  - External
    - External conflict
    - Foreign influence
- *Economic risk*
  - Domestic economy
    - Level of economic development
    - Income per capita
    - GDP growth
    - Investment over GDP
    - Inflation

- ▪ Fiscal and monetary policy
- ▪ Soundness of the banking system
- ○ External equilibrium
- ▪ External debt indicators
  - – Debt to export ratio
  - – Debt service
  - – Debt composition
  - – History of default and rescheduling
- ▪ Balance of payment
  - – Current account over GDP
  - – Terms of trade
  - – Export growth rate
  - – Access to capital markets
  - – International capital flows

Although Meldrum (2000) finds "a high degree of agreement in the ranking of investment risk" between the global country risk and the country credit risk ratings, this is not necessarily a sign of reliability for these methods. Indeed, they both suffer from flaws which make them imperfect and sometimes defective risk assessment tools, particularly when crises occur.

In general, they correctly describe the present situation and are able to discriminate between very high and very low risk. However, they seem to have some difficulties in clearly assessing the countries located in the medium range, especially when these countries exhibit specific dynamics and are likely to move from the medium-risk area into the low or the high-risk zone. Unfortunately, as explained by Exxon executive Leslie Cookenboo in Rummel and Heenan (1978), this is where they are the most needed: "Over the years, we've found it relatively easy to identify very stable and very unstable environments. But what bothers us the most are the borderline cases."

REFERENCES

Ascher W, 1989, Limits of 'Experts Systems' for Political-Economic Forecasting. *Technological Forecasting and Social Change*, 36, 137–51.

Banoo S, 1998, World's rating agencies should be regulated, says PM. *Business Times*, Apr 11.

Bellinger CS, 2001, Comment on Cooperation, Competition, and the Science of Pricing in the Political Risk Insurance Marketplace. *In:* TH Moran, ed. *International Political Risk Management*, Washington: The World Bank, 194–8.

BERI, 2001a, Business Environment Risk Intelligence. *In:* L Howell, ed. *The Handbook of Country and Political Risk Analysis*. 3rd edition. East Syracuse, NY: The PRS Group, 103–20.

BERI, 2001b, *Business Risk Service* [online]. Geneva: BERI. Available at: http://www.beri.com/brs.htm [Accessed 26 June 2002].

Brealey RA and Myers SC, 2000, *Principles of Corporate Finance*. 6th edition. New York: McGraw-Hill.

Business Week, 1980, Foreign Investment, the Post-Shah Surge in Political-Risk Studies. *Business Week*, Dec 1, 89.

Cantor R and Packer F, 1995, Sovereign Credit Ratings. *Current Issues in Economics and Finance*, Jun, 1 (3), 1–6.

Cantor R and Packer F, 1996a, Sovereign Risk Assessment and Agency Credit Ratings. *European Financial Management*, 2 (2), 247–56.

Cantor R and Packer F, 1996b, Determinants and Impact of Sovereign Credit Ratings. *Economic Policy Review (Federal Reserve Bank of New York)*, Oct, 2 (2), 37–53.

Clei J, 1994, La Méthodologie d'Analyse de la Coface. *Banque Stratégie*, Oct, 109, 5–6.

Coface, 2002a, *Country Rating Methodology* [online]. Paris: Coface. Available at: http://www.trading-safely.com/ [Accessed 25 July 2002].

Coface, 2002b, *About Coface Group* [online]. Paris: Coface. Available at: http://www.cofacerating.com/en/home/group.html [Accessed 25 July, 2002].

Coplin WD and O'Leary MK, 1972, *Everyman's Prince: A Guide to Understanding Your Political Problems*. North Scituate, MA: Duxbury Press.

Coplin WD and O'Leary MK, 1993, Mexico: A Long-term Pro-investment Forecast. *Planning Review*, Nov/Dec, 32–40.

Cosset JC and Roy J, 1991, The Determinants of Country Risk Ratings. *Journal of International Business Studies*, 22 (1), 135–42.

Cosset JC and Roy J, 1994, The Prediction of Country Risk Classification: The Case of the Export Development Corporation of Canada. *Revue Canadienne des Sciences de l'Administration*, Sep, 11 (3), 214–23.

Cosset JC, Daouas M, Kettani O and Oral M, 1993, Replicating Country Risk Ratings. *Journal of Multinational Financial Management*, 3 (1/2), 1–29.

Cruces JJ, 2001, Statistical Properties of Sovereign Credit Ratings. *Working Paper*, University de San Andres, Buenos Aires, Feb 9.

Eichengreen B and Mody A, 1998, What Explains the Changing Spreads on Emerging Market Debt: Fundamentals or Market Sentiment? *NBER Working Paper*, 6408, Feb.

EIU, 2001, Economist Intelligence Unit. *In:* L Howell, ed. *The Handbook of Country and Political Risk Analysis*. 3rd edition. East Syracuse, NY: The PRS Group, 121–52.

EIU, 2002, *About The Economist Intelligence Unit* [online]. London: Economist Intelligence Unit. Available at: http://www.eiu.com/site_info.asp?info_name=about_eiu [Accessed 24 July 2002].

Erb CB, Harvey CR and Viskanta TE, 1996, Political Risk, Economic Risk, and Financial Risk. *Financial Analysts Journal*, Nov/Dec, 52 (6), 28–46.

Estrella A, 2000, *Credit Ratings and Complementary Sources of Credit Quality Information*. Basle Committee on Banking Supervision Working Papers, Bank for International Settlements, August, 3.

Euromoney, 1987, How the Risks are Weighted. *Euromoney*, Sep, 357.

Euromoney, 1998, Country Risk Revisited. *Euromoney*, Dec, 356, 105–8.

Euromoney, 2001, *Methodology: Country Risk Ratings. In:* L Howell, ed. *The Handbook of Country and Political Risk Analysis*. 3rd edition. East Syracuse, NY: The PRS Group, 153–60.

Euromoney, 2002, *About Euromoney Magazine and Euromoney Confidential* [online] London: Euromoney. Available at: http://www.euromoney.com/magazine.about.html [Accessed 14 August 2002].

Feder G and Uy LV, 1985, The Determinants of International Creditworthiness and their Implications. *Journal of Policy Modeling*, 7 (1), 133–56.

Ferri G, Liu LG and Stiglitz J, 1999, The Procyclical Role of Rating Agencies: Evidence from the East Asian Crisis. *Economic Notes*, 28 (3), 335–55.

Fitch, 1998, Asia: Agencies' Harsh Lessons in a Crisis [online]. Available at: http://www.bradynet.com/e312.html [Accessed 20 February 1998].

Fitch, 2001, Rating Banks Above the Local Currency Sovereign Rating [online]. New York: Fitch Ratings, Jun. Available at: http://www.fitchratings.com/corporate/reports/report.cfm?rpt_id=128036 [Accessed 9 August 2002].

Fitch, 2002, Fitch Sovereign Ratings: Rating Methodology [online]. New York: Fitch Ratings. Available at: http://www.fitchratings.com/corporate/reports/report.cfm?rpt_id=116361 [Accessed 9 August 2002].

Flandreau M, 1998, *Caveat Emptor: Coping with Sovereign Risk without the Multilaterals*. Center for Economic Policy Research, Discussion Paper 2004, Oct.

Gherardi S, 1998, Nous sommes confrontés à un nouveau type de risque, celui du retrait brutal de capitaux. *Le Monde*, 13 janvier.

Goldstein M, Kaminsky GL and Reinhart CM, 2000, *Assessing Financial Vulnerability: An Early Warning System for Emerging Markets*. Washington: Institute for International Economics.

Haner FT, 1965, Business Investment Negotiations in Developing Countries. *Business Horizons*, Winter, 8 (4), 97–103.

Haner FT, 1966, Determining the Feasibility of Foreign Ventures. *Business Horizons*, Fall, 9 (3), 35–44.

Haque NU, Kumar MS, Mark N and Mathieson DJ, 1996, The Economic Content of Indicators of Developing Country Creditworthiness. *IMF Staff Paper*, Dec, 43 (4).

Haque NU, Mathieson DJ and Mark N, 1997, Rating the Raters of Country Creditworthiness. *Finance and Development*, Mar, 10–13.

Haque NU, Mark N and Mathieson DJ, 1998, The Relative Importance of Political and Economic Variables in Creditworthiness Ratings. *IMF Working Paper*, Apr, WP/98/46.

Howell LD, 1992, Political Risk and Political Loss for Foreign Investment. *The International Executive*, Nov/Dec, 34 (6), 485–98.

Howell LD, 2001, Introduction. *In:* L Howell, ed. *The Handbook of Country and Political Risk Analysis.* 3rd edition. East Syracuse, NY: The PRS Group, 3–16.

Howell LD and Chaddick B, 1994, Models of Political Risk for Foreign Investment and Trade: An Assessment of Three Approaches. *Columbia Journal of World Business*, Fall, 29 (3), 70–91.

Institute of International Finance, 2000, *Report of the Working Group on Country Risk.* Washington: Institute of International Finance, Sep.

Institutional Investor, 1997, It's Like Growth Stocks. *Institutional Investor*, Sep, 31 (9), 177–9.

Jüttner JD and McCarthy J, 1998, Modeling a Ratings Crisis. *Working Paper*, Sydney, Australia: Macquarie University.

Kennedy CR, 1991, *Managing the International Business Environment: Cases in Political and Country Risk.* Englewood Cliffs, NJ: Prentice Hall.

Kräussl R, 2000, Sovereign Ratings and Their Impact on Recent Financial Crises. *Working Paper*, Frankfurt/Main, Germany: Center for Financial Studies, Feb.

Kuhner C, 2001, Financial Rating Agencies: Are They Credible? – Insights Into the Reporting Incentives of Rating Agencies in Times of Enhanced Systemic Risk. *Schmalenbach Business Review*, Jan, 53, 2–26.

Lee SH, 1993, Are the Credit Ratings Assigned by Bankers Based on the Willingness of LDC Borrowers to Repay. *Journal of Development Economics*, 40, 349–59.

Luce E, 1998, Fitch IBCA: Credit Agency Accepts Criticisms over Asia. *Financial Times*, Jan 14.

Mathieson D and Schinasi G, 1999, *International Capital Markets: Developments, Prospects, and Key Policy Issues.* IMF Series: World Economic and Financial Surveys, Sep 24.

Meldrum DH, 2000, Country Risk and Foreign Direct Investment. *Business Economics*, Jan, 35 (1), 33–40.

Monfort B and Mulder C, 2000, Using Credit Ratings for Capital Requirements on Lending to Emerging Market Economies: Possible Impact of a New Basel Accord. *IMF Working Paper*, Mar, WP/00/69.

Moody's, 1999a, *Moody's Sovereign Ratings: A Ratings Guide.* New York: Moody's Investors Service, Mar, 43788.

Moody's, 1999b, *The Usefulness of Local Currency Ratings in Countries with Low Foreign Currency Country Ceilings.* New York: Moody's Investors Service, Jul, 46073.

Moody's, 1999c, *Opening The Black Box: The Rating Committee Process At Moody's.* New York: Moody's Investors Service, Jul, 46995.

Moody's, 2001a, *Revised Country Ceiling Policy: Rating Methodology.* New York: Moody's Investors Service, Jun, 67679.

Moody's, 2001b, Moody's Investors Services: Sovereign Credit Risk Analysis. *In:* L Howell, ed. *The Handbook of Country and Political Risk Analysis.* 3rd edition. East Syracuse, NY: The PRS Group, 161–83.

Moody's, 2002, *Sovereign Rating History: Special Comment.* New York: Moody's Investors Service, Jan, 73505.

Mulder C and Perelli R, 2001, Foreign Currency Credit Ratings for Emerging Market Economies. *IMF Working Paper*, Nov, WP/01/191.

Oral M, Kettani O, Cosset JC and Daouas M, 1992, An Estimation Model for Country Risk Rating. *International Journal of Forecasting*, 8 (4), 583–93.

PRS, 2001a, International Country Risk Guide. *In:* L Howell, ed. *The Handbook of Country and Political Risk Analysis.* 3rd edition. East Syracuse, NY: The PRS Group, 19–102.

PRS, 2001b, Political Risk Service. *In:* L Howell, ed. *The Handbook of Country and Political Risk Analysis.* 3rd edition. East Syracuse, NY: The PRS Group, 303–65.

Reinhart CM, 2001, Sovereign Credit Ratings Before and After Financial Crisis. *University of Maryland and NBER Working Paper*, Feb 21.

Reisen H, 1998, Credit Rating Agencies Need Radical Reform if They Are to Do their Job Properly. *Financial Times*, Feb 3.

Reisen H and von Maltzan J, 1999, Boom and Bust and Sovereign Ratings. *International Finance*, Jul, 2 (2), 273–93.

Rummel RJ and Heenan DA, 1978, How Multinationals Analyze Political Risk. *Harvard Business Review*, Jan/Feb, 56 (1), 67–76.

Shapiro HD, 2001, Institutional Investor. *In:* L Howell, ed. *The Handbook of Country and Political Risk Analysis*. 3rd edition. East Syracuse, NY: The PRS Group, 275–82.

Smith RC and Walter I, 2001, Rating Agencies: Is There an Agency Issue? *Working Paper*, New York: Stern School of Business, New York University, Feb 18.

Standard & Poor's, 2001, Standard & Poor's Ratings Group. *In:* L Howell, ed. *The Handbook of Country and Political Risk Analysis*. 3rd edition. East Syracuse, NY: The PRS Group, 225–72.

Standard & Poor's, 2002, *Sovereign Credit Ratings: A Primer*. New York: Standard & Poor's, Apr 3.

Terrier JL, 2001, Country Rating 2001–2002 by Nord Sud Export. *NSE*, Oct 24, 429.

West GT, 2001, Comment on Securitizing Political Risk Insurance. *In:* TH Moran, ed. *International Political Risk Management*, Washington: The World Bank, 158–62.

6

Econometric and Mathematical Methods

In this chapter we will briefly outline and review a wide range of techniques commonly used in risk assessment. We start with techniques that seek to determine an either/or outcome, such as discriminant analysis and logit and probit models. We then deal with regression analysis and model building and show how Monte Carlo simulations can be combined with model building to produce risk estimates. We also present value at risk and principal components analysis. We conclude the chapter with an overview of non-parametric techniques, artificial neural networks and multicriteria methods.

6.1 DISCRIMINANT ANALYSIS

Discriminant analysis is a statistical technique that makes it possible to classify an observation into one of several *a priori* groupings. Altman (1968) and Altman *et al.* (1977), for example, used this technique to predict firm bankruptcy. In the case of political/country risk analysis, the idea is to classify countries according to whether or not they are likely to default, expropriate or do something else perceived as unfavorable for the investment. Basically, three steps are involved:

1. Establish mutually exclusive group classifications. Each group is distinguished by a probability distribution of the characteristics.
2. Collect data for each of the groups.
3. Derive the linear combinations of the characteristics that best *discriminate* between the groups. "Best" in this sense means the discriminations that minimize the probability of misclassification.

For simplicity, consider the case where two variables, x_1 and x_2, are used to discriminate between two types of countries – those that will default on their foreign debt and those that will not default. Let x_1 stand for the country's growth rate and x_2 for the ratio of debt to exports. Now consider a linear combination of x_1 and x_2:

$$Z = a_1 x_1 + a_2 x_2 \tag{6.1}$$

The problem is to establish a criterion and use past data in order to determine the values of a_1 and a_2 that will make Z useful as an index for discriminating between members of the two groups. The idea, then, is to minimize the number of misclassifications. The problem is that the standard deviations of x_1 and x_2 may be so large that the two groups will overlap such that some of the defaulting countries will have higher Z-scores than those of the non-defaulting countries. The overlapping region is called the "zone of ignorance" and classifications in the zone of ignorance carry a greater likelihood of error. In a perfect model, there would be no misclassifications.

In order to minimize the number of misclassifications, we want to separate the Z-scores for the two groups as widely as possible relative to the variations within the groups. To do this we seek the values of a_1 and a_2 that maximize the function

$$G = \frac{(\overline{Z}_1 - \overline{Z}_2)^2}{\sum_{i=1}^{2}\sum_{j=1}^{n_i}(Z_{ij} - \overline{Z}_i)^2} \tag{6.2}$$

where the numerator represents the separation of the two groups and the denominator is a measure of the variation of Z within the groups. Z_{ij} is the Z value for the jth country in the ith group ($i = 1, 2$). n_i is the number of countries in group i and $\overline{Z}_i$ is the mean of the Z values in group i. By partial differentiation the values a_1 and a_2 can be found by the following linear equations:

$$a_1 Q_{11} + a_2 Q_{12} = d_1 \tag{6.3}$$
$$a_1 Q_{21} + a_2 Q_{22} = d_2 \tag{6.4}$$

where

$$Q_{pq} = \sum_{i=1}^{2}\sum_{j=1}^{n_i}(X_{pij} - \overline{X}_{pi})(X_{qij} - \overline{X}_{qi})$$
$$d_p = \overline{X}_{p1} - \overline{X}_{p2}$$
$$p = 1, 2$$
$$q = 1, 2$$
X_{pij} = value of X_p for the jth member of group i
$\overline{X}_{pi}$ = mean value of X_p for the n_i members of group i

Once the values of a_1 and a_2 have been found, the Z values for each country can be calculated and compared in order to determine the cut-off value. A cut-off value is necessary because of the "zone of ignorance" where some defaulting countries will have higher Z values than some non-defaulting ones. Suppose, for example, that the zone of ignorance lies between Z values of 1.91 and 2.62. The point of minimum misclassification might lie at 2.11. Thus, $Z > 2.11$ classifies a country as non-defaulting and $Z < 2.11$ classifies a country as defaulting.

As an example of how discriminant analysis can be used, suppose that HSBC is contemplating a sizeable loan to the Brazilian government. To see if the Brazilian government is statistically likely to default or reschedule over the life of the loan, the analyst assigned to Brazil uses the bank's in-house discriminant model to compute the country's Z value. He finds that the Z value is substantially lower than the cut-off point and that Brazil is classified as a country that is likely to default. With this classification in mind, he then proceeds with his own in-depth analysis of the country's economic, financial, social and political outlook, which shows that Brazil is effectively relatively risky compared with other countries in the region. This conclusion combined with the country's default classification derived from the discriminant analysis leads the analyst to recommend that the loan be refused.

Frank and Cline (1971) published the first systematic empirical study of debt rescheduling using discriminant analysis. Their fundamental unit of analysis was a country year. They examined data from 26 countries over a period of nine years but, because of holes in the data, they only had 145 country years with 13 reschedulings in their sample. Their original analysis included eight macroeconomic variables and they found that three of these – the lagged ratio of debt to export trend, the ratio of imports to international reserves, and the reciprocal of the maturity of the country's foreign debt – had significant explanatory power to discriminate between cases of rescheduling and cases of normal payment. Since the Frank and Cline study, many other models have been developed and the list of relevant explanatory variables has grown with them.

6.2 LOGIT AND PROBIT MODELS

Logit and probit models make it possible to model dichotomous variables, that is, variables that take a value of 1 or 0. These types of models are adapted to many types of political risk, which often have either/or outcomes: e.g. either the country defaults or it does not; either the country expropriates or it does not. The dependent variable y_i can thus be defined as

$$y_i = \begin{cases} 1 & \text{if default (expropriation) occurs} \\ 0 & \text{if it does not occur} \end{cases}$$

Let x_i be a $k \times 1$ vector of independent variables and a a $k \times 1$ vector of coefficients. The logit model assumes that the probability that y_i equals 1 is $e^{\alpha' x_i}/(1 + e^{-\alpha' x_i})$, which can be written as

$$\text{Prob}(y = 1) = \frac{e^{\alpha' x_i}}{(1 + e^{\alpha' x_i})} \tag{6.5}$$

The probit model is similar to the logit model except that it uses the normal distribution

$$\text{Prob}(y = 1) = \int_{-\infty}^{\alpha' x_i} \phi(t)\, dt \tag{6.6}$$

where $\phi(t)$ represents the density function for the normal distribution.

The a coefficients can be calculated using iterative techniques such as maximum likelihood methods. One drawback of the logit/probit models is that their power to discriminate is most sensitive near the midpoint when the probability is equal to 0.5. As the probability moves away from 0.5, changes in the independent variables have less and less impact on the probability that y_i equals 1. This is true for both the logit and the probit models. The question of which model should actually be used is difficult to answer. The logistic distribution resembles the normal distribution except that it has fatter tails, somewhat like a t-distribution. For intermediate values of $\alpha' x_i$, both distributions give about the same probabilities. For very small values of $\alpha' x_i$, the logistic distribution tends to give larger probabilities for $y = 0$ than the normal and for very large values of $\alpha' x_i$, it gives smaller probabilities for $y = 0$. Furthermore, as Greene (1997) points out, model predictions will differ if the sample contains very few values $y = 1$ relative to $y = 0$ or there are wide variations in one or more of the explanatory variables. Thus, on theoretical grounds it is difficult to justify one distribution over the other and, in most practical applications, it seems not to make much difference.

One popular way of using logit/probit models is to comb theory and practice for a set of variables that are likely to play a role in the event under consideration, estimate the model and then see which variables are actually statistically significant. The estimated model can then be used to forecast political events. Feder and Just (1977), for example, were the first to use a logit model for studying debt rescheduling. Like Frank and Cline (1971) their analytical unit was the country year. Their sample spanned 41 countries and eight years (1965–1972) but, because of incomplete data, it only included 238 country years with 21 cases of rescheduling. In fact, they experienced some difficulties in determining just when an episode of rescheduling had occurred. They ended up finding six macroeconomic variables that were statistically significant in explaining a country's likelihood of rescheduling debt:

- per capita income,
- the rate of growth of exports,
- the ratio of imports to foreign exchange reserves,
- the ratio of debt service payments to total exports,
- the ratio of capital inflows to debt service payments,
- the ratio of amortization to the outstanding stock of total foreign debt.

Many other studies using logit/probit models over different time periods have added to the list of significant explanatory variables for debt rescheduling (e.g. Feder *et al.*, 1981, for the period 1965–1976; Kharas, 1984, for the period 1965–1976; Hajivassiliou, 1987, for the period 1970–1982; Rahnama-Moghadam *et al.*, 1991, for the period 1980–1987; Dropsy and Solberg, 1992, for the period 1986–1989; Balkan, 1992, for the period 1971–1984; De Bondt and Winder, 1995, for the period 1983–1993; de Haan *et al.*, 1997, for the period 1984–1993). The upshot of all these studies is that, depending on the countries included in the testing and the period under consideration, there are many variables that can explain debt rescheduling. Herein lies the problem with the logit/probit models. The effects of the explanatory variables can differ from country to country and change over time. For example, a debt service ratio of one form or another enters many of the foregoing models with a negative sign and this is consistent with the leverage ratios developed in Chapter 3. However, it often has a positive sign and, based on the signaling hypothesis, it can reasonably be argued that the high debt reflected in high debt service ratios should be viewed as a good rather than a bad credit signal. Arguments such as these hold for many of the variables that enter the models. Thus, as effects vary from one country to another and over time, it is difficult to interpret the results. Furthermore, as an out-of-sample forecasting tool these models have proved to be unreliable.

6.3   REGRESSION ANALYSIS AND MODEL BUILDING

As applied to political/country risk, the logit/probit models developed above are generally lacking in a strong theoretical underpinning. They use a methodology that involves drawing up a list of variables that theory or practice suggests might have an influence on the phenomenon in question and testing whether they enter the model as significant explanatory variables. This procedure is not limited to the logit/probit models, however, and is applied in other regression models. For example, in their model on the determinants of secondary market prices for developing country syndicated loans, Boehmer and Megginson (1990) used the same procedure in an error components model.

The alternative procedure to this *ad hoc*, empirical approach is to develop a theoretical model and then test its ability to explain the phenomenon in question. Recent studies have started to adopt this approach. Some tests on bond pricing models can be found in Merrick (1999) for Argentine and Russian bonds or Keswani (1999) and Pagès (2000) for Latin American Brady bonds or Dullman and Windfuhr (2000) for European government credit spreads. Clark and Zenaidi (1999) develop an optimal stopping model for sovereign willingness to pay and test its relevance for 21 countries in four geographic regions.

As an example of model building for regression analysis, we can go back to the monetary approach to the balance of payments presented in Chapter 3. Let

MO_{1d} = quantity of nominal money balances demanded
MO_{1s} = country's money supply
$MO_0 = (D + F)$ = country's money base
D_0 = domestic component of the country's money base
F = foreign component of the country's money base
P = domestic price level
Y = real output
r = interest rate
a = price elasticity of demand for money
b = income elasticity of demand for money
c = interest elasticity of demand for money
m = money multiplier
g_i = growth rate of variable i
ε = error term

Remember that $PY =$ GNP. We begin with the traditional assumption that the complete demand function for money is positively related to GNP and inversely related to the interest rate. This can be written as

$$MO_{1d} = \frac{P^a Y^b \varepsilon}{r^c} \tag{6.7}$$

Since the money supply is a multiple of the country's money base, we can write:

$$MO_{1s} = m(D_0 + F) \tag{6.8}$$

In equilibrium, money supply equals money demand:

$$MO_{1d} = MO_{1s} = \frac{P^a Y^b \varepsilon}{r^c} = m(D_0 + F) \tag{6.9}$$

To get this equation into testable form, take the natural logarithm of both sides:

$$a \ln P + b \ln Y + \ln \varepsilon - c \ln r = \ln m + \ln(D_0 + F) \tag{6.10}$$

Differentiate (6.10) with respect to time:

$$a\frac{1}{P}\frac{dP}{dt} + b\frac{1}{Y}\frac{dY}{dt} + \frac{1}{\varepsilon}\frac{d\varepsilon}{dt} = c\frac{1}{r}\frac{dr}{dt} = \frac{1}{m}\frac{dm}{dt} = \frac{D_0}{D_0 + F}\frac{1}{D_0}\frac{dD_0}{dt} + \frac{F}{D_0 + F}\frac{1}{F}\frac{dF}{dt} \tag{6.11}$$

Remember that $D_0 + F = MO_0$, let

$$\frac{1}{P}\frac{dP}{dt} = g_p, \quad \frac{1}{Y}\frac{dY}{dt} = g_y, \quad \text{etc.}$$

and rearrange:

$$\frac{F}{MO_0} g_F = a g_p + b g_y + g_\varepsilon - c g_r - g_m - \frac{D_0}{MO_0} g_D \tag{6.12}$$

Equation (6.12) is the general form of the equation usually used in empirical tests of the balance of payments. It says that the weighted growth rate of the country's international reserves, $(F/MO_0)g_F$, is a function of the growth rates and elasticities of the different variables. It is interesting to note that the weighted growth rate of the country's reserves is negatively related to the weighted growth rate of the domestic component of the country's money base. In other words, other things being equal, a change in the central bank's credit to the economy, D_0, will produce an automatic equal and opposite change in F. Thus, under fixed exchange rates, a country can only determine the composition of the money base. It cannot control the size of the money base itself and, consequently, it has no control over its monetary policy.

Most risk models that drive economic and financial analysis are linear in their structure. Consequently, most tests are designed to detect a linear structure in the data. They are also parametric in that they specify a particular distribution for the variables in question. The techniques are many and varied and include straightforward regressions using least squares, maximum likelihood or generalized method of moments (GMM), as well as event studies, cointegration and error correction models, to mention only a few.

However, many aspects of economic and financial behavior are non-linear and in many cases the parametric form of the variables is unknown. Non-parametric estimation is a growing area of econometrics and will be taken up in a later paragraph. Parametric models that capture non-linearities in economic phenomena are also a growing area of econometrics. These models can generally be classed according to those that are non-linear in the mean and those that are non-linear in variance. Models that are non-linear in the mean depart from the martingale hypothesis while those that are non-linear in variance depart from the hypothesis of independence but not from the martingale hypothesis.

Consider the following model:

$$y_t = \mu(\varepsilon_{t-1}, \varepsilon_{t-2}, \ldots) + \varepsilon_t \sigma(\varepsilon_{t-1}, \varepsilon_{t-2}, \ldots) \tag{6.13}$$

where the ε_{t-i} represent shocks that are IID, $\mu(\cdot)$ is the mean of y_t conditional on past information and $\sigma(\cdot)$ is the standard deviation of y_t conditional on past shocks. The total innovation in y_t is proportional to the shock ε_t and equal to $\varepsilon_t \sigma(\varepsilon_{t-1}, \varepsilon_{t-2}, \ldots)$. An example of a simple model that is non-linear in the mean but linear in variance would be:

$$y_t = \varepsilon_t + \beta \varepsilon_{t-1}^2 \tag{6.14}$$

In this model $\mu(\cdot) = \beta \varepsilon_{t-1}^2$ and $\sigma(\cdot) = 1$. An example of a simple model that is linear in the mean and non-linear in variance would be:

$$y_t = \varepsilon_t \sqrt{\beta \varepsilon_{t-1}^2} \tag{6.15}$$

In this model $\mu(\cdot) = 0$ and $\sigma(\cdot) = \sqrt{\beta \varepsilon_{t-1}^2}$. This model is called a first-order ARCH model, that is, autoregressive conditionally heteroskedastic (Engle, 1982). A simple generalization of this model is called a GARCH(1, 1) model developed by Bollerslev (1986).

Let u represent the innovation in y and V the long-run average variance with γ as its weighting parameter. Then GARCH(1, 1) can be written as

$$\sigma_t^2 = \gamma V + \alpha \sigma_{t-1}^2 + \beta u_{t-1}^2 \tag{6.16}$$

with the constraint that $\gamma + \alpha + \beta = 1$. The model is usually estimated in the form

$$\sigma_t^2 = \omega + \alpha \sigma_{t-1}^2 + \beta u_{t-1}^2 \tag{6.17}$$

by setting $\omega = \gamma V$ and using maximum likelihood methods. For a stable GARCH, $\alpha + \beta < 1$ and $\gamma = 1 - (\alpha + \beta)$. The GARCH(1, 1) model can be generalized to a GARCH(p, q) model that estimates σ_t^2 from the most recent p observations of u^2 and the most recent q observations of σ^2. If $\alpha + \beta = 1$ we get an integrated or IGARCH model. Other important GARCH models are the absolute value GARCH and the exponential GARCH (EGARCH), to mention only a few. These models are clearly very useful for modeling time-varying volatility.

6.4 MONTE CARLO SIMULATIONS

Monte Carlo simulation is a well-known technique that is used in many economic and financial applications. Where political risk is concerned it is often employed for capital budgeting. Basically, Monte Carlo simulation is a sampling procedure that uses a table of random numbers to generate the probability distributions and risk estimates. The whole process involves three steps.

1. The first and most important step in the simulation process is to give the computer a precise model of the project under consideration. This requires identifying the relevant variables and their interdependencies across time. The complete model would include a set of equations for each variable describing their evolution over time. The more complete the model, the more complex the system of equations.

2. In the second step, the probabilities for forecast errors must be drawn up for each variable.

3. In the third step, the computer samples from the distribution of forecast errors, calculates the resulting cash flows for each period, and records them. After a large number of simulations, accurate estimates of the probability distributions of the project's cash flows are obtained.

In a Monte Carlo simulation, the effects of political risk are estimated directly and the role of the political risk analyst is to identify the relevant variables and the probabilities for forecast errors. Consider, for example, the proposal to build a textile plant in China. The cost of the plant is not known for certain but is expected to be between $100 million, if no problems are encountered, and $150 million, if a series of political events such as strikes, bureaucratic interference, surtaxes and other unfavorable government decrees occur. Revenues from the new facility, which will operate for many years, depend on the political variables as well as population growth and income in the target client region, competition and import quotas. Operating costs depend on the political variables, production efficiency, trends in the costs of labor and materials, etc.

Assuming that probability distributions can be assigned to each of the major cost and revenue determinants, a model can be developed and simulated. In effect, the computer selects one value at random from each of the relevant distributions, puts them together and produces an estimated profit and present value or rate of return on the investment. The process is repeated thousands of times to obtain a frequency distribution for the investment outcome.

The Hertz method (1976) is particularly well adapted to capital budgeting with political risk. Under the Hertz method the decision-maker is not required to assign specific probabilities to the individual variables. He is only required to choose:

1. The pertinent variables;
2. The expected value of each variable;
3. The upper estimate of each variable;
4. The lower estimate of each variable.

Thus, this system only requires what a good political risk analyst is likely to know or be able to estimate with some accuracy. The Monte Carlo simulation is then used to generate the required probability distributions.

The Monte Carlo method also permits assignment of values that reflect differing degrees of dependence between some events and other subsequent events. For example, the project's expected sales and prices might be determined by the intensity of competition in conjunction with the total size of market demand and the country's growth rate. A further advantage of the Hertz technique is that by separating the individual factors that determine profitability, the separate effects of each factor can be estimated and the sensitivity of profitability to each factor can be determined. If the effects of a particular factor on the final results are negligible, it is not necessary for management to spend time on analyzing that factor. Thus, certain aspects of the myriad possible sources of political risk can be ruled out at the beginning, thereby simplifying the analysis.

Monte Carlo simulation has several major drawbacks. It requires constructing a suitable model and obtaining probability distributions for a large number of variables. This in itself is extremely difficult. Furthermore, it is costly in programming and machine time. Therefore, full-scale simulation is not generally worthwhile except for large and expensive projects.

6.5   VALUE AT RISK (VaR)

Value at risk is an estimate, with a given degree of confidence, of how much one can lose from one's portfolio over a given time horizon. The concept of VaR is very appealing because it is consistent with the mean–variance paradigm and summarizes in a single statistical measure all possible portfolio losses over a short period of time due to "normal" market movements. It has become popular with senior management and corporate treasurers as well as with financial institutions and regulators and figures prominently in the BIS 1998 capital requirements for market risk. It is also a major element in the discussions on credit and counterparty risk.

For a more formal definition of VaR, let c represent the degree of confidence and δV the change in the value of a portfolio over a given period. Then VaR can be written as

$$\text{Prob}[\delta V \leq -VaR] = 1 - c \tag{6.18}$$

Suppose that VaR is $20 million and the degree of confidence is 99%, then if the time horizon is 10 days, $\text{Prob}[\delta V \leq -\$20m] = 1 - 0.99 = 0.01$ means that there is a 1% probability that the portfolio could lose $20 million or more over the next 10 days.

VaR is calculated assuming normal market conditions, meaning that extreme market conditions are not considered. Extreme conditions are considered separately. Most approaches to calculating VaR assume a joint normal/log-normal distribution of the underlying market parameters (Duffie and Pan, 1997; Jorion, 1996; Pritsker, 1997; RiskMetrics, 1996; Stambaugh, 1996). For short time periods, it is also customary to assume that the expected change in the price of the variable is zero. More complicated assumptions can also be accommodated, usually at the cost of time and/or tractability.[1]

---

[1] For more on VaR, see www.jpmorgan.com

6.5.1   VaR for a Single-Asset Portfolio

We start by estimating VaR for a single asset. Consider a portfolio of $50 million worth of Argentine Brady bonds. Since the BIS 1998 time horizon is 10 days, assume that this is the relevant time period. The confidence level is 99%, the annualized volatility of returns on Argentine Brady bonds is 47.5% and there are 250 trading days in the year. First, we calculate the standard deviation of the portfolio over the 10-day horizon:

$$\sqrt{\delta t} \times \sigma_{year} = \sqrt{\frac{10}{250}} \times 0.475 = 0.095$$

where $\sqrt{\delta t}$ represents the square root of the time horizon and σ_{year} is the annualized standard deviation or volatility. Second, we find the 99% confidence interval of the cumulative normal curve corresponds to 2.33 standard deviations from the mean. Thus, the 10-day 99% VaR on a portfolio of $50 million worth of Argentine Brady bonds can be calculated as:

$$0.095 \times 2.33 \times \$50m = \$11.0675m$$

6.5.2   VaR for a Two-Asset Portfolio

Now consider a $50 million portfolio with 50% in Argentine Brady bonds and 50% in Poland par Brady bonds. Assume as before that the time horizon is 10 days, the confidence level is 99%, the annualized volatility of returns on Argentine par Brady bonds is 47.5% and there are 250 trading days in the year. Assume further that the annualized volatility of returns on Poland par Brady bonds is 47.5% and the correlation between the two bonds is -0.5. First we estimate the annual volatility of the portfolio:

$$\sigma_p = \sqrt{\sigma_p^2} = \sqrt{\sum_{i=1}^{2} \frac{1}{n^2}\sigma_i^2 + \sum_{\substack{i=1 \\ i \neq k}}^{2}\sum_{k=1}^{2} \frac{1}{n^2}\sigma_{i,k}}$$

$$= \sqrt{0.5^2 \times 0.475^2 + 0.5^2 \times 0.475^2 + 2 \times 0.5^2 \times 0.475^2 \times (-0.5)} = 0.2375$$

where i, k = Argentina and Poland and $\sigma_{i,k}$ refers to the covariance between the Argentine and Polish Brady bonds.

Next, we calculate the volatility of the portfolio over the 10-day horizon:

$$\sqrt{\frac{10}{250}} \times 0.2375 = 0.0475$$

Thus, the 10-day 99% VaR on a $50 million portfolio with equal amounts in Argentine and Polish Brady bonds can be calculated as:

$$0.0475 \times 2.33 \times \$50m = \$5.53375 \text{ million}$$

The reduction in the VaR is due to the diversification effects associated with the low correlation between the two bonds. Extensions of VaR to portfolios containing n assets are straightforward.

6.5.3 Other Methods for Estimating VaR

Many other methods for calculating VaR also exist. Some have focused on developing methods that calculate the VaR more accurately using the ARCH/GARCH methodology described above.[2] Hull and White (1998), for example, suggest adjusting historical data on each market variable to reflect the difference between the historical volatility of the market variable and its current volatility. Other approaches such as those of Rockafellar and Uryasev (2000), Andersen and Sornette (1999), Basak and Shapiro (1998), Emmer *et al.* (2000), Gourieroux *et al.* (2000), Puelz (1999) and Tasche (1999) seek to develop more efficient algorithms for portfolio optimizations that minimize VaR. Bootstrapping and Monte Carlo simulations are used when the portfolio contains non-linear instruments such as options (Jorion, 1996b; Pritsker, 1997; RiskMetrics, 1996; Stambaugh, 1996).

Monte Carlo and bootstrapping are interesting because they are applied in many areas of financial and economic decision-making. Whereas Monte Carlo simulations, described above, are based on the generation of normally distributed random numbers, bootstrapping uses actual asset price movements taken from historical data. The method involves collecting daily data for the assets in the portfolio over a relatively long period. The popularity of bootstrapping is due to the well-documented observation that the distributions of daily changes in many market variables do not seem to be normal. They generally have fatter tails than the normal distribution and are often skewed. The bootstrapping method captures the features of the historical distributions when estimating the VaR.

It is clear from the foregoing discussion that VaR as a risk measure is only as good as the volatility estimate used to calculate it. When the measure is accurate, it is a powerful tool for risk management. Otherwise, it is worthless or worse than nothing. The problem is that there is no method for calculating VaR that has been shown to be superior to the others.

6.6   PRINCIPAL COMPONENTS ANALYSIS

Principal components analysis is a mathematical technique that uses the historical variance/covariance matrix of a data set to extract a set of indices that best explain the variance of the data. It proceeds sequentially. The first index generated by the methodology best explains the variance of the original data and is called the first principal component. After the first index is selected, the analysis proceeds to extract the index that explains as much as possible of the variance of the original data that is unexplained by the first principal component, given that this second index is constrained to be uncorrelated (orthogonal) with the first index. This index is called the second principal component. Principal components analysis proceeds sequentially to form additional indices, ensuring that each index formed explains as much as possible of the variance in the data that has not been explained by previous indices, under the constraint that each index is uncorrelated (orthogonal) with each of the previously extracted indices. The exercise can continue until the number of indices equals the number of variables in the data set. At this point, principal components can exactly reproduce the historical variance/covariance matrix. However, since the first principal component explains as much as possible of the historical variance/covariance matrix, the second explains as much as possible of the remaining variance and so on, the last few principal components have relatively little explanatory power. In fact, to the extent that there is any real underlying structure

---

[2] See Engle, (1982). for the ARCH model and Bollerslev (1986) for the GARCH model.

to the data, most of the correlation matrix should be explained by the first few principal components.

Suppose, for example, that we want to study Brady bond prices. Based on the ratio analysis of Chapter 3 and other studies, we identify 20 variables that are likely to affect Brady bond prices. However, we feel that there are two major problems. First of all, we find that there is a high degree of multicollinearity among the explanatory variables and, secondly, that there are too many of them. To solve this problem we can proceed as explained above to extract the principal components of the explanatory variables. We then use these components as the explanatory variables in a normal ordinary least squares (OLS) or generalized least squares (GLS) regression. Since the components are constrained to be orthogonal, the problem of multicollinearity is solved. By accepting a cut-off point for the amount of variance we want explained (80%, for example), we reduce the number of explanatory variables as well.

In a recent paper, Sherer and Avellaneda (2000) used principal components analysis to study the Brady bond debt of Argentina, Brazil, Mexico and Venezuela. They find that there are two statistically significant components or factors that explain up to 90% of the realized variance. The component that explains the most variance corresponds to variance attributable to regional (Latin) risk. The second component suggests the existence of a volatility risk factor associated with Venezuelan debt in relation to the rest of the region. A time-dependent factor analysis shows that the importance of the variance explained by the factors changes over time and that this variation can be interpreted in terms of market events such as the Mexican peso crisis, the Asian economic meltdown, the Russian default and the devaluation of the Brazilian real.

The problem with principal components analysis is that the components discarded in the components selection because they were relatively unimportant in capturing the variance of the explanatory variables, could nevertheless be important in explaining the dependent variable in the regression of the second step. There is no way to guarantee that the principal components are the best regressors.

6.7 NON-LINEARITIES AND NON-PARAMETRIC ESTIMATION

In much of what happens in political risk analysis we are faced with a functional relation between the dependent variable and the explanatory variables without the benefit of a structural model to restrict the form of the relation. When this is the case, non-parametric estimation techniques can be used to capture a wide variety of non-linearities without recourse to any one particular specification of the non-linear relation. In contrast to the highly structured parametric approach to estimating non-linearities such as ARCH/GARCH models, fractal analysis, Markov-switching models, threshold autoregression, etc., to mention only a few, non-parametric estimation requires few assumptions about the nature of the non-linearities. The problem is that non-parametric estimation is highly data intensive and generally not effective for small samples. Another problem is that non-parametric estimation is prone to overfitting and this cannot be easily overcome by statistical methods. Overfitting occurs when a model fits "too well" in the sense that it captures random noise as well as genuine non-linearities. The primary source of overfitting is having too many parameters with respect to the number of data points, in other words, too few degrees of freedom. A typical symptom of this effect is an excellent in-sample fit but poor out-of-sample performance.

Some of the most commonly used estimators in financial economics are the smoothing estimators where errors in observations are reduced by averaging the data in sophisticated ways. Some examples are kernel regression, orthogonal series expansion, projection pursuit, nearest-neighbor estimators, average derivative estimators, splines and neural networks.

The idea behind such averaging is straightforward. Suppose we want to estimate the relation between two variables X and Y, which satisfy

$$Y_t = f(X_t) + \varepsilon_t \qquad (6.19)$$

where $f(X_t)$ is an arbitrary fixed but unknown non-linear function and ε_t is a zero mean IID process. Suppose we estimate $f(X_t)$ at time t_0 where $X_{t_0} = x_0$ and that for this one observation repeated independent observations of the variable Y_{t_0} can be obtained: $Y_{t_0}^1 = y_1, \ldots, Y_{t_n}^n = y_n$. A natural estimator of the function $f(X_t)$ at the point x_0 is

$$\hat{f}(x_0) = \frac{1}{n}\sum_{i=1}^{n} y_i = \frac{1}{n}\sum_{i=1}^{n}\left[f(x_0) + \varepsilon_t^i\right] = f(x_0) + \frac{1}{n}\sum_{i=1}^{n}\varepsilon_t^i \qquad (6.20)$$

As n tends to infinity the error term becomes negligible.

When dealing with a time series, repeated observations for a given X_t are not available. In practice, this problem is overcome by assuming that $f(X_t)$ is sufficiently smooth so that observations of X_t near the value x_0 can be taken so that the corresponding values of Y_t will be close to $f(x_0)$. The idea is that if $f(X_t)$ is sufficiently smooth in the near neighborhood of x_0, $f(x_0)$ will be nearly constant so that it can be estimated by taking an average of the Y_t's that correspond to the X_t's near x_0. The closer the X_t's are to x_0, the closer the average of the corresponding Y_t's will be to $f(x_0)$. To account for this, the Y_t's are weighted where the weights decline as the X_t's get farther from x_0. Thus, for any arbitrary x, the smoothing estimator of $f(x)$ can be written as

$$\hat{f}(x) = \frac{1}{T}\sum_{t=1}^{T} w_{t,T}(x)Y_t \qquad (6.21)$$

where the weights $w_{t,T}(x)$ decrease for Y_t's associated with X_t's farther from x.

Besides the data and overfitting problems mentioned above, it is clear that choice of the neighborhood around x is of paramount importance. If the neighborhood is too large, the weighted average will be too smooth to capture the non-linearities of $f(X_t)$. If it is too small, the weighted average will be too variable, reflecting noise as well as the variations of $f(X_t)$.

Non-parametric estimation is widespread in financial economics (see, for example, Pasquariello, 2000 for a review of non-parametric interest rate modeling and Tkacz, 2000 for inflation). Kaminski and Reinhart (1999) have pioneered their non-parametric search into leading early warning indicators for banking and currency crises that seems to have some forecasting value. This approach, described in detail in Kaminski et al. (1998), takes as its basic premise that the economy behaves differently on the eve of financial crises and that this aberrant behavior has a recurrent systemic pattern. Currency crises, for example, are usually preceded by overvaluation of the currency; banking crises tend to follow sharp declines in asset prices. The diagnostic and predictive content is founded on the specification of exactly what is meant as an "early" warning, the definition of "optimal threshold" for each indicator and the choice of one or more diagnostic statistics that measure the probability of experiencing a crisis. They find that for currency crises, the best monthly indicators are an appreciation of the real exchange rate, a banking crisis, a decline in stock prices, a fall in exports, a high ratio of money (M2) to international reserves and a recession. The best annual indicators are a large current account deficit relative to both GDP and investment (Goldstein et al., 2000). For banking crises they find that the best monthly indicators are appreciation of the exchange rate, a decline in stock prices, a rise in the money (M2) multiplier, a decline in real output, a fall in exports and a rise in the real interest rate. The best annual indicators are a large ratio of capital inflows to GDP and a large current account deficit relative to investment (Goldstein *et al.*, 2000).

6.8 ARTIFICIAL NEURAL NETWORKS

The artificial neural network is an alternative to non-parametric estimation. Artificial neural networks draw their motivation from biological phenomena and are popular with practitioners. To get an idea of how they work, consider an output variable Y that is non-linearly related to a collection of n input variables x_i as follows:

$$y = f \left(\sum_{i=1}^{n} \beta_i x_i - \mu \right) \tag{6.22}$$

$$f(u) = \begin{cases} 1 & \text{if} \quad u \geq 0 \\ 0 & \text{if} \quad u < 0 \end{cases} \tag{6.23}$$

According to this setup, each input is weighted by a beta coefficient and summed across all inputs. If the weighted sum is greater than the threshold, denoted as μ, the artificial neuron is activated by way of the activation function $f(\cdot)$. Otherwise it stays dormant.

The model can be generalized to include continuous values of y, for example, by letting $f(\cdot)$ equal the logistic distribution. Further complications can be introduced by adding hidden layers and hidden units. In this case we have what is called a multilayer perceptron. Other types of artificial neural networks are radial basis functions, which were first used to solve interpolation problems, and projection pursuit regression, which is a statistical technique for analyzing high-dimensional data sets by looking at their low-dimensional projections. In fact, there is a wide range of models and many levels of complexity.

Neural networks are applied in a learning process that makes it possible to approximate non-linear functions. One problem with the neural network, however, is that there are no generally accepted procedures for choosing the architecture of the network such as the specification of the activation function, the number of hidden layers and units, etc. Furthermore, the network parameters are typically obtained by minimizing the sum of squared errors and, since the objective function may not be globally convex, there can be a multitude of local minima. It is also difficult to do significance testing.

6.9 MULTICRITERIA

The multicriteria method is a practical approach to political risk that aims at supporting the decision-maker, expert or analyst in his judgmental assessment. It has been applied to country choice in global index funds (Khoury *et al.*, 1994), to the prediction of business failure (Zopounidis, 1995), to portfolio management (Zopounidis *et al.*, 1994) and country risk (Cosset *et al.*, 1992; Clark *et al.*, 1998). It involves providing a decision-support tool that serves as an analytical guideline for conducting the assessment, thereby making the final decision easier and quicker to achieve. The final decision, however, is still based entirely on the analyst's judgment. In this approach, the idea is to tackle a decision problem rather than a modeling problem.

From a purely theoretical–economic point of view, the decision could be described in terms of preference theory. This means determining an aggregation function, which, in effect, is a utility function, and classifying the possible decisions in terms of the values of this function. However, as noted by several authors, a partial aggregation method seems more general, and closer to the actual decision-maker's practical approach to the decision problem. Broadly speaking, then, there are two main approaches to these multicriteria problems that seek to help the decision-maker toward the complex final decision. The first includes the so-called goal programming approaches, in which the decision problem is solved by reaching some goal according to the value of an objective function, which is tantamount to a utility function. In this method, applied to country risk by Cosset *et al.* (1992), the decision-maker is given a set of guidelines to help him find the way to the final decision. Typically, these methods employ a stepwise process, in which the departures from the initial goal are introduced into the problem while taking into account the relative importance of each criterion (Zionts and Wallenius, 1976, 1983).

The partial aggregation methods, such as those in the ELECTRE family used by Clark *et al.* (1998), also employ a complex stepwise process toward the final decision. However, there is neither an explicit nor an implicit utility function. The decision is guided by the total weight of the criteria that appear comparatively better in one decision than in another. This procedure allows for non-comparable decisions between which the decision-maker will hesitate.

There are several kinds of help that an ELECTRE analysis can supply. One is to sort out a set of actions that are not directly comparable to eliminate those that are clearly far behind in terms of most criteria, thereby reducing the decision to a restricted group of actions from which the final action will be chosen. Another use of some versions of the ELECTRE method, which is particularly relevant for political risk analysis, is the outranking of possible actions with several classes of ranking. Each class will correspond to actions or decisions, which are comparable, but clearly better than any of the actions that belong to a lower class.

The simplest partial aggregation method of the ELECTRE family that can be used as an outranking system is the ELECTRE I method. In this method, the first step is to establish a list of pertinent criteria and scale them according to the decision-maker's partial preference scheme. The values of the criteria should be strictly monotonous with respect to preference, either strictly increasing or strictly decreasing. However, for the actual calculations, the decreasing criteria will be transformed into increasing ones. The second step is to assign weights to each of these criteria. Finally, the decision problem is treated by comparing any ordered pair of actions according to the weight of the criteria. This approach is very similar to the approach that could be made of a decision through an election, with possible problems such as non-comparability and non-transitivity in some cases.

Thus, in an ELECTRE outranking exercise, we use the weighted criteria to establish a concordance index, which aims at assessing whether a majority of weighted criteria support the preference of one action with respect to the other. Let the n criteria be $1, 2, \ldots, i, \ldots, n$. The criteria can be quantitative, such as the economic and financial ratios developed in Chapter 3, or qualitative, such as economic freedom and corruption indices or measures of political stability, etc. For actions a and b, let $x_{1a}, x_{2a}, \ldots, x_{ia}, \ldots x_{na}$ and $x_{1b}, x_{2b}, \ldots, x_{ib}, \ldots, x_{nb}$ be the respective values of the criteria and finally, let $\alpha_1, \alpha_2, \ldots, \alpha_i, \ldots, \alpha_n$ be the weights ascribed to the criteria based on how important each criterion is with respect to the country risk. The concordance index c_{ab} is defined as:

$$C_{ab} = \frac{\sum\limits_{i=1}^{n} \delta_i \alpha_i}{\sum\limits_{i=1}^{n} \alpha_i} \qquad (6.24)$$

with $\delta_i = 1$ whenever $x_{ia} \geq x_{ib}$ and $\delta_i = 0$ otherwise. Clearly, one has always $c_{ab} \in [0, 1]$, and the majority rule requires that $c_{ab} \geq c_0$ for preferring action a to action b, with c_0 being some threshold ($c_0 > 0.5$, for example). Next, we calculate a discordance ratio, which expresses the possibility of vetoing the preference even if $c_{ab} \geq c_0$ whenever some of the criteria are such that $x_{ia} < x_{ib}$ with too large a discrepancy in favor of b. Thus, the discordance index d_{ab} is defined as:

$$d_{ab} = \frac{\sup(x_{ib} - x_{ia})}{R} \tag{6.25}$$

where $\sup(x_{ib} - x_{ia})$ is the largest (positive) discrepancy between x_{ib} and x_{ia}, and R is the largest interval in which the x_i are located. Clearly, again, $d_{ab} \in [0, 1]$, and the veto rule requires that $d_{ab} \leq d_0$ for preferring action a to action b, with c_0 being some threshold ($c_0 \in [0, 1]$).

The ELECTRE I method is the simplest method of the ELECTRE family. Other, more elaborate versions of the ELECTRE method, which we shall not describe in detail here, such as ELECTRE III, allow for indifference and weak preference thresholds and are even better suited to outrankings.

REFERENCES

Altman EI, 1968, Financial Ratios, Discriminant Analysis and the Prediction of Corporate Bankruptcy. *Journal of Finance*, 23, 589–609.

Altman EI, Haldeman R and Narayanan P, 1977, ZETA Analysis: A New Model for Identifying Bankruptcy Risk. *Journal of Banking and Finance*, 1, 29–54.

Andersen JV and Sornette D, 1999, Have Your Cake and Eat It Too. *Working Paper*, California: UCLA.

Balkan EM, 1992, Political Instability, Country Risk and Probability of Default. *Applied Economics*, 24, 999–1008.

Basak S and Shapiro A, 1998, Value at Risk Based Management: Optimal Policies and Asset Prices. *Working Paper*, Pennsylvania: Wharton School, University of Pennsylvania.

Boehmer E and Megginson WL, 1990, Determinants of Secondary Market Prices for Developing Country Syndicated Loans. *Journal of Finance*, 45 (5), 1517–40.

Bollerslev T, 1986, Generalized Autoregressive Conditional Heteroscedasticity. *Journal of Econometrics*, 31, 307–27.

Clark E and Zenaidi A, 1999, Sovereign Debt Discounts and the Unwillingness to Pay. *Finance*, 20 (2), 185–99.

Clark E, Cusin R and Lesourd JB, 1998, Risk Assessment and Sovereign Debt Instruments: A Multicriteria Approach. Presented at the International Conference on Forecasting Financial Markets, London, May 27–29.

Cosset JC, Siskos Y and Zopounidis C, 1992, Evaluating Country Risk: A Decision Support Approach. *Global Finance Journal*, 3 (1), 79–95.

De Bondt GJ and Winder CCA, 1995, An Empirical Indicator for Assessing Countries' Creditworthiness. De Nederlandsche Bank, *mimeo*, working paper no. 437, August.

De Haan J, Siermann CLJ and Van Lubek E, 1997, Political Instability and Country Risk: New Evidence. *Applied Economic Letters*, 4, 703–7.

Dropsy V and Solberg RL, 1992, Loan Valuation and Secondary Market for Developing Country Debt. In: RL Solberg, ed. *Country Risk Analysis: A Handbook*. London: Routledge.

Duffie D and Pan J, 1997, An Overview of Value at Risk. *Journal of Derivatives*, 4 (Spring), 7–49.

Dullman K and Windfuhr M, 2000, Credit Spreads between German and Italian Sovereign Bonds: Do Affine Models Work? *Working Paper*, Germany: University of Mannheim.

Emmer S, Kluppelberg C and Korn R, 2000, Optimal Portfolios with Optimal Capital at Risk. *Working Paper*, Germany: Munich University of Technology.

Engle R, 1982, Autoregressive Conditional Heteroskedasticity with Estimates of the Variance of United Kingdom Inflation. *Econometrica*, 50 (1), 987–1007.

Feder G and Just RE, 1977, A Study of Debt Servicing Capacity Applying Logit Analysis. *Journal of Development Economics*, 4, 25–39.

Feder G, Just RE and Ross K, 1981, Projecting Debt Servicing Capacity of Developing Countries. *Journal of Financial and Quantitative Analysis*, 16, 651–69.

Frank CR and Cline WR, 1971, Measurement of Debt Servicing Capacity: An Application of Discriminant Analysis. *Journal of International Economics*, 1, 327–44.

Goldstein M, Kaminsky G and Reinhart C, 2000, Assessing Financial Vulnerability: An Early Warning System for Emerging Markets. Washington: Institute for International Economics.

Gourieroux C, Laurent JP and Scaillet O, 2000, Sensitivity Analysis of Value at Risk. *Working Paper*, France: Université de Louvain la Neuve.

Greene WH, 1997, *Econometric Analysis*. 3rd edition. Upper Saddle River, NJ: Prentice Hall.

Gujarati DN, 1995, *Basic Econometrics*. 3rd edition. New York: McGraw-Hill.

Hajivassiliou VA, 1987, The External Debt Repayment Problems of LDCs. *Journal of Econometrics*, 36, 205–30.

Hertz DB, 1976, Uncertainty and Investment Selection. *In*: JF Weston and MB Goudzwaard, eds. *The Treasurer's Handbook*. Homewood, IL: Dow Jones-Irwin, Ch. 18, 376–420.

Hull J and White A, 1998, Incorporating Volatility Updating into the Historical Simulation Method for Value-at-Risk. *Journal of Risk*, 1 (Fall), 5–19.

Jorion P, 1996a, Risk2: Measuring the Risk in Value At Risk. *Financial Analysts Journal*, 52 (Nov/Dec).

Jorion P, 1996b, *Value at Risk: The New Benchmark for Controlling Market Risk*. New York: Irwin Professional.

Kaminsky G, Lizondo S and Reinhart CM, 1998, Leading Indicators of Currency Crises. *IMF Staff Papers*, 45 (1), 1–48.

Kaminsky G and Reinhart CM, 1999, The Twin Crises: The Causes of Banking and Balance of Payments Problems. *American Economic Review*, 89 (3), 473–500.

Keswani A, 1999, *Estimating a Risky Term Structure of Brady Bonds*. London: London Business School.

Kharas H, 1984, The Long Run Creditworthiness of Developing Countries: Theory and Practice. *The Quarterly Journal of Economics*, 415–39.

Khoury N, Martel JM and Yougourou P, 1994, A Multicriterion Approach to Country Selection for Global Index Funds. *Global Finance Journal*, 5 (1), 17–35.

Merrick J, 1999, *Crisis Dynamics of Implied Default Recovery Ratios: Evidence from Russia and Argentina*. New York: Stern School of Business, New York University.

Pagès H, 2000, Estimating Brazilian Sovereign Risk from Brady Bond Prices. *Working Paper*, France: Banque de France.

Pasquariello P, 2000, *Linear or Nonlinear: This is the Dilemma*. New York: Stern School of Business, New York University.

Pritsker M, 1997, Evaluating Value at Risk Methodologies. *Journal of Financial Services Research*, 12, 201–42.

Puelz A, 1999, Value at Risk Based Portfolio Optimization. *Working Paper*, Dallas, TX: Southern Methodist University.

Rahnama-Moghadam M, Samavati H and Haber LJ, 1991, The Determinations of Debt Rescheduling: The Case of Latin-America. *Southern Economic Journal*, 58, 510–17.

RiskMetrics, 1996, *Technical Document*. 4th edition. New York: JP Morgan, Inc., December.

Rockafellar RT and Uryasev S, 2000, Optimisation of Conditional Value at Risk. *Journal of Risk*, 2, 21–41.

Sherer KP and Avellaneda M, 2000, All for One, One for All?: A Principal Component Analysis of Brady Bond Debt from 1994 to 2000. Available at: http://www.math.nyu.edu/faculty/avellane/PCABrady.pdf

Stambaugh, F, 1996, Risk and Value at Risk. *European Management Journal*, 14, 612–21.

Tashe D, 1999, Risk Contributions and Performance Measurement. *Working Paper*, Germany: Munich University of Technology.

Tkacz G, 2000, *Non-Parametric and Neural Network Models of Inflation*. Bank of Canada, Working Paper 2000–7.

Zionts S and Wallenius J, 1976, An Interactive Programming Method for Solving the Multiple Criteria Problem. *Management Science*, 22 (6), 652–63.

Zionts S and Wallenius J, 1983, An Interactive Multiple Objective Linear Programming Method for a Class of Underlying Nonlinear Utility Functions. *Management Science*, 29 (5), 519–29.

Zopounidis C, 1995, *L'évaluation du risque de défaillance: méthodes et cas d'application*. Paris: Economica.

Zopounidis C, Godefroid M and Hurson C, 1994, Designing a Multicriteria Decision Support System for Portfolio Selection and Management. *In:* J Janssen, CH Skiadas and Zopounidis C, eds. *Advances in Stochastic Modelling and Data Analysis*. Dordrecht: Kluwer.

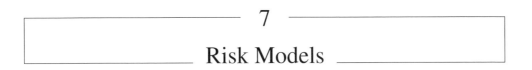

7

Risk Models

In this chapter we focus on how to quantify country risk and incorporate its effects in the investment decision. First, we look at the credit risk models and see how they can be applied to country risk to estimate default probabilities, maximum debt levels, implied volatility and credit value at risk. We then turn to the problem of country risk in portfolio and foreign direct investment. We show how country risk can be incorporated in the investment decision by adjusting either the cash flows or the required rate of return. We then present several methods for estimating the required rate of return to capture the country risk element. Finally, we show how the cost of country risk can be measured as a hypothetical insurance policy that pays off all losses accruing to political events.

7.1   CREDIT RISK

There are several approaches to estimating the probability of default. The first and simplest involves using historical data supplied by the rating agencies. A second method uses the interest rate spreads observed in the market and the third is based on modeling the value of the firm.

7.1.1   Probability of Default Using Historical Data

The rating agencies (see Chapter 5) publish data on average cumulative default rates such as that in Table 7.1. For example, a company with a credit rating of A at the beginning of the year has a probability of 0.04% of defaulting before the end of one year, a probability of 0.12% of defaulting before the end of two years and a probability of 0.21% of defaulting before the end of three years. The corresponding probabilities of a CCC rating are 19.79%, 26.92% and 31.63%.

The problem with historical probabilities is that they are averages across a heterogenous sample of firms or countries and over several business cycles. Thus, the actual probability of default can vary significantly between firms or countries with the same rating. They can also differ from one year to the next. This is true for countries as well as companies. Crouhy *et al.* (2000) point out that the rating agencies are slow to change their ratings and, consequently, the historical frequency of staying in a rating class overstates the true probability of keeping the same credit quality. This inertia causes the historical default rate for each class to be higher than it should be because each class contains firms which should have been downgraded. Where country risk is concerned, there is a further problem in that data is limited because there are relatively few countries and country ratings are a relatively new phenomenon.

7.1.2   Probability of Default Using Interest Rate Spreads

Another methodology uses interest rate spreads observed in the market to estimate the probability of default. The idea behind this methodology is that the probability of default can be

Table 7.1 Default probabilities

Rating	1 year	2 years	3 years
AAA	0.00%	0.00%	0.04%
AA	0.01%	0.04%	0.10%
A	0.04%	0.12%	0.21%
BBB	0.24%	0.55%	0.89%
BB	1.08%	3.48%	6.65%
B	5.94%	13.49%	20.12%
CCC	25.26%	34.79%	42.16%

Source: Standard & Poor's, January 2001. Reproduced with permission.

derived from the difference between the zero coupon yield curves for each rating category and the zero coupon risk-free yield curve. If there are seven rating classes, it will be necessary to estimate eight yield curves: one for each class and one for the risk-free asset.

A zero coupon bond is a bond that pays no coupons and a zero coupon yield curve is a plot of the zero coupon interest rate against time to maturity. Since most bonds carry coupons, the zero yield curve has to be estimated from information on coupon-bearing bonds. Bootstrapping and spline regressions are two popular methodologies for estimating the zero coupon yield curve.[1] The treasury curve is a natural choice for the risk-free zero curve and is often used by analysts. However, most analysts have come to use the LIBOR zero curve as the risk-free zero curve because of factors, such as special tax treatment, that cause treasuries to have artificially low yields. The methodology that follows shows how to calculate the probabilities of default. These probabilities are forward looking because they are based on the zero curve, which reflects the interest rates that are expected in the future. They are also risk-neutral probabilities because they are calculated with respect to the risk-free bond.

The principle of estimating default probabilities from bond prices is very simple. The assumption is that all issuers are credit-homogenous within the same rating class, that is, that all issuers of the same class have the same transition probabilities and the same default probability. In step one, the price of a corporate bond is compared with the price of a risk-free bond having the same maturity and the same cash flows in order to calculate the expected default losses. In this exercise it is usually assumed that the cost of default risk is equal to the total difference between the price of the risk-free bond and the price of the risky bond. This assumption attributes the total yield spread to default risk and is only an approximation since other factors, such as liquidity, can also influence the spread. In step two, the amount that will be recovered in the case of default is estimated and, in step three, this information is put together to estimate the default probability.

Consider the following notation:

$y_F(T) = $ the yield on a risk-free zero coupon bond with T years to maturity

$y(T) = $ the yield on a risky zero coupon bond with T years to maturity

$q(T) = $ the probability of default on the risky bond between time 0 and time T

$100 = $ the bond's principal

---

[1] Many models such as Carleton and Cooper (1976), Schaefer (1981), Vasicek and Fong (1982), Chambers *et al.* (1984), Mastronikola (1991) exist to estimate the term structure. Shea (1985) compares them and finds McCulloch's (1971) cubic spline model empirically tractable, easily computable by OLS and parsimonious.

The value of the risk-free bond is $100e^{-y_F(T)T}$, the value of the risky bond is $100e^{-y(T)}$ and the expected loss from default is $100(e^{-y_F(T)T} - e^{-y(T)T})$. If we assume that nothing will be recovered in the case of default, the bond pays 0 at maturity with a probability of $q(T)$ and 100 with a probability of $1 - q(T)$. We use this information to calculate the default probability:

$$[q(T) \times 0 + (1 - q(T))]100e^{-y_F(T)T} = 100e^{y(T)T}$$

$$q(T) = 1 - e^{-T[y(T)-y_F(T)]} \tag{7.1}$$

Now suppose that in the event of default the creditors are able to recover a portion of what is owed them. This assumption reflects reality since it is rare that creditors receive nothing at all. For example, recovery rates on corporate bonds in the US are currently about 50% of par value for senior secured debt and about 20% for junior subordinated debt. Let x represent the percentage of the bond's no default value that will be recovered in the event of default. The no default value of the bond is equal to the present value of the bond's principal discounted at the risk-free rate: $100e^{-y_F(T)T}$. Thus, the amount to be recovered with probability $q(T)$ is equal to $x100e^{-y_F(T)T}$. Putting this information together gives:

$$q(T) \times x100e^{-y_F(T)T} + [(1 - q(T))]100e^{-y_F(T)T} = 100e^{-y(T)T}$$

$$q(T) = \frac{1 - e^{-T[y(T)-y_F(T)]}}{1 - x} \tag{7.2}$$

As an example let $y_F(T) = 6\%$, $y(T) = 10\%$ and $T = 5$ years with the recovery rate $x = 20\%$. Using equation (7.2), the probability of default between year zero and year five is:

$$q(T) = \frac{1 - e^{-5[0.1-0.06]}}{1 - 0.2} = 22.66\%$$

The same type of methodology can be used to calculate default probabilities of coupon-bearing bonds. The advantage of the interest rate spread methodology is that it is straightforward and easy to apply. The problem for country risk analysis is that it only works for countries that have bonds that are traded.

7.1.3   Probabilities of Default Using Firm Value

The foregoing methods for calculating default probabilities are based on credit ratings, which are updated and revised relatively infrequently. There is also some question about their accuracy. The risk of default models that are based on firm value do not rely on credit ratings. They rely on market values and thus can give more timely information for estimating default risk.

The original Black–Scholes option pricing formula refers to a European-style call option on an underlying asset with no intermediate payouts. In their original article of 1973 Black and Scholes showed how options pricing theory can be applied to the equilibrium market pricing of corporate equity and debt. Corporate debt can be considered as a sale of the company's assets to creditors with shareholders owning an option to buy the assets back. On the exercise date, if the value of the assets is higher than the nominal value of the debt, the shareholders will exercise their option and buy back the assets by paying off the debt. In the opposite case, the company defaults and the creditors take possession of the assets. Merton (1974) formalized this idea.

Consider the following notation:

V_0 = value of the company's assets at time zero
V_T = value of the company's assets at time T
C_0 = value of the company's equity at time zero
C_T = value of the company's equity at time T
X = nominal value of a zero coupon bond that matures at time T
σ_V = volatility of dV/V
σ_C = volatility of dC/C

On the maturity date of the zero coupon bond, if $V_T < X$, it is optimal for shareholders to default on the debt. In this case the value of the equity is zero. If, on the other hand, $V_T > X$, it will be optimal for shareholders to pay off the loan. In this case the value of equity is equal to $V_T - X$. On the maturity date of the debt, equity will be worth either $V_T - X$ or 0, whichever is higher: $[\text{Max}(V_T - X, 0)]$, which is the same as the payoff on the European option in the Black–Scholes model. The Black–Scholes pricing formula gives the value of equity as:

$$C_0 = V_t N(d_1) - X e^{-rT} N(d_2) \tag{7.3}$$

where

$N(d)$ = the value of the cumulative normal distribution evaluated at d

$$d_1 = \frac{\ln(V_0/X) + \left(r + \sigma_V^2/2\right)T}{\sigma_V \sqrt{T}}$$

$$d_2 = \frac{\ln(V_0/X) + \left(r - \sigma_V^2/2\right)T}{\sigma_V \sqrt{T}}$$

The value of the debt is equal to the difference between the value of the company's assets less the value of equity: $V_0 - C_0$. $N(d_2)$ is the probability that the value of the assets will be greater than X, the nominal amount of debt outstanding. Consequently, $1 - N(d_2)$ or $N(-d_2)$ is the risk-neutral probability of default. In the terminology of KMV, a company in California now owned by Moody's that uses the Merton model in its risk estimates, d_2 is called the risk-neutral distance to default and $N(-d_2)$ is called the risk-neutral expected default frequency.[2]

To calculate $N(-d_2)$, we need to know V_0 and σ_V, neither of which is directly observable. In the case of a company whose shares are traded publicly, this problem can be overcome. The value of equity C_0 can be observed. The volatility of C, σ_C, although not observable, can be calculated from historical data or modeled, using a wide range of parametric and non-parametric techniques available in the literature. Using Ito's lemma and the definition of variance, it is easy to show that:

$$\sigma_C = \frac{\partial C}{\partial V} \frac{V}{C} \sigma_V = N(d_1) \frac{V}{C} \sigma_V \tag{7.4}$$

With C_0 and σ_C known, the values for V_0 and σ_V can be calculated by solving equations (7.3) and (7.4) simultaneously.

---

[2] In the KMV model, X is not equal to the nominal value of debt. Based on a sample of several hundred companies, KMV has observed that firms default when the asset value falls to somewhere between the value of total liabilities and the value of short-term debt. They call X the default point, calculated as short-term debt plus 50% of long-term debt.

7.1.4 Countrymetrics

Where countries are concerned, the Merton-based methodology is more difficult to apply because V_0 and σ_V are not observable and neither is C_0. However, Countrymetrics (www.countrymetrics.com) uses the Clark (1991, 2002) methodology to show how V_0 and σ_V can be calculated for a country. The estimation involves defining the economy's relevant cash flows in USD with respect to the balance of payments and discounting them back to the present at the economy's internal rate of return.

Consider the following notation:

EX = total exports not including investment income measured in USD
M = total imports not including investment income measured in USD
M^C = imports of final consumption goods measured in USD
CO = local consumption measured in USD
t = time
b = total income from the sale of the economy's output of final goods and services measured in USD
$b_t = EX_t + CO_t - M_t^C$
a = total expenditure by the economy for the purchase of final goods and services measured in USD
$a_t = M_t + CO_t - M_t^C$
$R = 1 + \rho$ where ρ represents the economy's internal rate of return
V_t = the international value of the economy's assets at the beginning of period t measured in USD

From the definitions of b and a it is clear that $b - a = EX - M$, the difference between exports and imports. This is important because the prices of exports and imports reflect international relative prices rather than domestic relative prices that can be distorted because of tariffs, subsidies and controls. The value of the economy in USD can be written as the present value of expected macroeconomic cash flows:

$$V_t = E\left[(b_t - a_t) + (b_{t+1} - a_{t+1})R^{-1} + \cdots + (b_n - a_n)R^{-(n-t)}\right] \qquad (7.5)$$

where all transactions take place on the first day of each period. It is interesting to see the relationship between this equation and the national accounts as they are usually presented. To see this, first calculate V_{t+1} and substitute into equation (7.5). Then multiply by $1 + r$ and rearrange. Ignoring interest on net exports, which disappears in continuous time, this gives:

$$EX_t - M_t + CO_t + (V_{t+1} - V_t) = \rho V_t + CO_t \qquad (7.6)$$

We recognize the left-hand side (LHS) of equation (7.6) as net domestic product where net investment in any year is equal to $V_{t+1} - V_t$. The right-hand side (RHS) is profits ρV_t plus cost (consumption) CO_t.

There are several ways to get an estimate of V_t. Since all the information in equation (7.6) is available in the national accounts, V_t can be estimated directly using the information in the national accounts. Another technique is to define a process for $(b - a)$, estimate the parameters of the process and calculate V_t from that.

Once a time series for the economy's international market value has been constructed, it can be used to estimate the economy's rate of return and its volatility (standard deviation). This information along with the risk-free rate on US treasuries or LIBOR, the nominal amount of foreign debt outstanding and its duration can then be used in equation (7.3) to estimate the default probability $N(-d_2)$.

The model can also be used to estimate three other important parameters: the theoretical financial risk premium, the maximum amount of foreign debt, and the economy's implied volatility (see Box 7.1). The theoretical financial risk premium is the difference between

---

Box 7.1   Using country implied volatility to analyze the Southeast Asian crisis of 1997

On 2 July 1997 the Thai baht was abruptly devalued by 20% despite weeks of desperate moves to prop up the currency, including central bank intervention of $8.7 billion on the spot market and $23 billion in forward contracts, interest rate increases from 12% to 18% and restrictions on foreign speculators. By the end of the year the baht crisis had spread around the world. The median devaluation of the five East Asian tigers hardest hit by the crisis – Indonesia, Korea, Malaysia, the Philippines and Thailand – was 80%. The International Finance Corporation's (IFC) emerging stock market index dropped by 20% between June and December and its Asian index fell by 53%. By the end of the year the baht had depreciated by 93%, the Hong Kong dollar, the Korean won and the Taiwan dollar were under attack and their stock markets were nose-diving, currencies and equity prices in Eastern Europe and Latin America were falling and in November, Korea, the world's eleventh largest economy and an OECD member country, became the recipient of the world's largest ever rescue package.

What happened? Conventional wisdom has it that in spite of a benign international background with high rates of growth in world trade and declining spreads on international borrowing, international investors suddenly awoke to the reality of structural weaknesses in the private financial sector, including resource misallocation and maturity and currency mismatches as well as public sector economic mismanagement regarding the exchange rate, financial regulation and implicit or explicit government guarantees. The rude awakening caused a crisis of confidence that the five countries, vulnerable because of the build-up of private sector, short-term, unhedged debt, were unable to overcome. Nevertheless, it is generally agreed that when the reckoning did come, the countries' underlying economic and financial situation did not warrant the humiliating treatment inflicted on them by the international financial markets. It is noted that public borrowing was subdued, most of the countries were running a fiscal surplus, inflation was low relative to most other developing countries and savings rates were high. With this in mind, conventional wisdom has it that the Asian crisis was another mindless overreaction by international investors.

There are several shortcomings to this attractive conventional view, which seems to fit the facts in general: (1) it fails to explain how otherwise sophisticated international investors could have remained oblivious so long to events that were known and had been developing over an extended period; (2) it also fails to explain what caused them to overreact when they finally did get wise; (3) it fails to explain what caused a crisis that was uniquely Asian in nature to spread to the other emerging markets in general, including those as far afield and economically different as Latin America and Eastern Europe. The information in the following table makes it possible to answer these questions.

Implied volatility of the Asian crisis countries 1993–1996

Year	1993	1994	1995	1996
Indonesia	55.0%	63.3%	56.2%	67.8%
Korea	77.7%	70.2%	67.9%	63.9%
Malaysia	43.6%	54.1%	47.0%	53.2%
Philippines	41.4%	49.8%	46.9%	46.2%
Thailand	63.3%	62.1%	56.5%	56.0%

Using the concept of implied country volatility suggests that markets were neither surprised nor overreacting. In the table above, we can observe that as far back as 1993, a year before the Mexican peso crisis, the market considered these countries as extremely risky with implied volatility ranging from 41% to 78%. When the peso crisis manifested itself in 1994, the markets were already expecting a large move in the Southeast Asian countries' economies. Furthermore, by 1996 implied volatility for Indonesia and Malaysia was at the levels reached at the height of the Mexican peso crisis in 1994. For Korea, Thailand and the Philippines, it had fallen only slightly. Over the whole period from 1993 to 1996, implied volatility rose for three countries (Indonesia, Malaysia and the Philippines) and fell for two (Korea and Thailand). These two countries that experienced a fall in their implied volatility were the two that had the highest implied volatilities in 1993. The reduction only brought them to the same level as the other three countries. All this suggests that as early as 1993 the market was anticipating the potential difficulties that would eventually materialize in 1997. It is interesting to note that Indonesia had the highest implied volatility on the eve of the crisis and was the country that suffered most when it hit. On the other hand, the Philippines had the lowest implied volatility and was the least affected.

the required rate of return estimated from the Black–Scholes formula and the riskless rate. It is the overall measure of the economy's creditworthiness. The maximum debt level indicates the amount of debt that equalizes the marginal cost of new borrowing with the economy's overall rate of return. A balance of payments crisis when the debt level is well below the maximum suggests that the problem is one of liquidity. When the debt level is close to or above the maximum, solvency is the problem. Implied volatility uses equation (7.3) with σ_V as the unknown to estimate the riskiness of the country's assets as reflected in bond prices traded on the market.

Example: The international value of the country's assets is $V_0 = \$100$ billion and $\sigma_V = 0.25$. The nominal amount of the country's external debt is $X = \$100$ billion with a duration $T = 5$ years. The zero coupon LIBOR rate on five-year USD is $r = 5\%$ per year. Using equation (7.3) gives $C_0 = \$32.23$ billion. The market value of the debt is $V_0 - C_0 = \$67.77$ billion. The distance to default, parameter d_2, is 0.1677 and the expected default frequency $N(-d_2) = 0.4298$. The theoretical financial risk premium can be calculated as $\ln(\$100/\$67.77)/5 - 0.05 = 0.0278$ and the total cost of the debt is 7.78%. Suppose that the rate of return on the country's assets is calculated from the historical data estimated from the foregoing model as $\rho = 7\%$. Since the required rate of return on the debt is higher than the return on the country's assets, this indicates that the country has a solvency problem. If we assume that to avoid insolvency the cost of debt should not exceed the return on assets, the maximum amount of debt that the country can carry can be found using equation (7.3) by holding the other parameters constant and letting X vary until the theoretical cost of debt falls to 7%. Using this methodology shows that the maximum debt level is about $88 billion. Implied volatility can also be calculated using equation (7.3). If the country's Brady bond debt is selling at 60% of its face value, the market value of the debt is $0.6 \times \$100$ billion $= \$60$ billion and the value of C_0 is $C_0 = V_0$ − market value of debt $= \$40$ billion. Using this in equation (7.3) with volatility as the unknown gives the implied volatility: implied $\sigma_V = 36.25\%$.

7.1.5 Loss Given Default

The loss given default refers to the loss that will be incurred if a default actually takes place. Going back to the example above, if the recovery rate is x, the loss given default rate is $(1-x)$ and the loss given default is $100(1 - x)$ with a present value of $100(1 - x)e^{-y_F T}$. The expected loss given default is equal to the probability of default multiplied by the present value of the loss given default $q(T) \times 100(1 - x)e^{-y_F T}$.

Example: We can go back to the example above, where $y_F(T) = 6\%$, $y(T) = 10\%$ and $T = 5$ years with the recovery rate $x = 20\%$. Using equation (7.2), the probability of default between year zero and year five was $q(T) = (1 - e^{-5[0.1-0.06]})/(1 - 0.2) = 22.66\%$. The expected loss given default is equal to $0.2266 \times 100 \times 0.8 \times e^{-5 \times 0.06} = 13.43$.

7.1.6 Credit Value at Risk

In Chapter 6 we defined value at risk as an estimate, with a given degree of confidence, of how much one can lose from one's portfolio over a given time horizon. Credit value at risk is an estimate, with a given degree of confidence, of how much one can lose from one's portfolio due to credit loss over a given time horizon. The time horizon for market risk is typically 10 days whereas for credit VaR the time horizon is typically one year. Remember that value at risk can be written as:

$$\text{Prob}[\delta V \leq -VaR] = 1 - c \qquad (7.7)$$

Credit losses occur when a counterparty defaults. They also occur when a counterparty is downgraded or when his creditworthiness degenerates. In the ratings terminology, a downgrade is called migration. To account for migration from one rating class to another, the rating agencies produce transition matrices based on historical data, which give the probability of a bond moving from one rating category to another. However, as we mentioned above, because of the infrequency of ratings changes, transition probabilities based on historical data are lower than in reality. The corollary of this is that the default probabilities are higher.

There are many ways to calculate credit VaR. CreditMetrics,[3] for example, relies on the estimation of the forward distribution of changes in the value of a portfolio of loans and bonds based on a rating system and the probabilities of migrating from one class to another, CreditRisk+ uses a Poisson distribution, and others use Monte Carlo simulations. In fact, the literature contains a wide range of parametric and non-parametric techniques for calculating credit VaR.

---

[3] CreditMetrics is a trademark of JP Morgan.

7.1.7   Credit VaR, Default Correlation and Contagion

As we showed in Chapter 6, VaR for portfolios of securities depends on the correlations between the different assets composing the portfolio. The same is true for credit VaR where the correlations refer to the tendency for two companies or countries to default at the same time. There are many reasons for default correlations. For example, countries in the same geographical region or producing the same type of commodities tend to be affected similarly by external events and as a result may experience financial difficulties at the same time. World economic conditions can also have similar effects on countries. In country risk analysis, the phenomenon of contagion figures prominently in the discussion of default correlations.

Generally speaking, contagion seems to refer to some kind of "excess" correlation between countries. Doukas (1989) defines contagion as the influence of news about the creditworthiness of a sovereign borrower on the spreads charged to the other sovereign borrowers, after controlling for country-specific macroeconomic fundamentals. Valdes (1997) defines contagion as excess co-movement in asset returns across countries. Eichengreen *et al.* (1996) define contagion as a situation where knowledge of a crisis in one country increases the probability of a crisis in another country above that warranted by the fundamentals.

There are several explanations to account for the tendency of country financial crises to occur in bunches. One explanation is based on the principal of "competitive devaluations" and holds that when countries trade with each other or compete in third markets, a devaluation in one country induces the other countries to devalue in order to remain competitive. Calvo (1998) explains contagion as a result of liquidity and asymmetric information, whereby a leveraged investor facing margin calls must sell his assets to uninformed investors who cannot distinguish between good assets and bad (lemons problem). A variant of this scenario is leveraged investors facing margin calls who sell assets whose price has not yet collapsed, thereby causing the collapse of these prices and spreading from market to market. Kaminsky and Reinhart (2000) emphasize the role of common lenders, such as commercial banks. In this explanation, the banks' need to rebalance their portfolios and recapitalize after initial losses causes an overall reduction in credit to most or all countries who rely on them for credit.

The most plausible family of contagion models focuses on the role of trade in financial assets and information asymmetries. Calvo and Mendoza (2000), for example, show how the costs of gathering and processing country risk information can cause herding behavior even among rational investors. Other models stress the role of cross-market hedging of macroeconomic risks by rational investors in the face of asymmetric information. In all these models the transmission channels for contagion are embedded in the international diversification of financial portfolios and the communication links that make them possible. The implication is that the financially open economies are more vulnerable to contagion, as are those whose asset returns are highly correlated with the original crisis country.

There are many ways to actually measure default correlations for countries. For example, in the Countrymetrics model presented above, default correlations between countries A and B can be introduced by calculating the historical correlation between the value of the two countries' assets. Another methodology obtains the correlations from the probability distribution of the time to default. In this methodology, an assumption is made about the joint distribution of the two countries' default probabilities. For example, if the joint distribution is assumed to be bivariate normal, the assumption is referred to as using a Gaussian copula.

7.2   INVESTMENT RISK

The orthodox theory of capital budgeting and investment under uncertainty taught in most business schools and economics departments revolves around the net present value (NPV) rule. According to this rule, expected flows of income and expenditure are estimated for each period and discounted at the appropriate rate. The present values for expenditure are then subtracted from the present values of income to find the NPV. Positive NPV indicates that the investment should be accepted, negative NPV that it should be rejected. There are three major methods for including country/political risk in the analysis. The first is to adjust the cash flows. The second is to adjust the discount rate. The third is to evaluate the project's NPV as if there were no political risk, quantify the political risk separately, and then subtract the quantified political risk from the project's NPV.

7.2.1   Adjusting the Expected Cash Flows

Adjusting the expected cash flows to account for political risk is a straightforward exercise. Let $u_t = $ a risk factor for year t that depends exclusively on the country where the investment is to be located with $0 < u < 1$. It can be interpreted as the probability that something bad *will not* happen. Suppose that in the absence of country-specific political risk, the expected net cash flow for year t is CF_t and the discount rate is R. With country-specific risk, the expected cash flow is reduced by $(1 - u_t)CF_t$ and the expected cash flow will be $u_t CF_t$. The project's NPV adjusted for political risk can thus be expressed as:

$$NPV = \sum_{t=0}^{n} u_t CF_t (1 + R)^{-t} \tag{7.8}$$

There is a theoretical difficulty with this method in that it assumes that political risk has no effect on the project's cost of capital. The practical difficulty is how to determine the u coefficients. Its advantage lies in the possibility of associating a specific coefficient with each period. This makes it possible to adapt the analysis so that it reflects the specific time profile of the country's political, social and economic cycles. For example, the u's in election years or renegotiation years for union contracts might be adjusted downward while in years when international agreements take effect it might be adjusted upward.

7.2.2   Adjusting the Discount Rate

The second way to include political risk in NPV analysis is to adjust the discount rate to reflect the incremental political risk. Let $\kappa = $ a risk factor that depends exclusively on the country in which the investment is to be located. It can be interpreted as the premium required to compensate the investor for the political risk. Also let $R = $ the project's required rate of return per period in the absence of the country-specific political risk. In the absence of country-specific political risk, the risk-adjusted discount factor is equal to $(1 + R)$. With country-specific political risk, the discount factor is adjusted to $(1 + R + \kappa)$. The project's NPV adjusted for political risk can thus be expressed as:

$$NPV = \sum_{t=0}^{n} CF_t (1 + R + \kappa)^{-t} \tag{7.9}$$

NPV will be smaller because the discount factor is larger. The question is how to determine k. A number of methods exist.

Determining the Required Rate of Return Using the CAPM

The most obvious method for calculating the required rate of return on an international investment is to use the Sharpe–Lintner–Mossin Capital Asset Pricing Model (CAPM) with an international market index denominated in a convertible currency, usually the USD:[4]

$$r_{aW} = r_F + \beta_W(r_W - r_F) \tag{7.10}$$

where r_{aW} is the required rate of return adjusted for systematic political risk, r_F is the risk-free rate of interest, r_W is the return on the world market portfolio and $\beta_W = \text{Cov}(r_a, r_W)/\text{Var}(r_W)$. The advantage of this procedure is that the CAPM is a centerpiece of economic evaluation, the formula is simple and, if implemented correctly, only systematic political risk would be captured. The disadvantages relate to the shortcomings of mean–variance analysis in general and the restrictive assumptions of the CAPM in particular. Furthermore, for equation (7.10) to give a reliable estimate of the required rate of return adjusted for political risk, all capital markets would have to be fully integrated. At the moment and for the foreseeable future, perfect market integration does not hold, especially for the emerging markets where political risk is most present.

A modified version of the CAPM developed by Bekaert and Harvey (1995) accounts for the possibility that markets are not fully integrated and that risk measures change over time. This time-varying, segmented/integrated solution to the problem proposes using the time-varying form of equation (7.10) if the country under consideration is fully integrated. If it is fully not integrated, the time-varying form of the traditional domestic CAPM should be used:

$$r_{aMt} = r_F + \beta_{Mt}(r_{Mt} - r_F) \tag{7.11}$$

where returns are measured in the same convertible currency, r_{aMt} is the required rate of return measured with the domestic index at time t and r_{Mt} is the return on the domestic market estimated at time t. If the country is only partially integrated, a combination of the two components should be used:

$$\bar{r}_a = \omega r_{aW} + (1 - \omega)r_{aM} \tag{7.12}$$

where $\bar{r}_a$ is the average required rate of return where the weight ω is time varying and determined by variables that proxy for the degree of integration such as the ratio of exports to GDP, market capitalization to GDP, etc.

Besides the problems with the CAPM in general, the problem with this model is that it is very difficult to implement in practice and it only works for countries with equity markets.

Ibbotsen Associates use an *ad hoc* adjustment to the world CAPM to estimate the required rate of return adjusted for political risk. Their methodology is to estimate the required rate of return using the world CAPM and then to add a risk premium estimated from the past performance of the country's market. The problem with this approach is that it is *ad hoc*.

The Goldman-Integrated methodology (see Mariscal and Lee, 1993) uses the CAPM to capture systematic operating risk. To reflect country risk, it adds the spread on a sovereign

---

[4] In Chapter 8, which deals with international portfolio analysis, we deal with the CAPM in more detail.

bond denominated in USD with respect to a US treasury of the same maturity. It has the advantage of being simple and straightforward to implement.

Credit Suisse First Boston (CSFB) has used a model that combines the yield on Brady bonds along with the US risk premium, the country beta and two constants of adjustment, one for relative coefficients of variation and the other for the interdependence between the risk-free rate and the equity premium. This model has no economic intuition or theoretical underpinning.

7.2.3 The Macro CAPM

The foregoing models for estimating the required rate of return that includes country risk depend on the existence of functioning equity markets and/or Brady bond spreads. They also depend on the degree to which the equity markets are integrated. The Macro CAPM of CreditMetrics uses the Clark (1991, 2002) methodology to estimate the country risk-adjusted required rate of return that is not constrained by the existence of certain markets or an estimation of their integration or degree of segmentation.

Equation (7.5) gives the international market value of an economy at the beginning of period t. Thus, the world index at time t is simply the sum of the capital values in dollars of all the individual national economies from 1 to m:

$$I_t = \sum_{i=1}^{m} V_{it} \qquad (7.13)$$

where I is the world index.

Let R_{wt} represent the return on this world index for period t. Since, at the world level, total exports equal total imports, the return on the world index is:

$$R_{wt} = \frac{I_t}{I_{t-1}} - 1 \qquad (7.14)$$

This index can then be used to calculate the risk-adjusted required rate of return on the country's overall economy:

$$\bar{R}_C = r_F + \beta_C(\bar{R}_W - r_F) \qquad (7.15)$$

where $\bar{R}_C$ is the required rate of return on the country's assets and β_C is the country's beta. Presented this way $\bar{R}_C$ includes all systematic risk, including systematic country/political risk.

The return on the country's international value can be used to capture the systematic risk if the investment with respect to the national economy is

$$\bar{R}_i = r_F + \beta_i(\bar{R}_C - r_F) \qquad (7.16)$$

where $\bar{R}_i$ is the required rate of return on asset i.

Substituting equation (7.15) into (7.16) gives the required rate of return with respect to the world index:

$$\bar{R}_i = r_F + \beta_i\beta_C(\bar{R}_W - r_F) \qquad (7.17)$$

Example: r_F = the three-month treasury bill rate = 6%, $\bar{R}_W$ = 10%, β_i = 1.2, β_C = 1.5. Using equation (7.17), the required rate of return on investment i in country C is: $\bar{R}_i$ = 6% + (1.2)(1.5)[10% − 6%] = 13.2%.

The advantage of this methodology is that all calculations are carried out in international relative prices and the index includes all cash flows accruing to all capital, physical, commercial and human. Thus, it is the most general market index. The disadvantage is the difficulty of calculating the individual country market values (V). The methodology has shown itself to be effective in forecasting high-performing, international portfolios of money market assets, long-term government bonds and market indices as well as sovereign debt defaults and reschedulings (Clark, 2002, pp. 350–354).

7.2.4   Measuring Political Risk as an Insurance Premium

The third approach for incorporating country/political risk in the NPV was developed by Clark (1997, 1998). It involves measuring the effects of political risk on the outcome of a foreign direct investment as the value of an insurance policy that reimburses all losses resulting from the political event or events in question. It makes a distinction between explicit events and ongoing change. Explicit events take the form of legislation or decrees such as expropriations, nationalizations, devaluations, etc. or the form of direct actions such as strikes, boycotts, terrorist acts, etc. The nature of explicit events is that they arrive intermittently at discrete intervals and that they generate an actual loss. Explicit events can be represented by a Poisson jump process. Ongoing change takes the form of continuous activity such as macroeconomic management and monetary policy, legislation, or social and political evolution that affects some or all aspects of the FDI's overall environment. Thus, in this model, ongoing change impacts on the level of what can be lost in the case of an explicit event and can be represented by geometric Brownian motion.

To see how this works, let x follow geometric Brownian motion and represent the exposure to loss in the case of an explicit political event:

$$dx(t) = (\alpha + \beta)x(t)dt + \sigma x(t)dz(t) \qquad (7.18)$$

where α is the rate of growth of the intensity of political risk with $\alpha < 0$; $\alpha > 0$; $\alpha = 0$. It measures the intensity of the political environment surrounding the particular risk in question. The interpretation of α is that as the intensity of the political risk increases, the severity or cost of the measures undertaken will be increased when an explicit event does occur. If $\alpha < 0$, the intensity of the political risk in question is expected to be declining on the average; if $\alpha > 0$, it is expected to be increasing on the average; if $\alpha = 0$, it is expected to remain the same.

β is the rate of growth of the investment and depends on the investment's internal rate of return and the rate of reinvestment out of profits. $dz(t)$ is a Wiener process with zero mean and variance equal to dt. σ^2 is the variance of $dx(t)/x(t)$ due to political risk. σ^2 can be interpreted as the level of the political risk.

Equation (7.18) says that exposure to political risk is expected to change at a rate of $\alpha + \beta$, the rate of growth of political intensity plus the rate of growth of the value of the investment, with a standard deviation due to political risk of σ times the random element in ongoing change represented by the Wiener process, $z(t)$.

Suppose that political events occur at random times according to an independent Poisson arrival process where q is a random variable that increases by steps of u every time a Poisson event occurs and λ is a constant intensity parameter such that:

$$dq(t) = \begin{cases} 1 & \text{with probability} \quad \lambda dt \\ 0 & \text{with probability} \quad 1 - \lambda dt \end{cases}$$

This means that losses arrive at a rate of λdt and that λ is the political risk probability parameter, that is, the probability that a loss-causing political event will actually occur over the interval dt.

If $x(t)$ represents the potential loss when a Poisson event occurs, the expected loss per interval dt is equal to $\lambda x(t)dt$. In the more advanced forms of the model, λ itself can be a random variable or even a dependent stochastic process.

To measure the cost of country/political risk we put this together and let W represent the value of a hypothetical insurance policy covering the investment against losses arising from the political risk so that when losses occur, they are reimbursed by the insurance. The expected total return on the insurance policy is equal to $E(dW)$ plus the expected cash flow generated by the explicit event, $\lambda x(t)dt$. Assume risk neutrality and a constant risk-free interest rate r, apply Ito's lemma and take expectations. This gives the following differential equation:

$$\frac{1}{2}\sigma^2 x(t)^2 W''(x(t)) + W'(x(t))(\alpha + \mu)x(t) - rW(x(t)) + \lambda x(t) = 0 \qquad (7.19)$$

where the primes denote first and second derivatives.

The solution to this equation depends on the values of the various parameters and the boundary conditions associated with each investment. For example, if we rule out speculative bubbles and assume that the policy has no value when there is nothing at risk, the value of the policy covering a series of losses is:

$$W = \frac{\lambda x(t)}{r - (\alpha + \mu)} \qquad (7.20)$$

The value of a policy covering expropriation is:

$$W = \frac{\lambda x(t)}{r + \lambda - (\alpha + \mu)} \qquad (7.21)$$

Once political risk quantified as the value of the insurance policy has been estimated, it can be integrated into the capital budgeting process in a two-step methodology:

1. Estimate the NPV of the project in the absence of political risk.
2. Subtract the value of the insurance policy from the project's NPV in the absence of political risk. This gives $NPV - W$, the net present value of the investment adjusted for political risk.

This methodology has the advantage of being theoretically consistent with modern portfolio theory. It also avoids the difficulty of forecasting risk parameters far into the future. In its more advanced forms, the policy can be valued to reflect various options available to managers, such as the option to abandon the project if things go badly. It can also be valued to reflect the change from one level of political risk to another, such as the case of South Africa from white to black rule or Hong Kong from British to Chinese rule (Clark, 1998). The political risk parameter, λ, can also be modeled to reflect uncertainty about the risk parameter itself and to be re-estimated in an endogenous Bayesian updating process. The difficulty lies in estimating the relevant parameters.

Example: The amount of the investment is $100 million and its risk-neutral growth rate is zero: $\mu = 0$. The risk-free rate can be observed: $r = 5\%$, the interest rate on a 30-year US government STRIPS (Separately Traded Registered Interest and Principal Security). The country risk analysts estimate that the probability of an expropriation is 0.02: $\lambda = 0.02$. In case of an expropriation, they estimate the recovery rate at 20%: $x = (1 - 0.2) \times \$100 = \$80$. They also estimate the risk-neutral change in the political climate as equal to zero: $\alpha = 0$.

Using this information in equation (7.21) gives:

$$W = \frac{0.02 \times \$80}{0.05 + 0.02 - (0 + 0)} = \$22.86$$

Suppose that the NPV of the investment in the absence of expropriation risk is $20 million. The NPV adjusted for political risk is $20 - \$22.86 = -\$2.86$ and should not be undertaken.

REFERENCES

Bekaert G and Harvey CR, 1995, Time Varying World Market Integration. *Journal of Finance*, 50, 403–44.

Black F and Scholes M, 1973, The Pricing of Options and Corporate Liabilities. *Journal of Political Economy*, 81, 637–59.

Calvo GA, 1998, Varieties of Capital Market Crises. *In:* GA Calvo and M King, eds. *The Debt Burden and its Consequences for Monetary Policy*. New York: Macmillan Press.

Calvo GA and Mendoza E, 2000, Rational Contagion and the Globalization of Securities Markets. *Journal of International Economics*, 51, 79–113.

Carleton WT and Cooper IA, 1976, Estimation and Uses of Term Structure of Interest Rates. *The Journal of Finance*, 31 (4), 1067–83.

Chambers DR, Carleton WT and Waldman DW, 1984, A New Approach to Estimation of the Term Structure of Interest Rates. *Journal of Financial and Quantitative Analysis*, 19 (3), 233–52.

Clark E, 1991, *Cross Border Investment Risk*. London: Euromoney Publications.

Clark E, 1997, Valuing Political Risk. *Journal of International Money and Finance*, 16, 477–90.

Clark E, 1998, Political Risk in Hong Kong and Taiwan: Pricing the China Factor. *Journal of Economic Integration*, 13 (2) 278–93.

Clark E, 2002, *International Finance*. London: Thomson.

Crouhy M, Galai D and Mark R, 2000, A Comparative Analysis of Current Credit Risk Models. *Journal of Banking and Finance*, 24, 59–117.

Doukas J, 1989, Contagion Effect on Sovereign Interest Rate Spreads. *Economic Letters*, 29, 237–41.

Eichengreen B, Rose A and Wyplosz C, 1996, *Contagious Currency Crises*, NBER Working Paper no. 5681. Cambridge, MA: National Bureau of Economic Research.

Kaminsky G and Reinhart CM, 2000, On Crises, Contagion and Confusion. *Journal of International Economics*, 51, 145–68.

Mariscal JO and Lee RM, 1993, *The Valuation of Mexican Stocks: An Extension of the Capital Asset Pricing Model to Emerging Markets*, Goldman Sachs.

Mastronikola K, 1991, *Yield Curves For Gilt Edged Stocks: A New Model*, Bank of England Discussion Paper (Technical Series) no. 49.

McCulloch HJ, 1971, Measuring the Term Structure of Interest Rates. *Journal of Business*, 44, 19–31.

Merton R, 1974, On the Pricing of Corporate Debt: The Risk Structure of Interest Rates. *Journal of Finance*, 29, 449–70.

Schaefer SM, 1981, Measuring a Tax-Specific Structure of Interest Rates in the Markets for British Government Securities. *The Economic Journal*, 91, 415–38.

Shea GS, 1985, Term Structure Estimations with Exponential Splines. *The Journal of Finance*, 40 (1), 319–25.

Valdes, RO, 1997, Emerging Markets Contagion: Evidence and Theory, Working Paper no. 7. Santiago: Banco Central de Chile.

Vasicek OA and Fong HG, 1982, Term Structure Modeling Using Exponential Splines. *The Journal of Finance*, 37 (2), 339–48.

8
International Portfolio Investment
Analysis

This chapter addresses the issue of country risk from a portfolio investment perspective, meaning investment in foreign stock markets or fixed income instruments. It is essentially concerned with financial investment as opposed to productive investment, based on well-established principles of modern financial theory. However, this approach is in no way restricted to financial portfolio flows, and can be applied to foreign direct investment in the same way that modern portfolio theory is applied to capital budgeting in a purely domestic context.

Country risk can constitute a significant amount of the overall risk for a portfolio invested abroad. Besides currency risk associated with fluctuations in the exchange rate, local characteristics in the political, macroeconomic or microeconomic fields can also affect the outcome of the investment. The various country risk assessment methods analyzed previously in this book could possibly be pertinent in this portfolio investment framework. However, the objective of this chapter is not to present them again, but rather to investigate how the specific methodology developed in modern financial theory can be extended to incorporate country risk. Indeed, as we showed in Chapter 7, it can provide an interesting alternative approach for estimating country risk, and can be extended to international capital budgeting. This is the path followed, for instance, by Deloitte & Touch Consulting Group, "to help telecommunications carriers and equipment vendors think like portfolio managers before jumping at cross-border opportunities in the burgeoning but risky international telecommunications marketplace" (Mooney, 1999). In this chapter we show how mean/variance portfolio analysis has been extended and applied to international portfolios.

8.1 MODERN FINANCIAL THEORY

This section briefly introduces modern financial theory and presents its main results, that subsequently will be used in an international framework for estimating country risk.

Quite surprisingly, the foundations of modern financial theory did not start in post-World War II America, but were conceived at the very beginning of the twentieth century in France by Bachelier (1900). This mathematician was the first to argue that asset price changes followed a random walk and as such could not be predicted. However, although the price changes could not be predicted, he found it possible to estimate their variability and consequently he decided to focus on their probability distribution. Therefore, he did not try to anticipate the direction of the prices but only investigated the way that price changes were distributed. He assumed that price changes were only caused by the random arrival of new independent bits of information. Thus, based on the central limit theorem,[1] he estimated that price variations should follow a normal (Gaussian) distribution. Instead of trying to forecast the evolution of something

---

[1] The central limit theorem stipulates that the sum of independent and identically distributed random variables, with a mean and a variance, tends toward the normal Laplace–Gauss probability law.

Figure 8.1   MSCI World stock market index 1969–1997

he thought unpredictable, he rather decided to approach the problem from a probabilistic perspective.

Figures 8.1 to 8.3 illustrate this approach. Figure 8.1 represents the evolution of the MSCI All Country World index[2] from 1969 to 1997. Figure 8.2 shows its monthly price changes,[3] and Figure 8.3 compares the distribution of the MSCI price changes with the normal distribution. As Figure 8.3 illustrates, at first glance, the normal distribution hypothesis (the bell curve) does not seem too far from the real world.

According to Bachelier's approach, since price changes follow a random path, it is impossible and useless to try to predict their evolution. Nevertheless, assuming they are normally distributed, it is possible to fully describe their behavior in probabilistic terms, with only two criteria: the mean and the variance of the Gaussian distribution. The mean corresponds to the expected price change (or return) of the asset. The variance determines the dispersion around the mean and, as such, measures the risk of the asset. Thus, in this mean/variance framework, any investment is completely characterized and must be analyzed according to a return/risk approach. This constitutes the cornerstone of the modern financial theory.

In 1952, working in this framework, Markowitz (1952) founded the basis of modern portfolio theory and established the rules of diversification. He showed how to reduce the overall risk of an investment by creating portfolios made of assets with low correlation between their returns. While the expected return of a portfolio $E(r_p)$ is simply the weighted average of the expected returns $E(r_i)$ of the individual assets, as reflected in equation (8.1), he demonstrated that its total risk depends on the individual risk of each asset, represented by the variance σ_i^2, as well as by the degree of interdependence between the returns on individual assets, represented by

---

[2] The MSCI All Country World index covers stock markets of 49 developed and emerging countries.
[3] More precisely it is the logarithm of the price changes that should follow a normal law, as Osborne (1959) demonstrated.

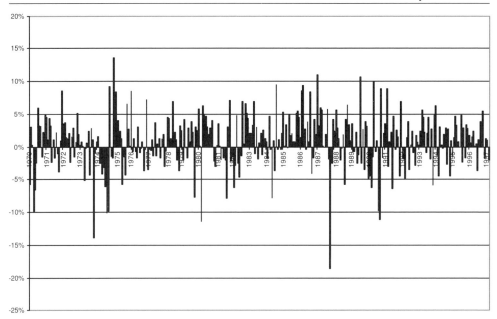

Figure 8.2 Monthly price changes of the MSCI World index 1969–1997

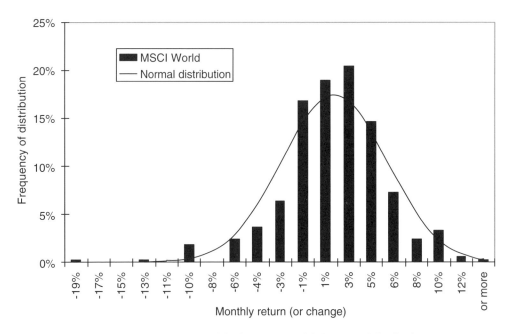

Figure 8.3 Comparison of the MSCI World price changes with the normal distribution

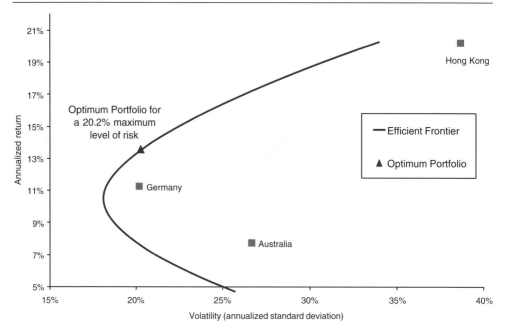

Figure 8.4 Example of an efficient frontier

the covariance σ_{ij} in equation (8.2).[4]

$$E(r_p) = \sum_{i=1}^{n} x_i E(r_i) \tag{8.1}$$

$$\sigma_p^2 = \sum_{i=1}^{n} x_i^2 \sigma_i^2 + \sum_{i=1}^{n} \sum_{\substack{j=1 \\ j \neq i}}^{n} x_i x_j \sigma_{ij} \tag{8.2}$$

Consequently, depending on the correlation between asset returns, the risk of a portfolio can be substantially reduced, and the risk/return trade-off dramatically improved. Indeed, if two assets are not perfectly correlated, when one drops, the other may rise and at least partially offset the negative impact of the former. Going further, Markowitz (1952) found the optimum portfolios, those that minimize the risk for a given expected return, or alternatively that maximize the expected return for a given level of risk. The whole set of these optimum portfolios was called the efficient frontier. It is composed of the best choices in a risk/return trade-off and is represented by the upper edge of a parabolic curve (see Figure 8.4).

Imagine, for example, that we have the opportunity to invest in the Australian, German and Hong Kong stock markets (see Figure 8.4). Based on MSCI historical data in Table 8.1, we can expect a long-term annual return of 7.7%, 11.2% and 20.2% respectively and a volatility of 26.7%, 20.2% and 38.7%. However these three portfolios are not necessarily optimum and, following Markowitz (1952), if we mix these assets appropriately, it is possible to optimize our investment to reach a point on the efficient frontier.

---

[4] σ_i^2 is the variance of the returns for the asset i and σ_{ij} is the covariance between the returns of the assets i and j.

Table 8.1 Risk/return trade-off for various portfolios

Portfolio	Return	Risk
Australia	7.7%	26.7%
Germany	11.2%	20.2%
Hong Kong	20.2%	38.7%
Efficient "triangle" portfolio	13.5%	20.2%

Assume, for instance, that we are ready to accept no more than 20.2% of risk.[5] By investing our entire portfolio in the German stock market, this constraint would be respected and an 11.2% return could be expected. However, this solution does not constitute the best choice. The efficient frontier shows that for the same level of risk (a 20.2% volatility), if we invest in the portfolio identified by the triangle on the graph, we could expect a higher yield of 13.5%. Some relatively simple calculations can give the exact components of the portfolio "triangle", which actually includes 3% Australia, 69% Germany and 27% Hong Kong.

Building on these foundations and assuming, among others, that every investor is Markowitz efficient in a mean/variance framework, Sharpe (1964) and Lintner (1965) almost simultaneously derived the Capital Asset Pricing Model (CAPM). The CAPM establishes that if we consider a portfolio investment made of several securities, rather than a single asset, the true relevant measure of risk is not given by the variance of its returns (σ_i^2) but by its contribution to the overall risk of the market portfolio, which is composed of all the available investable assets in proportion to their market capitalization. The impact of a specific investment on the overall risk of the market portfolio is determined by its so-called beta coefficient, which is given by the formula

$$\beta_i = \frac{\sigma_{im}}{\sigma_m^2} \tag{8.3}$$

where σ_{im} is the covariance of the returns of asset i with those of the market portfolio and σ_m^2 is the variance of the returns on the market portfolio.

More specifically, the CAPM states that $E(r_i)$, the expected return of any asset i, is a function of its beta β_i multiplied by the market risk premium $[E(r_M) - r_f]$ plus the risk-free rate r_f:

$$E(r_i) = r_f + \beta_i \lfloor E(r_m) - r_f \rfloor \tag{8.4}$$

Equation (8.4), represented graphically in Figure 8.5, is called the security market line (SML). Thus, the expected return of any security should depend only on its level of systematic risk as given by the beta coefficient, which represents the only relevant measure of risk for any asset. In this framework, an investment opportunity is fully described and must be analyzed as a function of beta and expected return.

The development of the CAPM shook up the portfolio management industry and caused some fundamental changes. Although empirical results were sometimes controversial and not always conclusive, this approach gained widespread support in the academic and professional worlds, and many investors adopted it in their day-to-day business. Consequently, modern financial theory provides some powerful tools to deal with international portfolio investment and with country risk in a broader perspective. It demonstrates the usefulness of reasoning in a

---

[5] Measured by the annualized standard deviation also called volatility and that corresponds to the square root of the variance.

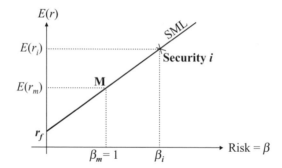

Figure 8.5   Expected return, beta coefficient and the security market line

risk/return trade-off. What really matters is not the risk itself, but rather how it compares with the expected return. In addition, it offers the beta as an analytical tool to estimate the level of risk.

8.2   INTERNATIONAL PORTFOLIO INVESTMENT AND COUNTRY RISK MANAGEMENT

8.2.1   The International Portfolio Investment Panorama

International portfolio investment is a key feature of the 1990s and, for the G7 countries, is estimated to have grown from 2% to 3% of GDP from the 1970s through the mid-1980s, up to more than 10% of GDP in recent years (Bank of Japan, 1999). It represents an important share of total cross-border investment, and has varied over the last decade between 9% and 53% of all private flows to developing countries (see Figure 8.6).

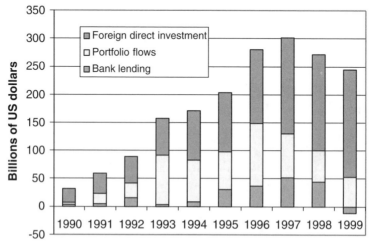

Source: World Bank Debtor Reporting System.

Figure 8.6   International private capital flows for developing countries

Since the advent of economic liberalism as the new world economic paradigm, and with the collapse of the Soviet Union, the case for international portfolio investment has been magnified by the implementation and development of new capital markets all over the world. Indeed, this expansion has diluted the relative weight of the major financial centers and induced the emergence of significant alternative investment opportunities in the international arena. For example, according to Brinson Partners (in Reilly and Brown, 2000), in 1969 the USA represented about two-thirds of the total investable capital markets. This share has fallen to less than half at the end of the 1990s. While 30 years ago, it was conceivable for an American investor, to reason on a strictly US basis, it now seems much more questionable to ignore at least 50% of the world.

8.2.2   Impact of Country Risk on International Portfolio Investment

The importance of country risk for an international portfolio investment has been demonstrated by many researchers. Some authors such as Erb *et al.* (1995, 1996b) or Diamonte and Liew (1996) explicitly investigate the influence of country risk on stock market returns. They show that specific country risk measures, such as those presented in Chapter 5 (ICRG, PRS, *Institutional Investor*), explain a large amount of the price changes. Based on these results Erb *et al.* (1996b) derive some successful, *a posteriori* trading strategies using the information embedded in these ratings. Madura *et al.* (1997) confirm these findings and conclude that "the most relevant variable for explaining disparate returns across markets is country risk". Erb *et al.* (1996a) or Fischer (1999) extend the investigation to fixed income instruments. Similarly, Scholtens (1999) studies the relationship between Eurobond yield spreads as provided by the secondary market, and country ratings. His research also indicates a strong impact of country risk on the interest rates paid by these assets.

Others, such as Agmon (1973), Lessard (1976), Solnik and de Freitas (1988), Beckers and Connor (1996) or Griffin and Stulz (2001), analyze the relative importance of domestic factors versus industry and global factors in the determination of returns. Most of them establish that markets are driven mainly by local factors. The explanatory power of local factors is up to four times higher than that of the industry. Rouwenhorst (1999) even ascertains that, as of 1998, the European integration process had not reduced the country effects within the EMU. Although Barnes *et al.* (2001) note a growing weight of the sector impact over the period 1992–2000, it is fairly limited to the technology/telecommunications stocks, and is probably due to the global asset bubble experienced by this industry over the period under consideration. Barnes *et al.* (2001) recognize that even in the Eurozone, country factors remain significant, and attribute this result to "rigid labor markets, linguistic and cultural differences, and the absence of tax and accounting harmonization". Furthermore, most empirical evidence indicates that the low correlation between countries is mainly the result of socio-political and economic features, and not the consequence of a possible industrial specialization. Financial assets behave differently from country to country because of socio-political and economic differences not because of country-specific sector specialization.

A third stream of research by Aliber (1973, 1975), Dooley and Isard (1980) or Dooley *et al.* (1995) focuses on the foreign exchange market. They study deviations from interest rate parity due to political risk, and country-specific shocks to exchange rates. They explicitly include country risk as a key determinant of their pricing model.

All this research points in the same direction and demonstrates that financial asset returns, whether in the equity, fixed income or foreign exchange markets, are strongly affected by country-specific factors. Choosing the right country is much more crucial than picking the

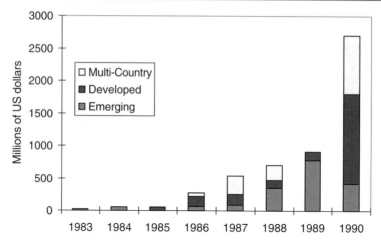

Source: Diwan *et al.* (1994). Reproduced by permission of Euromoney Institutional Investors PLC.
Note: The term "Emerging market" usually refers to those markets located in the low or middle-income economies as defined by the World Bank, meaning in 1999 a GNI per capita lower than $9266 (Standard & Poor's, 2001).

Figure 8.7   Launching of New Country Funds in New York

best stock, bond or currency. Country risk has a major impact on the return of cross-border financial investments. Therefore, this pleads in favor of a global top-down asset allocation, that should first concentrate on assessing the country risk/return trade-off, as opposed to a bottom-up approach that is primarily concerned with the characteristics of the individual assets. When considering international investment portfolios, country risk still appears as the main driving factor.

8.2.3   International Diversification

Since returns are strongly influenced by country-specific elements and because country-specific elements are often unrelated from country to country, the degree of cross-country correlation is often relatively low as well. Moreover, because of the diversification principle presented above, it seems obvious that investors and academics would be keen to pursue international portfolio diversification. Nonetheless, at the time of the Markowitz (1952) article, this was apparently not that straightforward. It was more than 15 years after he published his seminal paper that researchers like Grubel (1968), Levy and Sarnat (1970) or Lessard (1973) started to consider international diversification. In fact, Grubel (1968) noted: "Strangely, however, the analysis has not yet been applied explicitly to the explanation of long-term asset holdings that include claims denominated in foreign currency." Similarly, on the professional side, although a pioneer like Templeton had already massively invested abroad as early as the 1960s,[6] he remained an exception for many years, especially in the USA. It was only from the end of the 1980s that investors began to think about investing abroad. As a matter of fact, a sizeable part of the move to international investment can be attributed to the growing possibilities of investing via country funds[7] (see Figure 8.7).

---

[6] See, for example, Berryessa and Kirzner (1988).

[7] Country funds are some investment funds dedicated to a specific geographical area. Being listed in the home country of the investor they represent an easy way to invest abroad.

Table 8.2 Domestic ownership shares
of the world's five largest stock markets

France	89.4%
Germany	79%
Japan	95.7%
UK	92%
USA	92.2%

Source: French and Poterba (1991).

This bias of domestic investment to the detriment of international diversification is not US-specific. As shown in Table 8.2, it is shared by many other countries. Several authors, such as French and Poterba (1991) or Cooper and Kaplanis (1994), looked at this issue and concluded that investors generally have a costly home bias in their portfolio and could reach a more optimal risk/return combination by investing abroad.

The reluctance to invest overseas can be explained by an accrued perception of risk. One source of this risk is currency risk. Wide fluctuations in the exchange rate may increase the volatility[8] of a foreign asset when expressed in domestic currency. For instance, over the period 1990–1996, the US stock market index SP500 displayed a risk of 12% in US dollars, but around 16.5% when measured in German marks, French francs, pounds sterling or Japanese yen. Studying this additional volatility due to exchange risk, Eun and Resnick (1988) still advocate international portfolio diversification, even after including this supplementary source of uncertainty. However, they recommend hedging against it.

Other types of risk, such as those listed in Chapter 2, also apply to international financial investment. Regulations may fluctuate and induce supplementary costs. Foreign exchange controls or foreign ownership restrictions may be implemented. The fiscal environment may change. Controls and law enforcement may be weak. Local counterparts may be less reliable or financially sound. Delivery and settlement procedures may be less secure. Information and disclosure requirements can prove unreliable or incomplete. Liquidity can be highly variable, and can narrow very rapidly in bear markets, thereby preventing any rapid exit from the market. All these uncertainties can generate a substantial amount of additional risk, which could explain why investors tend to stay at home.

Yet, even after considering these potential drawbacks, many researchers still support an international portfolio diversification. Indeed, although some countries may appear as very high risk when taken individually, thanks to their low correlation with the rest of the world, they may induce some additional diversification gains. As a consequence, they make it possible to significantly reduce the overall risk of the portfolio. This is especially the case for the supposedly very risky emerging markets. Because their political and economic situation is largely different from those found in developed countries, their financial markets do behave in their own way and are fairly independent of the most developed countries. Consequently, in spite of their inherently high volatility, their inclusion in an international portfolio makes it possible to appreciably improve the risk/return trade-off. As we can see in Figure 8.8, emerging markets[9] taken individually present a high degree of risk, and are located at the right-hand side of the graph. However, when included in a global portfolio, their low correlation with the other countries moves the efficient frontier to the left. Thus, adding a bit of emerging markets

---

[8] The volatility is a measure of risk and corresponds to the annualized variance of the (logarithmic) returns.

[9] For example India, Korea, Thailand, Zimbabwe.

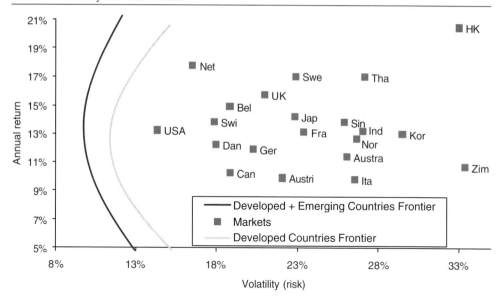

Figure 8.8 Efficient frontier without and with emerging markets

can dramatically improve the portfolio's risk/return trade-off. This is the stance followed by Errunza (1977), Divecha *et al.* (1992), Speidell and Sappenfield (1992), Cosset and Suret (1995) or Harvey (1995).

In corporate finance, many firms pursue such a strategy of geographical diversification. For instance, the German worldwide leader in cement, HeidelbergCement (2001), declares that: "Through a targeted geographical diversification, we make use of the opportunities identified in mature markets and the potential offered by growth markets". As evidence of the effectiveness of this strategic positioning, the company explains in its 2001 annual report that: "HeidelbergCement was able to limit the effects of the world-wide economic downturn due to its balanced international presence" (HeidelbergCement, 2002). Indeed, the firm is located in 50 countries, representing both developed and emerging markets. In 2001, it experienced a sharp increase of revenues in Eastern Europe and in the Africa–Asia–Turkey area, which partly offset some disappointing figures in the rest of the world.

8.2.4 International Capital Asset Pricing Model

The CAPM presented above holds that under certain conditions, beta rather than variance is the relevant measure of risk. Beta measures the impact of an asset with respect to the market portfolio. Under some restrictive assumptions, this model can be extended without any modification to the international context. Indeed, assuming that all investors share the same consumption basket, and that purchasing power parity holds all over the world,[10] the CAPM holds and the market portfolio is composed of all possible assets in the world.

In reality, it has been shown that, at least over the short term, purchasing power deviates from parity and international investors face some real exchange risk.[11] To account for this, Solnik

---

[10] Meaning that real prices are the same throughout the world.
[11] See for instance Adler and Dumas (1983).

(1974) developed the International Capital Asset Pricing Model (ICAPM). In this framework, the expected return of an asset is still a function of its beta with the market portfolio, but in addition, it also depends on the currency risk premia RP_k [equation (8.5)], that reflects the exposure to exchange risk:

$$E(r_i) = r_f + \beta_i[E(r_m) - r_f] + \sum_{k=1}^{K} \gamma_{ik} RP_k \qquad (8.5)$$

So far, the aforementioned CAPM and ICAPM assume static, constant relationships between the variables. However, we can reasonably assume that the level of risk is likely to be time-fluctuating, depending for example on the economic cycle. To take this into consideration, a dynamic version of the CAPM, called conditional CAPM, was developed by authors such as Gibbons and Ferson (1985) or Harvey (1989).

Whether unconditional or time-dependent, all these various ICAPMs imply an international market integration, with every security in the world freely tradeable by any investor. When investment barriers restrict the access to the capital markets for foreign investors, these models no longer apply. In the case of international market segmentation, as we pointed out in Chapter 7, a national CAPM is then more relevant, and the local securities should be priced according to the national market portfolio. Therefore, at the international level, the betas cannot be a correct measure of risk when markets are segmented. They must either be replaced by the variance of the returns or by another measure that captures systematic risk, such as the Macro CAPM by CreditMetrics.

The most sophisticated versions of the ICAPM were tested among others by Harvey (1991), Bekaert and Harvey (1995), Dumas and Solnik (1995) or De Santis and Gerard (1997). They tend to support the view of international integrated capital markets. When limited to the developed countries, the international beta is able to explain a significant amount of the changes in the return and seems to account for a good proportion of international portfolio investment risk. However, the ICAPM is far less conclusive for the developing markets. Bekaert and Harvey (1995) include some emerging countries in their analysis and find that some of them are segmented. In this case, Harvey (2000) shows that variance as a measure of risk does a much better job than beta in explaining the variations in expected returns.

It appears, then, that at least for the developed countries, the ICAPM provides a valid method for estimating the level of systematic risk, measured by beta, that includes the element of country risk. It can also be used as an indication of the minimum cost of capital, and serve as a hurdle rate for investment projects in corporate finance. However, for emerging countries, this model seems unable to discriminate between expected returns. This result makes sense if we think that these markets are not fully integrated into the world capital markets. Indeed, the presence of explicit or implicit investment barriers such as those documented by Demirgüç-Kunt and Huizinga (1994) or Bekaert (1995) pleads in favor of an at least partial segmentation in these countries. In this situation, another model, such as Clark's (1991, 2002) Macro CAPM or Bekaert and Harvey's (1995) weighted CAPM/ICAPM, is more accurate. The simple variance can also be used as an alternative measure of risk for these segmented countries.

8.3 THE LIMITS OF THE ICAPM

Although modern portfolio theory appears as a fruitful approach for tackling the issue of country risk for an international investment portfolio as well as for dealing with the international cost of capital in corporate finance, it does have some drawbacks that need to be clarified and investigated, in order to fully understand the limits of the mean/variance models.

8.3.1 The Normal Distribution

Because of the user-friendliness of the mean/variance framework, all the major discoveries of modern financial theory were initially based on the hypothesis of normally distributed returns. However, this Gaussian assumption is not universally accepted and was challenged as early as the 1960s by scholars like Mandelbrot (1963) or Fama (1965b), who favored a more general class of probability laws, known as stable distributions. Indeed, in most markets, returns tend to exhibit a leptokurtic shape with much fatter tails than supposed in the Gaussian case. This demonstrates a higher variability with large movements occurring much more frequently than what is implied by the normal distribution.

Harvey (1995) tested the Gaussian hypothesis for three developed and 20 emerging countries. Among the latter, and contrary to the three developed markets (Japan, UK and USA), normality was rejected in 14 cases. Following the approach of Mandelbrot (1963), Groslambert and Kassibrakis (1999) investigated the stable distribution hypothesis as an alternative to the normal hypothesis. They found that: "Due to their specific features [emerging markets] diverge much more strongly from the Gaussian distribution." They seem to follow probability laws with a much higher variability than the developed markets, whose distribution is not too far from the normal one. Groslambert and Kassibrakis (1999) concluded that: "The fund management industry must adopt a specific and dedicated approach when investing in emerging markets. It cannot apply the 'almost Gaussian' tools that it can use in the 'almost Gaussian' developed markets."

Moreover, remember that the hypothesis of the normal distribution is justified by the efficient market hypothesis, as presented in Fama (1970). If the market is informationally efficient and if new pieces of information arrive randomly, then prices should follow a random walk. Furthermore, if these random processes are independent, identically distributed and have a mean and a variance, then the central limit theorem states that price changes must follow a normal law. If, on the contrary, it is shown that the price variations are not independent, then the efficient market hypothesis is violated, which invalidates the theoretical underpinning of the Gaussian hypothesis. Concretely, it implies the possibility of making abnormal returns by using information not yet incorporated into the market prices. An obvious example of violation of the strong form of the efficient market hypothesis would be insider trading, when well-informed investors are able to lock in abnormal returns before their information is fully absorbed by the market. One traditional method of testing the weak form of market efficiency consists of investigating the autocorrelation properties of asset returns, in order to determine whether past prices help in explaining changes in future prices.

Fama (1965a) and Solnik (1973), in the US and European markets respectively, found that although it is present, serial correlation was not economically significant, and "probably negligible from an investor point of view" (Solnik, 1973). Harvey (1995) reaches the opposite conclusion when studying emerging markets. Most of them exhibit a high degree of autocorrelation that can explain a good amount of future returns. This is strong evidence against the weak form of the efficient market hypothesis in developing countries. As a corollary, however, it also shows that these markets are much more predictable, which suggests the existence of opportunities for abnormal profits.

8.3.2 Portfolio Diversification

As outlined above, portfolio diversification consists of improving the risk/return trade-off in a mean/variance framework by carefully spreading the portfolio over a wide range of assets. This strategy is very intuitive and appealing. Unfortunately, it has some shortcomings when applied in practice. Indeed, in order to be implemented, it requires *ex ante* knowledge of the expected returns, their variance and their covariance. If markets are unpredictable, these variables cannot be known with certainty and, thus, must be estimated. The standard approach consists of using past data as estimators for the true unknown inputs. To be valid, this method assumes that returns are stationary, so that *ex post* analysis can predict future data.

Jorion (1985) is among the first to have outlined how misleading this hypothesis could be in an international framework. He and many subsequent researchers have shown that the returns and the variance–covariance matrices were not constant, in particular for emerging countries, and could not be accurately estimated from past data. In addition, Goetzmann and Jorion (1999) found that the current historical international databases for emerging markets are probably too short and suffer from a survivorship bias[12] that may lead to an "overly optimistic picture of future investment performance". Moreover, Erb *et al.* (1994), Longin and Solnik (1995) or Solnik *et al.* (1996) showed that the correlation between markets increases substantially in periods of turbulence or when returns are negative. This is particularly worrisome, since it is precisely during these times that a well-functioning diversification would be needed most. Figure 8.9 represents the three-year rolling volatility for a few selected markets and shows how unstable this measure has been over the last decades.

Although these difficulties do not question the theoretical validity of the model, they make it very difficult to implement the model in practice, especially at the international level.

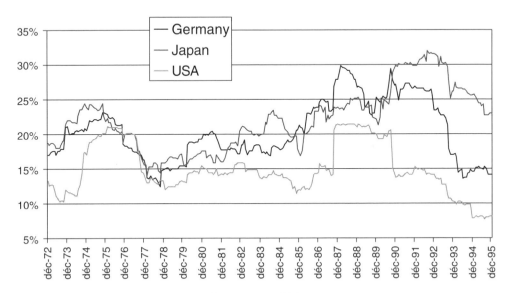

Figure 8.9 Three-year rolling volatility from 1972 to 1995

---

[12] The survivorship bias exists when the database does not include those markets or firms that disappeared in the past, for example due to bankruptcy or war, and whose performance was therefore very poor.

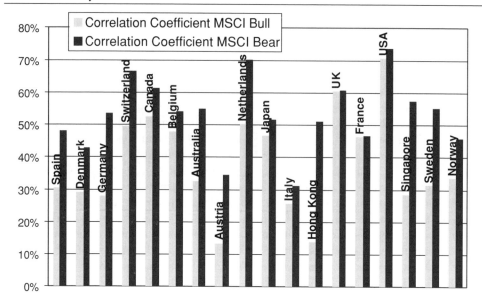

Figure 8.10   Comparison of the correlation coefficients with the MSCI World index during bear and bull markets

Nevertheless, the *ex post* studies of Jorion (1985) or De Santis and Gerard (1997) find that after taking into account these flaws, they do not fully cancel the benefits of an international portfolio diversification. They conclude that even though it is almost impossible to reach *ex ante* the optimum portfolios on the efficient frontier, international diversification can seriously improve the risk/return trade-off.

As an illustration, Figure 8.10 shows how different the correlation may be during bear and bull markets. When the MSCI World index is up, the correlation coefficient is much lower for most countries, while markets appear to be much more correlated during bear periods. Unfortunately, it is when the market is down that investors would prefer a lower correlation.

This asymmetrical behavior is found not only in the correlation coefficient but also in the volatility. Furthermore, returns in some countries are not evenly spread around the mean but rather present a certain degree of skewness.[13] This means that instead of being well balanced, the distribution of the returns has an abnormal number of positive or negative occurrences. Since the variance does not take into account this skewness, it is not a proper measure of risk when skewness is present. Volatility correctly estimates the level of uncertainty only if the returns are symmetrically distributed.

What really matters for investors is the downside risk, meaning when the performance is lower than what was initially expected. Variance encompasses both the negative and the positive outcomes. Consequently, it assesses not only downside risk, but upward potential as well. However, if the distribution is symmetrical, the amount of upside risk is exactly equivalent to the amount of downside risk. Therefore, in this particular case, the variance is a correct estimation of the downside risk, and can be used to compare various investment opportunities.

---

[13] See for instance McEnally (1974) or Bekaert and Harvey (1997) for emerging markets.

Thus, in the presence of skewness, which denotes an asymmetrical distribution, downside and upside risks differ, which makes variance irrelevant and requires other statistical tools, such as semivariance or lower partial moments, to adequately address the uncertainty characterized by the downside component. This is the path followed, for instance, by Sortino and van der Meer (1991) or Estrada (2000, 2001), when they establish the superiority of this approach over the traditional mean/variance method.

8.3.3   The CAPM

The validity of the CAPM was strongly challenged at the beginning of the 1990s, when Fama and French (1992) showed that other factors, such as the size of a firm or its book-to-market equity ratio, could explain variations in returns. These findings were confirmed at the international level by Fama and French (1998). However, after a decade of debate, researchers no longer question the ability of the beta to explain the cross-section of returns in developed markets, but rather focus on other parameters that, in addition to the beta, could complement and give more power to this model.

For the emerging markets, the story is different. Contrary to the developed countries, Harvey (2000) showed that measures of systematic risk were not sufficient to adequately reflect the degree of risk in emerging countries. Variations in returns were better explained when adding other measures of total risk such as the variance. This feature is probably due to a lower integration into the world capital markets.

In order to cope with these particularities, practitioners have developed a series of specific models to compute the cost of equity in foreign countries, including emerging markets. Most of these approaches are more or less derived from the CAPM. However, as mentioned in Chapter 7, most of them are lacking any theoretical justification, and merely constitute some catch-all adaptations of the traditional CAPM to the international setting. Because the standard CAPM seems to give discount rates that are too low, their methods consist of adjusting the beta coefficient, the risk premium or the risk-free rate upward so that the model's predictions better fit the empirical data. To get an idea of what these *ad hoc* methods include, we can look at Bank of America, Goldman Sachs or JP Morgan.

8.3.4   The Bank of America Approach

In order to allow for the features of the emerging markets, Godfrey and Espinosa[14] (1996) modify the CAPM, and incorporate some additional specific risks in their model. Their approach aims at finding the average cost of equity in a given country, and is not detailed enough to give the discount rate of a specific project.

They start by assuming that the risk can be split between political/sovereign risk, business risk and currency risk. With respect to currency risk, they consider that it should not be explicitly expressed in the required rate of return. It should be captured in cash flows denominated in home currency. This can be done by estimating future exchange rates or by taking the current forward rates. Then, the political/sovereign risk is taken into consideration by adding a country risk spread CR_i, where CR_i is given by the difference between the yield to maturity on a US dollar denominated bond of country i and a US treasury bond of similar maturity. Finally, they employ an adjusted beta β_{adj}, calculated as 60% of the ratio of the country's market volatility

---

[14] Godfrey and Espinosa were respectively Risk Analyst and Economist at Bank of America in 1996.

to that of the benchmark[15] [equation (8.7)], in order to account for the business risk [equation (8.6)]:

$$E(r_i) = r_f + CR_i + 0.6\beta_{adj\,i}\lfloor E(r_m) - r_f\rfloor \tag{8.6}$$

with

$$\beta_{adj\,i} = \frac{\sigma_i}{\sigma_m} \tag{8.7}$$

where the subscript m refers to the benchmark. This measurement of beta implicitly assumes that the correlation with the benchmark is equal to 1. To see this remember that the standard β can be written as:

$$\beta = \frac{\sigma_i}{\sigma_m}\rho_{im} \tag{8.8}$$

where ρ_{im} refers to the correlation coefficient between asset i and the benchmark. It is clear that the adjusted beta β_{adj} will always be greater than or equal to the traditional beta because the correlation coefficient ρ_{im} lies on or between -1 and $+1$.

Godfrey and Espinosa (1996) acknowledge that part of the extra risk embedded in the country risk spread can also be present in the adjusted beta. Therefore, they concede that their model could result in a double counting of the country risk, and induce an overestimation of the required rate of return. Variations in the level of risk could be reflected both in CR_i and $\beta_{adj\,i}$. To eliminate this possible double counting, and because Erb et al. (1995) found that between 30% and 40% of the variations in the expected return $E(r_i)$ are driven by changes in country credit rating (CR_i), only 60% of the adjusted beta is retained. This method, which in Godfrey and Espinosa's (1996) words intends "to generate only rough benchmarks for evaluating emerging market projects", yields some US dollar-based costs of equity that range from 14.7% in South Africa to 28.7% in Argentina.

8.3.5   The Goldman Sachs Approach

This model is based on Mariscal and Hargis (1999). It calculates the country discount rate in a way similar to that of Godfrey and Espinosa (1996). They add a country risk premium to the risk-free rate, and take the ratio of volatilities as beta [equation (8.7)]. They justify this choice "because research on emerging market equities has not been able to determine definitively whether markets are currently segmented or integrated. However measures of volatility have been found to be able to distinguish between high- and low-return markets better than betas". They also recognize some possible double counting between the credit spread and the volatility, and consequently, subtract the correlation of dollar returns between the stock market and the sovereign bond. However, contrary to Godfrey and Espinosa (1996), they do not assume this correlation to be constant at 0.40, and compute a specific correlation coefficient ρ_{im} for each country. The resulting formula is given by equation (8.9):

$$E(r_i) = r_f + CR_i + [1 - \rho_{im}]\beta_{adj\,i}\lfloor E(r_m) - r_f\rfloor \tag{8.9}$$

Equation (8.9) aims at calculating a country-specific discount rate. To find a stock-specific discount rate for a given firm x, Mariscal and Hargis (1999) add a specific company bond

---

[15] Godfrey and Espinosa (1996) suggest using the home market and not the world market as benchmark.

spread, that could be negative depending on the firm's characteristics. In addition, the beta of the firm on the local market index β_{xi} is incorporated, accounting for the specific sensitivity of the company with respect to the local environment. Putting all this together gives

$$E(r_{xi}) = r_f + CR_i + CR_x + [1 - \rho_{im}]\beta_{adji}\lfloor E(r_m) - r_f\rfloor\beta_{xi} \tag{8.10}$$

8.3.6   The JP Morgan Approach

The JP Morgan approach as presented in DeSwaan and Liubych (1999) is derived in the same spirit as the Bank of America and Goldman Sachs models. Again, the standard beta is replaced by an upward adjusted version, based on the ratio of volatility of the country to that of the world market [equation (8.7)]. And similarly, it is weighted down by a factor of 0.64. However, in the JP Morgan case, this factor is not used to alleviate the problem of double counting but is based on the assumption that the ratio of systematic risk to total risk in emerging countries should be the same as in developed countries, about 41%, meaning 64% when dealing with volatility.[16]

Contrary to the two previous examples, the country spread CR_i does not appear in the country discount rate $E(r_i)$, which can be written as:

$$E(r_i) = r_f + 0.64\beta_{adji}\lfloor E(r_m) - r_f\rfloor \tag{8.11}$$

It is only present in the calculation of the firm-specific cost of equity $E(r_{xi})$, where the country spread is added to the risk-free rate and subtracted from the market risk premium. As in the Goldman Sachs model, the systematic risk of the firm is included through its beta on the local market index β_{xi}:

$$E(r_{xi}) = r_f + CR_i + \lfloor 0.64\beta_{adji}\lfloor E(r_m) - r_f\rfloor - CR_i\rfloor\beta_{xi} \tag{8.12}$$

Note that when the whole local market is considered, $\beta_{xi} = 1$, equation (8.12) reduces to equation (8.11).

It is important to remember that the three foregoing practitioners' models are devoid of any theoretical justification and represent nothing more than *ad hoc* modifications to the standard CAPM. They aim at filling the gap between real empirical data and the unsatisfying results of the traditional models.

8.4   CONCLUSION

In modern finance, it is commonly accepted that international investments must command a higher discount rate in order to cope with the additional uncertainties, such as exchange risk, political risk or economic risk, generated by overseas operations (see for instance Shapiro, 1978 or Pettit *et al.*, 1999). Unless these uncertainties are completely undiversifiable, however, this stands in stark contrast to the dictums of modern portfolio theory, which holds that only risk that cannot be eliminated through diversification should be priced. The question, then, is how to account for these additional uncertainties that often manifest themselves as explicit, loss-causing events. One answer is that modern portfolio theory does not aim at forecasting

---

[16] 64% is the square root of 41%.

specific political events but rather at gauging the trade-off between risk and return and must be complemented by the techniques presented in Chapter 7 that include random, discrete jumps.

As it stands today at the practical level for international investing, outside of the well-known problems associated with mean/variance analysis, such as unstable statistical series, non-Gaussian returns and the weak explanatory power of the beta coefficient, the problem seems to boil down to whether markets are integrated or not. Most developed markets seem to be integrated and can be studied in the context of mean/variance analysis or, more specifically, with respect to beta. Emerging markets are another story, however. They do not seem to be integrated and, thus, the traditional beta is inappropriate. In the absence of a theoretical answer to the problem, practitioners have devised a number of procedures for adding risk premiums or modifying betas.

REFERENCES

Adler M, Dumas B, 1983, International Portfolio Choice and Corporation Finance: A Synthesis. *Journal of Finance*, Jun, 38 (3), 925–84.

Agmon T, 1973, Country Risk: The Significance of the Country Factor for Share-Price Movements in the United Kingdom, Germany, and Japan. *Journal of Business*, Jan, 46 (1), 24–32.

Aliber RZ, 1973, The Interest Rate Parity Theorem: A Reinterpretation. *Journal of Political Economy*, Nov/Dec, 81 (6), 1451–9.

Aliber RZ, 1975, Exchange Risk, Political Risk, and Investor Demand for External Currency Deposits. *Journal of Money, Credit, and Banking*, May, 7 (2), 161–79.

Bachelier L, 1900, *Théorie de la Spéculation*. Thèse pour le Doctorat ès Sciences Mathématiques. Paris: Annales de l'Ecole Normale Supérieure, 3 (27).

Bank of Japan, 1999, International Financial Markets as Viewed from BIS Statistics: Changes in the International Flow of Funds in the 1990s [online]. Tokyo: Bank of Japan, August. Available at: http://www.boj.or.jp/en/ronbun/ron9908.htm [Accessed 5 September 2002].

Barnes MA, Bercel A and Rothmann SH, 2001, Global Equities: Do Countries Still Matter? *Journal of Investing*, Fall, 10 (3), 43–9.

Beckers S and Connor G, 1996, National versus Global Influences on Equity Returns. *Financial Analysts Journal*, Mar/Apr, 52 (2), 31–9.

Bekaert G, 1995, Market Integration and Investment Barriers in Emerging Equity Markets. *World Bank Economic Review*, 9, 75–107.

Bekaert G and Harvey CR, 1995, Time-Varying World Market Integration. *Journal of Finance*, Jun, 50 (2), 403–44.

Bekaert G and Harvey CR, 1997, Emerging Equity Market Volatility. *Journal of Financial Economics*, Jan, 43 (1), 29–77.

Berryessa N and Kirzner E, 1988, *Global Investing: The Templeton Way*. Homewood, IL: Dow Jones-Irwin.

Clark E, 1991, *Cross Border Investment Risk*. London: Euromoney Publications.

Clark E, 2002, *International Finance*. London: Thomson.

Cooper I and Kaplanis E, 1994, Home Bias in Equity Portfolios, Inflation Hedging, and International Capital Market Equilibrium. *Review of Financial Studies*, Spring, 7 (1), 45–60.

Cosset JC and Suret JM, 1995, Political Risk and the Benefits of International Portfolio Diversification. *Journal of International Business Studies*, 26 (2), 301–18.

De Santis G and Gerard B, 1997, International Asset Pricing and Portfolio Diversification with Time-Varying Risk. *Journal of Finance*, Dec, 52 (5), 1881.

Demirgüç-Kunt A and Huizinga H, 1994, Portfolio Investments in Emerging Stock Markets: Direct and Indirect Barriers. *In:* Baring Securities, ed. *Investing in Emerging Markets*. London: Euromoney Publications, 255–70.

DeSwaan JC and Liubych A, 1999, Determining the Cost of Equity in Emerging Markets [online]. Policy Analysis Exercise, Master in Public Policy, John F Kennedy School of Government, Harvard

University. Available at: http://www.ksg.harvard.edu/PAE/DeSwaanPAE_Final.pdf [Accessed 10 September 2002].

Diamonte RL and Liew JM, 1996, Political Risk in Emerging and Developed Markets. *Financial Analysts Journal*, May/Jun, 52 (3), 71–6.

Divecha AB, Drach J and Stefek D, 1992, Emerging Markets: A Quantitative Perspective. *Journal of Portfolio Management*, Fall, 19 (1), 41–50.

Diwan I, Errunza V and Senbet LW, 1994, Diversification Benefits of Country Funds. *In:* Baring Securities, ed. *Investing in Emerging Markets*. London: Euromoney Publications, 199–218.

Dooley MP and Isard P, 1980, Capital Controls, Political Risk, and Deviations from Interest-Rate Parity. *Journal of Political Economy*, Apr, 88 (2), 370–84.

Dooley MP, Isard P and Taylor MP, 1995, Exchange Rates, Country-Specific Shocks and Gold. *Applied Financial Economics*, Jun, 5 (3), 121–9.

Dumas B and Solnik B, 1995, The World Price of Foreign Exchange Risk. *Journal of Finance*, Jun, 50 (2), 445–79.

Erb CB, Harvey CR and Viskanta TE, 1994, Forecasting International Correlation. *Financial Analysts Journal*, Nov/Dec, 50 (6), 32–45.

Erb CB, Harvey CR and Viskanta TE, 1995, Country Risk and Global Equity Selection. *Journal of Portfolio Management*, Winter, 21 (2), 74–83.

Erb CB, Harvey CR and Viskanta TE, 1996a, The Influence of Political, Economic and Financial Risk on Expected Fixed Income Returns. *Journal of Fixed Income*, Jun, 6 (1), 7–31.

Erb CB, Harvey CR and Viskanta TE, 1996b, Political Risk, Economic Risk, and Financial Risk. *Financial Analysts Journal*, Nov/Dec, 52 (6), 28–46.

Errunza VR, 1977, Gains from Portfolio Diversification into Less Developed Countries Securities. *Journal of International Business Studies*, Fall/Winter, 8 (2), 83–99.

Estrada J, 2000, The Cost of Equity in Emerging Markets: A Downside Risk Approach. *Emerging Markets Quarterly*, Fall, 4 (3), 19–30.

Estrada J, 2001, The Cost of Equity in Emerging Markets: A Downside Risk Approach (II). *Emerging Markets Quarterly*, Spring, 5 (1), 63–72.

Eun CS and Resnick BG, 1988, Exchange Rate Uncertainty, Forward Contracts, and International Portfolio Selection. *Journal of Finance*, Mar, 43 (1), 197–215.

Fama EF, 1965a, The Behavior of Stock-Market Prices. *Journal of Business*, Jan, 38 (1), 34–105.

Fama EF, 1965b, Portfolio Analysis in a Stable Paretian Market. *Management Science*, Jan, 11 (3), 404–19.

Fama EF, 1970, Efficient Capital Markets: A Review of Theory and Empirical Work. *Journal of Finance*, May, 25 (2), 383–427.

Fama EF and French KR, 1992, The Cross-Section of Expected Stock Returns. *Journal of Finance*, Jun, 47 (2), 427–66.

Fama EF and French KR, 1998, Value Versus Growth: The International Evidence. *Journal of Finance*, Dec, 53 (6), 1975–99.

Fischer B, 1999, Risks in Managing Emerging Market External Debt Portfolios. *Emerging Markets Quarterly*, Winter, 3 (4), 28–38.

French KR and Poterba JM, 1991, Investor Diversification and International Equity Markets. *American Economic Review*, May, 81 (2), 222–6.

Gibbons MR and Ferson WE, 1985, Test of Asset Pricing Models with Changing Expectations and an Unobservable Market Portfolio. *Journal of Financial Economics*, Jun, 14 (2), 217–36.

Godfrey S and Espinosa R, 1996, A Practical Approach to Calculating Costs of Equity for Investments in Emerging Markets. *Journal of Applied Corporate Finance*, Fall, 9 (3), 80–89.

Goetzmann WN and Jorion P, 1999, Re-emerging Markets. *Journal of Financial and Quantitative Analysis*, Mar, 34 (1), 1–31.

Griffin JM and Stulz RM, 2001, International Competition and Exchange Rate Shocks: A Cross-Country Industry Analysis of Stock Returns. *Review of Financial Studies*, Spring, 14 (1), 215–41.

Groslambert B and Kassibrakis S, 1999, The Alpha-Stable Hypothesis: An Alternative to the Distribution of Emerging Stock Market Returns. *Emerging Markets Quarterly*, Spring, 3 (1), 22–38.

Grubel HG, 1968, Internationally Diversified Portfolios: Welfare Gains and Capital Flows. *American Economic Review*, Dec, Part 1 of 2, 58 (5), 1299–1314.

Harvey CR, 1989, Time-Varying Conditional Covariances in Tests of Asset Pricing Models. *Journal of Financial Economics*, Oct, 24 (2), 289–317.

Harvey CR, 1991, The World Price of Covariance Risk. *Journal of Finance*, Mar, 46 (1), 111–57.

Harvey CR, 1995, Predictable Risk and Returns in Emerging Markets. *Review of Financial Studies*, Fall, 8 (3), 773–816.

Harvey CR, 2000, Drivers of Expected Returns in International Markets. *Emerging Markets Quarterly*, Fall, 4 (3), 32–48.

HeidelbergCement, 2001, Strategy [online]. Heidelberg: HeidelbergCement. Available at: http://www.heidelbergcement.com/html/e/page.asp?pageID=54 [Accessed 10 September 2002].

HeidelbergCement, 2002, Report to the Shareholders [online]. Heidelberg: HeidelbergCement. Availableat: http://www.heidelbergcement.com/html/e/uploads/a303/GB_2001_e_Lagebericht.pdf [Accessed 10 September 2002].

Jorion P, 1985, International Portfolio Diversification with Estimation Risk. *Journal of Business*, 58 (3), 259–78.

Lessard DR, 1973, International Portfolio Diversification: A Multivariate Analysis for a Group of Latin American Countries. *Journal of Finance*, Jun, 28 (3), 619–33.

Lessard DR, 1976, World, National, and Industry Factors in Equity Returns. *Journal of Finance*, May, 29 (2), 379–91.

Levy H and Sarnat M, 1970, International Diversification of Investment Portfolios. *American Economic Review*, Sep, 4, 668–75.

Lintner J, 1965, Security Prices, Risk and Maximal Gains from Diversification. *Journal of Finance*, Dec, 20 (4), 587–615.

Longin F and Solnik B, 1995, Is the Correlation in International Equity Returns Constant: 1960–1990? *Journal of International Money and Finance*, Feb, 14 (1), 3–26.

Madura J, Tucker AL and Wiley M, 1997, Factors Affecting Returns across Stock Markets. *Global Finance Journal*, Spring/Summer, 8 (1), 1–14.

Mandelbrot B, 1963, The Variation of Certain Speculative Prices. *Journal of Business*, 36 (4), 394–413.

Mariscal JO and Hargis K, 1999, Portfolio Strategy: A Long-Term Perspective on Short-Term Risk. *Global Emerging Markets*, Goldman Sachs Investment Research, Oct 26.

Markowitz H, 1952, Portfolio Selection. *Journal of Finance*, Mar, 7 (1), 77–91.

McEnally RW, 1974, A Note on the Return Behavior of High Risk Common Stocks. *Journal of Finance*, Mar, 29 (1), 199–202.

Mooney EV, 1999, Deloitte Develops Model to Assess Overseas Investment Risk. *RCR*, 18 (10), 20–24.

Osborne MM, 1959, Brownian Motion in the Stock Market. *Operation Research*, 7, Mar/Apr, 145–73.

Pettit J, Ferguson M and Gluck R, 1999, A Method for Estimating Global Corporate Capital Costs: The Case of Bestfoods. *Journal of Applied Corporate Finance*, Fall, 12 (3), 80–90.

Reilly FK and Brown KC, 2000, *Investment Analysis and Portfolio Management*. 6th edition. Fort Worth, TX: Dryden Press.

Rouwenhorst GK, 1999, European Equity Markets and the EMU. *Financial Analysts Journal*, May/Jun, 55 (3), 57–64.

Scholtens B, 1999, On the Comovement of Bond Yield Spreads and Country Risk Ratings. *Journal of Fixed Income*, Mar, 8 (4), 99–103.

Shapiro AC, 1978, Capital Budgeting for the Multinational Corporation. *Financial Management*, Spring, 7 (1), 7–16.

Sharpe WF, 1964, Capital Asset Prices: A Theory of Market Equilibrium Under Conditions of Risk. *Journal of Finance*, Sep, 19 (3), 425–42.

Solnik B, 1973, Note on the Validity of the Random Walk for European Stock Prices. *Journal of Finance*, Dec, 28 (5), 1151–9.

Solnik B, 1974, An Equilibrium Model of the International Capital Market. *Journal of Economic Theory*, Aug, 8 (4), 500–24.

Solnik B and de Freitas A, 1988, International Factors of Stock Price Behavior. *In:* SJ Khoury and A Ghosh, eds. *Recent Developments in International Banking and Finance*. Lexington, MA and Toronto: Heath, Lexington Books, 2, 259–76.

Solnik B, Boucrelle C and Le Fur Y, 1996, International Market Correlation and Volatility. *Financial Analysts Journal*, Sep/Oct, 17–34.

Sortino F and van der Meer R, 1991, Downside Risk. *Journal of Portfolio Management*, Summer, 17 (4), 27–31.

Speidell LS and Sappenfield R, 1992, Global Diversification in a Shrinking World. *Journal of Portfolio Management*, Fall, 19 (1), 57–67.

Standard & Poor's, 2001, *Emerging Stock Markets Factbook*. New York: Standard & Poor's.

9

Financial Crises in Emerging Market Countries: An Historical Perspective

9.1 INTRODUCTION

This chapter provides a succinct historical perspective of the emerging countries' financial crises, with a focus on the debt overhang problem.[1] Although we address the evolving relationships between debtor governments and private bondholders in the late nineteenth century, most of the analysis focuses on the EMCs' debt crisis of the 1980s and 1990s. During these two decades, debt restructuring took the form of an official concerted strategy under the aegis of the international financial institutions, acting as coordinating agencies between Paris and London Club creditors, on the one hand, and debtor country governments, on the other. Clearly, debt is only one instrument among a wide array of financial exposures that constitute "country risk", including bonds, equity and portfolio investment, trade and capital flows. Clearly also, country risk is not reduced to emerging market countries. Nevertheless, the justification for devoting one comprehensive chapter to the EMCs is twofold.

First, unlike any other financial instrument, external indebtedness has imposed a unique situation, given the systemic risk of a chain reaction that could threaten the stability of the banking industry worldwide, the economic and social situation in emerging market countries, and the soundness of the global trade and financial system. This threat was active in 1982, 1997 and 2002. A cooperative international strategy came into being as each group realized that pursuit of its perceived self-interest would have been detrimental to global economic and social welfare. Second, although September 11 is a reminder that there is no sanctuary for country risk, even in the most developed economies worldwide, it is, nevertheless, a fact that emerging market country risk constitutes the most complex and volatile category. Taken together, lending to emerging market countries has been and still is a formidable risk and opportunity.

Twenty years after the outbreak of the EMCs' foreign debt problems, to many observers, the debt crisis no longer represents a global threat to the international financial system. At the outbreak of Mexico's crisis in mid-1982, the systemic risk of a chain reaction enforced solidarity between debtors and creditors. Thousands of banks of all sizes and from numerous countries were brought closer together by credit syndication, debt consolidation and rescheduling procedures. At that time, international banks were overexposed and undercapitalized. Intervention from multilateral agencies and Paris Club governments imposed some order on the system. Developing countries were forced to adopt macroeconomic stabilization programs, while London Club banks had to participate in "defensive" loan operations, increasing their outstanding obligations to refinance interest payments and thus protect the quality of their assets.

The situation has since moved on. Although the banking system is marked by broad disparities, most banks have consolidated their balance sheets by increasing their equity and provisions

---

[1] See also the debt-focused Glossary at the back of this book.

Table 9.1   Total external indebtedness in US$ billion[a]

	1913	1970	1973	1975	1980	1986	1990	1994	2000	2001
Private	44	39	24	40	419	262	819	1124	1584	1539
Official		34	43	59	190	955	639	821	908	903
Total		73	67	99	609	1217	1458	1945	2492	2442

[a]World Bank, World Debt Tables, 1991–1995 and Global Development Finance, Summary Tables, 2000. For 1913: International Capital Movements during the Inter-War Period, Lake Success: United Nations, 1949, p. 2; cited in Hughes (1979).

while reducing their country risk exposure. A large number of debtors have adopted fiscal and monetary adjustment measures that allow market conditions to prevail. As of the end of 2002, more than 50 countries had implemented a stabilization program under the monitoring of the IMF, with financial support reaching over US$70 billion. Bilateral and multilateral official creditors have contributed to these efforts, both by supporting adjustment programs, and by allowing debt reduction and encouraging commercial banks to accept debt write-offs down the road. The initial policy of increasing exposure with fresh injections of capital under the so-called Baker Plan thus gave way to a policy of debt-burden alleviation initiated by the Brady Plan. In terms of official debt, the Paris Club outlined measures to promote substantial debt relief, particularly for highly-indebted, low-income countries, under the so-called Toronto, Naples and Lyon menus of debt restructuring. Despite the positive results of these strategies, they have not been able to solve the acute problem of severe indebtedness for a number of developing countries. Above all, the prospect of returning to capital markets remains uncertain, with a few notable exceptions in Latin America (Mexico, Chile) and in Eastern Europe (Hungary, Poland, Czech Republic).

Table 9.1 illustrates the rapid rise in external indebtedness during the 1980s and 1990s.

Debtor countries face three main categories of foreign lenders:

Private lenders	Commercial banks within or outside the London Club, bondholders and suppliers
Official bilateral lenders	National country governments within or outside the Paris Club
Official multilateral lenders	World Bank Group, IMF, as well as certain regional development banks (EBRD, IADB)

Developing countries still remain heavily indebted despite a concerted strategy carried out under the aegis of international institutions, aimed at reducing financial charges and restoring sustainable growth. Total foreign debt increased twofold between 1980 and 1986, and twofold again between 1986 and 2001 (Figure 9.1).[2] Total indebtedness is estimated at around US$2500 billion at end-2002. Debt to London Club commercial banks comes to US$870 billion, or 35% of the total.[3]

For most EMCs, indicators of solvency and liquidity are not improving (Figure 9.2); above all, the ratios of low-income countries are showing no improvement whatsoever. Exchange rate variations, i.e., the fluctuations between the currency of debt denomination and that of

---

[2] *Source:* World Bank, World Debt Tables 1991–1995 and Global Development Finance 2002, Summary Tables.

[3] *Source:* BIS, External Positions of Reporting Banks vis-à-vis Individual Countries. *BIS Quarterly Review*, Sep, 2002, Table 6A, p. A22.

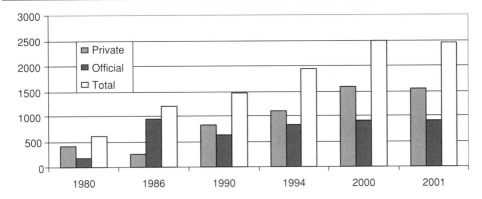

Figure 9.1   Total external indebtedness in US$ billion

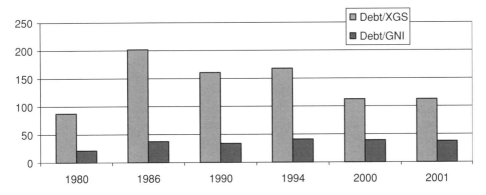

Figure 9.2   Solvency indicators (%) (*Source:* World Bank)

the debtor's export revenues, together with declines in real effective exchange rates of the countries themselves, have increased the relative proportion of debt. As a result, ratios of foreign debt/GNP have risen to an average of 40% from around 21% in 1980 and 34% in 1990.[4] For developing countries as a whole, external indebtedness is stubbornly larger than annual export revenues. There are clearly variations within this group of nearly 150 countries. The ratio of debt/exports in Asia reaches about 75% while that of Latin America is as high as 167%. Regarding income groups, the 85 "middle-income countries", with GDP per capita below US$9265, bear an external debt as large as their annual export revenues while "low-income countries", with GDP per capita below US$755, face ratios close to 200%. Protracted signs of slower growth in OECD countries will have a long-term impact on developing countries' access to trade and capital markets, at a time when commercial banks have to contend with competitive and regulatory pressure to satisfy capital adequacy requirements imposed by supervisory authorities. The new regulations, known as Basle II, will increase this overall pressure while making banks more discriminatory regarding "borderline" OECD countries such as Turkey, Korea, Mexico, Poland and Hungary.

---

[4] *Source:* World Bank, Global Development Finance 2002, Summary Tables, p. 222.

9.2   HISTORICAL PERSPECTIVE

9.2.1   Economic Growth-cum-Debt Process

Country risk stems from international capital and trade flows. Clearly, should countries live and grow in isolation (this is likely a contradiction), there would not be any exchange of goods and services, no portfolio or equity investment, nor any cross-border loans. Country risk emerges as countries begin exchanging products, services and capital. The international flow of capital dates back to the ancient civilization of the Mediterranean, and probably much further into the past of tribal societies. Though it is impossible to pinpoint the historical origin of international trade, the sixteenth century probably marks the inception of the era of an emerging international economic system centered in medieval Europe. It also marks the inception of country risk, including default, contract repudiation, confiscation and the impact of political turmoil on private investors and merchants. By the last quarter of the nineteenth century, Europe, led by Great Britain, had become the world's supplier of capital. As the industrial revolution crossed the Atlantic, the United States became a net exporter of capital at the beginning of the twentieth century. In particular, the half century before World War I saw a formidable liberalization of world trade, labor and capital movements, enhancing economic relations between industrialized Europe and North America, on the one hand, and Latin America, China and the Indian subcontinent, on the other.

   This is where country risk emerges, given that the accumulation of capital flows leads to debt stocks. The growth race between economic expansion and indebtedness creates concerns for both borrowers and their creditors. There is a critical point of debt accumulation beyond which the lender's risk exposure creates a forced solidarity with the debtor. Likewise, investment return depends not only on the country's overall economic expansion but also on the capacity and willingness of the country regarding capital and dividend repatriation. Creditors and investors become heavily dependent on foreign country governments' ability *and* willingness regarding repayment with interest.

9.2.2   Bonds versus Loans

In finance as in many other matters, history tends to repeat itself, though with some variation regarding who collapses and who, in turn, gets ruined. A sequence of lending waves occurred at intervals throughout the nineteenth and early twentieth centuries, with the 1820s, 1880s, 1910s and 1920s serving as prominent examples. Solvency, borrowing, financial crisis and default alternated. Latin American countries entered the London bond market in the early 1820s upon independence and stopped coupon payments soon thereafter. Mexico's foreign debt is as old as the republic itself. Mexico contracted its first bond in 1824 and defaulted as early as 1827 (Tenenbaum, 1985; Bouchet, 1987a, b; Aggarwal, 1989). As Eichengren points out: "In each of these cases large loans quickly lapsed into default, causing the same complaints of reckless lending and misuse of borrowed funds that were heard in the 1980s" (Eichengreen and Lindert, 1989). Until World War II, however, the bulk of capital flows was private lending through stock and bond issues, mainly for infrastructure-related projects. Loans were sold to a wide range of bondholders in Europe and North America. Defaults on foreign bonds were generally settled through debt-restructuring negotiations between the foreign borrowers and committees representing the bondholders. A combination of rescheduling, refinancing, discounted debt repurchases and the threat that creditor governments would link debt, trade and official loans, led to readjustment negotiations where bondholders settled for slightly less than half of contractual interest rates (Eichengreen and Portes, 1989).

During the interwar period, the bond market shifted from London to New York. An acceleration of loans to Latin American governments took place, notably to Argentina, Brazil, Chile, Colombia and Cuba. Contrary to the previous century, the bulk of bond lending took place between national governments, the United States leading the way. Official lending was paralleled by dynamic flows of private direct investment. When the general speculative surge in financial markets collapsed in 1929, Latin American borrowers were pushed into widespread default as the world economy tumbled into protracted depression. Most of them were cut off from access to world markets until the 1950s.

All in all, a distinctive feature of the 1930s is that global schemes to short-circuit the protracted bilateral negotiations proved unavailing. Nearly every aspect of the global solutions proposed in the 1980s, a special lending facility, discounted buybacks, matched injections of public and private funds, conversions of existing claims into new assets with different contingencies, was first suggested in the 1930s. Ultimately, those global schemes foundered on the issue of who should fund them and control their administration. The absence of supranational institutions to coordinate a fair burden-sharing between debtors and creditors was detrimental to concerted negotiations based on the preservation of mutual benefits.

The most salient difference between the 1930s and the 1980s was that default was a logical policy choice in the 1930s for the debtor countries. A great depression and a wave of protectionism in the industrial countries led to the collapse of international trade. Import substitution still paid off as a development strategy. The debt crisis was highly dispersed and did not threaten the stability of the financial system. Consequently, default was more tempting, as defaulting debtor countries were not threatened by large sanctions or penalties.

9.2.3   The Rising Importance of Commercial Bank Lending in the Post-WWII Era

Three events in the 1970s laid the groundwork fort the developing country debt crisis of the early 1980s, namely (i) the 1973–1974 oil price shocks, (ii) the resulting increase in international lending through the recycling of petro-dollars, i.e., the large current account surpluses of oil exporting countries, and (iii) the devaluation of the dollar in 1971 and the collapse of the fixed exchange rate system established in Bretton Woods at the end of World War II, with resulting floating rates. Between 1972 and 1981, the external debt of developing countries increased sixfold to US$500 billion and, in real terms, more than double the rate of increase in either GDP or export volumes. Most of the increased lending was private credit, mainly syndicated commercial bank loans, whose share in total debt rose from a third to a half.

In the mid-1970s, combined recession in the industrialized countries with the rising cost of oil imports, exchange rate instability and growing protectionist trends, substantially limited the expansion in world trade. Developing countries faced a mounting challenge regarding stagnation of official assistance flows, declining terms of trade and shrinking export markets. Since their current account deficit was largely financed through external borrowing from private sources and on market-based terms, specifically floating interest rate-based bank credits, financial vulnerability grew rapidly. Current account deficits of non-oil developing countries rose twofold between 1973 and 1977, to US$22 billion from US$11 billion.

The fledgling Eurocurrency market provided a conducive institutional framework for syndicated lending. And increased competition between international banks led to developing country borrowers being offered reduced spreads and longer maturities and grace periods.

Petro-dollar liquidity in international capital markets, combined with economic slowdown in the industrial countries, pushed real interest rates down to negative levels in 1975 and kept them abnormally low until the late 1970s. For developing country governments, these favorable terms made external borrowing an apparently cheap source of finance, particularly at a time when many were struggling to meet higher oil import costs. Optimism about ability to repay these loans was fostered by the parallel boom in export prices of oil and non-oil commodities and, to a lesser extent, earnings from manufactured products. Virtually all developing countries – both low and middle-income, oil importers and oil exporters – had access to commercial bank credit and participated in the rapid expansion of commercial bank debt. Banks of all sizes and diverse cultures entered the loan syndication market for a variety of reasons, including servicing client needs, defensive expansion to keep market shares, earnings growth and the opportunities offered by Eurocurrency markets. Without a turnaround in external conditions, such borrowing seemed sustainable. Certainly, heavy borrowing was not seen as overly risky by either borrower or lender. As *The Economist* summarized at that time: "The banks were awash with OPEC's surpluses; and ever-fancier syndicating techniques drew in thousands of institutions, including local and regional American and European banks that could hardly spell the names of half the capital cities they lent to."[5]

External debt was heavily concentrated, and Mexico and Brazil absorbed more than 40% of US bank claims on developing countries at end-1977.[6] At that time, many major US banks, the so-called "money-center banks", held portfolios outstanding in these two countries equivalent to more than half of their capital. In 1982, on the eve of the crisis, Latin American debt peaked at 180% of the nine money-center banks' equity capital.

9.2.4   The Debt Crisis and the Market-Driven Menu Approach

Stanley Fischer (1988) summarized the immediate origins of the crisis of 1982: "The debt crisis had three causes: imprudent macroeconomic management and borrowing by the debtor countries; imprudent lending by the international banks; and the increase in the real interest rate, decline in commodity prices, and recession associated with counter-inflationary policies in the industrialized countries in the early 1980s." Exchange rate appreciation encouraged capital flight from several of the large debtors. Excessive short-term borrowing, increase in international interest rates and decreasing export revenues were the triggers of a contagion of defaults and abrupt cut-offs in market access (Figure 9.3).

In August of 1982, Mexico announced to the international banking community that the country was unable to continue to service its public sector external debt obligations. Mexico's suspension of debt payments was noteworthy because of the sheer magnitude of its external liabilities. Mexico's bank debt of $75 billion was larger than the overall capital of many international banks. There were also fears that a failure to pay back the debt would lead to a complete breakdown of the international banking system, i.e., a systemic failure. To avoid that outcome, banks and creditor governments responded with a combination of time and money, i.e., including the rescheduling of payments and new loans. Within two years, more than 30 countries, representing half of all developing country debt, had fallen into arrears. This event and its after-effects form what is commonly labeled "the debt crisis".

---

[5] International Banking Survey. *The Economist*, 21 March 1987, p. 11.
[6] US Federal Reserve Survey, 1977.

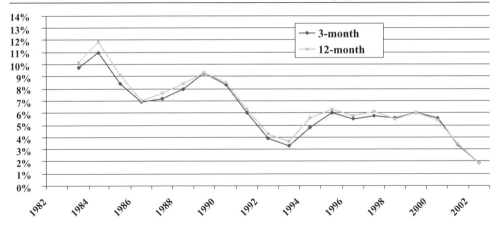

Figure 9.3   Evolution of euro/$ LIBOR

9.3   SOLVING THE DEBT CRISIS

9.3.1   Phase I – Buying Time with Rescheduling

Rescheduling is as old as finance. Creditors have always found ways of spinning out their repayments in preference to writing them off. In the 1970s, most of the reschedulings involved official bilateral, Paris Club, debt. They averaged three or four a year, reaching at most US$2 billion. In 1983–1984 alone, 30 countries rescheduled more than US$130 billion in medium-term loans and obtained in place short-term credit lines averaging US$32 billion. Buying time and preventing a confrontational approach was of the essence. The perception of the root causes of the financial difficulties was that debtor countries faced a bunching of payments coming due. Bankers treated the liquidity problem "piecemeal", through *ad hoc* rescue packages to bridge balance of payments gaps.

In the immediate aftermath of the crisis, the essence of private debt restructuring focused on country-specific pragmatism. As the Chairman of Manufacturers Hanover Corp., the most exposed US bank with two-and-a-half times shareholders' equity on loan to Latin America, declared in 1984: "There were those demanding a quick fix, while others were predicting imminent doom. What actually is transpiring is what most bankers had asserted all along – namely, that step-by-step, country-specific programs would work; panaceas would not" (Glynn, 1985). As the number of active bank creditors rapidly shrunk, commercial bankers argued that debt forgiveness, no matter how subtly wrapped up, involves moral hazard. The risk is that bad debt performers would be forgiven more easily than those that make macroeconomic and financial efforts to keep servicing their external borrowings.

The initial strategy was to count on the objective solidarity within the banking industry as well as between banks and debtor countries, with rising risk exposure, lower spreads and fees, and long-term rescheduling to avoid massive arrears accumulation. Spontaneous lending declined, however, as a growing number of banks turned into "free riders", while others got out by simply selling or swapping their assets. All of them strengthened their capital and reserves. Regarding the debtor countries, a combination of erosion in their terms of trade, capital flight and reduced capital market access led to worsening debt servicing capacity: debt-to-export ratios averaged nearly 300% in the first half of the decade while interest payments-to-export ratios remained stubbornly at close to one-third.

Despite heavy debt burdens, the solution of "default cartelization" was quickly discarded. The much-publicized 1984 inaugural meeting of 11 debtors in Carthegena, Colombia, generated widespread concern but few results. The March 1986 Punta del Este, Uruguay, meeting discussed ways and means of trimming the Latin American countries' interest bills on their US$350 billion debt with a market-driven approach, including interest capitalization, debt equity and securitization. The so-called Group of Eight's meeting in Rio, Brazil, in December 1988, did not intend to form a cartel either, but to debate technical debt reduction proposals. After the humiliating failure of Brazil's February 1987 moratorium on interest payments to secure negotiating advantages, the Rio summit held a non-confrontational stance. From the perspective of the debtor country, default would mean complete isolation from financial markets. This would have been highly detrimental in a highly interdependent financial world. Further, policies such as import substitution had been very much discredited. From the creditors' point of view, default could provoke a systemic risk of a "chain reaction" that could have brought about a breakdown of the international banking system.

9.3.2   Phase II – The New Money Approach

The thrust of the new strategy was "burden sharing". Banks were both overexposed and undercapitalized, hence the scope of systemic risk and the need to provide defensive lending. The initiative launched by US Treasury Secretary, James Baker, in October 1985, calling for new money from banks and international lending agencies together with a commitment to better economic management by the borrowers, set a statesmanlike seal on international cooperation. Banks were called on to provide US$20 billion of net new funds to 15 large debtor countries, mostly in Latin America, over a three-year period, implying annual growth in bank exposure on the order of 2.5%.

Further spontaneous new money packages, however, became more and more difficult to negotiate as a gradual fragmentation among the banking community evolved due to differences in regulations, long-term commercial interests and divergent balance sheet management policies. The debt refinancing strategy led to "debt fatigue" in both camps. The eroding cohesion among banks reflected growing skepticism about the debtor countries' prospect of eventually returning to financial markets and improving macroeconomic performance in the near future. This was due as much to external factors such as terms of trade as to bad economic policies in some indebted countries, including capital flight. In addition, the "free-rider" problem became more acute. As the number of active creditor banks kept decreasing, banking assets became more and more concentrated.[7] A landmark in the search for flexible market solutions was the publication of Chilean rules for debt/equity conversions, under which that nation reduced its total debt by almost US$1 billion between end-1986 and mid-year 1988.

The mid-1980s marked a peak in international banks' deteriorating loan portfolio quality. Falling profits, net charge-offs and non-performing assets were squeezing a rising number of institutions. In 1986, a record 144 banks went under in the United States, the number of "problem banks" reached 1457 and the number of unprofitable banks reached nearly 2800 (Barry, 1987). The signal that banks were both unwilling and unable to further add developing country risk exposure came from Citibank's abrupt decision to add US$3 billion to its loan-loss reserves to cover future losses on its US$15 billion worth of Third World loans, principally in

---

[7] At the end of 1990, the share of the nine major American banks in total banking commitments in Latin America was 80%, up from 60% in 1982.

Table 9.2   The world's largest banks by assets[a]

1986	2001
Dai-Ichy Kangyo	Sumitomo Mitsui
Fuji	Citigroup
Sumitomo	Deutsche Bank
Sanwa	JP Morgan Chase
Citicorp	Bank of Tokyo Mitsubishi
Norinchukin	UBS
Industrial Bank of Japan	HSBC CCF
Crédit Agricole	Bayerische Hypo
BNP	BNP Paribas

[a] Ranking the 200 largest banks, *Institutional Investor*, July 1987.

Latin America. Other international banks faced irresistible pressures from financial markets to follow suit. Banks used a combination of financial instruments in slashing developing country debt portfolios, including sales, charge-offs, debt-for-equity swaps, exchanges for other credits, external guarantees and substitution of local funding for cross-border funding. As risk exposure shrank, the new money base was also eroding. The Baker Plan had collapsed. (See Table 9.2.)

9.3.3   Phase III – The Official Concerted Approach to Debt Restructuring

As Bouchet and Hay (1988) summarize the limits of the new money approach: "The strengthening of the financial health of many banking institutions has led these banks to return to more traditional banking business, that is, transactional and specific purpose financing. As banks became stronger, much of the systemic pressure for defensive lending disappeared." The reluctance of the banking system to grant financing, together with weaker unity among the banks, undermined the "system's order" and replaced it with a more flexible "market order": the market-driven "menu" approach. A restructuring menu was devised for debt and debt service reduction with the formal adoption of the Brady Plan in 1989. The Brady initiative aimed not only at reducing the debt burden, but also at restoring conditions for sustainable development and paving the way for the return of these countries to capital markets. Drawing the conclusions from the failure of the new money approach of James Baker, Secretary Brady (1989) declared: "We should encourage debt and debt service reduction on a voluntary basis, while recognizing the importance of continued new lending . . . . We would expect debtor nations also to maintain viable debt/equity swap programs, and would encourage them to permit domestic nationals to engage in such transactions."

The US initiative also marked a turning point in official policy by replacing a refinancing strategy with concerted measures for debt reduction for middle-income countries, all within the framework of a voluntary case-by-case approach. The World Bank and the IMF, with the support of official bilateral creditors, set up specific financing measures to reduce the commercial bank debts of those developing countries implementing robust medium-term macroeconomic adjustment programs. The bilateral support program included assistance facilities set up by the G7 countries. These facilities, in the form of donations, encouraged the reduction of debts to private banks, including the funding of discounted buybacks and technical assistance programs.

All in all, the 18 debtor countries that have implemented debt restructuring agreements within the framework of the Brady Plan are: Argentina, Brazil, Mexico, the Philippines, Morocco,

Bulgaria, Jordan, Poland, Peru, Ecuador, the Dominican Republic, Venezuela, Uruguay, Congo, Côte d'Ivoire and Panama. For each of these agreements, a combination of moral suasion, active marketing by the bank advisory committees, and regulatory adjustments by OECD governments succeeded in achieving reasonable bank participation. The catalytic role of the IMF, the World Bank and regional development banks has been essential for the success of the transactions.

Multilateral Support Program: The Enhancement Role of IFIs

A key feature of the Brady Plan has been the "umbrella effect" of the preferred creditor status of the IFIs, shared with commercial banks, via payment guarantees or via collateral under the form of officially-financed zero coupon bonds. The multilateral support program for the reduction of commercial bank debt comprised a number of measures put in place by the World Bank, the IMF, and the regional development banks. As far as the IMF was concerned, 25% of drawings could be set aside to help reduce debt via buybacks and collaterals. More importantly, the IMF stood ready to "lend into arrears" if the debtor country was showing credible commitment toward a growth-oriented adjustment program, under the constraint of an unsustainable commercial bank debt burden.

On 31 May 1989, the World Bank Executive Directors approved the use of Bank resources to support debt and debt service reduction operations. As far as the World Bank is concerned, the funds allocated to support debt reduction operations amount to 25% of the structural adjustment loan program over three years, or 10% of the total loan program. In addition, bank regulators in OECD countries helped manage the systemic risk of a "chain reaction" of defaults by various tax and accounting adjustments. In all, the Bank and the IMF were prepared to release up to US$25 billion to support debt and debt service reduction to promote sustainable growth.

- *World Bank:* The World Bank allocates funds to support debt reduction operations that amount to 25% of the structural adjustment loan program over three years, or 10% of the total loan program. If need be, additional resources can be used to guarantee interest payments, up to 15% of the Bank's total loan program.
- *IMF:* Around 25% of a country's access to IMF resources can be set aside to support debt reduction operations. The IMF may approve additional resources up to 40% of the member's quota for interest support in connection with debt service reduction transactions.

Moreover, in mid-1989, the World Bank set up a special facility totaling 100 million dollars to support discounted buyback operations for low-income IDA debtor countries. Eligible debt includes commercial bank debt as well as short-term trade credits. The facility was funded with a transfer from the Bank's net income and was replenished in mid-1993. It is supplemented by bilateral financing from France, Japan, Switzerland, the USA and other donor countries. This facility has been used for a dozen low-income debtor countries since March 1991: Bolivia, Niger, Mozambique, Guyana, Uganda, Tanzania, Togo, Zambia, Nicaragua, Albania and Sierra Leone have gained access to IDA funds for discounted buyback operations at a weighted average price of 14 cents.

The Role of the Paris Club as a Forum for Official Bilateral Debt Negotiations

The Paris Club is the name of the *ad hoc* monthly meetings of creditor governments whose role is to negotiate coordinated and sustainable solutions to the external payment problems of developing debtor countries. The Club was set up in 1956 to deal with Argentina's request for rescheduling. Since then, the Paris Club has restructured the debt of close to 80 countries, for a total amount of US$400 billion.[8] Bilateral creditors restructure debt through this forum on a consensual and case-by-case basis consistent with equitable burden sharing. Paris Club debt includes intergovernmental loans and private export credits, guaranteed or insured by an export credit agency. To be valid, proposals for debt reduction must find a consensus within the Paris Club and then be ratified by each of the 19 creditor governments. The Paris Club has its offices in Paris and its secretariat is held by the French Treasury.

The Paris Club negotiations are unique in many respects. Contrary to commercial bank creditors, negotiations are wrapped up in one day. Debt negotiations start early in the morning and are to be completed during the evening or during the night at the latest. There are several reasons for this efficiency. First, there are only 19 Paris Club members, and not hundreds of creditor banks like in the London Club. On a case-by-case basis, additional official creditors are invited to join the talks if they hold a substantial share of claims on the debtor country. This has been the case, *inter alia*, of Brazil, Mexico, Korea, Portugal, Argentina and Israel. Second, the debtor country's borrowing and debt reduction requirements have been assessed prior to the talks by the IMF so as to fill the balance of payments gap. This gap-filling exercise limits the room for maneuver of both the debtor government and the creditor countries. Third, the ritual of the discussions is firmly cast. Accordingly, the debtor country cannot expect to obtain a larger debt reduction than what is necessary to close its financing requirements. Once the debt relief is agreed upon, the Paris Club secretariat uses a standardized format to incorporate the specific terms and conditions of the agreement. Those terms are *a priori* determined by the eligibility status of the countries, regarding their per capita GDP and their solvency indicators. Finally, the debtor country is often accompanied by a specialized financial adviser who ensures an optimal preparation of the negotiations, including a detailed reconciliation of creditors' claims and debtors' liabilities, and who can translate the creditors' negotiating position into debt relief numbers and balance of payments projections.[9] See Box 9.1.

Box 9.1   The consolidated debt in the Paris Club agreements

The principle of the cut-off date has been adopted since May 1984 for all Paris Club rescheduling agreements with the IMF member countries. The cut-off date is established in the first rescheduling agreement and only *pre-cut-off date loans* are eligible to be consolidated under the first and subsequent agreements. Post-cut-off loans must be serviced on schedule. This strategy is intended to protect the flow of "new money" to the developing countries, including official financial assistance and guarantees and insurance for export credits.

Short-term debt falling due during the consolidation period is also excluded from rescheduling. Only exceptionally have creditors agreed to consolidate arrears on short-term debts for first-time reschedulers.

Creditors have agreed to a more comprehensive coverage of pre-cut-off date debts. The agreements typically consolidate 100% of interest and principal payments (as well as arrrears when necessary). Rescheduling of previously rescheduled debt is also common even though the coverage generally excludes the previous or past two reschedulings.

---

[8] See the Presentation of the Paris Club, Paris Club website.
[9] For many years, Owen Stanley Financial has been actively involved in advising country governments in Paris and London Club debt negotiations.

Table 9.3   London-Interbank offer rate on US dollar deposits

Restructuring terms	Eligibility	Debt reduction conditions
Houston 09/90	GDP per capita< $2995 and debt/GDP> 50%	15-year rescheduling with 8–10-year grace
Toronto 10/88	Poorest countries	Menu options for a 33% debt servicing reduction
Naples 12/94	Poorest countries	67% debt relief menu
Lyon 11/96	Poorest countries	Cancellation up to 80%
Cologne 11/99	41 HIPC	90% reduction + swaps up to 20% of outstanding debt stock

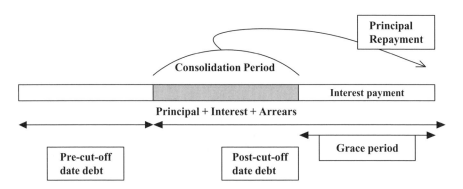

Figure 9.4   Paris Club debt and debt service reduction

Figure 9.4 describes the debt rescheduling process for Paris Club debt. When a debtor country first meets with its creditors, a "cut-off date" is set and is not subject to change in subsequent Paris Club negotiations. Only pre-cut-off date debt is eligible for rescheduling and/or debt relief. The amount of eligible debt is determined by a consolidation period that corresponds to a predefined structural adjustment program with the IMF.

In the first half of the 1980s, the Paris Club gradually expanded the scope and conditions of debt relief to low-income countries, including Multi-Year Rescheduling Agreements (MYRAs) in parallel with commercial banks' debt rescheduling packages. By the late 1980s, however, it became clear that the existing Paris framework for debt relief was inadequate for many highly-indebted poor countries. Paris Club negotiations moved from rescheduling to debt service reduction.

The G7's Toronto meeting of June 1988 was the first measure that looked at the problem of actually reducing debt servicing to Paris Club countries. The first country to benefit from these measures was Mali in October 1988. Around 20 other countries have taken advantage of the conditions for easing debt servicing, accounting for a total of nearly US$6 billion. The salient feature of the Toronto non-ODA debt relief terms is the menu of three options to fit the creditors' budgetary or legal constraints, with a one-third debt alleviation, namely, a debt servicing reduction option, an upfront debt reduction option, and a long-term rescheduling "commercial" option (Table 9.3).

A turning point occurred at the annual meeting of the IBRD and the IMF in Bangkok in October 1991. The G7 representatives announced new debt easing measures: "For the poorest and most indebted countries, the G-7 has acknowledged the need to adopt more concessional debt restructuring terms to support economic rationalization policies." A new flexible menu of "enhanced concessions" provided for a 50% reduction of debt servicing obligations in net present value terms. In a second step, creditors commit themselves to consider the issue of debt stock reduction after a period of three to five years. As usual, multiyear consolidation is conditional on the implementation of ESAF program annual reviews by the IMF Board. In addition, the Paris Club agreed to the principle of reducing debt stock through clauses stipulating conversion of part of the obligations into local currency. The Paris Club does not set a limit for conversions applied to official development aid. However, a limit of 10% to 20% is applied to the outstanding stock of officially guaranteed loans (for example Coface, ECGD and Hermes), or up to SDR15 to 30 million, whichever is higher. Conversion is a voluntary option, and should be ratified by each creditor government in a bilateral agreement. This opportunity has been offered to more than 20 countries including all countries benefitting from the enhanced Toronto terms, such as Senegal, Cameroon, Congo, Côte d'Ivoire, Jamaica, Peru, the Philippines, Morocco, Ecuador and Nigeria.

At the G7 Summit in Naples in July 1994, the main creditor countries agreed to consider British proposals for a further extension of the "enhanced Toronto terms" with a reduction in the stock of debt owed by the poorest countries. The agreement emphasized the case-by-case approach to debt and debt servicing reduction of up to 67% of eligible non-ODA debt to the Paris Club. According to the Paris Club secretariat, about 32 countries have benefitted from the Naples terms, including Honduras, Nicaragua, Haiti, Bolivia, Ghana, Madagascar, Yemen, Bosnia, Ethiopia and Senegal.

More recently, in November 1999, the Paris Club creditors agreed to reinforce the HIPC (highly-indebted poor countries) initiative by raising the level of debt cancellation for the poorest countries with robust track records of adjustment efforts to 90% or more if necessary. All in all, among the 41 eligible countries, 15 countries have benefitted from enhanced debt reduction including Tanzania, Bolivia, Chad, Guinea, Madagascar, Niger, Cameroon, Mali, Benin, Senegal, Uganda, Burkina, Mali, Benin and Mauritania.

Enabling legislation applying to official bilateral debt has opened the scope for debt conversion transactions. Former US President George Bush launched the "Enterprise for the Americas" in June 1990, aimed at reducing the debt of Latin American countries via debt conversion. Under the program, concessional debt is exchanged for new long-term debt with a reduced face value. The initiative also included the recycling of debt payments into local currency investment for sustainable development projects. In addition, the loans could be sold to eligible investors for debt-for-equity and debt-for-nature swaps.

The French Treasury started auctioning developing countries' claims in September 1992. The sales objective was to fund viable and productive local projects in the tourism, infrastructure and industry sectors, with either French, foreign or local private investors. The Treasury followed with Tanzania, Honduras, Morocco, Egypt, etc. The French Treasury's objective boiled down to maximizing the sales return, hence getting as high prices as possible in the auction process. Coface played a role of neutral intermediary, an "honest broker", with the approval of the debtor country to determine a basket of consolidated claims for sale.

In September 1992, the UK Export Credit Agency (ECGD) announced an ambitious program of selling Paris Club debt. The debts concerned are those which have been rescheduled under certain Paris Club and related bilateral agreements. The ECGD only sells claims provided the price it receives implies a higher level of income than the net present value of the expected recovery of the debt, within the framework of the Paris Club agreement.

The demand for ECGD paper has come from banks and from end-users for local investment projects.

All in all, the governments and export credit agencies of France, Belgium, Switzerland, the USA, Spain and Italy have implemented the trading and conversion of official bilateral debt.

Tax and Accounting Regimes and Debt Restructuring Menus

The Brady Plan consisted of a proposal for voluntary debt reduction, the terms of which would be negotiated between debtor and commercial bank creditors. A key "market" feature of these negotiations was a menu of options, including debt reduction, debt conversion and new money, from which commercial banks could choose.

The development of the market-based menu approach took into account the gradual fragmentation of the banking community owing to varying regulatory regimes, divergent long-term business interests and portfolio management policies, and large differences in country risk exposure. The extensive set of contractual provisions and legal covenants that were initially helpful in enforcing the cohesion of commercial banks in restructuring agreements and new money negotiations proved to be less and less effective in maintaining "forced solidarity" among creditor banks (Bouchet, 1988). Tax and accounting benefits for the creation of loan-loss reserves influenced not only the amount of reserves but also the willingness and ability to participate in debt restructuring negotiations. Bouchet and Hay (1989, pp. 157–158) concluded that the Brady Plan faced a collective action challenge: "The dominance of certain banks in the committee negotiating process, legal rigidities, and tax and regulatory disincentives suggest that the menu approach will face significant obstacles."

Table 9.4 summarizes the tax and accounting treatment of general loan-loss reserves in the major OECD countries at the time of the inception of the Brady Plan (Bouchet and Hay, 1989, p. 154).

Table 9.4 Tax and accounting treatment of sovereign debt during the implementation of the Brady Plan

Country	Reserve levels	Tax deduction	Reserve capitalization	Number of eligible countries
France	58%	YES 60% maxi	YES	42
Belgium	60% mini	NO	NO	50
Canada	35% mini	YES 45% maxi	NO	43
Germany	70%	YES	NO	*ad hoc*
Japan	35%	1% only	29%	38
Netherlands	45%	YES	NO	
Switzerland	70%	YES	NO	90
United Kingdom	65%	YES 50%	NO	*matrix*
United States	58% money center	NO	YES	*ad hoc*
United States	75% regionals	NO	YES	*ad hoc*

International banks' regulatory regimes with regard to provisions have been a key factor in the debt restructuring process. The essence of a loan-loss reserve against a claim is to absorb the accounting loss in case of default. And the essence of regulatory capital is to preserve the banks' financial stability in case of a non-performing loan portfolio. Commercial banks which include general reserves in capital (France and the United States) are likely to be reluctant to enter debt reduction schemes owing to the related upfront capital loss. Buybacks and discount bonds will probably meet strong opposition from the creditor banks due to the immediate recognition of the loss of regulatory capital, equal to the difference between the book value of the loan and the cash price received. These banks will prefer par bonds with temporary reduced interest rates in order to stretch the accounting loss in the income statement over the life of the loan. Commercial banks which must reserve against new money credits (e.g., France) face an additional cost compared to banks which have the discretion of increasing or maintaining reserves at existing levels. Finally, banks which benefit from very limited tax deduction on loan-loss reserves (e.g., in Japan) prefer selling discounted LDC claims in order to shrink their new money base and improve asset/capital ratios.

In the early 2000s, the new capital adequacy framework has a large impact on banks' cross-border risk portfolio. The "Cooke ratio" of the 1988 Basle Accord, based on risk-weighted assets, was clearly too rigid. The new Basle Accord, to be implemented in 2004, is more flexible in that it puts more emphasis on banks' own internal risk assessment methodologies. However, it will probably lead to rising banking reluctance to lend to former EMCs that have been promoted to "borderline" OECD countries, namely, Turkey, Mexico, Korea, Hungary and Poland. Bank regulatory regimes are important factors in credit negotiations because they determine the impact of financial transactions on a commercial bank's profit and loss account as well as on its capital position. Other things being equal, a bank will strive to maximize its profit while minimizing capital and reserve needs, so as to limit the funding costs of assets. The higher the level of loan-loss provisions, the greater the cost of carrying existing assets, the stronger the bank's capital position, and the less the additional cost of realizing a loss, both in terms of reported income and capital.

Because rating agencies and stockholders reward strong reserve and capital positions of financial institutions, commercial banks have considerably boosted their loan-loss reserves against LDC assets during the late 1980s and through the 1990s. In the meantime, international banks have increased their capital while shrinking LDC exposure. US banks doubled their capital between 1982 and 1990 while cutting by half their LDC assets as a result of loan sales, debt conversions and write-offs. Figure 9.5 illustrates the "scissor effect" between mounting equity capital and shrinking claims on EMCs of US banks, between 1981 and 2002. The short-lived Baker Plan coincided with a banking situation of capital weakness while the Brady Plan took off as regulatory capital had strengthened for most banking institutions.

Altogether, OECD governments' regulatory agencies have allowed the overexposed and undercapitalized banking system time to recover while treating what was widely perceived as a temporary cash flow problem in the developing countries.

9.4   DEBT REDUCTION INSTRUMENTS

Negotiations for debt restructuring between developing countries and foreign commercial banks are subject to a number of variable parameters, including the amount of debt out-standing, the accounting and fiscal environment, and the flexibility of the "menu" of options

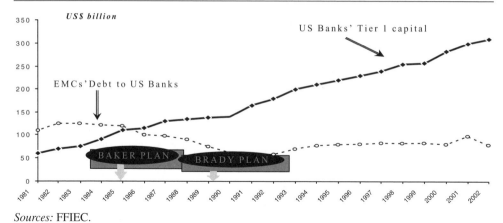

Sources: FFIEC.

Figure 9.5   US banks' claims on EMCs and regulatory capital

presented by the country. All other things being equal, the larger the menu, the more flexible the dialogue between the bank creditors and the debtor country. In most negotiations since 1990, comprehensive restructuring menus have included options for buying back debt, exchanging debt, converting debt, new money loans and debt rescheduling.

- *Par bond*: Exchange of old claims for a security with similar face value but with below-market interest rate, 30-year bullet maturity and principal guarantee.
- *Discount bond*: Conversion of old debt into new security with discounted face value, market-based floating rate of interest, 30-year bullet maturity and principal enhancements under the form of zero coupon bonds.
- *Front-loaded interest-reduction bond*: Exchange of old claims for new security at face value with below-market rate of interest for the first few years, increasing gradually to market-based floating rate and with shorter maturity and grace period.
- *Debt conversion bond*: Exchange of old claims for a security opening scope for conversion into local currency or into equity in domestic private firms.
- *New money bond*: Exchange of loans into tradeable securities with floating rates of interest (usually LIBOR-based) and market-based spread over LIBOR.
- *Discounted debt buyback*: Claim sale for cash by the creditor to the debtor country at a price close to that prevailing in the secondary market of commercial bank claims. The repurchase transaction extinguishes the debt.

Buying back debt at a discount either formally or informally enables developing countries to reduce their debt by exploiting the discount on commercial bank loans in the secondary markets. For highly indebted countries, one aim of buying back debt is to change the community of creditor banks by making it easier for small banks to leave. Debt repurchases provide an exit mechanism. For low-income countries with little commercial debt, the purchase can be used to eliminate market-based bank debt. Since debt buybacks boil down to prepayment of debt, they must be carried out uniformly for all creditor banks or they must be based on a waiver of *pari passu* clauses in loan agreements. Official buybacks with financial backing from multilateral bodies were made by Bolivia in January 1988, by Chile in November 1988, by the Philippines in January 1990 and by Niger and several other low-income countries in the framework of the IDA-debt reduction facility since 1991. These transactions use official funding from bilateral and multilateral creditors. They aim at cleaning up the countries' liabilities portfolios without any intention of restoring market access.

Debt exchange offers are based on the securitization of old debts in the form of bonds. The exchange of non-performing loans for tradeable and liquid bonds, in itself, constitutes an enhancement in the banks' portfolios. Discount bonds and par bonds have been used in most Brady debt restructuring agreements. Brady bonds have been frequently collateralized with special issues of zero coupon US treasury securities or comparable instruments (i.e., Banque de France) if the bonds are in a currency other than the US dollar (e.g., Côte d'Ivoire). Interest payments are often covered by 12–18-month rolling collateral, near-cash securities. These enhancements are purchased in part from the country's own resources or by credits from bilateral and multilateral donors. Collateralized defeasance involves extinguishing the debt through the provision of a financial asset to be held in a trust account as guarantee against the principal of the debt. The face value and maturity of the collateral instrument are designed to match those of the debt being defeased so that the proceeds of the guarantee at maturity may be used to fully repay the principal in a single balloon or "bullet" repayment. In essence, the debt is prepaid and, although still recorded in the books of the central bank or in the debt volumes of the World Bank, the payment at maturity has no bearing on the country's solvency and liquidity ratios. The US Federal Reserve Bank of New York has played the role of custodian for debt collateral in several instances as well as the BIS.

Discounted buybacks and debt exchange offers might generate moral hazard issues. Debtor countries may have the incentive to drive down the price in the secondary market of commercial bank claims in order to "recapture" a larger portion of the current discount. Creditors may thus be reluctant to accept deep discount exchanges while giving up the "upward" potential once the country gets its act together with restored sustainable growth conditions. This is why debt and debt service reduction workouts have always been agreed upon in parallel with structural adjustment programs under the auspices of the IFIs and along with official funding. This is also why several debt restructuring deals have incorporated "good fortune" recapture clauses. The agreements with Costa Rica, Mexico, Nigeria, Uruguay, Bulgaria and Venezuela have value recovery provisions. For Mexico, Nigeria and Venezuela, if the price of oil should rise above a reference price, bondholders can recapture part of the funds. For Uruguay, value recovery is based on a trade index for Uruguayan prices for wool, beef, rice and oil. The value recovery clause for Costa Rica is based on economic performance; recapture is triggered by GDP exceeding 120% of the 1989 figure in real terms. Regarding Bulgaria, the value recovery is related to the discount bonds only. The trigger mechanism is based on the real GDP index as measured in Bulgarian lev that must equal or exceed 125% of the 1994 reference.

All in all, the market value for Brady bonds stems from the following financial parameters:

> Face value of original debt
> Secondary market price
> Exchange rate (par bond/discount bond)
> Coupon level and interest rate (fixed/floating)
> Maturity and grace period of new debt
> Enhancements (guarantees, collateral and recapture clauses)

9.5   THE WAY FORWARD IN THE EARLY 2000s:
BACK TO THE 1890s?

One can observe several striking points of the post-Brady years, i.e., the late 1990s and early 2000s, that lead to an evolving structure in the financial flows to the emerging countries. First, private capital flows have risen sharply during the last decade and are larger than the volume of official flows. Second, within flows of private capital sources, one can notice a shift from bank loans to bonds. The surge in the share of bondholders in net financing stems from the combination of debt exchange offers and net issuance of bonds and notes. Third, there is a marked increase in non-debt-creating flows under the form of foreign direct investment (FDI) and equity portfolio investment. Fourth, loans and bonds often incorporate risk-mitigation instruments, under the form of political risk insurance, official and built-in country risk guarantees, and off-shore escrow accounts.

9.5.1   The Return of Private Capital Flows

Walter Wriston, former chairman of Citicorp, used to boast that "countries don't go bankrupt", as a justification for mounting risk exposure in Latin America and in other sovereign debtors. With his unique pragmatic, if not thorough, vision, Wriston added: "As long as a bank keeps its risks within its risk-taking capabilities, it survives; and if it doesn't, it dies."[10] When bankers realized that, contrary to countries, overexposed banks can go bankrupt, the net flow of spontaneous private capital dried up. During the mid-1980s, the IFIs provided emerging countries with the bulk of balance of payments financing. The black hole of balance of payment gaps or that of government budget deficits could no longer be filled up with syndicated eurocredits on market conditions. Banks restricted their cross-border financial activities to "defensive refinancing", specific-purpose project financing or short-term trade credits, with collateral.

As Table 9.5 illustrates, external private capital flows to emerging market countries have picked up during the second half of the 1990s. Most of the financing has been concentrated in the 15 middle-income countries whose debt has been restructured under the Brady Plan.

Table 9.5   Developing countries' access to international capital markets in US$ billion

US$ billion	BIS-reporting banks' claims and notes and bonds issues							
	1985	1990	1995	1998	1999	2000	2001	mid-2002
Loans								
Developing countries	506	525	770	839	805	742	717	709
Bonds								
Developing countries			313	324	357	456	490	529
Total	**506**	**525**	**1083**	**1163**	**1162**	**1198**	**1207**	**1238**
	1985	1990	1995	1998	1999	2000	2001	mid-2002
Loans	506	525	770	839	805	742	717	709
Bonds			313	324	357	456	490	529
Total	**506**	**525**	**1083**	**1163**	**1162**	**1198**	**1207**	**1238**

---

[10] International Banking Survey. *The Economist*, 21 March 1987, p. 4.

They include large borrowers such as Argentina, Brazil, Poland, Mexico, the Philippines and Chile. In addition, Turkey and Hungary, as well as several newly industrialized countries in Asia, most notably, Thailand, Indonesia, Singapore, Malaysia and South Korea, have received the bulk of private capital flows.

9.5.2 The Return of Bondholders

As early as 1991, one could observe the premises of restoration of access to voluntary capital market financing. As the IMF noted: "In contrast to the early years of the debt crisis, most new medium and long-term financing raised by re-entrants has been mobilized through bond issues as well as equity placements."[11] Contrary to loans that are easily rescheduled, bonds hold a *de facto* senior status. This status simply stems from the bearer nature of securities that makes it difficult to trace down the community of holders worldwide.

The rise in bond shares over bank loans came from the combination of two factors. First, widening the investor pool was a primary motive for emerging market countries, as they tapped the interest of other institutions, including insurance companies, investment funds and pension funds. Second, debt exchange offers throughout the 1990s changed the nature of the claims without changing the nature of the creditors, as banks swapped loans for bonds in their portfolios. These bonds are clearly more liquid than loans and can be traded in the secondary markets, providing the initial creditors with liquidity and the new holders with portfolio diversification.

The emergence of bonds as an important category of private investment has led to a better organization of this class of investors. Both ISMA (Box 9.2) and, more recently, EMCA (Box 9.3) play a coordinating role, including that of disseminating information for private creditors.

Box 9.2   International Securities Market Association (ISMA)

> ISMA was established in 1969. It is the self-regulatory organization and trade association for the global bond market. Its main purpose is to represent the interest of banks and securities houses worldwide. The driving factor behind the growth of the international securities market was a combination of tax issues and bank competition, and technology changes. ISMA performs a central role by providing a global framework of industry-driven rules and recommendations which regulate and guide trading and settlement in this market. In addition, ISMA provides reliable and accurate bond market data as well as risk management tools. The Association's membership comprises some 640 financial organizations based in around 50 countries. The majority of those members are banks and securities houses.
>
> See: www.isma.org

Box 9.3   The Emerging Markets' Creditor Association (EMCA)

> The EMCA was set up in the wake of Ecuador's US$6.5 billion default in 1999. The EMCA was established in November 2000 to help bondholders unite to represent their common interests. It represents international bondholder creditors in sovereign and corporate bond default situations.

---

[11] *Private Market Financing for Developing Countries*, IMF, December 1991, p. 15.

The EMCA includes mutual funds, institutional fund managers, insurance companies, total return funds as well as other investors. Its members hold more than US$50 billion in emerging markets debt. It also helps bondholders and issuers become better acquainted, thereby facilitating a fruitful dialogue between creditors and debtors.

See: www.emca.org

9.5.3   The Rise in Non-Debt-Creating Flows

Along with a surge in portfolio capital flows, a key feature of the 1990s is dynamic foreign direct investment flows. Privatization programs in many Latin American, Asian and Eastern European countries have been a driving force behind these flows. A very few countries, however, absorb the bulk of FDI. The share of middle-income countries has risen to as much as 94% of FDI flows in 2001, compared with 87% in 1991.[12] Mexico, Brazil, India, China, Malaysia and Indonesia get the lion's share. Latin American countries' ratio of FDI-to-GDP rose from 1% in the beginning of the decade to nearly 4% in 2001. FDI flows to developing countries increased to about US$150 billion annually in the 1997–2001 period, compared to less than US$50 billion in 1991–1992.

These non-debt-creating flows bring with them several benefits. Not only do they exhibit greater stability than other types of private capital flows, but reinvested earnings are procyclical, and FDI also brings technology and market-driven management. In addition, as private investors, both foreign and domestic, react positively to market size and investment climate, FDI tends to crowd in domestic investment.

Private capital flows to emerging markets have also been encouraged by country funds, mainly in Asia, Eastern Europe and Latin America. They played a crucial role in the development of domestic stock markets and, like FDI, brought with them incentives for further liberalization and better governance. These funds have often been promoted by IFC and by the EBRD and their listings in exchange markets enhance liquidity. As reported by the IMF, the number of so-called emerging market mutual equity funds increased from 91 in 1988 to 573 in 1993.[13] Growth kept up in the second half of the 1990s, mainly with mutual funds targeting Asian countries, including China.

9.5.4   The Emergence of Structured Financing

Mexico was the pioneer in using structured financing and collateralization to help reduce country risk and alleviate the reserve and capital requirements of its creditor banks. Mexico's market re-entry in the US and European medium-term capital markets used the pledging of long-distance receivables by Telmex, the national telephone company privatized in 1990. Other collateral-backed offerings used credit card receivables as well as receivables arising from cross-border electricity sales in the United States. Mexicana de Cobre pledged a loan repayment with copper export revenues in 1989 and 1991. Contrary to the external borrowing of the 1970s and 1980s, borrowers in the capital markets in the 1990s involved private corporations, through the issue of bonds and the overseas placement of Euro-certificates of deposits and commercial paper. Other borrowers have used the creation of specific-purpose off-shore vehicles, to which a secure income stream is assigned, hence reducing or even eliminating

---

[12] UNCTAD, World Investment Report 2001 and World Bank, Global Development Finance 2001.
[13] *Private Market Financing for Developing Countries*, IMF, March 1995, pp. 24–25.

country risk. Early redemption and conversion options constitute credit enhancements that have helped sovereign and corporate emerging market borrowers to regain market access. Political risk insurance is also used to mitigate country risk, thereby facilitating market access. In September 2002, a 15-year political risk insurance policy was issued in support of a US$50 million securitization of mortgage-backed bonds in Costa Rica. The transaction was rated AAA by the rating agencies. A higher rating than Costa Rica's sovereign rating was achieved thanks to the structure and enhancements of the market transaction.[14] Sovereign Ltd's global insurance portfolio, reportedly, exceeds US$6 billion, spread over more than 90 emerging markets.

Gradual improvements in the rating of corporate and sovereign debts by S&P and Moody's also help promote the EMCs' market re-entry. The World Bank was also instrumental in helping country risk reduction through its co-financing program, namely, the World Bank-sponsored B-loans. These guarantees are callable in the event of default. Thus, in mid-October 2002, the World Bank paid US$250 million to holders of Argentine bonds in a US$1.5 billion notes series backed by the Bank.

9.6 CONCLUSION

Country risk strikes wherever and whenever it is not expected, at least by the majority of risk analysts, creditors as well as investors. This is why risk translates into losses. In mid-1997, the abrupt devaluation of the Thai baht caught the IFIs and most international banks by surprise. The Asian "tigers" had all the credentials of newly industrialized countries. They had high savings and investment ratios as well as no major macroeconomic imbalances. They attracted large net inflows of FDI and portfolio investment. Nevertheless, the financial crisis engulfed the whole region in 1998 while the spill-over affected both Latin America as well as Eastern Europe in less than a year. LTCM's collapse, in 1999, was also a shock for private investors and correspondent commercial banks all over the world. The fund was managed by a superb team of seasoned financial experts including several Nobel Prize winners. Nevertheless, the confidence crisis was so deep and the losses so large that the Federal Reserve Board had to intervene, along with other G7 central banks, to inject liquidity into the system and to stem the risk of a liquidity crisis. Similarly, Argentina exhibited many apparent strengths throughout the 1990s, including a stable exchange rate and no inflation, large flows of FDI, positive growth until 1998, and the support of the IFIs in the form of World Bank guarantees. Finally, September 11 in the USA is also an example of a geopolitical crisis that simply proves there is no sanctuary from global terrorism.

In retrospect, one can multiply the examples and there will probably be many other examples in the future. Bouchet (1982) observed similar shortcomings of traditional country risk analysis at the time of the outbreak of the debt crisis in 1982. The point is that, in each of the crises, a complex combination of overconfidence, myopia, herd instinct and weak analysis has been at the root of excess country risk exposure followed by excess abruptness of withdrawal by investors and creditors (Box 9.4).

Box 9.4 Insolvency and creditors' rights committee of the International Bar Association

Committee J is the most prominent international association of lawyers interested in insolvency and creditors' rights law. It currently has more than 1100 members from over 85

---

[14] Sovereign Risk Insurance Ltd, Press Report, 9 September 2002.

countries. It serves as an Official Observer to the UNCITRAL Working Group on Insolvency Law. This association works on the existing and changing out-of-court workouts and international insolvency regimes in many countries. It gathers important details regarding information on the procedures, the role of creditors' committees and provisions for mutual assistance. Its objective is enhancing the harmonization of insolvency regulatory regimes to ensure certainty and effectiveness in cross-border trade and other financial transactions.

See: www.ibanet.org

Mounting volatility in the global economy adds an element of risk for investors. The transmission of national and regional economic disequilibria is growing faster than ever. Short-term capital flows shift from one financial market to another almost instantaneously. Information flows often create the paradox of intensifying the uncertainty (Bouchet, 2002). Short-term speculation, capital flight and the creditors' race to seize the assets of countries in financial difficulties compound country risk and even create self-fulfilling prophecies, thereby precipitating default. This is why the IMF has proposed a new bankruptcy system for indebted nations, with their own version of US-style "Chapter 11" bankruptcy laws. This framework would allow countries to temporarily stop paying their debts while putting their house in order under the protection of exchange controls. The system would also give seniority to those investors holding bonds issued after a bankruptcy-cum-restructuring process (Schwartz, 2001). The push for an internationally regulated sovereign bankruptcy procedure would help countries restructure their economies, under close IFI monitoring, without being sued by private creditors. In essence, this proposal is a direct follow-up of the Brady Plan, thereby enforcing concerted practices and solidarity between investors, creditors and countries. It implies that, in a globalized system, country risk is too important to be left to market forces alone.

The complexity of country risk, as presented in the preceding chapters, requires first of all timely and comprehensive information, as well as a robust base for thorough analysis of the country itself and of its economic, financial and geopolitical relationships with the rest of the world. Globalization of economic and political relations makes the challenge formidable. But the vast opportunities in the global economy are as impressive as the risks they generate.

APPENDIX: THE BRADY PLAN AT WORK IN EMCs[15]

Mexico

After nearly one full year of negotiations, Mexico was the first country to reach an agreement on debt and debt service reduction with its commercial bank creditors in February 1990. It was a comprehensive agreement, covering some 85% of all commercial debt. The agreement initially rescheduled all the eligible debt for 16 years with four years of grace, then offered banks the option of providing new money equal to 25% of their exposure over four years without enhancement or converting their rescheduled debt into bonds. Discount bonds held either a reduced face value (65%) and market-based interest rate (LIBOR + 13/16%), or the same face value but with a reduced and fixed interest rate (6.25%). Both bonds had 30-year "bullet" maturities, with defeasance enhancements under the form of a principal collateralization through

---

[15] Authors' data as well as World Bank, World Debt Tables, vol. 1, 1990–1995 and World Bank, Review of progress under the program to support debt and debt service reduction, Report to the Executive Directors, 21 March 1990.

the pledging of zero coupon US treasury securities and 18-month rolling collateral on the interest payments. Interest recapture provisions were linked to future oil prices. The enhancements were funded by resources drawn from the World Bank, IMF, Mexico's reserves and (indirectly) the Japanese EXIM Bank.

Philippines

In October 1989, the Philippines and its commercial creditors proposed granting waivers and implementing a debt buyback at a 50% discount. Debt not repurchased would have its interest rate reduced to 13/16% over LIBOR, and banks would be asked to provide new money in the form of either bonds or loans equivalent to about 15% of their holdings over two years on the same terms as the existing rescheduled debt (i.e., 15 years' maturity with an eight-year grace period). The bonds would be explicitly excluded from any new money base in the future. Banks contributing new money would be allowed to convert an equivalent amount of their earlier 1985 new money commitment (up to a maximum 50%) into bonds, thereby placing both the new money bonds and that share of the 1985 new money debt outside the base for future new money calls or rescheduling. All in all, the Philippines undertook two official buyback operations: one in 1990 that was linked to the new money call and another in May 1992 as an alternative to the conversion of Brady bonds.

Costa Rica

Costa Rica reached an agreement for a debt and debt service reduction operation in November 1989. The agreement between the debtor country and its advisory committee covered practically all commercial debt including arrears, a total of some US$1.8 billion. Banks were given the option of either selling their assets, including arrears, to Costa Rica at 16% of their face value, or exchanging them into long-term, low-coupon bonds. Principal and arrears were repurchased separately but at the same price. This was equivalent to about 19 cents per 1 US$ of original debt plus its accumulated arrears.

Venezuela

An agreement with the bank advisory committee was reached in December 1990. Banks were offered five options: temporary interest reduction bonds including a one-year rolling interest guarantee for the five-year period in which interest rates are fixed at rates below expected market rates; bonds with a 30% discount and market-based interest rates; interest reduction par bonds including recapture clauses linked to oil prices; buyback at a 55% discount; finally, about one-third of the banks chose the option of new money bonds, thereby providing the country with US$6 billion in new financing.

Chile

Since mid-1985, Chile operated two debt conversion programs, one open to both residents and non-residents (Chapter 18 scheme) and the other solely to non-residents (Chapter 19 scheme); the former scheme was intended to encourage repatriation of flight capital. The scheme restricted to non-residents carries rights of remittances of profits and capital, the other prohibits remittances. The Chapter 18 scheme was aimed at discounted debt repurchases, whereas the Chapter 19 scheme consisted essentially of conversions of debt into equity. In early December 1989, Chile repurchased $139.8 million of its outstanding commercial bank debt for cash through a voluntary auction procedure. The average price was $0.5825 but the government had set $0.59 as the cut-off price. The debt reduction operation was financed jointly by drawing upon the Copper Stabilization Fund (US$172 million), the quick-disbursing element of a World Bank loan (US$80 million), and the proceeds of the standby arrangement with the Fund (SDR64 million or about US$80 million). In accordance with the 1988 rescheduling agreement, banks holding a critical mass of claims equivalent to 66% of debt were required to approve the transaction.

Argentina

In July 1992, the debtor reached its agreement on DDSR terms that covered US$21 billion of long-term debt and an estimated US$8 billion of interest arrears. For the long-term debt, creditors chose between 30-year bullet maturity discount bonds (with a 35% discount) and par bonds, also at a 30-year bullet maturity. Both bonds are collateralized. Regarding past-due interest, US$400 million was paid in cash, US$300 million exchanged for notes (which will be immediately redeemed by the Argentine government), and the remaining US$7.7 billion converted into 12-year bonds with a three-year grace period.

Brazil

In August 1992, an agreement in principle was reached to restructure about US$44 billion of debt, with a six-option menu offering discount bonds, par bonds with permanent and temporary interest reduction, new money combined with conversion bonds, and a restructuring for temporary relief. The closing of the agreement took place in April 1994.

Brazil's debt was restructured with a menu of five instruments, namely:

- Par bonds = 30-year bonds at 4% rising to 6% in year 7 with principal guarantee and one year of rolling interest collateral;
- Discount bonds = 30-year bonds with 35% discount and a rate of LIBOR + 13/16%. The country provides principal and interest guarantees;
- FLIRBs = 15 years of which nine years of grace with rates rising from 4% to 5% in year 6 and LIBOR + 13/16% thereafter. Interest collateral is provided during the first six years;
- New money convertible bonds represent old debt converted into bonds with 18 years of maturity and 10 years of grace and a rate of LIBOR + 7/8%. New money representing 18% of eligible old debt has terms of 15/7 with a rate of LIBOR + 7/8%;
- FLIRBs with capitalization option are bonds with a 20-year maturity and 10-year grace and an effective rate of 8%. In the first six years, interest is paid in cash at fixed rates rising from 4% to 5%, the difference with fixed rate of 8% being capitalized.

Dominican Republic

The Dominican Republic reached an agreement in principle with commercial bank creditors on a Brady program, in May 1993, covering some US$775 million medium and long-term debt, incorporating three options: a cash buyback at 25 US cents on the dollar for debt principal and interest that remains after a downpayment; a collateralized discount bond at a 35% discount; and an uncollateralized interest reduction bond.

Jordan

In June 1993, Jordan reached an agreement to restructure commercial bank debt of about US$800 million. The package comprised three options: par bonds discount bonds and a buyback facility plus a potential replacement of some interest arrears with bonds. The par bonds have a bullet maturity of 30 years with interest rising up to 6% after year 6. The discount bonds also carry a 30-year maturity with 35% discount and interest at 13/16% over LIBOR. Both par and discount bonds were collateralized by US zero coupon bonds with six-month rolling interest guarantees. The interest arrears bonds held a 12-year maturity, with three years' grace and interest at LIBOR plus 13/16%.

Bulgaria

Bulgaria reached a Brady-type agreement with its creditors on 30 June 1994. The menu included a buyback at 25 cents to the dollar, bonds with a 50% discount, front-loaded interest reduction bonds with 18 years' tenor, eight years' grace, rising interest rates, and interest arrears bonds (17/7) with rising instalments. The deal provided for a 47% reduction in Bulgaria's hard currency debt of more than US$8 billion. The agreement was supported by official funding coming from the IMF, the World Bank and bilateral creditors.

Poland

Poland signed its Brady agreement with a debt reduction of about 45% on 30 August 1994 for the rescheduling of $13.2 billion of external debt. The deal included 30-year par bonds, discount bonds, past-due interest bonds and new money bonds on 35% of the base debt. No rollover interest guarantee was set up. The bonds have a 20-year maturity with seven-year grace, they pay 3.25% initially and step up to 7% by the ninth year. Poland had to reach an agreement with the Dart family, reportedly holding 6.2% of the London Club debt. The buyback required a waiver from holders of 95% of the debt paper.

Ecuador

Ecuador's Brady plan (June 1994) menu of principal options is constituted of a 45% discount bond and a par bond with a 30-year tenor, principal guaranteed with US zero coupon bonds, interest equalization bonds and PDI bonds with rising instalments, and respectively 10 years' tenor with no grace and 20 years' tenor and 10 years' grace. The interest rate was set at LIBOR+13/16%.

REFERENCES

Aggarwal VK, 1989, Interpreting the History of Mexico's External Debt Crises. *In:* B Eichengreen and PH Lindert, eds. *The International Debt Crisis in Historical Perspective*. Massachusetts: MIT Press.
Barry JM, 1987, 200 Banks Facing Failure this Year. *The Washington Post*, 22 May.
Bouchet M, 1982, Crise d'Endettement: Risque de défaut et défaut d'analyse. *Revue Banque*, Septembre.
Bouchet MH, 1987a, The Political Economy of International Debt: The Case of Mexico. PhD Dissertation, USC.
Bouchet MH, 1987b, *The Political Economy of International Debt: What, Who, How Much and Why*. Greenwood, IL: Quorum Books.

Bouchet M, 1988, Third World Risk: Long-term Treatment, No Quick Fixes. *International Financing Review*, London, September.

Bouchet M, 2002, Triangle Instable: Risque-Pays, Information et Nouvelles Technologies. *AGEFI*, Septembre.

Bouchet M and Hay J, 1988, *The Rise of the Market-based Menu Approach and its Limitations.* Washington, DC: World Bank, September.

Bouchet M and Hay J, 1989, The Rise of the Market-based Menu Approach and Its Limitations. *In:* H Husain and I Diwan, eds. *Dealing with the Debt Crisis*, World Bank Symposium. Washington, DC: World Bank.

Brady N, 1989, Remarks by The Secretary of the Treasury Nicholas Brady to the Brookings Institution, 10 March. *Treasury News*, Washington, 4–5.

Eichengreen B and Lindert PH, 1989, *The International Debt Crisis in Historical Perspective.* Massachusetts: MIT Press, 2.

Eichengreen B and Portes R, 1989, After the Deluge: Default, Negotiation, and Readjustment During the Interwar Years. *In:* B Eichengreen and PH Lindert, eds. *The International Debt Crisis in Historical Perspective*. Massachusetts: MIT Press, 26–7.

Fischer S, 1988, *Economic Development and the Debt Crisis.* World Bank Policy, Planning and Research Working Papers, June, 8.

Glynn L, 1985, Government Finance – Is The Latin Debt Crisis Over? Don't Kid Yourself. *Institutional Investor*, May, 86.

Hughes H, 1979, Debt and Development: The Role of Foreign Capital in Economic Growth. *World Development*, Feb, 7 (2), 96.

Schwartz E, 2001, *IMF Proposes Bankruptcy System for Indebted Nations.* Bloomberg.com, 27 November.

Tenenbaum BA, 1985, *Mexico en la época de los agiotistas, 1821–1857.* Fondo de Cultura Economica, México.

10
Country Risk and Risk Mitigation Instruments

10.1 INTRODUCTION

This chapter addresses the ways and means investors and creditors can employ to mitigate country risk. They can use a wide array of financial and institutional instruments to get protection against cross-border risk and return volatility. Export cover, investment insurance and a market-driven menu of financial innovations can enhance liquidity while reducing country risk (Figure 10.1).

According to an international survey of risk investors conducted by MIGA (Multilateral Investment Guarantee Authority), approximately 50% expressed the views that political risk is more of a concern today than five years ago (Ikawa, 2001). According to Ducroire – Belgium's export guarantee agency – 90% of credit losses in overseas export markets accrues from country risk. In a world of mounting uncertainty, where the September 11 terrorist attack on the US boosted the awareness of political risk, Hiscox, the provider of specialist business insurance, and the Control Risk Group, the international business risk consultancy group, claim they have handled over 1100 kidnap or extortion cases across 87 countries. The CRG's RiskMap 2002 survey has increased the number of countries rated at High or Extreme Security Risk by 30% to 60 countries (http://www.crg.com).

All in all, the new global economy has increased both risks and opportunities for investors, project finance lenders, creditors and exporters involved in cross-border strategies. Risk in today's global marketplace can take a wide array of forms. Risks are illustrated by the high volatility of short-term capital flows with resulting destabilizing speculation, the international transmission of financial crisis through "spill-over effects", transnational mafia networks, terrorism and the like. Meanwhile, despite global nervousness, strategic investors use sovereign emerging market debt as suitable instruments of diversification. A mid-2001 emerging markets investor survey by JP Morgan, covering some US$127 billion under management, concluded that in an environment where risk aversion is on the rise, risk diversification toward sovereign emerging market debt gets a higher priority.[1]

As a result of mounting risks in a more complex global market, investors and lenders try to mitigate their vulnerability. This can be done by obtaining "comfort" from official bilateral and multilateral agencies through insurance coverage or co-lender status. It can also be done through market-based instruments that alter an investor's risk exposure, thereby achieving superior risk–return combinations. These financial instruments include asset securitization, asset-backed securities and debt conversion transactions that provide an implicit access to a preferential exchange rate.

---

[1] Investors look to emerging sovereigns, *Financial Times*, 30 July 2002.

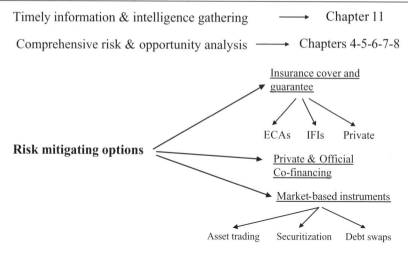

Figure 10.1   How to mitigate country risk

10.2   THE ROLE OF NATIONAL EXPORT CREDIT AGENCIES

Risk-averse corporate managers can rely on export cover and insurance guarantees. Regarding the promotion and protection of trade flows, most OECD countries have set up official export credit agencies (ECAs) to enhance exports and foreign investment while mitigating country risk. Since 1978, all OECD-based ECAs have achieved the elimination of trade-distorting tied aid and they all provide exporters with a level playing field equal to the OECD minimum risk fees. At stake behind export and investment promotion is the support of domestic economic activity, employment expansion and geopolitical influence. These agencies grant cover for exports to around 160 or more countries. Political risk insurers, both public and private, provide a broad range of coverage to investors, including that against expropriation, currency blockage, breach of contract, sequestration, confiscation, *inter alia*. They provide such coverage on the assumption that if the insurers are required to pay compensation, they will then have a legal basis to pursue recovery against the host government. With the support of dynamic guarantee facilities, around 20% of OECD countries' exports to developing countries are guaranteed against country risk.

From the borrower's and importer's standpoint, export credit financing is well suited to projects involving substantial investment for imported capital equipment, since export credits typically offer longer maturities than standard commercial bank loans. The fixed interest rate usually applicable to officially supported export credits is also an advantage for the country's overall creditworthiness. In addition, export credit agencies help mobilize export credit for medium-size private enterprises in developing countries, which have limited access to medium and long-term credits. From the investor's standpoint, export credit co-financing goes with balance of payments support as well as the monitoring of technically sound procurement arrangements.

The major ECAs in the OECD countries are the following:

- *Austria*: Oesterreichische Kontrollbank AG
- *Belgium*: Office National du Ducroire
- *Canada*: Export Development Corporation (EDC)

- *France*: Compagnie Française du Commerce Exterieur (Coface)
- *Germany*: Hermes Kreditversicherungs AG
- *Italy*: SACE
- *Japan*: Export–Import Insurance Department
- *Spain*: Compañia Española de Seguros de Crédito a la Exportación, SA (CESCE)
- *United Kingdom*: Export Credits Guarantee Department (ECGD)
- *United States*: Export–Import Bank of the United States (Exim-Bank)

The Coface Group (Box 10.1) has emerged as a major player in the field of country risk assessment and risk insurance, with more than 50 years of cover experience in 99 countries. The Group's two core businesses are credit insurance and credit management services, including country risk analysis, credit information, management and recovery. It is rated AA by Fitch IBCA. Risk analysis is performed in partnership with Unistrat Insurance, a company specializing in the coverage of political risk in 170 countries. About half the exposure is concentrated in Latin America and the Middle East. Political risk is defined as any event or decision of a political or administrative order, be it national or international, which can cause financial, commercial or economic loss to a business. Political risk insurance covers the direct impact of said events on export, import, investment and financing activities. The following risks are included in this definition:

- Events: riots, civil commotion, strikes, wars and malicious acts.
- Arbitrary decisions by a public entity: breach of contract, discrimination, boycott
- Political decisions: embargo, revocation of license, currency inconvertibility, non-transfer of assets, confiscation, expropriation, nationalization, deprivation, etc.

Box 10.1   Coface

The Coface Group facilitates and secures trade throughout the world. The Group offers more than 78 000 companies – whether large or small, whatever their business and wherever they are – a range of solutions spanning rating, protection and services. By furnishing market survey information and investment guarantees along with credit insurance, receivables management and business information, the Group gives its clients the opportunity to outsource the entire management of their customer data accounts.

The Common Risk System, built around a database containing information on 41 million companies worldwide, represents the backbone of the Group's @rating Solution, a unique web-based rating system allowing enterprises to insure trade debt throughout the world. @rating Solution, which forms part and parcel of all Coface products, helps enterprises to expand in today's global marketplace and will provide them with the keys to success in their future e-business initiatives.

Country risk analysis is expressed in a rating/ranking format but based on a qualitative analysis aimed at integrating the socio-political and economic specificities of each country. Coface takes into account and assesses six types of risk around six different analytical modules: political risk; liquidity and non-transfer risk; sovereign risk; market crisis risk; systemic banking crisis; macroeconomic growth risk.

http://www.coface.org

In Belgium, the role of Ducroire (Box 10.2) is worth noting as the Brussels-based ECA has taken the lead in implementing debt conversion transactions in the early 1990s to reduce its cross-border exposure while enhancing the liquidity of its portfolio.

Box 10.2   Ducroire

Ducroire insures all forms of cross-border investment against infringement of rights of ownership and non-payment, including the following:

- participating interest in the capital of a foreign company
- loans equivalent to investments
- guarantees for bank loans
- reinvestment of profits

The loss due to infringement and/or non-payments must be the direct result of one of the following events:

- expropriation
- non-transferability of currency
- war and riots
- government action
- breach of contract

The standard policy has a term of 15 years and the losses are compensated up to 90% of the investment value. The premium is paid annually and it is related to the country risk classification and the insurance scope.

http://www.delcredere.be/ducroire

In the United States, the Exim-Bank (Box 10.3) performs a key role of export and investment promotion while being actively involved in official debt reduction and debt conversion schemes, particularly in Latin American countries.

Box 10.3   Exim-Bank

The Export Credit Insurance Program helps US exporters develop and expand their overseas sales by protecting them against loss should a foreign buyer or other foreign debtor default for political or commercial reasons.

Exim-Bank's guarantees provide repayment protection for private sector loans to credit-worthy buyers of US exports. In the event of default, it will repay the principal and interest on the loan. The foreign buyer is required to make at least a 15% cash payment.

Exim-Bank's comprehensive guarantee program covers 100% of the commercial and political risks for medium-term insurance, guarantees and loans. It also guarantees lease financing. Eligible participants are any US or foreign bank, located in the United States or overseas. Political risks include transfer risk, expropriation and political violence, excluding devaluation of a foreign currency as a risk of default.

Exim-Bank is the US government's arm to promote trade and FDI in emerging markets. As such, the bank plans to increase the volume of credit given to Russia for financing exports from the USA, totaling around USD300 million. Exim-Bank's total credit portfolio currently stands at USD58 billion. Russia's share of this is around 3.5%. Over the 1999–2001 period, the bank has financed the shipping of exports worth around USD3 billion to Russia.

http://www.exim.gov/

10.3 THE ROLE OF OFFICIAL MULTILATERAL RISK GUARANTEE INSTITUTIONS

The "country risk mitigation" role of international financial organizations is rooted in their preferred creditor status. Simply said, obligations to World Bank institutions rank preferred to other "subordinated" obligations. As Moran (2001) notices: "As part of their effort to facilitate flows of private capital to emerging markets, MIGA and multilateral lending agencies are spreading the "umbrella" of their preferred status over other parties who participate with them in supporting infrastructure and other private investment projects, presumably protecting these parties from reschedulings or default as well." Defaulting on a World Bank loan will surely create a chain-reaction process that will cut the rogue state off from international market access. This is why virtually all governments give priority to keeping current on loans from the IFIs. Should the country demonstrate genuine efforts to service debt while facing a liquidity crunch, the IFIs might tolerate an exceptional payment deferral. This was the treatment granted by the IMF to Argentina in 2002 to save the country from defaulting.

Country risk mitigation can take many forms. It includes the World Bank "partial risk" and "partial credit" guarantees of government financial obligations, covering specified risks and specified maturities, respectively. Usually, the World Bank guarantees the late maturities of a long-term infrastructure project loan. As such, the World Bank Group institutions provide "comfort" to private co-lenders with regard to emerging market country borrowers. They provide an element of deterrence against sovereign risks. These risk mitigation tools provide an "enabling environment" conducive to larger and longer-term private capital flows to developing countries.

In Latin America, multilaterals such as the Inter-American Development Bank (IADB) and the Andean Development Corporation (CAF) work to develop regional capital markets by providing partial loan guarantees, issuing bonds in local currencies, partnering with insurance companies and offering joint "A/B" loans with private lenders. In Eastern Europe, the London-based EBRD (European Bank for Reconstruction and Development) is also active in sharing risk with private investors via a dynamic co-financing program.

10.3.1 The World Bank's Co-financing Program

Multilateral development banks play an important risk mitigating role in several ways. First, they provide private investors with comprehensive information regarding the risks and opportunities in emerging market countries. As we will see in Chapter 11, IFIs are a key source of intelligence-gathering to assess the overall external indebtedness of developing countries as well as their macroeconomic, liquidity and solvency situation. Second, IFIs are a major source of balance of payments financing along with the monitoring of structural adjustment programs.

Conditional financing ensures that countries implement market-driven reform programs aimed at maintaining or restoring market access. Third, apart from the direct lending operations, IFIs play an important catalytic role in mobilizing sources of financing through various techniques of co-financing with official and commercial lenders.

Co-financing is a major source of country risk mitigation, particularly in the infrastructure sector. It describes funds committed by official bilateral partners, export credit agencies, or private sources to specific Bank-funded projects. Co-financing amounted to US$15 billion during the 2000–2001 fiscal years. Creditors participating in co-financing benefit from the IFIs' analysis of projects, supervision of their implementation, administration of loans until their full repayment, and the IFIs' preferred creditor status. The four principal techniques for co-financing include direct financial participation under the B-loan program, guarantees of later maturities, contingent participation in later maturities, and sale of participation or complementary loan contracts. These techniques provide commercial banks with varying degrees of financial protection.

In parallel with the implementation of the Brady Plan, the World Bank initiated an Expanded Co-financing Operations (ECO) program in July 1989 (Box 10.4). ECOs aim at assisting borrowers in gaining or broadening their access to the international capital markets, especially through private placements and public bond offerings. Credit enhancements under an ECO program can take a variety of forms including the following:

- Guarantees of commercial loans in the context of financing for Bank-approved projects;
- Guarantee on medium and long-term bond issues;
- Contingent obligations such as bond issues with an option to "put" them to the Bank under predetermined circumstances;
- Support for limited recourse project finance.

Box 10.4   The World Bank's credit enhancement and co-financing program

---

Co-financing refers to any arrangement under which Bank funds or guarantees are associated with funds provided by third parties for a particular project or program. Official co-financing, either through donor government agencies or multilateral financial institutions, constitutes the largest source of co-financing for Bank-assisted operations. The World Bank's objectives in encouraging co-financing are to:

- Mobilize resources to fill a financing gap in a specific project or program.
- Establish closer coordination with official donors on country programs, policies and investment priorities.
- Provide donors with a cost-effective way of extending assistance by using the Bank's country experience and capacity to manage projects and programs.

Official co-financing can be channelled in two forms – parallel or joint – each of which has distinct procurement arrangements. Under parallel co-financing, the Bank and co-financiers finance different goods and services and normally administer procurement separately, under their own procedures. Most co-financing is extended on a parallel basis. Under joint co-financing, the Bank and co-financiers finance expenditures from a common list of goods and services in agreed proportions, following the Bank's procurement guidelines.

10.3.2   The Role of the International Finance Corporation

The International Finance Corporation (IFC) is a special affiliate institution of the World Bank designed to boost private sector investment in emerging market countries. Although it does not lend to governments, the IFC participates in private investment promotion. Since its founding in 1956, the IFC has committed more than US$31 billion of its own funds and has arranged around US$21 billion in syndications and underwriting for more than 2600 companies in more than 135 countries. Since its first investment in 1958, the IFC has helped mobilize FDI to developing countries by:

- Sharing the risk of projects with private investors, through a mixture of debt, equity and quasi-equity;
- Acting as one of the co-lead managers of the underwriting of investment funds' assets;
- Helping reduce perceived project and political risk by its presence in a project;
- Providing information on investment opportunities and advisory services regarding the legal and regulatory environment;
- Establishing closed-end registered and specialized equity funds for individual developing countries;
- Facilitating the steps in the investment process from approval to ground-breaking.

With regard to risk mitigation, the IFC sponsors a B-loan program in which the Corporation acts as lender-of-record on behalf of a larger syndicate and agrees to collect debt service and distribute payments on a *pro rata* basis. As a result, the IFC has successfully secured financing for many borrowers that would not otherwise have had access to long-term project funds on reasonable terms from the international financial markets. From the investors' standpoint, bank regulatory authorities exempt IFC loan participations from country risk provisioning. The IFC has also set up in late 1986 a guaranteed recovery of investment principal (GRIP) for encouraging equity investment. Under the GRIP, instead of making a direct equity investment the private investor deposits the funds with the IFC which, in turn, makes the equity investment in its own name. Dividends and capital gains are to be shared by the IFC and the investor in agreed proportions.

Participants in IFC loans also share in the IFC's tax benefits in the host country, including exemption from withholding taxes on loan interest. Over four decades, the IFC has invested in more than 500 companies that have foreign investors. In addition, the IFC provides technical assistance aimed at promoting foreign direct investment. Since its establishment in 1985, the Foreign Investment Advisory Services (FIAS) has conducted more than 250 advisory assignments in 100 countries.

The IFC's risk mitigation role also involves the management and promotion of investment funds in emerging markets. The IFC's objective is to provide international investors with opportunities to invest through professionally managed vehicles, with careful diagnosis and professional structuring and advising of the fund. Five main kinds of fund vehicles have helped achieve risk mitigation objectives:

- International portfolio equity funds, including index funds, to mobilize large volumes of international private savings and stimulate the development of emerging stock markets;
- Private equity funds in unlisted firms;
- Venture capital funds to invest equity and provide management support to new firms;

- Domestic mutual funds to mobilize funds from local investors and to help develop local stock markets;
- Pension funds to help mobilize private domestic savings. (www.ifc.org)

10.3.3 The role of MIGA (Multilateral Investment Guarantee Agency)

Since its creation in 1988, MIGA's objective has been to facilitate the flow of foreign direct investment to developing and transition economies by alleviating investors' concerns about non-commercial risks, including the following four specific risks:

- currency transfer,
- expropriation without due compensation,
- war/civil disturbance, and
- breach of contract.

MIGA insures new cross-border investment originating in any MIGA member country (157 as of 2002), destined to any other developing country. Types of foreign investment that can be covered include equity, shareholder loans and shareholder loan guarantees, provided the loans have a minimum maturity of three years. Equity investment can be covered up to 90% and debt up to 95%, with coverages typically available for up to 15 years, and in some cases, for up to 20. MIGA may insure up to US$200 million, and if necessary more can be arranged through syndication.

Since its creation in 1988, MIGA has performed a distinctive and evolving role as a multilateral insurer in the political risk investment insurance market. MIGA operates a "Cooperative Underwriting Program" (CUT) in which the Agency agrees to pursue recovery on behalf of all participants and share proportionally in any claims losses and recoveries. The CUT program is a political risk insurance, in which MIGA "fronts" for participating private insurers in cooperatively insured projects.

As a member of the World Bank Group, MIGA claims preferred creditor status, or the right to get paid first, when developing country governments prove unable or unwilling to service all of their external financial obligations. MIGA performs a catalytic role in enhancing foreign direct investment as the Agency's coverage has a multiplier or "springboard" effect in terms of private capital flows. Since its inception, MIGA has issued more than 500 guarantees for projects in nearly 80 countries and total coverage issued reaches around US$10 billion, bringing the estimated amount of facilitated FDI to more than US$41 billion (www.miga.org/screens/about/about.htm).

10.4 THE RISK MITIGATION ROLE OF PUBLIC AND PRIVATE RISK GUARANTEE INSTITUTIONS

The US Exim-Bank and the US Overseas Private Investment Corporation (OPIC) are both US government agencies. OPIC is a self-sustaining bilateral US government agency that combines the functions of lending to private projects, like the IFC, and a political risk insurance, like MIGA (Box 10.5). It operates as a business-oriented quasi-private corporation. It became an independent institution within the executive branch of the US Federal government in 1971. OPIC is not a multilateral agency, but its all-risk-guaranteed loans have historically been exempted from reschedulings, thereby obtaining an implicit preferred creditor status. Its main role is to support US private investment in developing nations and emerging market economies, with such instruments as long-term political risk insurance and limited recourse project financing. OPIC clients are exclusively American companies. It does not provide direct government-to-government aid or grants.

OPIC supports business projects in virtually every industrial and economic sector including agriculture, energy, construction, natural resources, telecommunications, transportation and distribution, banking and services among others. Insurance is available for investments in new ventures or expansions of existing enterprises. Insurance can cover the following three political risks:

- Currency inconvertibility (but not against currency devaluation);
- Expropriation;
- Political violence, including war damage and civil strife damage.

Box 10.5   OPIC as premier provider of political risk insurance

OPIC has provided investment protection since 1949. Reportedly, OPIC:

- Issued around 7000 contracts
- Holds reserves of close to US$4 billion
- Paid US$1 billion in claims
- Can cover investments in some 145 developing countries
- Is backed by the full faith and credit of the US government
- Can offer up to US$400 million in total project support for any one project – up to US$250 million in project finance and up to US$250 million in political risk insurance, for up to 20 years. OPIC has coverage available for equity investments, parent company and third-party loans and loan guarantees, technical assistance agreements, cross-border leases, capital market transactions, contractors' and exporters' exposure, and some other forms of direct investment.

http://www.opic.gov

10.5   THE ROLE OF PRIVATE PROVIDERS OF SPECIALIST INSURANCE FOR COUNTRY RISK

Lawyers and insurers have put global risk and terrorism on the front burner of the insurance industry's agenda in the aftermath of the September 11 attack on the United States. Priority was given to find a coordinated coverage definition of the terrorism threat. Concerned that future terrorism could bankrupt them, most reinsurers and primary insurers exclude terrorism coverage from property and casualty policies.[2] The specialist insurance business with regard to political risk expanded since the beginning of 2000, reflecting mounting concerns with the risks that the business community faces in cross-border transactions. This risk includes that of corruption, organized crime, terrorism, civil war, money laundering, and any "anti-market" and "non-transparent" measures that impact investment returns. As the Control Risks Group

[2] See Morris, Manning & Martin, LLP, Global Definition of Terrorism Urged for Insurance Industry, Press Release, 8 July 2002.

concludes: "Even prior to September 11th, the economic decline and growing tensions involved in running global businesses were leading senior managers to take a less confident approach to international investment."[3]

Considering that information and intelligence are two good ingredients of risk mitigation strategy, a number of specialized consultancy groups provide the international business community with advisory services regarding organized crime. Hiscox is considered as the largest provider of specialist insurance for the "global elite" at risk with political risk, reportedly accounting for two-thirds of worldwide premium income. Hiscox covers against kidnap, bodily harm, extortion, hijack and malicious detention, with a capacity of up to US$100 million.

Often private insurers team up with official financial institutions to help mitigate risks for lenders and investors. The CAF (Corporacion Andino de Fomento), which is a treaty organization among Andean governments that has never suffered a default, formed a joint venture with US private insurance company AIG Global Trade & Political Risk Insurance Company, in mid-2000, to set up the Latin American Investment Guarantee Company. This is a political risk insurance company, based in Bermuda, with US$50 million of paid-up capital to underwrite and co-insure loans. CAF's chairman, Enrique Garcia, considers that after two years of existence the company has provided around US$600 million in underwriting insurance and helped attract close to US$2 billion in private investment to Latin America.[4]

10.6   THE MARKET-BASED "MENU" APPROACH

The most dramatic form of country risk is, from the creditors' and investors' standpoints, default and contract repudiation. Inadequate risk analysis *ex ante*, or inadequate loan-loss provisions *ex post*, translate into capital losses and, for the most fragile investors, liquidation threats. The number of emerging market crises over the last 20 years has resulted in a widening of financial instruments to better fit the constraints of the creditors and the financing requirements of the borrowers. In particular, risk mitigating financial schemes have expanded through a market-driven menu approach (Box 10.6). This approach emerged in the aftermath of the failure of the Baker Plan, given the lack of appetite of international banks for new money loans. It aims at tailoring the financing mechanism to the specific preferences of the different classes of private creditors.

One can distinguish various categories of new debt instruments that provide more liquid and less risky assets. The first category aims at changing the ownership of the claims via the secondary market of commercial bank debt, by swapping assets with other creditors or by consolidating the claims in the hands of a new intermediary. The second category involves changing the financial conditions and hence the value of the original claims with interest rate reduction, currency redenomination and collateralization. The third category of country risk mitigating schemes involves changing the financial profile of the claims through rescheduling, retiming, indexed loans and value recovery rights. The fourth and last category involves changing the legal nature of the bank claims by converting loans into some other kind of assets with securitization and debt conversion instruments. Each of these market-driven risk mitigating financial instruments can help the investors improve their cross-border profit scope.

---

[3] Press Release, 10th Annual RiskMap Survey, Control Risks Group, 2002 Edition.
[4] A Bridge for the Markets, *LatinFinance*, June 2002, p. 24.

In several of these "menu" alternatives, the secondary market of bank claims provides investors and creditors with a reservoir of liquidity and risk mitigation opportunities.

Box 10.6   Financial engineering for EMCs' market reaccess strategy*

Collateralized bonds

As a result of difficulties in accessing international capital markets, emerging market countries have used collateralized bonds, including future-flow securitization through export receivables, to reaccess markets. Brady bonds are securities issued in the framework of concerted debt restructuring operations, with guaranteed repayment under the form of long-term zero coupon bonds, often co-financed by the country's reserves and by official financing.

Step-ups and step-downs

Sovereign fixed-rate bonds which include a step-down (step-up) feature have coupon payments that are higher (lower) for a short initial time period, but then decrease (increase) over the medium to long term.

Dual currency notes

These notes generally take the form of paying principal in foreign currency, and interest in domestic currency. By offering the up-side gains associated with high domestic interest rates, coupled with protection against exchange rate depreciation, these instruments seek to attract foreign investors concerned about exchange risk.

Structured notes

Structured notes are fixed income securities linked to derivatives. The embedded derivative transactions are most commonly swaps, although options and futures/forwards may be used as well. The notes involve fairly complex transactions, with varying contingent payoffs that generally allow for the hedging of almost any risk.

Warrants

Bond warrants allow the holder of the warrant the right, but not the obligation, to buy a certain, usually long-term bond, at a predetermined price at some future date. Warrants can be seen, from the issuers' perspective, as call options, issued out-of-the-money (i.e., they become interesting to exercise if spreads come down before the exercise date) that can be combined with an otherwise "plain vanilla" bond.

Put options

By embedding a put option in a bond, an issuer gives the holder the right to demand payment of the bond at a specified date before its maturity date. Put options can be "hard", that is the put date is unconditional, or "soft", that is exercise of the put option is linked to a specific event.

Augmentation

Augmentation refers to the reopening of existing bonds in international capital markets. The benefit of this instrument is that it reopens an existing issue, with which investors are already familiar and do not have to evaluate separately. Augmentations can also be done in an opportunistic manner and in relatively small amounts.

Swaps and debt exchange

Swaps can result in debt service reductions, and improve the maturity structure of external debt by replacing short-term bonds with medium and long-term debt instruments. Swaps can also reduce debt obligations in NPV terms, and free up collateral against certain debt instruments such as Bradys.

Buyback transactions

Low and middle-income countries use buyback operations for different purposes. The former use straight buyback operations to retire external debt with the support of official donor countries, often with the funding of the IDA Debt Reduction Facility. The latter use buybacks within bond exchange transactions to issue new securities with extended average maturity.

*"Assessing the determinants and prospects for the pace of market access by countries emerging from crises", IMF Policy Development and Review Department, 6 September 2001, pp. 21–22. Reproduced with permission (with authors' inputs).

In several of these "menu" alternatives, the secondary market of bank claims provides investors and creditors with a reservoir of liquidity and risk mitigation opportunities.

10.6.1   The Rise of the London Club Debt Secondary Market of Emerging Market Loans

The *secondary market* for commercial bank claims is the market where buyers and sellers can trade sovereign debt. Emerging markets debt trading is a global over-the-counter trading market that serves a broad range of creditors and investors. As the EMTA observes: "Investors have a wider selection of geographically diversified investment opportunities than ever before with a broader spectrum of investment instruments and risk characteristics" (EMTA, 2001 Annual Report, p. 5). Currently the debt of close to 40 developing countries sells at below its face value on the secondary market, the discount reflecting the risk associated with holding such debt. The price represents the net present value of the claims. The marketplace for emerging markets debt instruments is an OTC market of dealers and investors located worldwide. Market participants include major commercial banks, investment banks and various local entities, as well as a wide range of institutional investors and investment fund managers. They are linked informally through an efficient telecommunication network.

An active secondary market in LDC debt began to emerge in the mid-1980s in which banks traded their portfolios on an inter-bank loan swap basis in order to consolidate or diversify their claims or to take advantage of accounting and tax benefits. The market expanded in 1987–1988 owing to the rise in reserves and a growing number of debt–equity conversion programs. The market rose from about US$95 billion in 1990 to about US$2700 billion in 1995, fuelled by a succession of sovereign reschedulings of London Club debt, debt conversion programs, and later by new bond issuances. In 1996–1997, the market rose to a US$6000 billion turnover as a result of improved liquidity of officially guaranteed Brady bonds, before declining sharply in the wake of the Asian and Russian financial crises. In 2001–2002, the secondary market picked up again following several years of slowdown in the aftermath of the contagion effect that affected virtually all emerging market countries' debts. Trading volumes began to rebound in 2001 reaching US$3500 billion. As a result, overall liquidity has strengthened for the market's benchmark instruments, in comparison with most other sectors of the fixed income markets.

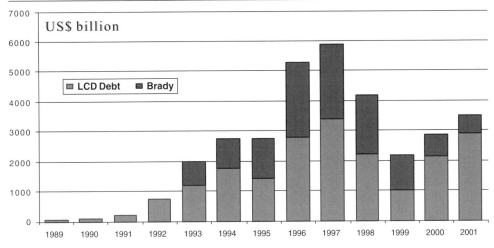

Source: EMTA-London.

Figure 10.2   Trading volume in secondary market of EMCs' debt

In 2002, however, investors flocked to the safety of OECD government bonds amid unsettling news regarding economic and geopolitical developments. In a context of jittery stock markets, risk-averse investors shifted assets from equities into US treasury bonds. In addition, the signs of bond market contagion from political uncertainty and financial weaknesses in Brazil and Argentina, respectively, affected the emerging bond markets. This spill-over effect occurred despite the fact that emerging markets' debt outperformed all asset classes with the exception of US treasuries (Ostrovsky, 2002) (Figure 10.2).

Secondary market trading is dominated by Latin American country debt, in particular debt from Brazil, Mexico, Argentina and Venezuela, accounting for close to 70% of volume (Figure 10.3). Many investors consider the Mexican par bond as a benchmark as it is reportedly one of the most liquid markets in the world after the US treasury market. Outside Latin America, the debt of Morocco, the Philippines, Bulgaria, Russia and Poland is traded in a market which is considered reasonably liquid. Privatization programs and conversion schemes which have been active in several countries such as Argentina, Chile, Venezuela, Brazil and the Philippines have stimulated trading of sovereign country debt. Improving policy

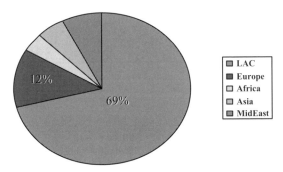

Source: EMTA-London.

Figure 10.3   Secondary market trading volume by region

and sovereign credit rating in some developing countries also contributes to the expansion and "depth" of the secondary market. As emerging market borrowers strive to re-enter the capital markets, Brady bonds have been supplemented by an ever-wider variety of Eurobonds and local currency instruments, with greater liquidity and innovation in the use of derivative instruments.

Developments in the market have led to the creation of an Emerging Markets Traders Association (EMTA) in New York in December 1990 (Box 10.7). The Association came in response to the rapid growth in the LDC debt trading market, the increasing variety of instruments traded, the growing number of investors and the need to coordinate these items. The Association is instrumental in formalizing transaction records and setting reporting and accounting guidelines.

Box 10.7   EMTA

Formed in 1990, the EMTA is dedicated to:

- Promoting the orderly development of fair, efficient and transparent trading markets in developing countries' debt;
- Helping integrate the emerging markets into the global capital markets;
- Building and promoting the emerging markets asset class.

The EMTA was set up by the financial community in response to the new trading opportunities created by the sovereign debt restructurings under the aegis of the Brady Plan; EMTA's membership includes most of the world's leading financial institutions that actively participate in the emerging markets as creditors, investors and investment fund managers.

Through the exchange of information and the adoption of general trading principles and more specific market practices, he EMTA helps insure an orderly market, hence operating efficiency and liquidity.

Through a variety of projects, including its annual and quarterly Volume Surveys of trading activity and its Pricing Surveys, the EMTA promotes greater market transparency. It also provides a forum for market participants to develop industry positions and present them to official national and multilateral institutions, similar in that respect to the Washington-based Institute for International Finance.

http://www.emta.org

The table below shows the trading volume and liquidity estimates for developing countries' debt:

Weak liquidity
Angola, Nicaragua, Cameroon, Albania, Senegal, Iraq, Congo, Tanzania, Zaire, Zambia
Reduced liquidity
Algeria, Vietnam, Cuba, Ivory Coast, Egypt, Jordan, Madagascar, Panama, Uruguay
Average liquidity
Nigeria, Morocco, Costa Rica, Bulgaria, Peru, Russia, Turkey
Good liquidity
Brady bonds = Argentina, Brazil, Ecuador, Mexico, Philippines, Poland, Venezuela

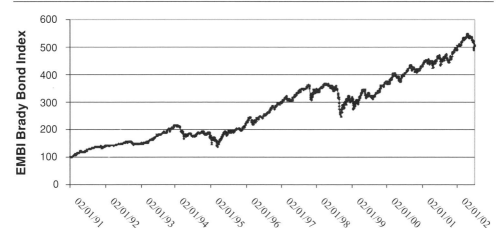

Figure 10.4   JP Morgan Emerging Markets Brady Bond Index

10.6.2   Price Developments

Secondary market prices have been volatile over the last decade. Figure 10.4 illustrates the evolution in the emerging markets' Brady bond index as reported by JP Morgan's EMBI, over the 1991–2002 period. One can observe three marked declines corresponding to the Mexican debt crisis in late 1994, the Asian financial crisis in 1997–1998, and the Argentine crisis in early 2002.

10.6.3   Technical Supply and Demand Factors Affecting Debt Prices

One can distinguish a number of variables that influence the direction and the volatility of secondary market prices. They comprise both endogenous and exogenous parameters. The first set of variables reflects macroeconomic and financial trends in a given country, hence relative yield perspectives in comparison with alternative investments. The second set reflects the evolution in the financial markets as well as in other countries which compete to attract investors.

1. *Macroeconomic situation*: Factors such as liquidity, solvency and privatization programs tend to affect price volatility. In addition, structural reforms, adoption of credible corrective macroeconomic policies and IMF support are all positive factors behind price changes. The socio-political situation will also influence bond spreads and debt prices.
2. *Debt restructuring agreements* with Paris and London Club creditors open the way for debt relief, improved liquidity and scope for market reaccess.
3. *Ranking by risk rating agencies*: the major credit rating agencies (such as S&P, Fitch IBCA and Moody's) have formalized ratings of LDC debt, including Brady bonds and other market-based bond issues.
4. *Interest rate volatility*: Evolution in the US treasury 30-year bond rate has been a driving force behind the evolution in fixed-rate Brady par bonds.
5. *Market liquidity*: The combination of Brady debt restructuring agreements and officially supported privatization programs has strengthened the secondary markets. With the securitization of the LDC debt market, liquidity has improved through the Eurobond clearing institutions and CEDEL.

6. *Information and transparency*: Information on market prices and liquidity is available through Bradynet, Wesbruin Capital for exotic debt prices, and New York-based EMTA for overall market trends. In mid-2000, Wesbruin and Bradynet joined forces to offer hard-to-find exotic debt information, including pricing on defaulting and distressed country paper (http://www.bradynet.com/e868.html).
7. *Securitization*: The exchange of bank loans into long-term bonds with guarantees funded by international institutions enhances the quality of claims. Likewise, debt buyback and bond exchange programs aim to extend bond maturities and reduce near-term amortization and interest payments.
8. *Instrument diversification*: New instruments have emerged in the 1990s such as new money bonds, exit bonds and interest reduction bonds, restructured loans, promissory notes, trade paper and others. As a result, the relative share of Brady bonds has fallen. In 2001, Brady bond paper comprised about 16% of trading volume compared with 50% over the 1995–1997 period.
9. *Regional contamination and "spill-over" effect*: bandwagon effects and herd behavior create regional ramification effects with resulting impact on spreads and debt prices. In funds portfolios, emerging markets are usually considered as one single asset class. Risk aversion and contagion reached a peak during Russia's 1998 financial crisis.
10. *Deal-driven transactions*: A well-managed debt–equity program opens the way for swap transactions adding liquidity to the market as well as investment opportunities in the domestic economy.

10.6.4 Debt Conversion Transactions[5]

Debt conversion provides creditors and investors with risk mitigation opportunities. A debt swap constitutes the legal and financial transformation of a country's liability from a hard currency debt into domestic currency obligations. Debt conversion boils down to prepayment of debt at a discount in local currency. Assets can be of various natures, such as equity (debt for equity conversions), exports (debt for exports), or wildlife protection, health, education and/or environmental conservation (debt for sustainable development).

The vehicle for such debt conversions is often the secondary market of commercial bank claims where banks can sell or swap their LDC assets, investors can obtain bank loans at a discount for subsequent conversion into domestic currency assets, and debtor countries can repurchase their own discounted debt. The secondary market discount is the driving element behind debt conversion dynamism.

The emergence of debt conversion coincided with the expansion of secondary market transactions. At the inception of the so-called Brady Plan, on 10 March 1989, Treasury Secretary Nicholas Brady called for encouraging debt reduction on a voluntary basis while recognizing the importance of continued new lending. In the proposed market-based menu approach, he emphasized "the need to maintain viable debt/equity swap programs in debtor nations while encouraging them to permit domestic nationals to engage in such transactions", as a vehicle for capital flight repatriation.[6] Debt conversion became a standard feature of debt restructuring negotiations with London Club creditors, and conversion clauses have been introduced in

---

[5] For a comprehensive presentation of debt conversion, see: "Review of Experiences with the Implementation of Debt Conversion", Owen Stanley Financial, Bouchet et al, Report to Ministry of Foreign Affairs, The Hague, November 1996.
[6] Remarks by The Secretary of the Treasury to the Brookings Institution and the Bretton Woods Committee, 10 March 1989, US Treasury News.

virtually all debt agreements during the 1990s. In December 1991, Paris Club debt became eligible for debt conversion. The scope for debt conversion using official claims is large, in particular in the "social sectors" (education, health, environment) as well as in the restructuring of privatized companies. Since mid-1996, the Paris Club agreed to increase debt conversion up to 20% of guaranteed credits without limitations for official development aid. Official debt can be purchased in the framework of auctions sponsored by creditor governments. Non-OECD official creditors have also begun disposing of claims for conversion purposes.

Debt–equity swaps comprise about 40% of the total volume of debt conversions. Latin American countries constitute the bulk of debt conversion, with close to 70% of total operations. In these countries, however, the increase in secondary debt prices has gradually eroded the discount, hence the driving incentive behind conversion. Chile managed to reduce a substantial part of its external debt while stimulating FDI and privatization, thereby pushing prices back to near par value. In the aftermath of Mexico's liquidity crisis in December 1994, the combination of lower prices and dynamic privatization reignited interest in debt conversion. Although debt conversion peaked in the early 1990s, debtor country governments have shown renewed interest in swaps in the early 2000s, as a vehicle for improving average debt profiles and for boosting domestic and foreign investment. As the IMF observes regarding the slowdown of conversion following the Brady Plan: "High debt prices in the secondary market, regularization of relations with commercial bank creditors, and advances already made in most privatization programs were responsible for declining conversion activity."[7] According to Fund's estimates, no less than US$52 billion of external debt was converted during the 1984–1994 decade.

10.6.5 Mechanics of Debt Conversion

Debt conversion boils down to accessing a preferential exchange rate, or to a subsidy for obtaining local currency for domestic investment purposes. The debt conversion mechanism enables an interested party who wishes to obtain local currency for spending or for domestic investment purposes to purchase sovereign debt with a *discount in hard currency* and receive in return *local currency with a premium* under the form of equity, bonds or other types of domestic assets. Usually debt conversion is managed under the auspices and regulation of the debtor country's central bank. The monetary authorities' objective is to reduce the risk of inflationary tensions as well as that of round tripping. Figure 10.5 shows the different steps of a debt conversion transaction.[8]

In exchange for debt cancellation, the central bank of the debtor country agrees to make a payment in local currency or domestic assets (e.g., in the context of privatization). In order for each party to draw benefits from the transaction, the value of the payment made by the debtor country should exceed the discounted price paid by the investor for the debt. It should also be greater than the amount of local currency the investor could have obtained through a regular foreign exchange transaction. The price paid by the debtor country for what boils down to buying back the debt at a discount in local currency should also be less than the face value of the original liability. Figure 10.6 illustrates the various incentives to the participating parties in a debt swap transaction where the initial discount is 60% in the secondary market, hence a price equal to 40% of face value. The original claim is worth US$1000. The transaction process

---

[7] Private Market Financing for Developing Countries. *World Economic and Financial Surveys*, IMF, March 1995, p. 10.

[8] For further analysis of debt conversion, see: "Manual on the Conversion of Official Bilateral Debt", Owen Stanley Financial (in cooperation with ING Bank), UNCTAD, Geneva, July 1995, pp. 13–15.

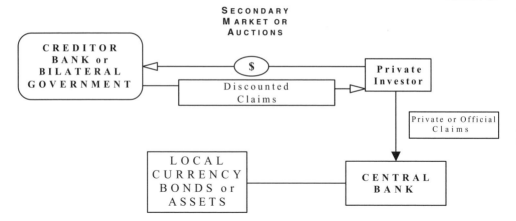

Figure 10.5   Debt conversion transaction

is an example of a positive sum game that will satisfy the demands of the initial creditor bank, the private investor, as well as the debtor country government.

There are various forms of central bank payouts in debt conversion transactions, including the following payments:

  (i) Transfer of ownership of equity in a public company in a privatization program;
 (ii) Local currency for local cost component of investment or operating costs;
(iii) Local currency and/or financial instruments to fund humanitarian or environmental projects of NGOs;
(iv) Non-traditional exports aimed at hard-currency revenue diversification;
 (v) Informal scheme under which residents retire their debt to the central bank by delivery of external debt acquired in the market;
(vi) Tax vouchers, customs duties, oil exploration bonuses etc.;
(vii) Monetary stabilization bonds designed to mitigate the inflationary impact of the expanding money supply.

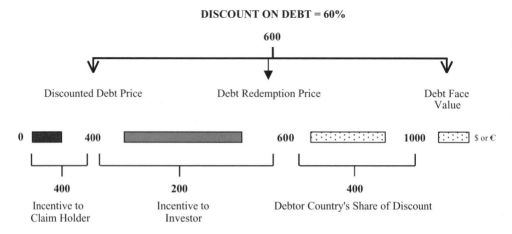

Figure 10.6   The positive-sum game of debt conversion (*Source*: Owen Stanley Financial)

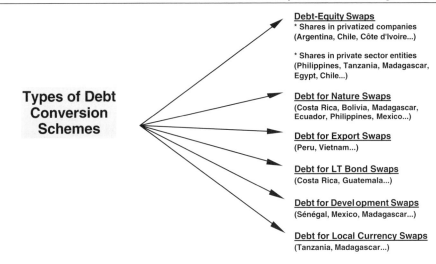

Debt-Equity Swaps
* Shares in privatized companies
(Argentina, Chile, Côte d'Ivoire...)

* Shares in private sector entities
(Philippines, Tanzania, Madagascar,
Egypt, Chile...)

Debt for Nature Swaps
(Costa Rica, Bolivia, Madagascar,
Ecuador, Philippines, Mexico...)

Debt for Export Swaps
(Peru, Vietnam...)

Debt for LT Bond Swaps
(Costa Rica, Guatemala...)

Debt for Development Swaps
(Sénégal, Mexico, Madagascar...)

Debt for Local Currency Swaps
(Tanzania, Madagascar...)

Figure 10.7   The variety of debt swap schemes (*Source*: Owen Stanley Financial)

A key prerequisite in debt conversion and buyback transactions is the formulation of *enabling legislation* so as to waive various legal clauses that prohibit a debtor country from inequitable treatment of its debt obligations. In addition, restrictions on permissible assignees must be waived if creditor banks are to be able to sell debt to private investors. These transactions require specific accommodative covenants because they can be considered the legal equivalent of debt prepayments (Bouchet and Hay, 1988). Debt swaps enable creditors to settle foreign currency claims before contractual maturity in return for the payment of local currency at an agreed discount. Consequently, mandatory prepayment and "sharing" clauses in loan and refinancing agreements are legal obstacles that must be circumvented. Chile's new money agreement in 1985 was the first to incorporate specific clauses opening the way to large debt conversion operations in relation with recapitalization and privatization programs.

10.6.6   Range of Debt Conversion Transactions

Various types of debt conversion have been carried out in numerous regions of the world. Figure 10.7 gives a succinct overview of the wide array of debt swap arrangements.[9]

Various Forms of Debt Conversion

- *Debt-for-export swaps* enable a private creditor to receive export products and/or commodities of a debtor country to offset part of its outstanding claims on the concerned country. A number of transactions have taken place in Latin America (Peru), Asia (Vietnam) and Africa which involved the repayment of external debt service obligations through exports of "non-traditional" products. The system aims at promoting export diversification and exploring new markets while reducing external liabilities. Blocked foreign currency claims can be made liquid via these conversion schemes involving specialized trading companies.

---

[9] See: "Review of Experiences with the Implementation of Debt Conversion", op. cit. Also: "Debt Conversion Programs", Appendix G, *World Debt Tables*, vol. 1, 1994–1995, World Bank, pp. 163–169.

• *Debt-for-debt swaps* are interbank transactions done for portfolio rebalancing motivations as well as tax, accounting and regulatory incentives. Loan swaps originate from different perceptions of country and credit risk or from a strategy of portfolio adjustments, aimed at consolidation, diversification and liquidity.

• *Debt-for-development swaps* constitute one variety of debt conversion dealing with debt forgiveness. The combination of the debt crisis and the environmental challenge provides considerable opportunities for countries, non-government entities and commercial banks with this type of operation. Debt-for-nature swaps typically involve a foreign bank or a creditor country, a non-profit organization dealing with environment preservation programs, and the country's central bank. In exchange for the cancellation of external debt, the foreign organization will obtain a commitment from the debtor government to fund programs of nature, environment and wildlife protection over a number of years. Such conversions have been financed mainly through official bilateral resources, inflows from non-governmental organizations and debt donations by commercial banks. These swaps have been dynamic, particularly in low-income countries where commercial bank debt trades at deep discounts in the secondary market (Bolivia, Honduras, Costa Rica, Senegal, Côte d'Ivoire, Madagascar, etc.).

• *Debt conversions in employee stock ownership plans* are a special case of debt–equity conversion transactions. Debt owed to private banks is sold, either in a block or over time, to a company-sponsored employee stock ownership business which pays for the employee's equity out of the company's business revenues. The corporation could also incur debt in order to acquire the assets owned by the lenders for the employees. The scheme would consist of a debt–equity conversion followed by a "leveraged buyout".

• *Debt-for-local currency conversion* occurs when a domestic resident acquires a portion of its country's external debt for subsequent conversion into local currency, thereby providing a mechanism for capital flight repatriation. This scheme has been particularly instrumental in Latin America.

• *Loans-for-bonds exchange offers* aim at replacing existing debt documented as loans by security instruments which are usually bearer instruments and thus possess greater tradeability in the secondary market than loans. Officially funded credit enhancement under the form of principal and interest guarantees may lead banks to extend concessions to the borrower through a lower interest rate on the bond or a lower-than-par exchange price. Exchange offers with collateralized defeasance against the principal of the new debt reduce the debt service obligations of the debtor, and hence the risk of the creditors. The exchange can provide lenders with tax and accounting benefits as well as enhanced liquidity.[10] Debtor country strategies aim at increasing the average debt maturity and reducing the overall debt servicing cost, hence alleviating budgetary and balance of payments constraints. In 2001–2002, Mexico, Brazil, Argentina, Colombia and Turkey completed large debt swap operations involving external or domestic debt, or both.

• *Onlending and relending* are mechanisms that give creditor banks the right to reallocate credit within a debtor country. Relending occurs when the original borrower has the domestic currency to repay its debt (at the going exchange rate), but the central bank is unable or unwilling to deliver the foreign currency. In such a case, the foreign creditor becomes the owner of foreign currency deposits with the central bank instead of receiving his

---

[10] In June 2002, Argentina carried out one of the largest debt swap operations ever conducted by a developing country. The operation replaced about US$30 billion of domestic and external bonds with five new securities. The swap extended the average maturity of the government's debt by nearly three years. See World Bank, Global Development Finance 2002, pp. 134–135.

repayment. The basic idea of relending is to defer the outflow of foreign currency from the borrowing country, while allowing the credit, and hence business risk, to be reallocated by the foreign creditor among different public and private sector entities in the same country. Onlending uses the same procedure in connection with new money loans. The concept of these facilities was created by the steering committee of banks in the context of the Brazilian rescheduling of 1982–1983. Thereafter, provisions for these loan conversion facilities were included in the restructuring packages of Argentina, Chile, Mexico, the Philippines and Venezuela.

 • *Debt-for-cash transactions* are discounted buyback operations, implemented under the auspices of the central bank. Commercial banks sell their claims to debtor countries or private investors or to other banks which have long-term business interests in the country. Cash sales give small exposure banks a way out of the debt rescheduling process. From the country's standpoint, the efficiency of buyback schemes stems from the implicit internal rate of return given the resources used to retire the external liabilities. Under exceptional circumstances, a country buys back its debt with its own resources, resulting in an informal operation outside the auspices of the World Bank and the IMF. Otherwise, a debtor country would implement such debt reductions with donor funds or financing borrowed from the official sector. Formal buyback operations have been implemented by various countries like Bolivia in January 1988, Chile in November 1988, the Philippines in January 1990 and Niger in early 1991. For low-income and highly-indebted countries, the buybacks have been operated through the IDA debt reduction facility. In 2001, Honduras, Tanzania and Yemen implemented IDA-sponsored buybacks.

 • *Debt "conversion rights" for domestic investment*: In Mexico, Argentina, Honduras and Venezuela, foreign investors have exercised "conversion rights" awarded in auctions under the aegis of the central bank, the proceeds of which were used mostly for investment in infrastructure projects (transportation and communication). To qualify for debt conversion-funded investment, projects must respect sectoral as well as magnitude criteria (petrochemicals, steel and aluminum, pulp and paper, banking, tourism, etc.). In most countries, foreign investment in the context of swap transactions is accompanied by strict capital and interest remittance repatriation restrictions.

 • *Debt–equity conversions* are deals transforming an LDC's external debt into an equity holding in a domestic company. A growing number of debtor countries have set up the necessary regulatory framework for debt conversions to stimulate private investment and, in the context of a privatization program, shrinking state intervention in the economy. In several countries such as the Philippines, Brazil, Argentina, Chile and Mexico, privatization programs have provided a new impetus for debt–equity swaps. Mexico converted interbank credit lines into privatization notes, subsequently redeemed at par, for investment in newly privatized Mexican banks (Figure 10.8).

10.6.7 Official Bilateral Debt Conversion

During 1991, the Paris Club agreed on the principle of reducing debt through clauses stipulating the conversion of part of the obligations into local currency. The Paris Club does not set a limit for conversions applied to development aid. However, a limit of 10% to 20% is applied to officially guaranteed commercial loans (for example those covered by Coface, ECGD and Hermes). Conversion is a voluntary option and should be ratified by each creditor

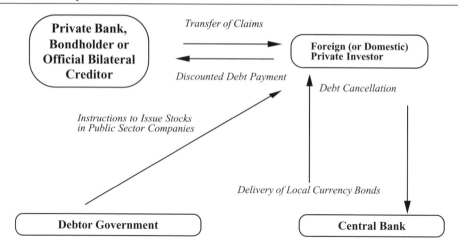

Figure 10.8   Debt–equity swap structure with privatization

government in Paris Club bilateral agreements. Currently, more than half a dozen OECD countries have established regular sales or auctioning of sovereign debt for debt conversion purposes.

Paris Club agreements contain a provision which makes it possible for creditors to voluntarily undertake debt swaps. These operations may be debt-for-nature, debt-for-aid, debt-for-equity swaps or other local currency debt swaps. These swaps often involve the sale of the debt by the creditor government to an investor who in turn sells the debt to the debtor government in return for shares in a local company or for local currency to be used in projects in the country. In order to preserve comparability of treatment and solidarity among creditors, the amounts of debt swaps that can be conducted are capped at a certain percentage of the stock of the claims of each individual creditor.

The terms under which these operations can take place are contained in the standard terms of treatment. To ensure full transparency between creditors, participating creditor countries and the debtor's government must inform the Chairman of the Paris Club regarding the debt swap transactions, in a semi-annual basis report. A specific provision stipulates the framework and limits of swap operations: "On a voluntary and bilateral basis, the Government of each Participating Creditor Country or its appropriate institutions may sell or exchange, in the framework of debt for nature, debt for aid, debt for equity swaps or other local currency debt swaps: (i) all ODA loans; (ii) amounts of outstanding credits, loans and consolidations on debts not granted under ODA conditions, up to 20% of the amounts of outstanding credits as of a specific date, or up to an amount of SDR 30 million, whichever is higher."

10.6.8   Debt Conversion: A Positive Sum Game?

Debt conversion can be a useful risk mitigating vehicle from the investor's standpoint. The transaction allows private investors to get access to discounted external claims on emerging market countries while obtaining a preferential exchange rate. From the debtor's viewpoint, debt conversion reduces external liabilities while stimulating foreign direct investment and, in the context of privatization, alleviating the budget constraint. However, swaps also have an impact on the country's monetary, budgetary and balance of payments situation. First, the local currency payout may result in an increase in the money supply which could have a potentially inflationary impact. This has been the case in Latin American countries, particularly in Brazil. Second, budgetary allocations for the service of the converted debt at the time of conversion may not be sufficient to cover the local currency payout, thereby creating a deficit. Finally, as regards the balance of payments, the debtor country foregoes a foreign currency inflow, in the form of a potential foreign direct investment, in exchange for external debt cancellation. New money is therefore a key parameter of successful debt conversion operations.

Another risk for the debtor country is what is termed "round tripping". This is a situation where local currency funds resulting from a conversion are used by the investor to purchase foreign currency at the official rate and re-transfer it out of the debtor country. Not only does this practice defeat the debtor country's objective in authorizing the conversion, but it also results in a double negative impact on the country's balance of payments. Countries with convertible, or quasi-convertible, currencies must take special care to ensure that sufficient controls are imposed to avoid such practices. This is of particular importance for debtor countries in strong money supply zones, e.g., the franc zone of West and Central Africa. Round-tripping has reportedly been at work in countries such as Peru, Argentina and Nigeria.

Clearly, the investor will look carefully at the country's regulatory framework with regard to debt swaps. Of particular concern are the regulations concerning the nominal and real foreign exchange rate, dividend and capital repatriation restrictions, new money requirements, domestic inflation and real interest rates, tax laws and wages, and sectoral allocation of the debt conversion proceeds. The investor's objective in pursuing a debt conversion operation is to increase the impact of his investment in local currency terms. This translates into a payout level which provides the investor with an acceptable leverage, or "multiplier" of the funds invested via the conversion. To arrive at the real multiplier, the investor has to take various elements into consideration, including parallel exchange rates (official or unofficial) existing in the debtor country, and whether the local currency is stable or likely to depreciate (or be devalued) substantially before the local proceeds of the conversion have been absorbed. The leverage gained via a conversion will be quickly neutralized unless the funds are invested immediately or means of protection from depreciation or devaluation built into the structure of the conversion.

To protect the investor against depreciation or devaluation of the local currency, countries have issued foreign currency-denominated instruments payable in the future in local currency at the exchange rate prevailing at the date of payment. Likewise, country governments have accepted the immediate disbursement of conversion proceeds to be placed into an interest-bearing local currency account (sometimes in the form of an endowment fund). In addition, local currency instruments bearing positive real interest rates to compensate for future depreciation can be issued. Finally, should the investor accept a payout in the form of a financial instrument payable in tranches over a period of time, he is assuming a disbursement risk on the debtor country. The disbursement risk is directly related to the priority of the project and surrounding political risk.

In conclusion, foreign investors and creditors contemplate a wide spectrum of risk mitigating instruments to reduce country risk exposure. Guarantee schemes and debt swap transactions boil down to one main objective, namely, lowering the risk scope to compensate for the inherent uncertainty in cross-border investment.

REFERENCES

Bouchet M and Hay J, 1988, *The Rise of the Market-based "Menu" Approach and its Limitations*. World Bank, CFS Informal Financial Note no. 5, September, 153.

Ikawa M, 2001, Introduction. *In:* TH Moran, ed. *International Political Risk Management: Exploring New Frontiers*. Washington, DC: The World Bank Group.

Moran TH, 2001, Preferred Creditor Status: Overview. *In:* TH Moran, ed. *International Political Risk Management: Exploring New Frontiers*. Washington, DC: The World Bank Group, 23.

Ostrovsky A, 2002, IMF sees signs of Brazil effect on bond market, *Financial Times*, 13 September.

11

Country Risk Assessment: A Matter of Information and Intelligence Gathering

11.1 INTRODUCTION

In quantum mechanics, Heisenberg's 1927 principle stipulates that the more precisely the position is determined, the less precisely the momentum is known in this instant, and vice versa. In layman's terms, this means it is impossible (and a source of diminishing returns) to attempt measuring both the exact position and the exact momentum of a particle at the same time. This relation has important implications for such fundamental notions as causality and the determination of future behavior.

There is a useful analogy between quantum mechanics and country risk, in that both deal with uncertainty. Pinpointing the risk boils down to influencing the risk momentum. Each crisis, be it in the 1890s, 1930s, 1980s or late 1990s, stems from an information deficit that leads to mounting uncertainty. However, in today's global economy, efforts at transparency and communication networks are the name of the game. Countries compete with each other to get market access via a regular flow of quality information. In turn, fund managers, investors, creditors and bank depositors get flooded by an excess of information that requires careful discrimination and cross-checking. Consequently, globalization of information can generate rising volatility of capital flows and crisis propagation. The wide availability and instant transmission of information combine to possibly trigger a herd instinct and self-fulfilling prophecy that result in spill-over effects and crisis contamination. In the new global environment where Ulrich Beck (2002) regards risk as being the norm, there is the so-called information paradox on which Charles Perrow (1999) casts light: too much information and knowledge leads to mounting uncertainty.

The concept of risk stems from a twofold set of values that relate to its measurement and its perception. The latter is rooted in a society's fears and threats at a specific moment in time and in a specific place. It follows that risk is assessed and measured in different ways today compared with the nineteenth century or even the late 1980s, before the fall of the Berlin Wall. It also means that risk is looked at differently in the United States, Europe and China, today and probably tomorrow. The measurement of risk is thus closely related to its perception. And as perception varies across space and time, the measurement of risk is a volatile issue. One measures well only what one perceives and defines clearly. Given that risk is made up of uncertainty, information is thus a key input in accurate risk measurement.

Country risk analysis is only as good as the quality of the underlying information. The latter is the key behind decision-making, resulting in either good assessment or excess exposure with related losses. To anticipate and assess the riskiness behind macroeconomic discontinuities, one needs good data. As Mobil Corporation's senior economist for country risk summarizes (Painter, 1999): "The first responsibility is to have the appropriate resources available."

The issue of country risk information emerged only in the early 1980s, alongside growing trade and financial transactions, and with the debt crisis in emerging market countries. As Ruth A. Pagell (1998) puts it: "International business information is relatively new and mirrors the increase in cross-border business." The international banking industry faced a formidable "information gap" when banks started to recycle petrodollars during the 1970s and early 1980s. AMEX Bank (1984) reports: "Lack of data on the debts of developing counties is widely cited as a major difficulty facing the international credit market, perhaps itself contributing to the debt crises of 1982–83." In August 1982, Mexico's Finance Minister, Jesus Silva Herzog, abruptly sent a telex to Citibank's William Rhodes, then chairman of a number of international banking credit syndications. Mexico's debt servicing suspension sent a shock wave through the banks' credit committees, resulting in a frantic search to get a comprehensive picture of the banks' global risk exposure in Mexico. For many banks, this exposure aggregation resulted in a painful and frustrating exercise. Most of the banks had scattered credits throughout their branch and subsidiary networks worldwide for tax and regulatory purposes. Many had been attracted by international loan syndications without much knowledge of the underlying risk. Comprehensive and timely information was lacking, then, regarding debt servicing capacity. In addition, banks had underestimated the contagion risk of payment defaults triggered by protracted recessions and competitive devaluations in many emerging market countries. Worse, many banks had insufficient capital and loan-loss reserves to mitigate the risk of bankruptcies. Comparing the sovereign default crises of the 1920s and 1980s, Eichengreen and Portes (1988) note: "There is little evidence that capital markets have grown more sophisticated over time, or that banks have a comparative advantage in processing the relevant information."

The deficit in reliable country risk intelligence precipitated the creation of the Washington-based Institute for International Finance in 1983. The threat of systemic risk on the international banking system abated only in the late 1980s, after some progress had been made by the debtor countries in restructuring and reforming their economies. All in all, the abruptness of the crisis, the ongoing uncertainties arising from the debt overhang, and the lack of robust country risk information resulted in a mounting reluctance of commercial lenders to provide new funds to those countries, even on a concerted basis. During the 1983–1988 period, commercial banks provided US$47 billion in new long-term money through concerted lending to 17 countries and restructured more than US$405 billion of claims (World Bank, 1988–89). Since then, international banks have strengthened their portfolio with larger loan-loss reserves, better capital adequacy ratios and stronger risk analysis methods. More prudent, more demanding and better informed creditors inevitably result in sharper discrimination among borrowers.

The root causes of financial crises, however, changed over the 1990s, illustrating the gap between the focus of country risk assessment – namely, balance of payments and liquidity indicators – and the diverse root causes of financial imbalances. Although the ultimate manifestation of a debt crisis is often protracted balance of payments tensions, the crises of the late 1990s and the beginning of the twenty-first century have shifted attention to microeconomic imbalances, where information is still a formidable challenge. In particular, the causes of banking crises, with subsequent capital account tensions, include lending booms, weak governance and "crony capitalism", destabilizing external factors, precipitous financial liberalization, inadequate prudential supervision, and weaknesses in the legal and institutional framework (Eichengreen and Arteta, 2000). These are more complex causes of crises than a rising debt servicing ratio or a drop in official reserve assets. As Michel Camdessus observed, the 1994 devaluation of the Mexican peso was the first financial crisis of the twenty-first century. At the heart of the currency collapse were investors' souring expectations, creditors' herd behavior and a rapid reversal of capital flow (Edwards and Frankel, 2001).

As the global economy and the spill-over effects compound the magnitude and abruptness of country risk crises, timely information has never been so crucial in risk assessment and prediction. Robert Dunn (2001) concludes: "The herdlike behavior of lenders and investors in removing funds from many developing countries, after one encountered trouble, was based in part on the fact that the bankers lacked detailed and trustworthy knowledge about their economic and financial conditions. Operating with very limited knowledge, they flee at the first sign of trouble."

Today, more reliable information and data have become the basis for sophisticated risk analysis methods. In that regard, the role of international institutions is crucial, in particular that of the Bretton Woods institutions. As José Angel Gurria (2002) sums up: "Multilaterals cannot eliminate country risk but they can attenuate it, allowing access to markets that otherwise would be closed."

One can differentiate between the most reliable sources of country risk intelligence by their official or private origins. We shall distinguish the supply of information from international organizations, central banks and private risk agencies as well as the academic community.

11.2   SOLVENCY AND LIQUIDITY RISK: THE SUPPLY OF DEBT-RELATED INFORMATION

11.2.1   Official Sources of Country Risk Data and Information

Solvency and liquidity risk always ends up in balance of payments and debt servicing difficulties in over-indebted countries. The debt overhang stems from a typical mismatch between financial obligations and revenues. This mismatch (in terms of volume, timing, currency and interest rates) can stem from a combination of domestic and external problems. It can also be compounded by a gap between domestic savings and investment, by structural weaknesses and exogenous shocks. However, most country risk analysts focus on the demand side of the debt overhang, i.e., the over-indebtedness. The supply of capital available to emerging countries is not tackled as it should be, according to the CIA's economist James W. Harris. He argues (Harris, 2000) that "we, country risk specialists, assess the likelihood of financial crisis badly because we do not incorporate an adequate understanding of the supply side of the global credit markets." Financial turbulence, indeed, can be originated or accentuated and prolonged by capital volatility on the supply side. Tight credit, rising spreads, abrupt shortening of maturities and global credit contraction in international liquidity are all factors that put pressure on emerging markets, whatever the soundness of their internal financial situation. Liquidity and solvency information must thus be assessed in close parallel with the global financial environment. This information is within the hands of multilateral financial organizations.

The Role of the International Monetary Fund as Provider of Financial Data: Balance of Payments, Adjustment Programs, Exceptional Financing and Debt Relief

The IMF provides a key role in country risk data availability. The Fund collects, from each member country, detailed statements of external current and capital accounts, including details on the capital flows relevant for measuring changes in external debt. Countries submit these data at least once a year; many report on a quarterly basis and some on a monthly basis. The Fund is more focused on "flow data" and there is no systematic procedure for collecting and publishing data on external debt as such. The IMF's data are published on a monthly basis in the *International Financial Statistics* (*IFS*), combining balance of payments information on each of the 183 member countries.

However, the 1997–1998 emerging market crisis revealed deficiencies in the international financial system both on the debtor side and on the creditor side, namely in the capacity of investors to undertake adequate risk assessment and of supervisory authorities to monitor properly international and national liquidity. The Asian crisis shed light on the need for enhancing collaboration and information exchanges between international organizations. The financial crisis reminded risk analysts to look more closely at a country's external liquidity composition, including the structure of debt by debtors, creditors, currency, maturity and interest rates. At the time of the July 1997 abrupt devaluation of the Thai baht, the World Bank's *World Debt Tables* had released end-1995 external debt data while the BIS had only available end-1996 external liabilities to international banking institutions. Risk analysts and investors had little visibility of the Asian countries' financial deterioration. As Camdessus (1999) put it: "There is a strong consensus for making transparency the 'golden rule' of the new international financial system. A lack of transparency has been found at the origin of each recurring crisis in the emerging markets; and it has been a pernicious feature of the 'crony' capitalism that has plagued most of the crisis countries and many more besides."

The IMF has made a three-pronged effort regarding country risk information availability, regarding the *timeliness*, *quality* and *standardization* of economic and financial data. The Fund's work on data dissemination standards began in late 1995, when the Interim Committee endorsed the establishment by the Fund of standards to guide member countries in the public circulation of their economic and financial data. Those standards consist of two tiers: the *General Data Dissemination System* (GDDS) that applies to all Fund members, and the more demanding *Special Standard* for those countries having or seeking access to international capital markets. A key part of the Special Standard is a template for publishing comparable data on international reserves and liquidity. The reserves template includes information on credit lines and contingent claims on official reserve assets. A growing number of developing countries publish a comprehensive Net International Investment Position, within the IFS. The Fund's technical and financial assistance staff helps countries prepare metadata with comprehensive plans for improvements of dissemination practices. The Fund's board approved this initiative in 1996 and 1997, and it was upgraded in 2002 (World Bank, 2001). As a result, a growing number of countries provide investors and creditors with comparable and timely financial and economic information. As of late 2002, according to Fitch, 50 countries have signed up for the Special Standard, including a majority of investment grade countries. A further 40 countries are committed to meeting the less demanding General Standard. In addition, country governments that accept the need to systematically publish the concluding statements of IMF "Article IV" missions are highly praised by the Fund and by investors. This is the case, for instance, with Tunisia, the only country in the region that has subscribed to the IMF Special Data Dissemination Standard.[1]

Since the 1997–1998 Asian financial crisis, the IMF's role of fireman to extinguish debt crises has been strongly questioned. G7 policymakers and academic scientists have placed pressure on the Fund to promote a pre-emptive role based on early warning indicators. As former US Treasury's Caroline Atkinson (2002) notices: "The IMF is the only body with political legitimacy and technical ability to make judgments . . . regarding when a country cannot pay its debts without crippling its economy."

---

[1] See IMF Managing Director Horst Köhler's Remarks in Tunisia, *IMF News Brief*, 02/18, 23 October 2002.

Table 11.1 IMF financial statistics on Thailand

US$ million	1995	1996	1997	1998	1999	2000	2001
Official Reserves	35 982	37 731	26 179	28 825	34 063	32 016	32 355
Trade Balance	−7968	−9488	1572	16 238	14 013	11 700	8582
Current Account	−13 554	−14 691	−3021	14 243	12 428	9313	6195
Current Account/GDP %	−12.8%	−12.4%	−1.3%	8.4%	7.2%	4.7%	2.1%
Net Errors & Omissions	−1196	−2627	−3173	−2828	33	−677	626
Net International Position	−53 850	−62 737	−74 269	−63 693	−46 691	−31 284	−18 339
Total Debt Outstanding	100 832	108 742	109 276	105 084	95 647	79 715	67 350
o/w Medium & Long-term	48 434	60 999	70 982	76 644	75 688	65 021	53 980
Reserves/Imports Cover (ratio in months)	6.8	7.1	5.7	9.5	9.6	6.8	6.6
Total Debt Payments	8253	9024	11 629	14 430	14 134	12 893	15 817
Trade Openness Ratio %	90.2%	84.5%	94.2%	101.6%	104.3%	125.7%	126.6%
Investment/GDP %	40.9%	40.8%	33.4%	22.2%	20.1%	21.3%	22.9%
Export Competitiveness (index in terms of US$)	121.1	108.9	104.9	91.2	87.7	85.9	87.3

Source: IMF *IFS* and national authorities.

The international community attaches increasing importance to the IMF's work on standards and codes as a crucial element of crisis prevention. Accordingly, the Fund has intensified its efforts to help countries improve the quality and timeliness of their financial data. It has developed quarterly reports on compliance with the Special Data Dissemination Standard to promote greater financial stability and transparency. In addition, the IMF embarked on greater openness while expanding public access to its own operations and activities, including the release of information notices on the Fund's Article IV consultations with member nations and disclosure of a range of background documents for those consultations.

Table 11.1 illustrates the usefulness of the IMF's *IFS* regarding Thailand's external liquidity position over the 1995–2001 period.

Of particular usefulness is the International Investment Position (IIP) that captures a country's financial openness and vulnerability. The IIP is a balance sheet concept that provides a comprehensive snapshot of the magnitude and structure of a country's full range of external claims and liabilities (IMF, 2002).

Beyond external payments data, however, the IMF's *IFS* tables are a key source of information regarding the central banks' balance sheets, hence casting light on the direction of the debtor country's fiscal and monetary policies. It helps analysts to determine whether or not sovereign borrowers live beyond their means. The balance sheet is a handy way to determine whether the countries possess the political will and ability to adjust the macroeconomic situation to create the underlying conditions for sustainable growth. In particular, the financing of the country's public sector borrowing requirement (PSBR) appears in the evolution of the main monetary parameters, including the monetary base, domestic credit expansion and domestic money supply. Given large and rising PSBR, financing can originate either from larger taxes, or a larger resort to external financing, or monetary expansion and credit creation through central bank purchasing of government bonds. The latter will give rise to an expansion in net domestic assets. The country will be able to maintain its lax monetary policy and obtain low recorded rates of monetary expansion and inflation so long as it can attract the foreign currency required to prop up the exchange rate. Otherwise, when the country has run out of exchange reserves, or should the central bank adopt a more independent stance vis-à-vis the government's budget deficit, devaluing will become unavoidable.

The central bank balance sheet can be reduced to three main categories, as follows:

Liabilities	Assets
Monetary Base = Currency in circulation + Bank deposits	*Net Foreign Assets + Net Domestic Assets* (including Loans to the public sector and Loans to the domestic banking system)

The balance sheet of Thailand's central bank at end-1996 and at end-2001 sheds light on the usefulness of these data. Before the eruption of the crisis, i.e., at end-1996, the dramatic expansion in the domestic money supply stemmed from a sharp increase in domestic credit in parallel with a drop in net foreign assets. One year later, in the aftermath of the Thai baht devaluation of July 1997, the central bank's official reserve assets dropped by US$11 billion, to a low of US$26 billion. Observing then the counterparts of the money supply is illuminating. Net foreign assets turned negative to the tune of −US$563 million while net domestic credit rose to nearly US$5 billion. It wasn't until end-2001 that the country rebuilt official reserves to a comfortable level of US$32 billion, thanks to booming net foreign assets and a tightening of domestic credit together with a sharp rise in interest rates:

1996		1997		2001	
Money Supply = 3727	Net Foreign Assets = −81	Money Supply = 4340	Net Foreign Assets = −563	Money Supply = 5302	Net Foreign Assets = +1326
	Net Domestic Assets = 3809		Net Domestic Assets = 4973		Net Domestic Assets = 4067

As John M. Atkin (1984) puts it: "Changes in the components of a central bank balance sheet will convey timely signals about the direction of fiscal and monetary policies and about the foreign exchange operations of the central bank."

The World Bank Group: Macroeconomic Fundamentals, External Indebtedness and Economic Restructuring

Whereas the IMF focuses on debt flows in the balance of payments, the World Bank focuses on debt stocks. The Bank, as a major creditor, maintains a full record of the external debt of its member countries. The World Bank's debtor reporting system was set up in 1951 and its main objective is monitoring long-term public or publicly guaranteed debt. In 1970, the system was extended to incorporate private, non-guaranteed long-term debt. The Bank has an internal system of cross-checks and it supplements reported data with information collected in country missions and by other organizations. The Bank requests information from member countries on all long-term debt, which consists of external liabilities with an original maturity of more than one year. The debt data, both aggregated and on a country-specific basis, are published in the annual report *World Debt Tables*, currently entitled *Global Development Finance*.

The Bank's statistical data comprise a long-term debt breakdown into creditors (official bi-lateral and multilateral, banks, bonds and private suppliers) as well as between debtors (public

Table 11.2   Total external debt stock of Thailand

US$ million	1994	1995	1996	1997	1998	2000
Total Debt	65 596	83 093	90 778	93 731	86 172	79 675
o/w						
Long-term	36 418	41 998	53 164	56 466	59 410	
Short-term	29 179	41 095	37 613	34 836	23 523	
Net Resource Flows*	4863	10 630	14 220	9615	8987	
Net Transfers**	2375	7501	10 598	5596	4651	
Debt/Exports of G&S	111.8	112.2	120.4	123.1	124.5	92.5
Debt/GDP %	46.4	50.5	51.4	62.8	76.5	66
Debt Servicing Ratio %	13.4	11.6	12.7	15.5	19.2	16.2

* Net long-term debt flows + FDI + portfolio equity flows + grants.
** Net flows − interest payments and profit remittances.
Source: World Bank/*World Debt Tables* and *Global Development Finance.* Reproduced with permission.

sector/private sector without public guarantee). The World Bank releases debt tables with an 18-month lag. Accordingly, these data are useful for academic research and are not considered sufficiently operational and timely for market-driven risk assessment. The analysis and summary tables included in *Global Development Finance* present aggregate data on international capital flows by region or by income and indebtedness classification criteria. These data comprise major economic and debt ratios, as well as information on Paris and London Club restructuring agreements.

Table 11.2 summarizes the World Bank's debt data regarding Thailand's external indebtedness.

Beyond debt data, the World Bank is a key source of macroeconomic and structural information on developing countries. A handy annual publication, namely the *Little Data Book*, is a useful source of succinct social, financial and economic information on more than a hundred developing countries.[2] This pocket version of the World Development Report is intended as a quick reference for economists and risk analysts. In addition, the Annual Report and the World Development Report tackle such issues as infrastructure, sustainable development conditions, social indicators as well as trade and capital flows.

In addition, the World Bank pays growing attention to governance issues in member countries. OECD country governments have recognized that corruption is a transnational phenomenon that requires global coalition building. The World Bank has pioneered efforts toward combating corruption in member countries in the early 1990s (Gray and Kaufmann, 1998; Klitgaard, 1998; Mauro, 1998). The Bank set up an "Anticorruption Knowledge Center" as well as a Development Forum discussion on anti-corruption strategies. It focuses on a number of emerging market countries in Africa, Latin America, Asia and Eastern Europe. All in all, 48 countries are involved in specific anti-corruption and governance measures under the Bank's auspices. As a senior manager of the Development Institute says: "The multilateral organizations have accepted that corruption is not just a moral issue, but a developmental issue, as well."[3] On 18 August 2001, James Wolfensohn (2001) declared: "The biggest obstacle to the development of legal and judicial systems is a situation in which the economic elite uses the system in its own interests. Legal reform is not only a technical but also a political task."

---

[2] *Little Data Book*, World Bank, Washington, DC (annual publication).
[3] See *Latin Finance*, 2000.

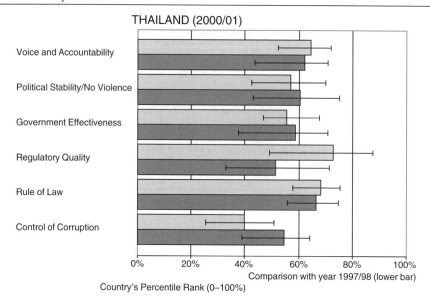

Figure 11.1   Composite Governance Indicators (*Source*: World Bank)

Recent efforts of the World Bank to tackle governance and corruption have paved the way for a regular flow of information and data, including a composite Governance Indicator that uses six different underlying parameters. The indicators reflect the statistical compilation of perceptions of the quality of governance of a large number of survey respondents in industrial and developing countries, as well as non-governmental organizations (NGOs), risk agencies and think-tanks. Figure 11.1 illustrates the World Bank's appraisal of governance and corruption in Thailand (World Bank, Anti-corruption Initiative).

The Bank for International Settlements: International Banking Claims and Liabilities

The BIS is a key source of aggregate data on external sovereign liabilities and assets. The Basle-based institution provides debt stock and flow data collected by official monetary institutions on the international assets and liabilities of commercial banks. The BIS also gathers data on international bonds, Euronote issues and certain derivative instruments. Much of this information is published in the *BIS Quarterly Reports on International Banking and Financial Market Developments*.

The statistics were originally introduced in 1964 to monitor the development of the Eurocurrency markets. However, the consolidated banking statistics were launched in a comprehensive form following the onset of the Mexican debt crisis in 1983, with the purpose of monitoring international banks' exposure to developing countries. The data cover contractual lending by the head office and all its branches and subsidiaries on a worldwide-consolidated basis. The BIS data also contain breakdowns by maturity and by sector as well as information on unused credit commitments and facilities. Most of the data are from the consolidated accounts of banks with head offices in the industrial reporting countries, but the system supplements these data with the business of branches and affiliates in the BIS reporting area of banks which have head offices outside the reporting area. The information is available on a quarterly basis since March

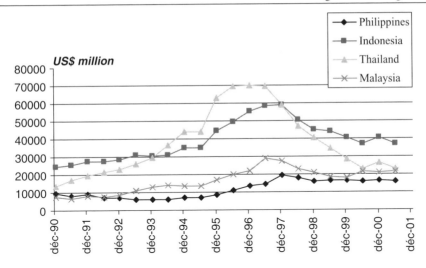

Figure 11.2   Total BIS bank claims

2000, with a six-month lag. There are currently 28 countries reporting these data. Figure 11.2 illustrates the rise and fall in international banks' overall risk exposure in four Asian countries between 1990 and 2001.

One of the main contributions of the BIS data is to shed light on countries' short-term liabilities. Calculating the actual short-term debt requires some statistical manipulations in order to exclude the residual liabilities from the original debt falling due during the current year. Figure 11.3 illustrates the abrupt swing in Asian countries' net short-term debt on the eve and in the aftermath of the crisis.

The BIS data are the only available comprehensive and timely data on international banks' cross-border claims. Its breakdown by sector and maturity has recently been expanded to include the creditor composition of private capital flows. The BIS thus provides a useful

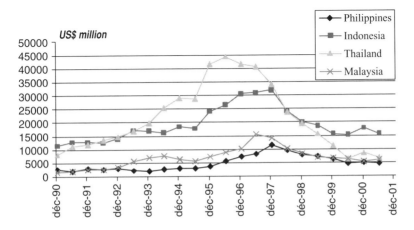

Figure 11.3   Net short-term BIS bank claims

quarterly presentation of the consolidated foreign claims of reporting banks regarding the specific exposure of 17 national groups of reporting banks, within the OECD. The risk analysts accordingly can monitor the inflows and outflows of bank lending for each of the major creditor countries. Table 11.3 illustrates the BIS's presentation of the evolution in international bank claims on Thailand.

BIS data clearly point out the abrupt rise in Thailand's short-term liabilities to international banks during the 1994–1996 period. The short-term debt accounted for 46% of total external obligations at end-1996, rising by nearly 50% compared with 1994. At the time of the devaluation of the Thai baht, in July 1997, these data were readily available and could have helped assess the deterioration in the country's international liquidity, along with other data such as that of the IMF. The key, indeed, is not transparency but rather how lenders use the information. When things are going well, all claims look creditworthy, and vice versa. As BIS's William White (2000) notices: "As far back as 1996, the BIS international banking statistics clearly indicated a dangerous build-up of foreign short-term liabilities by many Asian countries. This was not sufficient to stop the boom in international lending."

Joint Official Aggregation Efforts: The BIS, the IMF and the OECD

The number of EMCs' protracted crises during the 1980s and 1990s exemplified the need for both timely and reliable information on balance of payments and debt data. The debt crises also confirmed the pressing need for enhanced debt gathering collaboration between official institutions, namely between the IMF, the World Bank, the BIS and the OECD. Recognizing the need for more intense dialogue to reconcile differences in debt compilation systems, the four institutions and the Berne Union formed the International Working Group on External Debt Statistics in 1984. The IMF chaired the task force. Toward this end, the BIS and the OECD have worked more closely. The latter focuses on a comprehensive measurement of official and private resource flows to developing countries in support of its Development Assistance Committee (DAC).

The OECD provides debt stock and flow statistics that it receives through the DAC creditor reporting system, including market sources. The data also include information provided by the debtor countries themselves. The 19 member countries of the DAC that report to the creditor reporting system supply data on official development assistance (ODA), and on officially guaranteed private export credits. In the process of compiling estimates of debt the OECD makes various checks on and adjustments to its own creditor-reported data as well as drawing on external data sources.

The first step in estimating debt data for each borrowing country is the integration of BIS-reporting banks' external assets and OECD data on officially supported export credits by official insurance agencies such as ECGD, Hermes, Coface and Exim-Banks in the United Kingdom, Germany, France, the United States and Japan, respectively.

Taking as starting point the semi-annual reports prepared jointly by the BIS and the OECD on the claims of bank and non-bank trade creditors, the OECD's *External Debt Statistics* aggregate tables provide for each borrower a comprehensive and comparable measurement of gross external indebtedness and other liabilities, broken down by category of debt together with the estimated amortization payments on long-term debt.

The second step is eliminating double-counting in the combination of BIS and OECD data. Some suppliers' credits reported to the OECD are also held by banks, for instance. The data from the World Bank's debtor reporting system are also used to complement and cross-check the data from the creditor reporting system. As such, the OECD issues a comprehensive picture

Table 11.3 Thailand: BIS-reporting bank loans and deposits

US$ million	1994	1995	1996	1997	1998	1999	2000	2001	Q1/02
External debt to international banks									
all sectors	54 465	92 178	98 693	77 511	51 689	36 451	27 670	23 065	20 747
o/w short-term < 1 year	30 968	43 606	45 702	38 791	23 698	14 223	10 317	9451	10 170
non-bank private sector	9828	12 561	13 995	11 770	10 462	10 144	8426	7661	7339
banking sector	44 637	79 617	84 698	65 741	41 227	26 307	19 244	15 404	13 408
Deposits in international banks									
all sectors	7041	11 807	9180	9465	12 031	12 137	14 076	15 534	14 782
non-bank private sector	1840	2131	1921	2020	2306	2701	3017	3683	3654
banking sector	5201	9676	7259	7445	9725	9436	11 059	11 851	11 128
Net external position									
all sectors	−47 424	−80 371	−89 513	−68 046	−39 658	−24 314	−13 594	−7531	−5965
non-bank private sector	−7988	−10 430	−12 074	−9750	−8156	−7443	−5409	−3978	−6516
banking sector	−39 436	−69 941	−77 439	−58 296	−31 502	−16 871	−8185	−3553	3789

Source: BIS Quarterly Review. Reproduced with permission of Bank for International Settlements, Basle, Switzerland.

of a country's external liabilities including lending by multilateral institutions and non-OECD creditor countries, private export credits that are not officially guaranteed, and certain private sector borrowing. As the OECD declares: "The Annual Report, containing statistics on the volume and composition of the external debt, covers more countries than any other publication of its kind. The way in which the figures were compiled enables the reader to make more comparisons than is usually possible."[4] As the OECD recognizes, however, the two main gaps are intercompany claims that are understated, and some information on military debt, particularly for countries like Syria, Jordan, Libya and Iraq.

Since March 1999, the IMF joined the World Bank, the BIS and the OECD in publishing joint external debt statistics in response to requests for dissemination of more timely debt and international reserves indicators. They bring together for the first time the best international comparative data available on external debt stocks and flows. The new Inter-Agency Task Force, chaired by the Fund, uses a creditor and market-based reporting system, with particular emphasis placed on short-term debt.[5] Special effort is made to cut the time lag before publication. The purpose of the joint series is to facilitate timely and frequent access on the joint website by a broad range of users to one data set that brings together data that are currently compiled and published by the contributing international agencies on components of countries' external debt (see Table 11.4 for the example of Thailand). The joint quarterly publications of the Inter-Agency Task Force on Finance Statistics show the following data:

- the *stock of debt*, with a minimum two-month lag, for the last five quarters, and
- *flow figures* for the latest complete two years and two recent quarters.

Commercial Banks' Country Exposure Lending Surveys

Financial and currency crises in the 1990s have been compounded by abrupt reversals of capital flows, both with regard to mounting capital flight and sharp cuts in foreign lending and

Table 11.4 Total external debt stock of Thailand

US$ million	1987	1988	1999	2000	2001 (e)*
Total Debt	24 006	23 489	91 531	75 863	64 527
O/W					
Long-term bank loans	7104	7197	32 268	23 576	18 907
External debt securities	2505	2610	13 198	12 222	10 271
Brady bonds	0	0	0	0	0
Non-bank trade credits	2073	1328	5754	4458	3686
Multilateral claims**	5398	4262	8761	8150	6880
Official bilateral loans***	3495	3536	14 552	13 376	12 500
Short-term liabilities to banks	2641	3667	14 206	10 305	9451
Short-term debt securities	641	695	939	2446	1661
Short-term non-bank trade credits	149	194	1853	1330	1171

* (e) denotes estimate.
** Including use of Fund credit.
*** Including guaranteed bank credits.
Source: Joint BIS–IMF–OECD–World Bank statistics. Reproduced with permission.

---

[4] OECD External Debt Statistics, Paris, 1989.
[5] The statistics are hosted at www.oecd.org/dac/debt

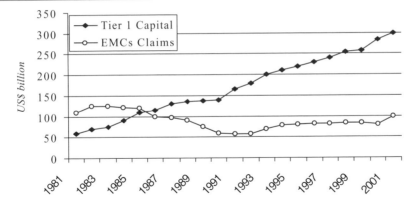

Figure 11.4   US banks' claims on EMCs and equity capital

direct investment. This "scissor effect" accentuated the impact of balance of payments deficits on liquidity ratios (e.g., short-term debt/reserves ratio). Hence, monitoring international bank exposure is a key component of country risk analysis, not only to closely follow the confidence or nervousness of international banks in a particular country, but also to assess the likelihood and extent of contagion effects.

In that regard, central banks in OECD countries have enhanced the quality and timeliness of national banking systems' cross-border risk exposure over the last 20 years, i.e., in the aftermath of the 1982 debt crisis.[6] Most of the OECD country central banks report bank claims on a regular basis, with a breakdown regarding borrowing country. This is the case, in particular, of national banking institutions in the US, the UK, Canada, France, Germany and the Netherlands.

In the United States, the Federal Financial Institutions Examination Council (FFIEC) is an umbrella organization that collects and warehouses data for the Federal Reserve, Office of the Comptroller of the Currency, and Federal Deposit Insurance Corporation. Much of the information collected is made public, aggregated over all reporting banks, in quarterly tables. The time lag is about one quarter. The reported data provide considerable detail on US bank claims on foreign countries, with itemization by individual country, maturity and borrowing sector. Figure 11.4 casts light on the financial strengthening of US banks over the 1981–2001 period, with a sharp rise in capitalization paralleled by declining cross-border claims on EMCs at the time of the 1985 Baker Plan and the subsequent Brady Plan. Banks were able to resist new money calls as their capital to exposure ratios improved substantially, hence making them more independent.

Table 11.5 describes the evolution of US bank claims on Thailand before and after the Asian crisis. As the FFIEC reports information on US banks' capital, one can observe that the ratio of US banks' claims on Thailand to their Tier 1 capital dropped from 2% in 1996 to hardly 0.31% in 2002.

All in all, the driving force behind the improved availability of quality data on emerging market countries' economies has been a combination of financial crises and international official and market pressure. Policymakers and regulators have been developing and implementing a set of standards and codes under the aegis of a number of international bodies. The IFIs and

---

[6] The German Central Bank issues the Reihe 3 quarterly report, while the Banque de France issues its Quarterly Bulletin as does the Bank of England.

Table 11.5   Total external claims of US banks on Thailand

US$ million	1995	1996	1997	1998	1999	2000	2001	2002*
Cross-border claims	2926	5339	2633	1380	828	945	1279	963
O/W owed by banks	1290	1832	980	339	177	245	743	461
Short-term claims	2504	4326	1985	782	560	679	1035	735

* Mid-year.
Source: US FFIEC.

national supervisory authorities have put the emphasis on data quality and availability, fiscal and financial policies' transparency, and banking supervision. Following the IMF's initiative in 1996, "efforts to encourage countries to apply high standards in the statistical and supervisory fields were given more political focus by the Asian and Russian sovereign debt crisis, and this led to the establishment in April 1999 of the Financial Stability Forum (FSF) (Fitch, 2002). Today, country governments compete to get market access and to satisfy investors' demands and expectations with two main instruments: a market-based regulatory framework, and timely, complete and internationally comparable data in key economic and financial fields. Creditworthiness thus stems from adherence to transparency and good governance.

Table 11.6 presents the main 12 standards and those official agencies involved.

11.2.2   Private Sources of Country Risk Data and Information

The Institute of International Finance: The Global Banking Industry's Country Risk "Think-Tank"

The IIF represents the private banking industry worldwide. Macroeconomic data transparency was widely recognized as a problem after the 1995 Mexican "Tequila" crisis. This problem became still more acute at the time of the 1997 Asian crisis. In the aftermath of the Asian crisis, the IIF increased pressure on country governments to provide better information on capital

Table 11.6   Standards

Macroeconomic policy and data transparency	
Data dissemination and quality	IMF
Fiscal transparency	IMF
Monetary and financial policies	IMF
Financial regulation and supervision	
Banking supervision	BIS-Basle Committee
Securities regulation	IOSCO
Insurance	IAIS
Institutional and market infrastructure	
Systematically important payment systems	CPSS
Corporate governance	OECD
International accounting standards	IASC
International auditing standards	IFAC
Insolvency	World Bank
Market integrity and money laundering	FATF

movements, bank deposits, holdings of securities, derivatives and reserves. The IIF declared: "Investors in emerging markets should have more timely and meaningful economic data to enable them to assess risks."[7]

The Washington-based IIF (see Box 11.1) provides member banks with three main sources of data:

1. Country-specific data, where the most noticeable value-added of the IIF lies in the meticulous reconciliation of balance of payments data and debt servicing flows;
2. Global surveys of capital flows to emerging market economies;
3. Reports on the international financial system's architecture and regulatory issues.

Box 11.1   The Institute of International Finance (IIF)

The IIF is the world's global association of financial institutions. Created in 1983 in response to the international debt crisis, the IIF has evolved to meet the changing needs of the financial community. Members include most of the world's largest commercial banks and investment banks, as well as a growing number of insurance companies and investment management firms. Among the Institute's Associate Members are multinational corporations, trading companies, export credit agencies and multilateral agencies. The Institute has more than 320 members headquartered in 60 countries. Activities fall broadly into three areas: (i) *analyzing risks* in emerging market economies; (ii) *serving as a forum* for member firms on key policy issues in emerging markets' finance and regulatory matters; and (iii) *promoting collaboration* between members and multilateral financial institutions. The IIF has two primary goals beyond that of serving as a discussion forum:

1. To support members' risk management, asset allocation and business development in emerging markets. To this end, the IIF provides members with reliable data and analysis of economic and financial developments and prospects.
2. To provide economic intelligence on emerging market economies. The IIF has established a robust reputation for the quality of its macroeconomic and financial analysis of risks in emerging markets and for its database. In addition to coverage of individual economies, the Institute publishes reports on regional and global financial issues.

See: www.iif.org

International Rating Agencies and Country Risk Information

Rating agencies provide investors and analysts not only with risk assessment but also with web-based real-time credit ratings and research. A sovereign rating, indeed, is a quantitative assessment of a government's ability and willingness to service its foreign debt obligations in full and on time. As such, a rating is a forward-looking estimate of default probability and is based on a wide number of economic and social parameters. The appraisal is thus both quantitative as well as qualitative even though the ultimate output is a grade or a rank. As Standard & Poor's (2002) considers: "The quantitative aspects of the analysis incorporate a number of measures of economic and financial performance and contingent liabilities, although

---

[7] Report of the Working Group on Transparency in Emerging Markets Finance.

judging the integrity of the data is a more qualitative matter. The analysis is also qualitative due to the importance of political and policy developments."

Standard & Poor's is a premier source of weekly updated sovereign ratings regarding local and foreign currency debt, both for short and long-term horizons. The analytical framework of sovereign ratings is based on 10 categories that incorporate economic and political risk. In addition, S&P's financial and economic research includes a glossary of financial terms, as well as solvency and liquidity indicators, including estimates and forecasts for a limited number of developing countries. Moody's and Fitch provide similar research services. Likewise, BradyNet provides a range of country indicators for about 40 countries, over a nine-year horizon, including balance of payments as well as debt and macroeconomic data, up to the previous year.

Table 11.7 illustrates S&P's external debt data on Thailand and other countries, as of mid-2002.

Commercial and Merchant Banks as Sources of Country Risk Intelligence

The quality of bank research is closely related to the scope and depth of international exposure of the banks. Research, indeed, is not only made of quantitative data but also of a resilient network of contacts in the local private and public arenas. Several banking institutions have cut to the bone their country risk staff in the wake of the Mexican, Asian and Argentine crises. Other banks consider that emerging markets are there for the long haul and they constitute a key risk diversification market. According to Citicorp's calculations, 86% of the world population lives in emerging market countries, and their economies account for 43% of the world's purchasing power, yet most of these markets are far from saturated. It follows that some emerging markets might have been hit hard over the last few years, but more are climbing back from the economic doldrums.

Global Finance's 2002 annual survey of the best emerging market banks is a useful source for assessing the quality of country risk research. Citibank comes out on top year after year, with a presence in 80 countries it defines as emerging. Despite the downturn in Argentina, Citigroup says its emerging market core income for year-end 2001 rose 22% over the prior year, to nearly US$3 billion. "The bank's localized approach extends to assessing global and corporate creditworthiness and it tailors credit policy to the king of information available in each country", says Eilen Fahey, managing director of financial institutions at Ficht Investors Services.[8] In Argentina, international banks such as Citigroup, SCH, BBVA and FleetBoston control about 37% of the local banking industry and are thus a prime source of country risk information.

Global Finance's survey gives the following classification of the best banks in the following regions:

Latin America	BBVA
Central & Eastern Europe	RZB Group of Austria
Asia	HSBC
Middle East/Africa	Citigroup

[8] Annual Survey of Best Emerging Market Banks, Global Finance, May 2002, p. 28.

Table 11.7 Sovereign risk indicators: external debt data

Country	Foreign currency rating	Net external liabilities/current account receipts (%)		Gross external debt/current account receipts (%)		Net external debt/current account receipts (%)		Narrow net external debt/current account receipts (%)		Net public sector external debt/current account receipts (%)		Net investment payments/current account receipts (%)		Net interest payments/current account receipts (%)	
		1998–2002	2002	1998–2002	2002	1998–2002	2002	1998–2002	2002	1998–2002	2002	1998–2002	2002	1998–2002	2002
Taiwan	AA	−102	−124	26	30	−80	−101	−80	−101	−77	−100	(2.7)	(2.7)	0.0	0.0
Japan	AA −	−145	−136	221	222	−167	−159	−22	−14	−55	−65	(8.1)	(7.5)	N/A	N/A
Hong Kong	A +	−67	−92	124	103	−80	−92	−80	−92	−36	−38	(1.5)	(2.2)	0.0	0.0
Korea	A −	35	27	77	66	10	−6	11	−5	0	−22	1.7	0.8	1.7	0.8
Malaysia	BBB +	51	49	44	44	5	4	7	6	−9	−7	5.6	5.4	2.1	2.1
China	BBB	74	69	62	50	−36	−43	−35	−41	−41	−47	8.7	8.6	(1.1)	(1.5)
Thailand	BBB −	64	18	107	82	42	8	44	11	−3	−14	2.5	0.6	2.3	0.1
India	BB	132	140	155	169	74	64	82	73	60	57	4.2	1.6	4.3	7.3
Vietnam	BB −	−79	45	74	75	−97	27	−97	27	−101	39	4.6	5.1	1.6	1.6
Indonesia	CCC+	N/A	N/A	228	205	162	141	162	141	72	64	11.6	8.5	9.0	4.5
Argentina	SD	367	443	388	382	243	312	299	359	177	225	21.2	23.6	16.7	17.7

Source: Standard & Poor's. Reproduced with permission.

These banks constitute reliable sources of country risk information. A few additional banks have accumulated a seasoned track record as far as emerging market research is concerned. These banks are, *inter alia*, Caisse des Dépôts et Consignations (CDC), JP Morgan, ABN Amro. Standard Bank has a comparative advantage in South African research (Economics Division's *Economics Weekly*), while Barclays Capital's Emerging Market research team closely follows Brady debt developments and global prices in Latin America. Regarding investment banks' research, one should point out three indices monitored by:

- IFC (International Finance Corp.): Emerging Stock Market Factbook (www.ifc.org) and Emerging Markets Database (EMDB). Standard & Poor's EMDB is a leading source for information and indices on stock markets in developing countries. EMDB was first launched by the IFC in 1981 to collect data on emerging markets for in-house use. Over time, demand from the financial community for this data increased. In 1987, IFC began offering its indices and underlying data as a commercial product. In January 2000, Standard & Poor's acquired EMDB from IFC. EMDB covers 54 markets and more than 2200 stocks. Drawing a sample of stocks in each EMDB market, Standard & Poor's calculates indices designed to serve as benchmarks that are consistent across national boundaries. http://www.spglobal.com/indexmainemdb.html
- JP Morgan's EMBI Global (Emerging Markets Bond Index) was introduced in mid-1999. It is a comprehensive EMCs' debt benchmark composed by a market capitalization-weighted index. It comprises 27 countries, and includes a wide range of financial instruments, such as Brady bonds, Eurobonds, traded loans and local market debt issued by sovereign and quasi-sovereign entities. To be considered as "emerging", countries must have a low or middle income per capita of <US$9635 as reported by the World Bank, and must have restructured their external or local debt outstanding. Argentina, Brazil and Mexico constitute more than half of the index. http://www2.jpmorgan.com/MarketDataInd/EMBI/embi.html
- Morgan Stanley Capital International: MSCI is a leading provider of global indices and benchmark-related products and services to investors worldwide. The MSCI's Standard Index represents 85% of free float-adjusted market capitalization, including several emerging markets such as Mexico, Turkey, Hong Kong, South Africa, Korea and Mexico. http://www.msci.com/equity/index.html

Special attention must be given to CDC's emerging market research, given the quality of its economist staff and that of its outputs. CDC provides free access to its monthly publications on emerging markets, comprising a monthly rating, external debt and spreads data, equity research and regional focus. The economist and analyst research staff offers international issuers and investors an extensive array of economic and financial research services,[9] including the following:

- Economic monitoring of about 40 emerging markets;
- Financial and exchange rate forecasts;
- Country-specific analysis, including macroeconomic and political developments.

---

[9] CDC IXIS Service des Etudes Economiques et Financières (www.cdc.fr).

11.3   FDI-RELATED COUNTRY RISK ASSESSMENT

Assessing the financial risk related to cross-border lending can be helped by a large number of intertwined financial indicators to predict currency devaluation, deposit blockages, arrears, debt rescheduling and default. These risks can be quantified thanks to the data that have been presented earlier in this chapter. The various risks that are related to cross-border direct investment, however, are broader and more complex. The return on the investment is not based only upon the country's ability to generate foreign exchange to service its obligations. The balance of payments, the reserves and the debt servicing ratios are no longer the key variables behind the market's liquidity and solvency. Other parameters get into the picture, such as the socio-political situation, structural deficiencies, real wages and domestic prices, infrastructure bottlenecks, loose regulatory framework, neighboring countries' economic health, etc.

The analysis, both at the micro and at the macro levels, of the host country's overall economic and social situation becomes a prerequisite before a multinational company's long-term investment decision strategy. As David Raddock (2001) concludes: "Good strategic planning should encompass the whole tapestry. The more apparent political threats to the financial well-being of an enterprise stem from such government actions as expropriation or the imposition of crippling legal restrictions that will lead to expropriation, freezing of foreign company's assets or insistence on divestment, a government's failure or the sort of paralysis that can induce political uncertainty, restrictions on repatriation of profits, social confusion or chaos, and disruptions from various types of civil disorders including strikes, terrorism, and revolution."

11.3.1   The Role of Specialized Country Risk Assessment Companies

- *The Political Risk Services Group (PRS) and the International Country Risk Guide*: Since 1979, the PRS has been supplying private investors with the data and analysis needed to assess and forecast the global business marketplace. The database includes 140 countries. Quarterly revised country reports feature concise analysis of potential political, financial and economic risks to business investments and trade in a consistent format. A monthly political risk letter tackles recent political and social developments, including rather descriptive statements regarding government stability, party and coalition splits, corruption, terrorism, civil unrest, democratic accountability, as well as law and order. It also offers a political and economic forecast table that gives a probability of turmoil. A composite risk rating incorporates political inputs with a 50% weighting as well as financial and economic inputs that each contribute 25%.
- *The Economic Intelligence Unit (EIU)*: The London-based company is an independent organization and a sister company of *The Economist* newspaper. It provides global macroeconomic forecasts as well as comprehensive reports for nearly 200 individual countries. In addition to reports, the EIU also delivers country ratings and rankings (see Chapter 5). http://www.eiu.com/site_info
- *Lehman Brothers and Eurasia Group's Political and Economic Stability Index*: Eurasia Group is a research and consulting firm that focuses on political risk analysis and industry research for emerging markets around the world. Eurasia Group has expertise on Africa, East and Southeast Europe, Former Soviet Union, Latin America, Middle East, and Southeast and East Asia. Staring in October 2001, the monthly index aims at measuring relative stability in 22 emerging markets by integrating political science theories with financial market

developments. The evaluation of 20 composite indicators of political and economic stability uses a combination of quantitative and qualitative data to produce scoring. Stability components include institutional efficiency, political legitimacy, political violence, economic performance and government effectiveness. The LEGSI provides an "early warning" system which helps anticipate critical trends and provides a measure for country capacity to withstand political, economic, security and social shocks. http://www.legsi.com

11.3.2 National Public and Private Information Sources

- National agencies in OECD countries produce and publish research and information on emerging market countries. In particular, export credit agencies (ECAs) provide investors and exporters with a combination of analysis and insurance. Paris-based *Coface* (Box 11.2) is France's leading private credit risk guarantee agency. Risk rating is supported by a comprehensive database of economic and financial indicators, including a "risk outlook" that encompasses assets and weaknesses of investment scope.

Box 11.2   Coface

The Coface Group facilitates and secures trade throughout the world. The Group offers more than 78 000 companies – whether large or small, whatever their business and wherever they are – a range of solutions spanning rating, protection and services, including country risk data and analysis.

Country risk analysis is expressed in a rating/ranking format but based on a qualitative analysis aimed at integrating the socio-political and economic specificities of each country. Coface takes into account and assesses several types of risk around six different analytical modules: political risk; liquidity and non-transfer risk; sovereign risk; market crisis risk; systemic banking crisis; macroeconomic growth risk.

See: www.coface.org

- The Washington-based *Central Intelligence Agency* produces the annual CIA world fact book on about 50 developing countries, including a wide range of economic and social data. http://www.cia.us
- Central banks and public institutions in emerging countries: Whereas IFIs and OECD countries' central banks provide key data on the cross-border exposure of international banks, i.e. on the supply of hard-currency loans to emerging market countries, local central banks are also a source of important data regarding the domestic economy. The following table presents a range of central banks' websites among those that are the most useful. The full list of central banks' sites is available through the BIS.

Peru: http://www.bcrp.gob.pe/
Nigeria: http://www.cenbank.org/welcome.htm
Mexico: http://www.banxico.org.mx/
   siteBanxicoINGLES/index.html
China: http://www.pbc.gov.cn/english/

Poland: http://www.nbp.pl/home_en.html
Chile: http://www.bcentral.cl/
South Korea: http://www.bok.or.kr/index_e.html
Brazil: http://www.bcb.gov.br/

11.3.3   Think-Tanks and Risk Analysis Companies

There are a large number of think-tank and private research institutions that devote research to country risk issues. A few institutes go beyond academic work and offer assessment of government policies as well as policy advice and proposal for reforms.

Heritage Foundation (www.heritage.org/whoweare): Founded in 1973, the Heritage Foundation is a research and educational institute whose mission is to formulate and promote conservative public policies based on the principles of free enterprise. Its ideological posture is firm and clear: encouraging market-oriented economic policies in the United States and beyond. This stance means that the Heritage Foundation prepares analyses, policy papers and reports that promote privatization, sound macroeconomic adjustment, limited government and individual freedom. Chile is praised more highly than Cuba. In particular, the Center for International Trade and Economics (CITE) provides research on the role of market-driven economic policies in fostering growth in countries around the world. CITE produces the annual Index of Economic Freedom.

Cato Institute (www.cato.org): Publishes regular reports evaluating government policies and offering proposals for reform. Although the Cato Institute is not intended to provide access to macroeconomic and financial data *per se*, its policy papers on emerging market economies are based on a wide range of information sources that make its analyses highly valuable for the risk analyst.

Country risk information is not only available in external sources of information, even though analysts tend to rely more on the creditor than on the debtor. Regarding microeconomic analysis, as well as the analysis of the political and institutional situation, local sources of information have a clear comparative advantage. This source of information includes the local branches of foreign banks and companies, but also a number of competent local companies whose job is to provide investors with seasoned risk and opportunity assessment reports. Former government officials often set up or join local think-tanks. Their most interesting contribution is socio-political risk analysis from their local vantage point, including work conditions, legal and regulatory framework, political stability, social tensions, political alliances, union influence, etc. They also show a strong comparative advantage regarding sectoral analysis, including the banking and corporate sector.

The high degree of risk at stake with foreign investment calls for a comprehensive analysis that encompasses the analysis of the firm's vulnerability in a dynamic framework. The French company Thierry Apoteker Consulting (TAC) has developed an innovative tool for analyzing investment risks and opportunities. The analytical framework is based on the concept of "threshold" or breaking point where a number of economic and financial imbalances converge to pave the way for imminent crisis. TAC and the European Commission have also developed a risk assessment methodology that can be used both in international comparison for FDI attraction, and within a given country to identify strengths and weaknesses in the policies or economic factors of interest for international companies' strategies. The so-called FACTOM analytical framework (Box 11.3) has been used on a limited number of Asian countries.

Box 11.3   FACTOM: An instrument to assess developing countries' FDI attractiveness

Competition between countries to attract FDI has increased significantly, and international trade patterns tend to be much more fluid than before. A growing number of emerging market countries are dependent on FDI as a means to catch up in terms of technology and managerial know-how, as a tool to fasten capital accumulation and foster domestic growth, and as a foreign financing resource flow.

The European Commission has funded a limited research project aimed at constructing a quantitative instrument that could be used both in international comparison for FDI attraction, and within a given country to identify policy strengths and weaknesses with regard to FDI attractiveness. The model incorporates a broad conceptual design to define the major factors behind FDI stimulation.

The conceptual design of FACTOM assumes an international company considering an investment in a developing country will focus on three broad sets of variables, namely: policy framework (including economic and political stability, rules regarding entry and operations, privatization policy, tax policy, enabling legislation), business facilitation environment (including facilitation services, hassle costs and corruption, cluster effects, etc.), and three economic determinants, domestic market seeking, resource or asset seeking, efficiency seeking or export oriented.

The *overall result AFDI* (overall measure of country attractiveness for foreign investment) can be broken down into *broad variables*, themselves broken down into relevant economic *variables*, and again broken down into elementary *indicators*, with a total *variable homogeneity* in terms of range (from 0 to 100), and direction (0 is always the most negative measure and 100 is always the most positive measure). The overall measure includes 84 *indicators*, grouped into 25 *variables* and five *broad variables*. The statistical calibration of the weights of each indicator has been made using a statistical instrument called a "Genetic Algorithm" which is designed to test billions of possible combinations between variables, under "expert-determined" constraints for the overall weights of broad variables.

The following figure illustrates the results for a comparison between Vietnam and six other Asian countries:

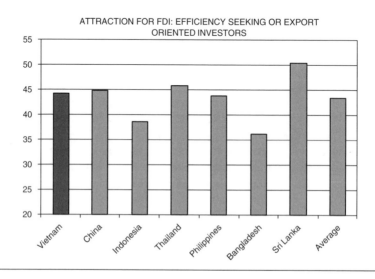

11.4   CONCLUSION

Country risk analysis is only as good as the information that underlies it. Gone are the days when international banks embarked on a frantic search to assess the magnitude of Mexico's external liabilities. The 1982 debt crisis was the starting point of an international effort, both public and private, to improve the timeliness and reliability of economic and financial data. Today, countries, both developed and emerging, compete to provide investors with information and intelligence. Websites of central banks, international institutions and rating agencies provide daily information that can feed analysis and forecasting models. This wealth of information has not reduced the risk of default in emerging market countries. Creditworthiness goes with governance and transparency and, to that extent, better information reduces uncertainty. However, instant transmission of information in the global economy tends to accentuate the herd instinct of creditors, local savers and investors (Bouchet, 2002).

Table 11.8   Main information sources of relevance to country risk analysis

1. Academic community
The Harvard Institute for International Development (Boston)
New York University (www.ntu.edu.sg/library/statdata.htm)
CERAM's Global Finance Chair (www.globalfinance.org)
Rabid Tiger Project Jeff Deutsch's Political Risk Consulting and Related Research
Dr. Nouriel Roubini (NYU) (www.stern.nyu.edu/globalmacro/)
Dr. Harvey Campbell (Duke University) (www.duke.edu/~charvey/Country_risk/couindex.htm)
2. IFIs
www.imf.org
www.worldbank.org
IFC Emerging Stock Market Factbook (www.ifc.org)
Web sites of central banks (www.zagury.com/cbanks.htm and www.bis.org)
International banking and financial market developments (www.bis.org)
Inter-American Development Bank (www.iadb.org/)
UNDP (www.undp.org)
UNCTAD (www.unctad.org)
3. Private and public think-tanks and specialized institutions
Handbook of Economic Statistics, Central Intelligence Agency (www.cia.us)
Political and Economic Risk Consultancy, Ltd. – PERC Gateway to news and country data
Credit Risk International
Frost & Sullivan
Cato Institute (www.cato.org)
Institute for International Economics (Washington, DC)
Institute of International Finance, Inc. (Washington, DC)
The Economist Intelligence Unit (London) (www.eiu.com)
The Davos World Economic Forum (www.weforum.org)
Morgan Stanley Capital International Data
Coface (www.coface.org)
Bradynet Info (www.bradynet.com)
Political Risk Services (country risk indices)
Global Risk Assessment, Inc. – Country Risk Services (www.grai.com)
****
Transparency International (corruption and governance) (www.transparency.org/cpi)
Freedom House (www.freedomhouse.org)
PricewaterhouseCoopers (www.opacityindex.com/)
World Competitiveness Yearbook – IMD (http://www02.imd.ch/wcy)
Heritage Foundation (www.heritage.org/whoweare)

APPENDIX: EXTERNAL DEBT, OFFICIAL INFORMATION SOURCES

Data Series	Source	Description
External debt – all maturities		
A Bank loans	BIS	Loans from banks *resident* in 32 countries.
B Debt securities issued abroad	BIS	Money market instruments, bonds and notes issued in international markets by both public and private sector borrowers.
C Brady bonds	World Bank	Bonds issued to restructure commercial bank debt under the 1989 Brady Plan.
D Non-bank trade credits	OECD	Official and officially guaranteed non-bank export credits from 25 OECD countries.
E Multilateral claims (African Development Bank, Asian Development Bank, IDB, IMF, World Bank)	African Development Bank, Asian Development Bank, IDB, IMF, World Bank	Loans from the African Development Bank, Asian Development Bank, and Inter-American Development Bank, use of IMF credit, and IBRD loans and IDA credits from the World Bank.
F Official bilateral loans (DAC creditors)	OECD	Concessional (aid) and other loans provided mainly for developmental purposes by the 21 member countries of the OECD Development Assistance Committee and Korea as of 2000.

Debt due within a year

Liabilities with an original maturity of one year or less, plus repayments due within the next 12 months on liabilities with an original maturity of over a year, plus arrears.

Data Series	Source	Description
G Liabilities to banks	BIS	Liabilities to banks which are *nationals* of (i.e. headquartered in) 23 countries and which report their claims on a worldwide consolidated basis. The data include holdings of short-term securities which are also included in line H.
H Debt securities issued abroad	BIS	Money market instruments, bonds and notes issued in international markets by both public and private sector borrowers. The data include securities held by foreign banks which are also included in line G.
I Non-bank trade credits	OECD	Official and officially guaranteed non-bank export credits from 25 OECD countries.

Memorandum items

Data Series	Source	Description
J Total liabilities to banks (locational)	BIS	Liabilities to banks *resident* in 32 countries (i.e. line A plus banks' holdings of debt securities which are partly included in line B plus other claims which are not loans or debt securities).
K Total liabilities to banks (consolidated)	BIS	Liabilities to banks which are *nationals* of (i.e. headquartered in) 23 countries and which report their claims on a worldwide consolidated basis, both short-term (line G) and long-term liabilities.
L Total trade credits	OECD	Official and officially guaranteed export credits from 25 OECD countries.
M Total claims on banks (locational)	BIS	Claims on banks *resident* in 32 countries.
N International reserve assets (excluding gold)	IMF	Monetary authorities' holdings of SDRs, reserve position in the Fund and foreign exchange assets.

Source: Joint BIS–IMF–OECD–World Bank statistics on external debt. Background summary, www1.oecd.org/dac debt/htm/backsum.htm. See also BIS joint press release 11/1999E, 15 March 1999. Reproduced with permission.

REFERENCES

Amex Bank, 1984, *International Debt: Banks and the LDCs*, The Amex Bank Review Special Series no. 10, March.

Angel Gurria J, 2002, Stand, Strengthen and Deliver. *Latin Finance*, Mar, 60.

Atkin JM, 1984, Country Risk: What the Central Bank's Figures may be Signaling. *The Banker*, Nov, 44.

Atkinson C, 2002, Forget Sovereign Bankruptcy Plans. *Financial Times*, 17 May, 15.

Bouchet MH, 2002, L'Information, un nouveau risque d'implosion pour les nations. *AGEFI-Finance & Technologie*, Sep, 177, 42–4.

Camdessus M, 1999, Camdessus Stresses Needs for Improved Standards. *IMF Survey*, 28 (11), 179.

Dunn R Jr, 2001, The Routes to Crisis Contagion. *Challenge*, Nov/Dec, 56.

Edwards S and Frankel J, 2001, Preventing Currency Crises in Emerging Markets: Introduction. NBER Currency Crises Prevention Project Draft Paper, April, 2.

Eichengreen B and Arteta C, 2000, Banking Crises in Emerging Markets: Presumptions and Evidence, Working Paper, August.

Eichengreen B and Portes R, 1988, Dealing with Debt: The 1930s and the 1980s, World Bank Workshop on LDC Debt, December, 2.

Fitch, 2002, Fitch Ratings, Special Reports: Standards and Codes – Their Impact on Sovereign Ratings, 10 July, 2.

Gray C and Kaufmann D, 1998, Corruption and Development. *Finance & Development*, Mar, 35 (1), 7–10.

Harris JW, 2000, Weighing Emerging Market Risk: The Supply of Capital. *Business Economics*, Jan, 52.

IMF, 2002, Statistics Department: Development of International Position Statistics, 13 August.

Klitgaard R, 1998, International Corruption against Governance. *Finance & Development*, Mar, 35 (1), 6.

Mauro P, 1998, Corruption: Causes, Consequences, and the Way Forward. *Finance & Development*, Mar, 35 (1), 11–14.

Pagell RA, 1998, Finding International Credit Information. *Business Credit*, Mar, 15.

Painter DH, 1999, The Business Economist at Work: Mobil Corporation. *Business Economics*, Apr, 34 (2), 52.

Perrow C, 1999, Organisations à hauts risques et "accidents normaux", Actes de la XIV° séance du séminaire du programme Risques Collectifs et Situations de crise, CNRS, Paris, 2 juin.

Raddock DM, 2001, *Navigating New Markets Abroad*. 2nd edition. Rowman & Littlefield, 73.

Standard & Poor's, 2002, *Sovereign Credit Ratings: A Primer*, 3 April.

Ulrich B, 2002, *La Société du Risque: Sur la voie d'une nouvelle modernité*. Paris: Fayard.

White WR, 2000, Recent Initiatives to Improve the Regulation and Supervision of Private Capital Flows. BIS Working Paper no. 92, October.

Wolfensohn J, 2001, Corruption Bars Effective Legal Systems. World Bank AFP Report, 13 August.

World Bank, 1988–89, *World Debt Tables*, vol. 1, External Debt of Developing Countries, Appendix III, Tables 1 & 4. Washington, DC: World Bank.

World Bank, 2001, *Assessing the Implementation of Standards: A Review of Experience and Next Steps*. International Monetary Fund, 11 January. Washington, DC: World Bank.

Glossary

Acceleration Clause: A clause providing that the entire principal of a note (or a loan) shall become immediately due and payable in the event of default.

Accrued Interest: Interest which has accumulated but which is not legally due before a specified payment date.

ADB (Asian Development Bank): A Manilla-based regional development bank, focused on promoting growth in Asia, specialized institution of the United Nations.

Advance Payment: Money received by a supplier in advance of shipment or fabrication.

Adverse Selection: Consider a market in which products of varying quality are exchanged and only the sellers are aware of the quality of each unit they sell. This implies an incentive for them to market poor-quality merchandise leading to a gradual reduction in the average quality of goods and also in the size of the market. It is important to underline that the asymmetry of information occurs *ex ante*. George Akerlof was the first to illustrate this market inefficiency with his famous "lemon problem" (*See also* Asymmetric information, Credit rationing, Moral hazard).

AfDB (African Development Bank): An Abidjan-based regional development bank, focused on enhancing sustainable growth in Africa, specialized institution of the United Nations.

Agent Bank: A commercial bank (may not be a creditor bank) that collects all payments from a restructuring loan or a syndicated loan, and distributes them to each participating creditor bank.

Allocated Transfer Risk Reserves (ATRRs): Country-specific reserves which banks registered in the United States are required to set aside against assets which are deemed to be "value impaired" by the Inter-Agency Exposure Review Committee (ICERC). The reserve is a charge against income and tax deductible but it is excluded from primary capital. It is calculated by multiplying the reserve percentage dictated by ICERC by the face amount of exposure classified as "value impaired", after adjustments for guarantees and previous write-downs. Generally, the provision covers all loans except performing trade credits and interbank lines. Amounts in excess of the ICERC requirement may be set aside as ATRRs at the discretion of bank management.

Amortization: Repayment of principal balances during a given accounting period.

Arrears: Contractual debt service which is not paid on schedule. In practice, payments may be delayed for a few months because of administrative problems before they are classified as arrears.

Asset-Backed Securities: A "fixed income" security that pays its coupon and principal from a specific revenue stream and has a specific asset as collateral to reduce or even eliminate the underlying risk. The collateral includes US or any AAA T-bills, accounts receivables, mortgages, zero coupon bonds, real property, etc.

Asymmetric Information: In a world in which agents have different information about the economic environment, agents' behavior may partially or fully reveal information they have but which is not universally known. Hence, "neutral" variables may contain potentially valuable information in a world of asymmetrically informed agents (*See also* Adverse selection, Moral hazard).

Aval: An endorsement on a bill guaranteeing payment.

Baker Plan: The debt strategy outlined in Seoul, Korea by the US Treasury Secretary Baker at the annual meetings of the World Bank and the International Monetary Fund in September 1985. The focus was on 15 heavily indebted countries, namely, Argentina, Bolivia, Brazil, Chile, Colombia, Ecuador, Ivory Coast, Mexico, Morocco, Nigeria, Peru, Philippines, Uruguay, Venezuela and Yugoslavia. The Plan proposed annual increases (2.5% or US$7 billion per year) in commercial bank lending to these countries, annual increases (US$3 billion) in net disbursements by multilateral development banks for growth-oriented programs, and growth-oriented structural reforms (privatization, trade liberalization, etc.) by debtor countries. The Plan was superseded by the Brady Initiative on 10 March 1989.

Basis Points: A standard unit of measure for bond yields, 1% equals 100 basis points.

"Basle I": *See* Cooke ratio.

"Basle II": The Basle Committee on Banking Supervision is working on a new Accord on capital adequacy guidelines that more exactly represent the inherent risks. "Basle II" consists of three main "pillars": Capital requirements based on the internal risk ratings of individual banks, expanded and active supervision, and information disclosure requirements to enhance market discipline. Supposed to be imposed by 2006. From an emerging markets' perspective, relatively creditworthy countries that are not members of the OECD like Singapore, Hong Kong, Taiwan and Israel, whose risk weightings fall from 100% to either 20% or 0%, will be among the winners. On the contrary, OECD members with a credit rating worse than AA like Slovakia, Turkey, South Korea, Mexico and Poland *inter alia* will face tougher conditions.

Basle Committee on Banking Supervision: Established in 1974 by the central bank governors of the Group of Ten countries to provide a basis for international cooperation in bank supervision (*See also* "Basle I", "Basle II", BIS, Cooke ratio).

Bilateral Loans: Loans from governments and their agencies (including central banks), loans from autonomous bodies, and direct loans from official export credit agencies.

BIS: Basle-based Bank for International Settlements set up in 1930 at the Hague Conference to manage Germany's war reparation payments (*See also* "Basle I", "Basle II", Basle Committee on Banking Supervision, Cooke ratio).

Bond, Exit: A tradeable instrument bearing a low interest rate and extended maturity which is issued to a creditor (in lieu of the original debt service payments) who wishes to withdraw from the debtor country.

Bond Spread: Difference of yields between US Treasury bonds with Emerging Markets bonds of comparable maturity. Assuming the first to be a risk-free rate, the difference can be seen as a risk premium demanded by international investors for the more risky and opaque business environment in emerging markets.

Bond, Zero Coupon: A bond which pays neither principal nor interest until maturity. It merely states the face payment which is due at maturity and is sold at a discount which reflects the timing of payments (i.e., face value of the discounted value of the future bullet payment at maturity).

Brady Bond: Named after the 1989 US Treasury Secretary Brady, who sponsored the restructuring of the London Club's distressed sovereign loans and interest arrears into long-term, guaranteed, liquid debt instruments.

Brady Plan: Also known as the "Brady Initiative". Describes the proposal made by US Treasury Secretary Nicholas Brady on 10 March 1989 to reduce the debt overhang of countries heavily indebted to commercial banks. The Treasury estimates that the Plan will lead to a reduction of roughly US$70bn (20%) in repayments to banks by 39 heavily indebted countries over three years. These estimates assume that the World Bank and the IMF would provide US$20bn and US$25bn respectively in guarantees and other incentives for banks to discount their debts voluntarily. Thirteen countries have reduced their commercial bank debt through Brady-style operations with funding provided by IFIs and official bilateral creditors: Mexico, Uruguay, the Philippines, Nigeria, Jordan, Ivory Coast, Costa Rica, Venezuela, Argentina, Nicaragua, Brazil, Dominican Republic and Poland.

Bridge Loan: Used in the context of managing a country's debt profile, it is short-term financing provided to a debtor country – usually by the monetary authorities of industrial countries in conjunction with other central banks, governments, multilateral institutions and commercial banks – to supplement the country's foreign reserves prior to finalizing adjustment programs and concerted lending packages. This short-term advance is made pending receipts of funds by the borrower.

Bullet Maturity: One-time payment of principal at maturity (*See also* Bond, zero coupon).

Capital Flight: From emerging markets, can be explained by economic theory as a product of natural and economically rational behavior of wealthy residents of these debtor countries to diversify their portfolios in order to protect themselves against riskiness of any particular investment. The calculation of the amount of annual capital flight is a byproduct of balance of payments and official reserve levels analysis coupled with the change in BIS banks' liabilities vis-à-vis private non-bank residents.

Capitalization, Interest: An arrangement by which interest due is added to the principal of the loan and converted into a capital liability, effectively deferring payment beyond the original schedule.

Co-financing: A mechanism by which creditors provide project loans in parallel with loans granted by multilateral agencies such as the World Bank. Such "co-financiers" receive the benefit of the multilateral agencies' evaluation of the project and can share in certain benefits resulting from the special relationship between the debtor country and the multilateral agencies. In principle, cross-default clauses prevent debtors from defaulting on amounts owed to co-financiers without defaulting on the official institutions.

Collateral: Financial or real guarantee used as risk mitigation instrument. In Brady bonds, collateral consists of 30-year US Treasury zero coupon bonds as well as cash accounts usually at the Federal Reserve Bank in New York. The collateral's purpose is to pay the principal and/or the interest should a debtor country not honor its financial obligations.

Cologne Terms: In November 1999, the Paris Club creditor countries, in the framework of the initiative for "Heavily Indebted Poor Countries" (HIPC) and in the aftermath of the Cologne Summit, accepted to raise the level of cancellation for the poorest countries up to 90% or more if necessary in the framework of the HIPC initiative. 41 countries are potentially eligible for the HIPC initiative and may benefit from the Cologne terms. As of 2002, 15 countries have benefitted from the Cologne terms.

Commercial Credits: (i) Credits granted by a bank or a supplier to a debtor country for importing goods and services. When these credits are guaranteed by the appropriate institution of a Paris Club creditor, they are included in the claims treated in the context of the Paris Club. (ii) Non-ODA credits are sometimes referred to as commercial credits.

Concerted Bank Lending: Loans made by commercial banks, coordinated by a bank advisory committee, and based on equiproportional increases in bank exposure (*See* Free riders).

Contingent Lending Agreements/Facilities: Agreements or facilities which establish a linkage between additional financing and specific, predefined trigger mechanisms.

Cooke Ratio (BIS Capital Adequacy Guidelines): The capital adequacy or risk-weighted asset ratios prescribed by the Capital Accord of July 1988 under the aegis of the Basle Committee on Banking Supervision; named after Peter Cooke, who chaired the Committee for over a decade and sometimes also referred to as "Basle I" (*See also* "Basle II", Basle Committee on Banking Supervision, BIS).

Credit Rationing: As demonstrated by Joseph Stiglitz and Andrew Weiss, information asymmetry can lead to credit rationing in which some borrowers are arbitrarily denied loans. This occurs because a higher interest rate leads to even greater adverse selection: the borrowers with the riskiest investment projects will now be the most likely to seek out loans at a higher rate. If the lender is not able to discriminate between good and bad borrowers, he may want to cut down the number of loans he makes, leading to a further rise in interest rates and further worsening (*See also* Adverse selection, Asymmetric information).

Cross-default Provision: A legal wrinkle which allows one creditor to declare default and exercise its remedies against the borrower in cases where other loans of the borrower have been suspended, terminated, accelerated or declared in default by other creditors.

Currency Board: A monetary regime based on explicit legislative commitment to exchange domestic currency for a specified foreign currency at a fixed exchange rate, combined with restrictions on the issuing authority to ensure the fulfillment of its legal obligation.

Currency Redenomination: Switching of loans denominated in one currency or currencies into the currency of the creditor country or into ECUs (the mechanism is intended to bring about a better match between the currency mix of debt service payments and the currency composition of external receipts).

Cut-off Date (Paris Club clause): When a debtor country first meets with Paris Club creditors, the "cut-off date" is defined once and for all and is not changed in subsequent Paris Club treatments. Accordingly, new money credits granted after this cut-off date are not subject to future rescheduling. Thus, the cut-off date helps restore access to credit for debtor countries facing payment difficulties.

Debt Defeasance: It involves extinguishing debt through the provision of a financial asset (zero coupon or other financial instrument) to be held in a trust account as collateral against the principal of the debt. The face value and maturity of the collateral instrument are designed to match those of the debt being defeased so that the proceeds of the collateral instrument at maturity may be used to fully repay the principal in a single balloon payment. Since the principal of the debt is secured, the debt service obligations of the debtor are reduced to the payment of interest.

Debt/Equity Swap: An exchange of foreign currency debt for local currency equity in a domestic firm. This may be done by the bank holding the loan or by an investor who purchases the debt paper in the secondary market. The exchange may involve a public debt and equity in a private sector company; a private debt and equity in the same company; or public debt and equity in a public enterprise which is being privatized.

Debt-for-Debt Swap: Exchange of one type of foreign debt for another with different terms and conditions. Debt exchanges involve par swaps and discount swaps.

Debt-for-Export Swap: These swaps enable a creditor to receive export products and/or commodities of a debtor country to offset part of its outstanding claims on the concerned country.

Debt-for-Nature Swap: An exchange of a foreign currency debt for local currency which is used to finance the conservation of environmental assets such as parklands and tropical forests. A private conservation organization, for example, purchases a country's commercial bank debt (usually at a discount) or receives the debt paper as a donation. The debt is then canceled in exchange for the issue of local currency assets to be invested in the protection of an environmentally sensitive area like a tropical rainforest or a biodiversity reserve.

Debt Outstanding and Disbursed: Total outstanding debt at year end.

Debt Overhang: Indicates a huge pile of (foreign) debt that cannot be settled by short-term liquidity injection but that rather longs for long-term rescheduling or write-off (*See also* Cologne terms, Solvency ratios).

Debt Swaps: These operations may be debt-for-nature, debt-for-aid, debt-for-equity swaps or other local currency debt swaps. These swaps often involve the sale of the debt by the creditor government to an investor who in turn sells the debt to the debtor government in return for shares in a local company or for local currency to be used in projects in the country. Paris Club creditors and debtors regularly conduct a *reporting* to the Paris Club secretariat of the debt swaps conducted. Debt–equity swaps involve the conversion of debt into local currency equity in a domestic firm.

Deferment: Short-term roll-over of current maturities.

De minimis **Provision**: Paris Club agreements define a *de minimis* level, when the claims of a Paris Club creditor covered by the rescheduling agreement are less than this level, this creditor participates in the meeting as an observer and does not reschedule its claims. This rule aims at preventing debt treatments that do not have a significant impact in terms of debt relief and would be costly to implement.

Disbursements: Drawings on loan commitments by the borrower during the year.

Discount Bond (Brady): Registered 30-year bullet amortization issued at discount, with floating market-based interest rate.

Discounted Debt Buyback: Transaction whereby the debtor country purchases all or part of its outstanding debt in the market, usually at a discount. Accordingly, the outstanding debt will decline by the nominal value of the debt that has been bought back.

Emerging Market: The IFC uses income per capita and market capitalization relative to GNP for classifying equity markets. If either (1) a market resides in a low or middle-income economy (in 1998, high income was defined by the World Bank as US$9361 per capita GNP), or (2) the ratio of investable market capitalization to GNP is low, i.e. not in the top 25% of all emerging markets for three consecutive years, then the IFC classifies a country as *emerging*. The IFC identified 81 such countries in their *Emerging Stock Markets Factbook 2000*. Meeting the latter requirement, a country becomes part of the Emerging Market Data Base (EMDB) index. Countries are "graduated" from the EMBD index if their income rises into the high-income category for three consecutive years.

Equity-Linked Bonds: Convertible bonds or bonds with equity warrants.

Escrow Account: Special account in local or foreign currency, established on behalf of the debtor country in a domestic or in a foreign bank, in which deposits are made by the debtor periodically. Such an account ensures creditors that debt payments will be made on time as a portion of the debtor's revenues are set aside for this purpose.

EURIBOR: In its concept similar to LIBOR, EURIBOR, established by the European Banking Federation and ACI, applies a country quota approach encompassing a panel of 47 reference banks (*See also* LIBOR).

Eurobonds: Long-term financial instruments issued by MNCs or country governments, and denominated in a currency other than that of the country of placement. Eurobonds are under-written by a multinational syndicate of investment banks and simultaneously placed in many countries. They are issued in bearer form, and coupon payments are made yearly. The US dollar accounts for about 70% of eurobonds. Liquidity in the secondary market is monitored by Euro-clear.

Euro-commercial Paper: Short-term euronotes issued by private companies.

Eurodollar Market: International banking market for US dollar-denominated claims and deposits arising from note, credit line and loan, or bond held by a non-resident institution or private person of the United States.

Events of Default: Any event which allows creditors to declare the outstanding principal, as well as all accrued interest, due and payable on demand.

Exceptional Financing: A special "below the line" category in the IMF balance of pay-ments used to accommodate transactions undertaken on behalf of the monetary authorities to compensate for any overall imbalance.

Exit Instrument: Exchange offer which allows a creditor to withdraw voluntarily from future concerted lending packages through the conversion of their claims into more tradeable finan-cial assets such as long-term, low-interest rate bonds, commonly known as exit bonds. Exit bondholders are to be exempted from future requests for new money and debt restructuring.

Exit Rescheduling: An exit treatment is the last rescheduling a country normally gets from the Paris Club. The aim is that the debtor country will not need any further rescheduling and will thus not come back for negotiation to the Paris Club.

External Debt: External obligations in hard currency owed by public and private entities resident in a country to non-resident public and private creditors. External indebtedness has a direct impact on the debtor country's balance of payments and liquidity position. External public debt is defined as the amount, at any given time, of disbursed and outstanding foreign currency liabilities contracted by a country or by public or private companies with the guarantee of the state. The corresponding credits are held by three categories of lenders:

- *Private lenders* (commercial banks and suppliers);
- *Bilateral lenders* (individual countries within or outside the Paris Club);
- *Multilateral lenders* (World Bank, IMF, as well as certain regional banks such as the Inter-American Development Bank and the Asian Development Bank).

Face Value: Full amount of the original debt obligation.

Fiduciary Fund (or Trust Fund): Fund in which assets are safeguarded and whose stream of interest income is used to fund a specific project.

Floating Rate Notes (FRNs): Medium-term CDs where the interest is fixed as a percentage above six-month LIBOR. Negotiable and transferable securities with flexible interest rate, fixed interest periods, and issued in predetermined and uniform amounts.

Force Majeure: State of emergency or exceptional condition that permits a creditor or an investor to depart from the strict terms of a contract because of an event or effect that cannot reasonably be anticipated or controlled.

Free Rider: Individual banks may refuse to participate in a bailout loan with the international banking community, thereby not matching their expected share of the concerted loan package. Similarly, small-exposure banks might refuse to join debt reduction operations while requiring full payments on their claims. Such "free-riders" would then see the value of their lending portfolios rise as other banks write down a country's debt (*See also* Mandatory repayment clause).

Goodwill Clause: A statement in Paris (or London) Club agreements which would allow the creditors in question to extend the life of a stated rescheduling arrangement, but which is not legally binding. Creditors agree to consider further debt relief after the expiration of the consolidation period, and a commitment to meet at the end of three to four years to consider the matter of the stock of debt.

Grace Period: Time period during which the debt is not amortized, i.e., no principal gets paid by the borrower, and only interest payment obligations are serviced against the total debt stock.

Gross External Debt: Amount, at any given time, of disbursed and outstanding contractual liabilities of residents of a country to non-residents, and denominated in hard currency.

Gross Financing Gap (% of reserve assets): Current account deficit plus scheduled principal repayments on external debt plus stock of short-term liabilities as a percentage of official foreign exchange reserves.

Guarantee: A written, legally-binding promise by one party to be liable for a specific obligation of a second party in the event that the second party does not fulfill its financial obligation at a due date. IFIs such as the IADB provide emerging market countries with a financial guarantee to enhance local currency long-dated bond markets, hence offering a triple-A financial guaranty insurance.

Herd Behavior: To be able to "herd" an investor must be aware of and be influenced by others' action. Herd behavior consequently results from an obvious intent by investors to copy the behavior of other investors.

HIPC (Highly Indebted Poor Countries): *See* Cologne terms.

IADB (Inter-American Development Bank): An affiliate of the World Bank Group.

IBRD (International Bank for Reconstruction and Development): Also referred to as the World Bank (Group), based in Washington, DC.

IDA (International Development Association): An affiliate of the World Bank, established in 1960, to promote development in the world's poorest countries. It is the largest single multilateral source of concessional lending to low-income countries. It has 150 member countries. Borrowing countries typically have 1991 per capita incomes of less than US$765.

IDA Debt-Reduction Facility: A US$100 million fund established by the International Development Association in June 1989 through a transfer of the World Bank's net income. The money in this fund goes to help severely indebted, low-income countries reduce their commercial debt. The fund has been replenished several times since 1993. Various countries have reduced their debt through the IDA Facility, namely, Bolivia, Niger, Mozambique, Guyana, Zambia, Sierra Leone, Tanzania and Senegal.

IFIs: Abbreviation for International Financial Institutions like for instance the World Bank Group, the International Monetary Fund (IMF) and the Institute for International Finance (IIF).

IIF (Institute for International Finance): Founded in the year 1983 in response to the international debt crisis. The Institute counts more than 320 members, including most of the world's largest commercial banks, investment banks and multinational companies and provides the following services: emerging markets analysis, forum for discussion with members and dialogue of the private financial sector with the official community on emerging markets policy issues of mutual interest.

Inter-Agency Exposure Review Committee (ICERC): The Committee was set up in 1979 by the Federal Reserve, the Office of the Comptroller of the Currency and the Federal Deposit Insurance Corporation of the United States primarily to evaluate transfer risks of US commercial banks.

Interbank Lines: Short-term working capital extended between banks to cover short-term claims on a revolving basis. Such claims are generally not included in reschedulings.

Interest Margin: Percentage "basis" points above LIBOR. This rate is used for convenience to measure the approximate cost to banks of funds which they obtain in the interbank markets.

Interest Rate Switching: Selection of a new basis for interest calculations on an existing loan. The options may include LIBOR, a domestic rate, the prime rate or a fixed rate, to which a margin is added.

Interest Retiming: Changing the frequency of interest payments, essentially allowing a debtor to defer one or more interest payments. Retiming boils down to short-term interest rescheduling in that it permits a debtor country to stretch out interest payments.

International Financial Institutions (IFIs): They comprise the so-called Bretton Woods organizations (the IMF and the World Bank Group) as well as other multilateral agencies such as regional development banks, the European Investment Bank, etc.

LIBOR (London Interbank Offered Rate): The interest rate offered by the British Bankers' Association (BBA), a group of London banks, for US dollar deposits of a stated maturity. LIBOR is the primary benchmark used by banks, securities houses and investors to fix the cost of borrowing in the money, derivatives and capital markets around the world. The basis for pricing Eurocurrency loans. *See also* EURIBOR.

Liquidity: The capacity of a financial instrument to be converted easily, speedily and with minimum loss into cash. Very short-dated treasury notes are an example of a liquid financial instrument. A liquid market is one in which there is enough activity and "depth" to satisfy both sellers and buyers.

Liquidity Ratios: Gauge the ability to service debt and redeem or reschedule liabilities when they mature, and the ability to exchange other assets for cash, for instance debt service ratio [(principal + interest)/exports], interest ratio (interest/exports), import coverage (reserves/imports), current account/GDP, *inter alia*.

London Club: An *ad hoc* association of commercial lenders to a debtor country. Within that association, a representative body which serves on behalf of the creditors in negotiations and is usually composed of the major commercial creditors is the Steering Committee, sometimes also referred to as the Advisory Committee.

Loss Exposure: Risk posed by a financial transaction or a portfolio of transactions with respect to loans and claims.

Mandatory Repayment Clause: A standard clause in loan agreements between debtor countries and commercial bank creditors. It stipulates certain circumstances under which repayment is accelerated. The debtor, by being obligated to prepay any one creditor, must repay all lenders on a *pro rata* basis. In the context of rescheduling agreements and new money loans to rescheduling countries, the provision is intended to neutralize "free-rider" banks which do not participate in debt restructuring and new money agreements. In that regard, debt conversion and debt buyback transactions amount to payment prior to contractually defined maturity. The provision applies across the universe of public sector borrowers so that a voluntary prepayment of one or more credits by one borrower would trigger mandatory prepayment not only by that borrower but also by the other public sector borrowers.

Maturity: The date on which a loan, bill or other debt instrument falls due for repayment.

"Menu" Approach, Market-Based: Describes a series of instruments which are used voluntarily by creditors and debtors to resolve problems of external indebtedness to commercial banks. The instruments seek to change the *nature* of bank claims through exchange offer and securitization, the *ownership* of bank claims through debt conversion mechanisms and discounted repurchases, and the *financial profile* of debt obligations through interest retiming and long-term consolidation. A typical menu comprises the following instruments:

- *Par bond*: An exchange of old claims for a bond with the same face value but a below-market interest rate and, generally, a bullet maturity of 30 years.
- *Discount bond*: Converting old claims into a bond with discounted face value (negotiated by debtors and creditors) and offering floating rate of interest. These bonds, too, have a bullet maturity of 30 years.
- *Front loaded interest reduction bond*: Old claims are exchanged for a bond with the same face value with a below-market rate for comparable credit risk for the first few years, increasing gradually to a generally market-based rate.
- *Debt conversion bond*: Exchange old claims for a bond with an option to convert into equity in firms in developing countries.
- *New money bonds*: Purchases of new instruments with a variable rate of interest, usually a spread over LIBOR, and maturities of 10 to 15 years.

Moral Hazard: A variant of an imperfect market, where the participants have the same information when the relationship is established, and the informational asymmetry arises from the fact that, once the contract has been signed, the principal cannot (adequately) observe the action of the agent. Regarding country risk and debt crisis, the argument says that the expectation of bailouts from IFIs encourages commercial banks and bondholders to make "irresponsible" loans that governments cannot reasonably repay on their own.

Moratorium: A declaration by a debtor that debt service payments will not be made for a certain period of time beyond the original maturity of the loan.

Multi-Year Rescheduling Agreement (MYRA): An arrangement for postponing more than two years' principal repayments. It first emerged in 1984 and was introduced in commercial bank negotiations to "smooth" amortization profiles and reduce the administrative and other costs associated with more frequent (annual) reschedulings.

Negative Pledge Clause: Granting of security interests by a debtor country over its assets to its creditors. In the case of a debt refinancing agreement, the debtor country agrees with the banks not to provide any other group of creditors with security interest on the country's reserves, exports of goods and public sector companies' assets. The objective of such a clause is to prevent a situation where a debtor would allocate significant assets to other creditors, thereby effectively subordinating the unsecured bank credits.

Net Debt/GDP %: Gross external debt minus general government financial assets (cash, deposits, loans and equity holdings) as a percentage of GDP.

Net Flows on Debts: Disbursements minus principal repayments, i.e., excess of new lending over amortization payments.

Net Present Value (NPV): Measure that takes into account the degree of concessionality. It is defined as the sum of all future debt service obligations (interest and principal) on existing debt, discounted at the appropriate market rate. Whenever the interest rate on a loan is lower than the market rate, the resulting NPV of debt is smaller than its face value.

Net Resource Flows: Sum of net resource flows on long-term debt plus net foreign direct investment, portfolio equity flows and official grants.

Net Transfers: New disbursement minus amortization (i.e., principal debt service) and interest payments. As such, net transfers are equivalent to net flows minus interest.

New Money: Loans arranged for budgetary or balance of payments support in conjunction with debt rescheduling, usually in proportion to each creditor bank's exposure, in order to enforce comparability of treatment among creditors.

New Money Bonds: Bonds issued by debtor countries in exchange for additional financing. Such instruments are usually more senior and tradeable than old claims.

Non-debt-Creating Flows: Net foreign direct investment, portfolio equity flows and official grants (excluding technical cooperation).

OECD: Paris-based Organization for Economic Co-operation and Development, with a membership comprising 29 "industrialized" developed countries. It was set up in 1960 to promote economic growth and the expansion of world trade. Its most recent members are Mexico (just before the 1994 Tequila crisis) and South Korea (just before the 1998 Asian crisis).

Off-balance Sheet Activities: Bank activities, often fee-based, that do not involve booking assets or taking deposits (insurance, swaps, forwards, LCs, advisory assistance, M&As, etc.).

Official Creditor: This covers (a) official bilateral creditors (governments or their appropriate institutions), including Paris Club members; (b) multilateral creditors (international institutions such as the IMF, the World Bank or regional development banks).

Official Development Assistance (ODA): It consists of disbursements of loans (net of repayments of principal) and grants made on concessional terms by official agencies of the members of the Development Assistance Committee of the OECD to promote economic development and welfare in recipient developing countries. Loans with a grant element of more than 25% are included in ODA, as are technical cooperation and assistance.

On-lending: The process by which funds borrowed by one party are made available to a third party, with the agreement of the creditor. Typically, the funds are recorded as a deposit in the central bank. However, the creditor and the contractual borrower (often the central bank itself) agree to make the loan proceeds available to a third party within the country in local currency equivalent.

Optional Prepayment Provision: The optional prepayment provision permits the borrower to prepay all or part of the loan provided it prepays all lenders under the agreement on a *pro rata* basis.

Outstanding Amounts (Paris Club issue): This amount is divided into three parts: principal, interest and total amount. The amount of total outstanding debt must be equal to the sum of all the maturities and arrears. The amount of principal outstanding is the sum of all arrears (principal and interest) plus all future maturities in principal. The amount of interest outstanding must be equal to the sums of all the future maturities in interest.

Par Bonds (Brady): Registered 30-year bullet amortization issued at par, i.e., at the original face value of the sovereign loan, with fixed rate semi-annual below market coupon. Usually, par bonds carry a principal collateral as well as a rolling interest guarantee.

Paris Club: Informal group of official creditors whose role is to find coordinated and sustainable debt workout solutions to the payment difficulties experienced by debtor nations. Paris Club creditors agree to rescheduling, refinancing or restructuring debts due to them, with prior macroeconomic adjustment programs under the aegis of the IMF. Rescheduling is a means of providing a country with debt relief through a postponement and, in the case of concessional rescheduling, a reduction in debt service obligations. The first meeting with a debtor country was in 1956 when Argentina agreed to meet its public creditors in Paris. Since then, the Paris Club creditors have reached 344 agreements concerning 77 debtor countries. Since 1983, the total amount of debt covered in these agreements has been US$391 billion. In spite of such an activity, the Paris Club has remained strictly informal. It is the voluntary gathering of creditor countries willing to provide developing countries with debt relief. It can be described as a "non-institution". Although the Paris Club has no legal basis nor status, agreements are reached following a number of *rules and principles* agreed by creditor countries.

Prepayment Clause: The prepayment clause is a standard clause in loan agreements between a debtor and a creditor bank. In its various forms, it can provide the debtor with the opportunity to accelerate repayment of the loan on a voluntary basis and/or provide for acceleration of repayment due to changes in laws affecting the creditor. In rescheduling agreements, the clause is intended to prevent the obligor from granting a preferential repayment schedule to other banks which have not signed the convention and which would be paid ahead of normal maturity terms.

Primary Balance/GDP %: Deficit minus interest payments on general government debt, as a percentage of GDP.

Principal in Arrears on Long-Term Debt: Principal repayment due but not paid, on a cumulative basis.

Principal Repayments: The amounts of principal (amortization) paid in foreign currency, goods or services in the year specified.

Private Non-guaranteed External Debt: External obligation of a private debtor that is not guaranteed for repayment by a public entity.

Provisioning: The setting aside of a financial institution's resources to cover potential losses from bad loans. Loan-loss provisions against bad claims can be tax-deductible according to specific national banking regulations.

Public Debt: External obligations of a public debtor, including the direct and guaranteed debt of the central government, obligations of regional and local governments, and the non-guaranteed debt of other public sector entities, as well as autonomous public bodies.

Public Sector: Public sector is defined (unless otherwise specified) as the government of the debtor country, as well as the companies or other entities under governmental control (where the government has a direct or indirect share of 50% or more).

Quota (IMF): When a country joins the IMF, it is assigned a quota that fits in the structure of existing member quotas considered in the light of the member's economic characteristics relative to those of other countries of comparable size. The size of the country's quota determines voting power and access to Fund resources as well as shares of SDR allocations.

Regulatory Capital: The minimum amount of capital imposed by the national regulatory authorities (8% of risk-weighted assets under the Cooke I ratio regime).

Regulatory Regime: The guidelines, laws and practices as determined by the regulatory authorities of the creditor's country which govern commercial banking with respect to activities such as lending, securities purchases, acceptances and define what provisions banks should make for probable losses in their loan portfolios. Banks have faced intensified pressure, both competitive and regulatory, to strengthen their balance sheets and to comply with the capital requirements of the Bank for International Settlements (BIS). General loan-loss provisions and equity capital are two key components of the so-called Cooke ratio of 8% of risk-weighted assets (*See also* Basle Committee on Banking Supervision, BIS, Cooke ratio).

Relending: An operation in which the external debt repaid by one debtor is lent to another entity in the debtor economy. The second debtor may repay prior to the definitive repayment date and the foreign creditor may relend again to a third debtor within the debtor country. In practice, relending has occurred when the original borrower had the domestic currency to repay its debt (at the going exchange rate) but the central bank was not able or willing to provide the foreign exchange.

Repudiation: Unilateral disclaiming of a liability by a debtor.

Refinancing: Conversion of arrears and all or part of the original debt into a new loan.

Rescheduling: Formal deferment and retiming of the principal due on a loan, with the application of new maturities to the deferred amounts. Regarding Paris Club debt agreements, they include interest rescheduling in place of new money.

Reserves: "External assets that are readily available to and controlled by monetary authorities for direct financing of external payments imbalances, for indirectly regulating the magnitudes of such imbalances through intervention in exchange markets to affect the currency exchange rate, and/or for other purposes" (*Balance of Payments Manual*, 5th edition, BPM5).

Reserves/Imports (months): Official foreign exchange reserves (including gold at market prices) divided by monthly imports of goods and services.

Revolving Underwriting Facility (RUF): Medium-term facility on which the borrower can draw at any time of its life, usually certificates of deposits (CDs) or short-term promissory notes.

Round-Tripping: Speculation that can take place in conversion transactions where an investor with access to foreign exchange purchases a loan in the secondary market and receives local currency repayment from the original debtor. The investor then converts the local currency at the black market rate and repeats the transaction. The larger the secondary market discount and the smaller the difference between the official and black market currency exchange rates, the larger the potential gain for the speculator engaged in round-tripping.

Securitization: The process by which banks' assets become more marketable and gain enhanced liquidity through the substitution of floating rate notes for syndicated lending, the introduction of transferability into international credits, the exchange of loans for collateralized bonds and the packaging of existing assets for resale.

Set-Aside Funds: The World Bank approved procedures to support debt reduction in May 1989 by setting aside 25% of a country's adjustment lending program over a three-year period (or 10% of its overall lending program) to guarantee principal reduction. An increment of up to 15% of the overall three-year program can be made available for interest support. The IMF's Executive Board approved that around 25% of a country's access to IMF resources be set aside to support operations involving debt principal reduction. The IMF may also approve additional funding up to 40% of the member's quota for interest support in connection with debt service reduction transactions.

Sharing Provisions: A legal covenant in commercial bank agreements which specifies that debt service payments are to be made through the agent bank for allocation on a *pro rata* basis to all creditor banks. Further, payments received or recovered by any one lender must be shared on a *pro rata* basis with all co-creditors under the loan agreement. Thus, no one lender may be placed in a more favorable position than its co-lenders with respect to payments received and/or recovered.

Short-Term Credits: Credits that have an original maturity of one year or less. Maturity is defined as the difference between the last principal repayment and the date when the credit starts (usually from the disbursement or the delivery of the goods). All other credits, having an original maturity of more than one year, are medium and long-term credits.

Short-Term External Debt: Debt that has an original maturity of one year or less. Available data permit no distinction between public and private non-guaranteed short-term debt.

Solvency: Country's ability to meet the present value of its external obligations. In theory, countries are solvent as long as the present value of net interest payments does not exceed the present value of current inflows (primarily exports) net of imported inputs. In practice, countries stop servicing their debt (long before) when the country's economic and social costs are perceived to be high. Hence, the willingness to pay is more important than the theoretical ability.

Solvency Ratios: Ratios assessing the stock of debt of a debtor country, for instance total external debt/exports and total external debt/GDP (*See also* Debt overhang, Reserves/imports).

Sovereign Credit Ratings: Quantitative assessment of a government's ability and willingness to service its foreign debt in full and on time. A rating is a forward-looking estimate of default probability.

Special Drawing Rights (SDRs): Unconditional reserve assets that are created by the IMF to supplement existing reserve assets. The first SDR allocation took place in January 1970. The SDR can be used in a wide variety of transactions and operations between central banks and international organizations.

Spread, Interest Rate: Usually expressed in percentage points over and above a reference rate such as LIBOR or the prime rate in the country of the creditor. The spread added to the reference rate constitutes the interest rate applicable to the loan (*See also* Bond spread).

Standby Credit: A commitment to lend up to a specified amount for a specific period, to be used only in a certain contingency (commitment fee paid on the unused portion of a facility).

Stock Treatment (Paris Club clause): As opposed to standard *flow treatments*, some Paris Club treatments apply not only to the payments falling due in a particular period of time, but to the whole stock of debt from which those payments fall due. The aim of any agreement which deals with the stock of debt in this way is to provide a country with a final treatment by the Paris Club called an "exit rescheduling".

Subordinated Debt: Debt that is payable only after other debts with a higher ranking have been repaid; it is generally listed in a firm's capital structure between equity and senior debt.

Subrogation Rights: In contracts of indemnity, they allow the insurer to take over the rights of the assured against any third party who is responsible for a loss in respect of which the insurer has made a claim payment.

Supplier's Credit: Export finance which is available to a supplier of items as distinct from credits to the foreign purchasers under buyer's credit.

Syndication: Loan syndication in the Eurodollar market takes the form of a contractual arrangement by a group of banks (the "lead banks") to share a loan that is too large for one bank to make. Loan syndication is a risk mitigation tool in the banking industry.

Systemic Risk: The risk of an event affecting the whole international financial system, arising from a major spill-over effect. A chain reaction-driven collapse can be triggered by regional crisis contamination and/or by the liquidity or solvency crisis of a leading financial institution.

Term Deposits and CDs: Negotiable instruments that can be traded on the secondary market. Because of higher liquidity, CDs pay lower interest rates ($\leqslant$ 10 basis points: a basis point is 0.01%). Very popular with company treasurers, because of low risk and high flexibility.

Tombstone: An advertisement which lists the managers and underwriters and sometimes the providers of a recently completed syndicated facility or issue.

Topping-up (Paris Club clause): In a subsequent debt reduction, granting more debt reduction on debt the Paris Club previously reduced to provide even further debt relief (e.g., when increasing the cancellation level from 33.33% under Toronto terms to 67% under Naples terms and 80% under Lyon terms).

Unallocated Loan-Loss Reserves: Value of anticipated future charge-offs on the existing loan portfolio that cannot yet be identified with any particular asset.

Value Recovery Clause: Clause included in some commercial bank debt restructuring agreements that entitle creditor banks to recover a larger portion of their loans, subject to a specific condition related to a better than expected performance of the debtor country. It is usually associated with the international price of a good or a basket of goods exported by the debtor country, or to its real GDP growth rate (e.g. Mexico, Côte d'Ivoire).

Variable Interest Debt: External debt with interest rates that float with movements in a key market-based rate such as the six-month LIBOR or the US prime rate.

Waiver: Voluntary relinquishment of a legal right as provided for in the loan agreement for the duration of a specified time period or an indefinite period.

Warrant: Options which permit the holder to buy stock for a stated price, thereby providing a capital gain if the price of the stock rises. Bonds that are issued with warrants, like convertibles, carry lower coupon rates than straight bonds.

Write-off Debt: Removal from the creditor's balance sheet of obligations due from a debtor but unpaid and regarded as uncollectible. While this presents a "clean" balance sheet for the creditor bank, it need not mean that the creditor is abandoning claims against the debtor. In contrast, if a debt is forgiven, it has to be written off.

Zero Coupon Bonds: Bonds that do not pay periodic interest so that the total yield is obtained entirely as a capital gain on the final maturity date.

Index

Index compiled by Annette Musker